THE NEW LA
OF MOBILE LEARNING

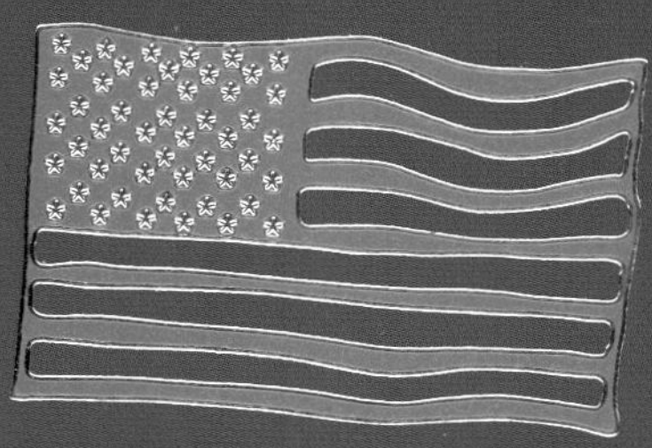

THE NEW LANDSCAPE OF MOBILE LEARNING

Redesigning Education in an App-based World

Edited by Charles Miller and Aaron Doering

NEW YORK AND LONDON

First published 2014
by Routledge
711 Third Avenue, New York, NY 10017

Simultaneously published in the UK
by Routledge
2 Park Square, Milton Park, Abingdon, Oxon OX14 4RN

Routledge is an imprint of the Taylor & Francis Group, an informa business

Library of Congress Cataloging-in-Publication Data

The new landscape of mobile learning : redesigning education in an
app-based world / edited by Charles Miller, Aaron Doering.
pages cm.
Includes bibliographical references and index.
1. Mobile communication systems in education—United States. 2. Distance education—United States. 3. Educational technology—United States. 4. Education—Effect of technological innovations on—United States. I. Miller, Charles, 1943– editor of compilation. II. Doering, Aaron Herbert editor of compilation.
LB1044.84.N49 2014
371.33—dc23 2013024093

ISBN: 978-0-415-53923-4 (hbk)
ISBN: 978-0-415-53924-1 (pbk)
ISBN: 978-0-203-10842-0 (ebk)

Typeset in Palatino
by Apex CoVantage, LLC

Cover illustration by Marcel Mueller
Cover design by Charles Miller
Book layout and design by Charles Miller, Aaron Doering, and Alex Lazarou

Printed and bound in the United States of America by Sheridan Books, Inc. (a Sheridan Group Company).

For Kyra, Eli, and Parker

Contents

Foreword

The Failure of Education's First Mobile Device

Michael Searson
School for Global Education & Innovation, Kean University
President, Society for Information Technology & Teacher Education (SITE)

Consider for a moment, the *book* as education's first mobile device; specifically, the type of book driven by the invention of Johannes Gutenberg's printing press. While the moveable type, the centerpiece of the printing press, was invented hundreds of years earlier in China, Gutenberg's creation had a much greater impact in the transformation of society. In fact, in 1999, leading up to the new millennium, *Time* magazine recognized Gutenberg's invention as the most important event of the 1000–2000 millennium.

Of course, one cannot understate the profound and transformative impact that the Gutenberg press had across society, from the rise of science to the Reformation, from the Age of Enlightenment to the establishment of a widespread middle class; from action as a vehicle to disseminate the ideas and art of the Renaissance to the ultimate decline in the influence of the Church, as well as its impact on education.

Perhaps more than any other thinker of his time, Martin Luther understood the profound potential the printing press had unleashed. Luther saw the Church as corrupt, too controlling, centralized and out of touch with the common person. The printing press aided Luther's cause in two ways: first, as Gutenberg's first major mass publication was the Bible, Luther understood that all printed materials could now be widely distributed, and no longer required interpretation (or control) by a centralized figure, i.e. the Pope. Without this understanding, it would not have made sense for Luther to translate the Bible into the vernacular, rather than Latin (the language of Gutenberg's version and the acceptable standard of the time). He understood that the printing press had transformed the book into a mobile device; it could now be placed into the hands of the common person. The locus of religious discourse had now shifted from a church leader to the individual. Armed with a copy of the Bible any person would now have direct access to his or her god.

A second role that the printing press played in Luther's campaign is the widespread distribution of his "95 Theses." Luther himself composed only hand written versions of this document. While he felt that the posting of this document on a church door would challenge the authority of the Church (which it did), his colleagues recognized that the increased voice that the printing press could provide would have an even greater impact. They translated Luther's version from Latin to German, and then had multiple copies printed. It caused quite a stir in Germany, and shortly thereafter, throughout Europe. The Reformation had begun and the central authority of the Church (at least, in the West) would forever be diminished. Arguably this is the first example of using the new mobility the printing press afforded the book as a protest tool. A mobile tool had forever altered the authority of the Church. Luther's message had gone *viral*.

And then there is education: calling into question the largely unrealized potential of the book as true mobile device in education is not meant to undermine its otherwise profound impact on education. Aided by the publication of the Gutenberg Bible, the first mass printing of the new press, Bibles were now widely available to the public. However, since few could read, the teaching of literacy and an increase in formal schooling began to spread throughout Europe. Learning how to read, followed by an education in the "Classics" would no longer be restricted to only the most wealthy and powerful.

The impact of this new mobile device on the *authority* of the teacher and classroom is another matter. Prior to the invention of the printing press, books, with limited publishing and distribution networks, were only available to the rich and powerful, e.g., the Church. When the content of the text was to be "distributed," it would commonly take place when the *learned* person stood behind the lectern (or podium) and read directly from one of the few copies of the book to those gathered before him (always a "him" in those days). In fact, the term "lecture" is derived from the lectern. Follow the logic here: limited availability to texts leads a person of authority standing behind a lectern to deliver a text-based lecture. With the invention of the printing press resulting in the widespread mobility of books, why did we not have a Luther-type attack on educational authority? Why were all lecterns not thrown out of the classroom? After all, students now had their own texts that they could read at home. Did the teacher need to read or lecture from the same texts that students could now read on their own? And, the point of having students read passages aloud from content-based texts? For example, is understanding of science increased when a series of students reads aloud one passage after another from a science textbook? Why should a notion like "flipping the classroom" seem novel or innovative today, if teachers had relinquished authority for control of knowledge and learning to students hundreds of years earlier, with the advent of the printing press, and the new mobile book? Shouldn't Gutenberg-spawned books have provided the basis for a flipped classroom, if teachers had handed over the authority for learning to the student?

Of course, the mobile devices referred to in *The New Landscape of Mobile Learning: Redesigning Education in an App-based World* are different from printed books in key ways. They are essentially small computers with powerful communications capabilities.

Most of today's mobile devices possess the following features that distinguish them from the mainframe to desktop to laptop lineage: front- *and* rear-facing cameras; location-based tools (often including a GPS); an accelerometer and gyroscope (usually in tandem); multiple communications systems, which could include some combination of the following: Wi-Fi, Bluetooth, NFC, cell-based networks; and a flexible set of efficiently designed programs, generally, referred to as "apps." Additionally, these devices can be driven by touch, gesture, and voice input commands. Yet, their full potential as innovative educational tools has largely *not* been unleashed in the classroom. As with books before them, many of the constraints to their full potential are imposed by an entrenched school-based culture, where the locus for learning is controlled by a central authority and outdated pedagogies.

Unshackling the toolset that collectively distinguishes the mobile device from its predecessors could have a profound impact on education. It could lead to powerful learning opportunities, especially those driven by the learner. One way to assess the extent to which tools within mobiles are being fully utilized is when the learning opportunity could *only* be realized through a mobile device (exploiting the features described above). For example, the collective experience of "reading" the app version of Al Gore's *Our Choice* and its interface that fully leverages touch tablets simply cannot be realized through a printed text or even a traditional "electronic text" on a computer. The publishing team for this new type of "book" has gone out of its way to use gesture-based features; full multimedia content; intuitive navigation; location-based content; and other innovations for unique reading experience.

Another potential area where mobile devices have yet to make a meaningful impact is *where* learning takes place. Students can now readily be led out of the classroom (after all, they are called *mobile* devices). Rich place-based learning experiences would be greatly enhanced if educators were to fully embrace the power of mobile devices. Using location-based features, coupled with the front- and rear-facing cameras would allow students to engage in rich collaborative networks, where they would work with others to collect data to document their findings in a variety of diverse environments (see Project Noah for an example of this type of work). Full engagement with the power of today's mobile tools could complement other innovative learning practices. For example, students could use some of the tools described above to engage in powerful augmented reality experiences. In recent years, games and simulations have begun to have an impact on education. Just imagine the power of collaborative gaming tools on mobile devices that can be carried with the student 24/7!

As with the advent of the printing press, where a new tool (the printing press-produced book) had a more transformative impact in renegotiating the power structure of other aspects of society than it did in the classroom, we are at a similar juncture with mobile devices. While many schools have moved toward adoption of mobile tools in the classroom, very few have articulated a vision that would suggest a change in pedagogy to truly leverage the power of these new tools. In particular, the locus of authority remains the same—unchanged since before the printing, missing an opportunity that the wide availability of books should have afforded. Mobile learning could be headed in the same direction. Ironically, mobile devices provide learners greater access to information than any book could ever hope to do. Yet they, too, are shackled by the constraints of restrictive pedagogies, where the student remains a passive recipient of knowledge under the instruction of the teacher. To date, there is little evidence that adoption of mobile devices has had much impact on classroom practice. The collaborative richness that learners experience outside of the classroom is often shut down upon entering school doors. Inventive apps, that may utilize some of the features described above, are rarely used. Rather, applications that continue the passive dissemination of knowledge, from teacher to student, are often placed front and center on students' devices.

Under the critical guidance of professors Charles Miller and Aaron Doering, *The New Landscape of Mobile Learning* suggests some remedies to this situation. Working with a group of very talented authors, they collectively present a vision of how educators can move forward and leverage the opportunity mobile tools offer to transform learning. They provide exciting perspectives from researchers and practitioners, designers to developers, ranging from the K–12 classroom to the university level and beyond. While it would be an unfair burden on any set of authors to claim that they have posted the "95 Theses" of mobile learning, *The New Landscape of Mobile Learning* does provide a vision for the types of issues and practices we must consider if mobile learning has any chance of reshaping education. Let's not miss this opportunity with education's second mobile device.

References

Gore, A. (2011). *Our choice: A plan to save the climate crisis* (Version 1.0.3). [Mobile application software]. Retrieved from http://itunes.apple.com/.

Project Noah. (2013). Project Noah. Retrieved from http://www.projectnoah.org.

Preface

> Mobile learning is the point at which mobile computing and eLearning intersect to produce an anytime, anywhere learning experience. We are there.
>
> (Harris, 2001)

> The future of learning: From eLearning to mLearning.
>
> (Keegan, 2002)

These bold forecasts, from a decade past, preceded the emergence of the now ubiquitous app world, the true "anytime, anywhere" digital experience that resides in pockets, purses, and backpacks around the globe. Educational apps for mobile devices such as smartphones (e.g., iPhone, Android, BlackBerry, etc.) and digital tablets (e.g., iPad, Galaxy Note, Surface, Nexus, etc.) represent an extraordinary and largely untapped array of potential tools for educators and students in the multifaceted contexts of face-to-face, hybrid, and distance education. Moreover, with more than 150 million Apple iPads and 350 million iPhone and iPod Touch devices in use, rising numbers of universities, K–12 schools, and institutions are selecting the iPad as the tablet-based platform of choice for their face-to-face and online classrooms. For example, at the University of Minnesota every incoming freshman in the College of Education and Human Development receives an iPad at the beginning of their first semester. However, with enthusiastic integration comes pessimistic criticism and debate, a healthy and necessary balance exhibited throughout the history of the educational technology field.

"There's an app for that" has quickly become the technology catchphrase of the decade as the app revolution sweeps the world, in concert with the increasing availability and capabilities of the iPhone, iPad, and iPod Touch. Beyond the value of apps for everything from work utilities and communication, to entertainment, art, and even research, there is another key component to the app craze that constitutes fertile ground in the educational technology field—the *accessibility* of app design and development. Today, one need not be a consummate programmer with expertise in the intricacies of programming languages to enter the arena of app design.

Although many believe that apps have the potential to create opportunities for transformational mobile education, a disparity exists between the individuals responsible for creating the apps (i.e. development companies, some with little to no instructional experience, masked behind the business-minded protection of the iTunes App Store) and the ultimate consumers in the classroom (i.e. PK–20 educators and students). To this extent we believe *The New Landscape of Mobile Learning* will bridge this gap and illuminate the critical design, integration, and research narratives from leaders in the instructional design, distance education, and mobile learning fields.

This book is organized into the following five sections:

- The Emerging Role of Mobile Learning
- Mobile Learning Design Guidelines and Frameworks
- Mobile Learning Design and Development Narratives
- Mobile Learning Integration, Research, and Evaluation
- The Future of Mobile Learning.

Each section begins with an introduction that highlights the key elements and foundations of each included chapter. Likewise, each chapter begins with an overview, rich author biographies, and a brief summary for app educators, designers, and researchers. Furthermore, we present several visionary pullout sections threaded throughout the book to add additional and diverse voices to our dialogue of mobile learning.

The Mobile Learning Iceberg

The cover of this book was designed to illustrate and create a new metaphor for mobile learning. As the density of pure ice is approximately 920 kg/m^3, and that of sea water roughly 1,025 kg/m^3, only 11 percent of an iceberg is visible above the water surface. The primary contour, structure, and physical elements of an iceberg, those that exhibit the true character of the formation, past and present, as well as shape the future narrative of the object, are difficult to visualize by a cursory glimpse of the visible portion.

The "tip of the iceberg," a common expression that denotes a small portion of a larger problem to be solved, is what we believe to be the current perspective of mobile learning: The 11 percent.

Similar to an iceberg, a partial view of a classroom does not illustrate the complexities of the social interactions, pedagogical foundations, and technology integration that shape the full narrative of learning in this context. Icebergs float freely in the ocean, bumping into and crashing against constraints such as land, man-made structures, and other icebergs. These constraints continue to shape the formation beyond simple melting or calving, and also serve a vital role in the iceberg's narrative. We aim to cast these complexities, constraints, and narratives as opportunities to understand, shape, and embrace the future of mobile learning.

As you explore the following sections and chapters, our challenge to you, the reader, is to ask yourself, "What lies beneath the water?"

Section 1
The Emerging Role of Mobile Learning

Mobile learning, an obvious and understandable extension of the now commonplace moniker "e-learning," has substantiated its presence as a critical area of interest for academic design, development, integration, and research, as well as an attractive headline in national news, educational policy, and government funding. The fields of instructional design, educational technology, learning sciences, and educational psychology have rich histories detailing the oft-enthusiastic exploration of education in the digital landscape. However, these fields also share an observable track record of "jumping the gun" with new technologies, promising considerable learning gains with repeatedly little return. The well-documented journey (cf. Saettler, 1990) through vast landscapes of instructional libraries, radio broadcasts, motion pictures (with and without sound), television, the PC, and most recently the Internet is fraught with elevated expectations of transformation balanced with lackluster outcomes. The "Great Media Debate" notwithstanding (cf. Clark, 1994; Kozma, 1994), these advances in technology are routinely perceived as means to an end and solutions to a problem, rather than opportunities to transform.

Enter the Apple iPad.

In less than three years since the time of this writing, the iPad was initially and outspokenly questioned as a failure-ridden larger PDA to being lauded as the future of education. Much like Thomas Edison prophesized that movies would replace books, many believe the iPad is the twenty-first-century learner's sole backpack. Before we continue to "jump the gun," we begin this book with an exploration through several foundational lenses focused on the emergence of mobile apps in education.

Mr. Mundie and Dr. Hooper open this section with a connectivist view of mobile learning—"one that attempts to understand mobile learning based on the learners' ability to use mobile technology to cultivate and exploit connected networks of information for problem solving." The authors first examine the innovative opportunities of mobile learning through characteristics of technology and context, and suggest, "these alone are insufficient to produce innovative learning." Secondly, Mundie and Hooper explore both the information model and information space of mobile learning, ultimately concluding that "if education is to change in a real sense . . . the conditions that produce such outcomes need to be identified and integrated into education designs."

Dr. Dennen and Ms. Hao continue this introduction to mobile learning by presenting several paradigms of app use in multiple contexts. Dennen and Hao illuminate mobile learning examples through the foundational learning theories of behaviorism, cognitive information processing, cognitive constructivism, and social constructivism. The authors then share several of their own app prototypes, as well as commercially available exemplars, and discuss specific representations of pedagogical use. Finally Dennen and Hao challenge designers to "not simply replicate existing tools for a mobile medium, but take advantage of the affordances of a mobile device" through considerations of portability, connectivity, input capability, and recording ability.

Next, Dr. Hokanson shares his perspective on the promise of mobile learning through an exploration of current and historical practices such as field notebooks, sketchbooks, and commonplace books. Through a rearward transition from digital to analog, Hokanson suggests, "the complex condition that is learning does not come from sitting passively and viewing presented information, but more effectively when the learners create the materials themselves, when the learner is active in a variety of ways such as writing, moving, or recording." Hokanson focuses his efforts on a hybrid use scenario between digital and analog, and recommends that mobile apps "must be the means to make connections between media, between ideas, and between the remote and the digital."

Through an innovative lens of mobile learning, Mr. and Mrs. George address the nature of collaboration within the context of mobile education and focus on "the lessons that the Montessori approach to education has to teach us about creating in a digital, mobile landscape." The authors, award-winning children's app designers (see Section 3, Chapter 9), argue that in traditional education "competition trumps collaboration" through modes of competition including opponents, adversaries, and rivalries. To this effect they present the "*and*," a contemporary design perspective on learner collaboration that affords designers and teachers with "the opportunity to help children learn, based on their individual needs, and in accordance with their specific development."

Dr. Scharber concludes the section with an overview of the iPad invasion in K–12 education, specifically in the context of English teaching and learning. Scharber presents several conceptualizations of the intersection between literacy and mobile learning, and challenges teachers to "harness the power of our beloved language in all of its forms and mediums (i.e. written, verbal, pictorial, digital, multimodal) to redirect the perception of and dialogue around the importance of incorporating technology (including iPads) meaningfully into classrooms and schools." For Scharber, "technology tools (past, present, and future) must be understood for their impact on definitions of and expectations for literacy" to transform learning in this context, as well as K–12 education as a whole.

References

Clark, R. (1994). Media will never influence learning. *Educational Technology Research and Development*, *42*(2), 21–29.

Kozma, R. (1994). Will media influence learning? Reframing the debate. *Educational Technology Research and Development*, *42*(2), 7–19.

Saettler, P. (1990). *The Evolution of American Educational Technology*. Englewood, Colorado: Libraries Unlimited, Inc.

Dr. Curtis J. Bonk
Professor,
Instructional Systems Technology,
Indiana University

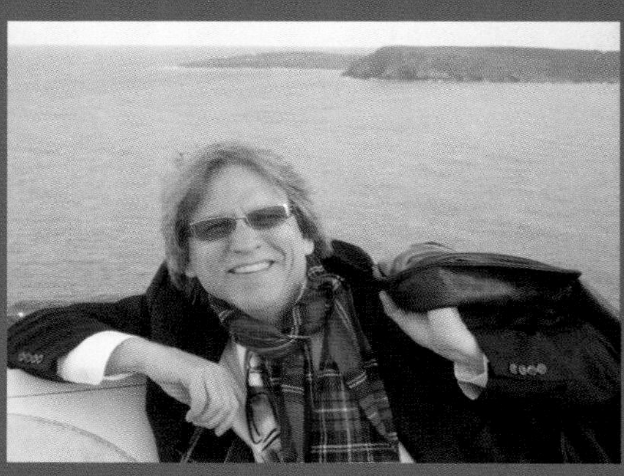

A key problem of education today is the fixation on formal learning environments as the solution for our test score, economic, and personal woes. The gigantic educational funding machine throughout the world spins out proclamations, laws, policies, and projects in the direction of schools and universities. There are fierce debates about teacher credentials, assessment practices, accreditation, accountability, and so on. Unfortunately, these battles mask where the vast majority of learning is now occurring. Increasingly, the stages in which human learning takes place are not the bounded and contrived classrooms, study halls, and courtyards of K–12 schools and institutions of higher learning. Today learning is typically informal and often quite casual and ubiquitous.

My research team and I are interested in pushing the frontiers of such informal learning into the extreme. As we are documenting, in the twenty-first century we learn when in planes, trains, boats, and cars as well as when on polar ice, hiking in the Rocky Mountains, or sitting in a cafe. We learn on our way to school, but often not in it.

Learners seek and find information when and where they need it. If they want to learn a new language, they can be tutored through it in Livemocha or Babbel with peers from other countries. If they want to obtain an update on an intriguing scientific expedition in the Amazon basin, they venture online, not to their textbooks. Alternatively, they might have heard about an inspiring TED talk that they can watch when they get home from school. Or, more commonly, they might go online to find out how to fix a mobile phone that fell in a puddle during a rainstorm as they got off the bus. And, today's learners can also join online groups of global peers to discuss these issues and share what they have found.

This age, or "learning century" as I like to refer to it, is the most momentous and fast-changing period for human education ever recorded. Mobile technologies are evolving to bring unique and often quite extreme forms of learning to us each second of the day. What a wonderful time to be a human learner.

Bridget Gilormini
Director,
PACER Center's
Simon Technology Center

The response to mobile technology has been a bit overwhelming in my world of assistive technology. As the gap between technology and specialized technology gets smaller, my hope is that in five years I would be out of a job more or less. Over the years I've watched technology get faster, smaller, and decrease in price. Many have looked to technology to solve an educational need, but for a variety of reasons they have been unable to find the right tool. Mobile technology like the iPad and the vast array of apps that are available have given many parents and educators hope that this technology will be *the* technology. Specifically, for children and adults with disabilities who do not have a voice, the iPad has been revolutionary. The price point, the "cool factor," and the many good, bad, and ugly app communication choices (more than 100 are currently available) together have made the iPod and iPad the new shiny communication tools of choice. Many feel so strongly about the potential of the devices that they are buying without benefit of having touched, felt, or tried the technology in the scope of a communication device, hoping that it will open up a new door of possibility. Social networking has brought communities of these users together and helped them through the process. As fast as naysayers are constructing barriers, groups of talented and creative people are creating solutions: solutions to mount the device, access the device, manipulate the device, protect the device, and more. And Apple has been responsive to the community of users who see so much potential in this type of technology for children and youth with disability. Their attention to accessibility makes it available and important to a much larger pool of consumers because they have designed with a larger number of people in mind (i.e. universal design for learning). Ultimately, it is also my hope that more developers will embrace this value as a design criterion for the benefit of more people, *including* those with disabilities.

Chapter 1
Considering the Potential of Connected Mobile Learning

In this paper, we present a connectivist view of mobile learning—one that attempts to understand mobile learning based on the learners' ability to use mobile technology to cultivate and exploit connected networks of information for problem solving. Through the cultivation of knowledge networks, learners develop skills such as finding and filtering information in order to construct solutions to problems and evaluate their effectiveness. From this perspective, mobile technology can be understood as a means for learners to dramatically expand the kind of meaningful information (information model) in context with the total information (information space) available for problem solving. Mobile learning, in this context, then becomes an act that is determined by the learner, as they use mobile technology to create and exploit knowledge networks to support their learning goals.

For Designers

Mobile learning designers must decide whether they are designing to reach a wider audience or to support learners' unique learning needs. If the latter, they should consider how their designs support individual learning and how they can incorporate the affordances and networking capabilities of mobile technologies to expand learners' access to information, tools, and activities that expand personal knowledge.

For Teachers

Teachers must decide whether they are using mobile technologies to strengthen traditional curricula or to support their students' unique learning needs and interests. If the latter, they should consider how their teaching will be impacted by the affordances and networking capabilities of mobile technologies to expand learners' access to information, tools, and activities that expand personal knowledge.

For Researchers

Researchers must decide whether they are interested in investigating how mobile technologies might strengthen traditional instructional practice or support students' unique learning needs and interests. If the latter, they should investigate how the affordances and networking capabilities of mobile technologies can expand learners' access to information, tools, and activities that expand personal knowledge.

In five years mobile learning will be common, increasing access and creating the potential to seek and solve problems face to face and online.

James Mundie
Manager of Educational Technology or
World Campus,
Penn State University

Dr. Simon Hooper
Associate Professor,
Learning, Design, and Technology,
Penn State University

James oversees the development and delivery of online courses, and maintains the technology vision and strategic direction for Penn State World Campus. His research investigates how people use mobile devices to support teaching and learning. He has developed several iPad applications including a collaborative environment for communicating concepts that are not easily communicated via text and a mobile video annotation application for digital ethnographers. Simon designs and develops software to support teaching and learning. His research interests include interaction design, learning analytics, and information visualization.

Considering the Potential of Connected Mobile Learning

In a world of connected, ubiquitous information, it is neither sufficient nor possible to amass a store of content knowledge in order to be considered "learned." Over the past decade, scholars have been developing the idea that the value in knowledge is not what is contained within informational content, but rather in the meaning that is created when pieces of information relate to each other (Downes, 2012). This is the central idea behind connectivism, an epistemology suggesting that while the notion of knowledge as a concrete collection of objective, observable facts served us well in the Industrial Age, the Information Age has different problems that require new ways of thinking (Siemens, 2005).

The deficiency in the industrial model is not that our collections of facts and procedures are wrong. Rather, problems have become more complicated and less defined. Whereas in the Industrial Age, knowledge was relatively scarce to the point that it could be bound up and sold as property (e.g., textbooks), our collections of facts and procedures have become so prolific that it is no longer possible to keep pace with some fields, let alone master them in their entirety.

Moreover, our understanding of what constitutes knowledge is continually evolving. How knowledge is represented and the role of technology in that process has been investigated in diverse disciplines for thousands of years. More recently, Elias (2011) described a four-phase process through which data become increasingly usable through a series of transformations. During this process, known as the knowledge continuum, data change to information, then knowledge, and finally into wisdom. Raw data become useful when meaning is applied thereby allowing declarative questions to be answered (i.e. who, what, when and where). More sophisticated questions (i.e. why and how) can be answered when information is further processed resulting in the generation of knowledge. When transformed into wisdom it becomes fully "actionable" (Elias, 2011).

Researchers have also challenged the notion of knowledge as internal representations of "justified true beliefs." Instead, knowledge is conceived of as being distributed—it is the set of connections to which an individual has access (Hutchins, 1996; Pea, 1993). These connections might exist within the individual but include links to other networks in the world. For example, it might include connections that exist within machines or between sets of people. Most importantly, when these sets of connections are accessible to the individual they expand personal knowledge. Taken to its conclusion, knowledge is believed to be most valuable when it is formed into networks with many connections.

If our notions of what defines knowledge are changing, then we should revisit our notions of how knowledge is acquired. Current educational practice is largely influenced by manufacturing models to achieve economies of scale. Through practice in controlled environments, learners achieve replicable results by applying remembered facts and procedures to problems with definitive answers. The curricula supported by these practices may no longer be relevant, requiring different pedagogies to help learners to cope with the sheer volume of information that is available today. Consequently, it is becoming increasingly important to be able to draw from a widely distributed body of knowledge, to be able to judge quickly the value of information, and to be able to apply what has been learned to diverse circumstances (Ledward & Hirata, 2011).

Connectivists propose that knowledge is more enduring when learned through activities that promote inter-connectivity, rather than when learned as facts and procedures. That is, when one bit of information is linked to another, a meaning is formed that is more valuable than either of the individual pieces. People derive meaning from the process of forming relationships by connecting information. It is in this context that we wish to take a closer look at mobile learning as a new form of learning for the Information Age. But is mobile learning really new and different in comparison with traditional learning methods? And if so, what is its purpose?

What Makes Mobile Learning Innovative?

It is important to distinguish between definitions of mobile learning in order to understand their design potential. Although mobile technologies have matured over the past decade, to date there is little evidence of the impact of mobile learning on educational practice beyond increasing access. Indeed, if history is a guide, the evolution of mobile learning designs will follow a familiar path. The genesis of each new educational technology involves replicating existing instructional models: Educators attempt to translate extant practices onto each new technology. We have known for a long time that when new technology is implemented without changes in pedagogy, the only educational outcome that can be reliably predicted is improved efficiency (Clark, 1983).

So what qualifies as mobile learning and what makes mobile learning innovative? In the literature, definitions of mobile learning often focus on two characteristics: technology and context. Technology generally refers to the mobile device and its integrated feature set that allows users to capture, measure, manipulate, and transmit information and events that occur in the course of learning. Mobile devices are always portable, thus allowing the context for learning to be expanded beyond the traditional classroom to support on-demand access to educational materials. Learning is often considered mobile when learners can access educational materials at their convenience (i.e. anywhere and at any time) (Quinn, 2000).

Although technology and context define the necessary characteristics of any mobile learning environment, these alone are insufficient to produce innovative learning. Providing access to an ever-expanding set of affordances likely increases educational potential. Likewise, freeing learners from the classroom makes educational content ubiquitous, but it does not imply the pedagogical changes associated with contemporary notions of knowledge. The result, too often, is that the infusion of the devices is considered to be the innovation rather than the use of the device to solve problems in novel ways.

Moreover, the mobile devices that students bring into the classroom are often viewed as distractions, interfering with the assembly-line model of educational practice rather than being used to develop twenty-first-century skills. Such skills imply the ability to learn quickly by cultivating knowledge networks that support information-gathering practices in authentic environments, applying mental filters to find, sort and extract information, using that information to solve problems, and evaluating the results of one's own work.

When armed with these skills students develop the ability to find information, think critically about its relevance and authenticity, construct and apply solutions, and evaluate solutions in terms of the original problem criteria. In the following sections we expand briefly on these abilities and suggest how mobile technology may promote their development in learners.

Finding Information

With access to vast connected networks of knowledge, learners must be able to find information sources that can be used to solve problems. This involves cultivating and organizing knowledge networks into structures that make sense to the learner. Cultivating knowledge networks is a lifelong endeavor that requires active and ongoing social processes and varying degrees of community participation by the learner. However, the portability of mobile devices combined with mobile networking infrastructure offers the opportunity for learners to extend their participation in knowledge networks to encompass nearly all aspects of daily life. For example, Instagram allows users to send digital photographs to Facebook directly from a mobile device, and therefore from virtually any context. These photographs can then be used to engage existing participants and attract new ones. Mobile learning applications could take the same approach, allowing learners to send artifacts generated during a learning activity to the learner's social networks, potentially encouraging further participation and expansion of the network.

Mobile applications might also be developed to do the opposite, allowing content found in social networks to be incorporated back into a learning activity. Using mobile devices in this way may give students the opportunity to practice finding and organizing content, encouraging practice and supporting the idea that networks are problem-solving tools. Mobile learning activities designed to utilize social networks in the context of problem solving may also give learners the opportunity to evaluate which networks are best suited for solving different types of problems.

Filtering and Extracting Relevant Information

Once information sources have been found, mobile devices can help the learner to decide which are relevant, which are accurate and trustworthy, and so forth. Software can be configured to provide meta-information about information sources that guide learners to judge the veracity of the information. For example, this could take the form of community rating systems that help the learner to judge the value of a data source. Likewise, software might automatically favor or restrict the use of certain sources of information over others. Mobile devices have location-based affordances that might link the information more directly to the problem context, giving the learner the ability to more granularly fine-tune the problem solution.

After finding credible and reliable information sources that help solve a problem, learners must extract relevant information from the source. This requires the development of critical thinking skills. Mobile software can be configured to make intelligent recommendations at a granular level, similar to how Amazon.com makes purchasing recommendations. Recommendation can be based on what the device knows about the learner over the history of its usage, what the device knows about the environment in which the mobile learning activity is situated, and other factors personalized to the learner.

Constructing and Evaluating Solutions

Real-world problems often contain many variables, are ill-defined or too complex to fully articulate, and their solutions may not be solvable in one attempt, often resulting in multiple iterations and a range of possible solutions before achieving a satisfactory resolution (Brown, 1992; Collins, 1992).

Evaluating real-world problem-solving ability is similarly complex. As a result, assessment is commonly used for summative evaluation: to assign a grade or to rank a performance. Yet, the most valuable form of feedback uses diagnosis, correction, elaboration, and explanation to modify performance. Technology can accelerate the evaluation process thereby increasing the likelihood of providing formative evaluation. For example, the use of an online assessment tool slashed the time required to provide feedback to undergraduate students learning American Sign Language from weeks to days (or even hours) (Miller et al., 2008).

Likewise, mobile learning supports the notion that evaluation need not be the sole purview of the expert (i.e. the teacher). Connected technology supports the development of metacognitive strategies by enabling students to judge their own and peers' performance against rubrics that reflect the key learning objectives. As such, the evaluation process becomes an extended learning opportunity as learners internalize desired models of learning. Mobile technology can be used to help learners construct and evaluate appropriate solutions in a number of ways: through access to expert knowledge and opinions from participants in social networks, through instant feedback from mobile devices and applications, and by aggregating artifacts for later analysis, discussion, or reflection.

Mobile Learning and Connected Information

In order to explore its potential as a pedagogical support, mobile learning can be considered in terms of the *information model* that the technology supports, and the *information space*, or total information available within the context of the learning activity. From a connectivist perspective, the learner uses technology to exploit knowledge networks to discover and apply the information needed to solve problems, and to judge the solutions. Mobile technology dramatically expands access to information networks available for problem solving, and assists the learner in both predicting and judging the efficacy of potential solutions.

Mobile technology expands the learner's knowledge networks dramatically, in ways that were not possible before the advent of mobile technology, and it does so in a way that is personalized, placing the locus of control literally in the learners' own hands. Mobile technology, used to its full potential, allows the learner to choose what problems to solve, what information to use, where that information comes from, and how any solution makes sense within each learner's prior knowledge and experience. In mobile learning, as in traditional learning, what is important is *how* the learner solves the problem. However, whereas in the Industrial Age mobile devices would have been seen as tools that *contained* the right answers to questions, in the Information Age mobile devices contain the means to find and synthesize the answers to questions, and to pose new questions.

Information Model

Information models are collections of information, made meaningful through interconnections, and relevant to the problem at hand. Too often, knowledge is presented as isolated facts and procedures. However, learners need information *and* meaning in order to solve problems and make effective decisions. For example, Downes (2012) illustrates that although it is true that Paris is the capital of France, this information alone has limited use. One must consider that Paris is a city, that cities can be capitals, the role of capitals in trade networks and politics, that nations have capitals, and so on. Information models supply learners with logical frameworks that can support decision making and problem solving.

For example, information models emerge when the curator of an art gallery selects and arranges exhibition artifacts to help visitors identify relationships among the artwork. Paintings (i.e. information) may be organized by room and chronologically (i.e. given meaning), with Baroque painters such as Velazquez occupying one space, Surrealists such as Dali occupying another, to help the viewer discover the relationship between the two. There also may be information models containing meta-information, such as note cards next to paintings to signify the dates of the paintings, the artists' names, and historical information in context. Mobile technology can provide learners with more diverse and personalized information about exhibits. This information can be tailored to have varying levels of meaning—with many connections, so that the learner may be explicitly shown that which they are expected to gain an understanding of, or with few connections so that they may discover an understanding on their own. To support highly sophisticated information models, mobile technology can leverage advanced tools (often referred to as Learning Analytics Systems) that use historical course databases, individual student histories, and artificial intelligence to customize support in a way that is individualized, and thus potentially more useful to the learner.

When instructional content fits well within a learner's zone of proximal development and attention span, simple information models may be all that is needed for learning to occur. The simplest systems provide little meaning, they simply present content and it is up to the learner to form the connections that lend meaning. In contrast, intelligent systems may be most effective when a learner needs help to remain engaged and on-track throughout a learning activity. Thus, when content is familiar, a lecture may be an efficient way to learn content. However, when content is unfamiliar a learner may require access to a range of guidance and support tools to learn effectively.

Information Space

The **information space** is the total available information in the context of the learning activity. The affordances of mobile technology expand the information space in three ways: through storage capacity, through networking capabilities, and through sensors built into the device that capture and process data in ways that humans cannot. Storage capacity expands the information space by allowing learners to carry vast libraries of digital assets with them wherever they go, in ever increasing quality. Networking capabilities allow learners to cultivate and access personal, professional, and academic social networks so learners have potentially instant access to expert and novice opinions on any topic imaginable. Sensors built into mobile devices such as cameras, microphones, global positioning systems, gyroscopes, magnetometers, motion detectors, and near-field communications systems give learners the ability to gather and analyze a wide variety of data about the immediate environment in order to consider heretofore unseen aspects of the environment and better understand their own relationship to it. Taken together, the careful integration of a device's affordances into the mobile learning activity provides learners with diverse tools to access, manipulate, organize, integrate, and store content.

For example, the previously mentioned art gallery may be thought of as an information space bounded by its own walls, with additional constraints such as the number of people who can fit into its galleries, a limited number of index cards containing metadata that it makes sense to hang alongside exhibits, limited operating hours and limited times during which art experts may be present to engage visitors, and so on. In the absence of mobile technology, a visitor to the gallery has only limited access to resources with which to understand its content. Mobile technology can dramatically expand the gallery's information space by connecting visitors with knowledge networks that would have been difficult (if not impossible) to interact with without the technology. Visitors can connect with art experts around the world synchronously or asynchronously, rather than those that could be personally available before. They can carry with them into the gallery *every* art textbook, rather than one or a few, and they can capture details of the gallery using cameras and other sensors that they previously would have had to draw on paper or memorize.

Conclusion

Mobile learning theorists have questioned the role of mobile technology in the learning process. If traditional epistemology holds that knowledge exists within the mind of the learner then learning has little to do with the inherent capabilities of any technological medium. Thus, the role of technology in education has largely been to deliver consistent and replicable instruction to large numbers of people (Clark, 1983). This orientation downplays the role of technology to that of content delivery. Instructional technology has been designed to favor efficiency of delivery and comparison of individuals as they amass a personal storehouse of knowledge, and thus learning is assumed to be the result of the manner in which instruction is designed rather than shaped through technology. The focus of education has been on learners achieving an objective in the most efficient way possible. To this end, we have developed systems that limit access to relevant information, may or may not provide guidance, and we generally do not want the learner to be divergent in their thinking. Mobile learning challenges this efficiency model. Instead of all learners achieving the same outcomes, we now have the ability to customize learning outcomes to the individual.

Researchers have proposed that mobile technology is most useful when used to explore the information space (Laouris & Eteokleous, 2005; Sharples et al., 2009), untethering learners from the classroom so that they may freely explore or collaborate in authentic environments to derive insights through practice. Thus, the value of mobile learning is thought to be that we can pose (or students can discover) educational problems that exist outside the confines of the traditional classroom. However, from this perspective the classroom is merely being transposed to another location.

Although constructivist learning theories are considered to be social theories of learning because they rely on processes that occur *between* individuals, they have been used to date as a way of building knowledge *within* individuals. The logical endpoint for knowledge in connectivist learning, in contrast, is in information models that are external to individuals. These orientations do not necessarily conflict; however, they have significantly different implications for pedagogical practice, particularly in the assessment and comparison of learners, learning outcomes, and curricula. Moreover, a connectivist view of knowledge as connected information implies a different value for connected knowledge than knowledge isolated in individuals. Information has its greatest value when it has a greater number of connections; therefore knowledge will have its greatest value when it has the potential to be accessed by many rather than by a few.

Navigation of knowledge networks for problem solving requires different skills from mere assimilation of information. If education is to change in a real sense, that is if technology is to support emerging notions of knowledge, the conditions that produce such outcomes need to be identified and integrated into education designs. In time, designs that reflect the inherent affordances and capabilities of the mobile medium will evolve that will shift pedagogical and design practice to support the development of skills in learners to better serve their needs and the needs of society.

optimistic

References

Brown, A. L. (1992). Design experiments: Theoretical and methodological challenges in creating complex interventions in classroom settings. *The Journal of the Learning Sciences, 2*(2), 141–178.

Clark, R. E. (1983). Reconsidering research on learning from media. *Review of Educational Research, 53*, 445–459.

Collins, A. (1992). Toward a design science of education. In E. Scanlon & T. O'Shea (Eds.), *New directions in educational technology: Vol. 96*. New York: Springer-Verlag.

Downes, S. (2012). Connectivism and connective knowledge: Essays on meaning and learning networks. Retrieved October 9, 2012, from http://www.downes.ca/files/Connective_Knowledge-19May2012.pdf.

Elias, T. (2011). Learning analytics: Definitions, processes and potential. Retrieved October 9, 2012, from http://learninganalytics.net/LearningAnalyticsDefinitionsProcessesPotential.pdf.

Hutchins, E. (1996). *Cognition in the Wild*. Cambridge, MA: MIT Press.
Laouris, Y., & Eteokleous, N. (2005). We need an educational relevant definition of mobile learning. Retrieved October 9, 2012, from http://www.mlearn.org.za/CD/papers/Laouris%20&%20 Eteokleous.pdf.
Ledward, B. C., & Hirata, D. (2011). An overview of 21st century skills. Retrieved October 9, 2012, from http://www.ksbe.edu/spi/PDFS/21st%20Century%20Skills%20Brief.pdf.
Miller, C., Hooper, S., Rose, S., & Montalto-Rook, M. (2008). Transforming e-assessment in American Sign Language: Pedagogical and technological enhancements in online language learning and performance assessment. *Learning, Media and Technology, 33*(3), 155–168.
Pea, R. D. (1993). Practices of distributed intelligence and designs for education. In G. Salomon (Ed.), *Distributed cognition: Psychological and educational considerations. Learning in doing: Social, cognitive and computational perspectives* (pp. 47–87). Cambridge: Cambridge University Press.
Quinn, C. (2000). mLearning: Mobile, wireless, in your pocket learning. *LineZine*, Fall 2000. Retrieved October 31, 2012, from http://www.linezine.com/2.1/features/cqmmwiyp.htm.
Sharples, M., Arnedillo-Sanchez, I., Milrad, M., & Vavoula, G. (2009). Mobile learning: Small devices, big issues. In N. Balacheff, S. Ludvigsen, T. de Jong, and S. Barnes (Eds.), *Technology enhanced learning: Principles and products* (pp. 233–249). Heidelberg, Germany: Springer.
Siemens, G. (2005). Connectivism: A learning theory for the digital age. Retrieved October 9, 2012, from http://www.elearnspace.org/Articles/connectivism.htm.

Chapter 2
Paradigms of Use, Learning Theory, and App Design

Learning apps have the potential to transform both formal and informal educational experiences. To realize this potential, they must be pedagogically sound, designed with both learning theory and learning objectives in mind. This chapter presents paradigms of app use in a learning context, then explores how major learning theories and design principles relate to these paradigms. Finally, examples of learning apps within each paradigm are shared, with a focus on their pedagogical design.

For Designers

This chapter encourages designers to think about the underlying pedagogy of app-based learning interactions so they can design specifically for those interactions. Additionally, it challenges designers to consider innovative ways of maximizing the iPod, iPhone, and iPad's features in support of learning.

For Teachers

This chapter guides teachers in both determining what types of apps might help them best meet specific learning goals and evaluating apps for pedagogical soundness and innovation. Ultimately, it helps teachers be savvier when selecting and integrating apps in their curriculums.

For Researchers

This chapter provides researchers with a classification system for apps based on pedagogical and learning interaction factors. Additionally, it can help researchers identify areas in which studies of mobile learning pedagogy might be warranted.

In the next five years, mobile learning will find its niche in formal education settings, and will remain ubiquitous in informal settings.

Dr. Vanessa P. Dennen
Associate Professor,
Instructional Systems,
Florida State University

Shuang Hao
Doctoral Candidate,
Instructional Systems,
Florida State University

Vanessa Dennen is an associate professor of Instructional Systems at Florida State University where she researches learning and knowledge management in networked and mobile settings. Additionally, she teaches courses on learning theory and instructional design for technology-mediated learning. Shuang Hao is a doctoral candidate at Florida State University. She has also worked as a training specialist at the Florida Department of Highway Safety and Motor Vehicles in designing distance learning modules. Her research interests include online and mobile learning strategies and performance improvement technologies. Together, Vanessa and Shuang have designed and developed apps and mobile learning-based activities and have taught classes on mobile learning design. Additionally, they are researching factors and attitudes related to mobile learning adoption across different cultures.

Paradigms of Use, Learning Theory, and App Design

Mobile apps are attractive options for educators and learners alike, offering the ability to extend technology-based and technology-mediated learning opportunities into new settings as well as bringing a different set of features in a relatively low-cost package to more traditional educational settings. As Quinn (2011) notes, mobile learning "is *not* about putting e-learning courses on a phone . . . [it] is about *augmenting* our learning—and our performance." Further, app designers should take advantage of some of the features that mobile devices afford over more traditional forms of learning media such as personalization, location-based services, crowdsourcing (Kukulska-Hulme, 2010), and integrated non-keyboard input devices (e.g., touchscreen, camera, GPS), and also consider the environment in which apps will be used (Kukulska-Hulme, Traxler, & Pettit, 2007) with potential variability as one shifts from iPod to iPhone to iPad. However, there is another set of design issues to be raised in a mobile learning context, and those are related to pedagogical design. In this chapter, we discuss the ways in which both pedagogical use and learning theories influence app design.

Paradigms of Learning App Use

This chapter presents pedagogical design issues for four different types of apps, summarized in Table 2.1, which was inspired by Taylor (1980) and Koschmann's (1996) earlier work examining how computers are used in education. We have consciously omitted certain categories of apps, such as productivity tools. While these types of apps certainly are used in the service of learning, those provided and supported by existing

Table 2.1 Overview of app paradigms

Paradigm (App as . . .)	App Function	Example(s)	Primary Underlying Learning Theory
Tutor	Direct instruction and assessment	Flash cards, drill and practice, quiz games	Behaviorism
Information source	Presents information	eBooks, animations	Cognitive information processing
Simulator	Presents an environment	Virtual worlds, role-play games	Cognitive constructivism
Collaboration enabler	Connects people and helps them work together	Discussion forums, Web 2.0	Social constructivism

software companies in conjunction with their desktop and Web-based applications or tools are most likely to be adopted by instructors. Although there may be other ways in which apps may be classified (e.g., Park's (2011) system which is based on the level of transactional distance), we believe that these four categories represent the most useful classifications and differences for learning app developers to consider.

Learning Theory and App Design

Behaviorism

One of the hallmarks of behaviorism, and in particular of operant conditioning, is the use of a reinforcing stimulus—positive or negative—to help shape an individual's behavior. Based on Thorndike's Law of Effect, which states that people are inclined to do activities that are pleasing and avoid activities that are not, a behaviorist approach to learning would involve finding out what stimuli people like and dislike and then using those stimuli to either encourage or discourage a particular behavior. This principle of behaviorism is often visible in technology-based learning environments in the form of feedback systems. Feedback may come in the form of functional interaction indicators (e.g., auditory or visual affirmation that the learner has clicked a button) as well as learning performance indicators (e.g., affirmation that the learner selected a correct reply).

Shaping and chaining are two other strategies derived from behaviorism that can be used to support learning via a multi-step approach. Shaping involves successive approximations of a behavior; a learner will progress from an initial general attempt that will, over time and with practice and feedback, gradually come to resemble the target behavior. Chaining, then, involves stringing smaller behaviors together to create a longer one. Regular, immediate feedback is a critical part of both shaping and chaining, and the strategies may be used together or separately. Both strategies can be used to help learners master a new behavior, moving through different levels of difficulty.

Most apps include at least some form of behaviorist interaction simply because they include some sort of feedback mechanism within the interface. Common pedagogical applications of behaviorism to app-based learning include quiz-type interactions, such as flashcards, and drill and practice games; behavior modification programs, such as apps that track behaviors like time spent studying or practicing and provide encouragement and feedback; and push technologies, which can send daily reminders, automatic learning tips, and other learning-related messages.

Behaviorism's implications for app designers include rewards, instant feedback, personalized learning, and mastery. Providing rewards within a learning system is a way of capitalizing on the Law of Effect; receiving acknowledgement of their achievements motivates many learners. Conversely, it is generally recommended to avoid punitive systems in a learning scenario, since those are thought to discourage learners. Rewards can be set up in various ways, including scoring systems, prizes, or badges for reaching new levels, and token economies (e.g., virtual coins which may be won, lost, or spent for virtual goods).

Instant feedback is an important part of behavioral learning. When feedback is delayed or provided at a later point in time, it is less meaningful to the learner. Immediate feedback helps the learner. In terms of learning app design, this means that designers should strive to provide learners with feedback at the point of interaction or input.

Personalized learning can be enabled in a behavioral context by providing a learning system, such as an app, that supports students working at the pace that best suits them individually. This type of learning control was initially advocated by Keller (1968), who described a personalized system of instruction (PSI) that was not dependent on a live, human teacher for instructional delivery. Selection and sequencing of content is not left up to the student's discretion in a PSI, and the student is encouraged to work toward mastery. Computer-based learning applications are well suited to the PSI model of instruction in part because the computer can tirelessly provide consistent and standardized feedback to a learner, whatever pace he or she is working at.

Finally, behaviorist approaches focus on mastery learning. Typically this means that a learner must continue to work on a given content or skill-based objective until it has been sufficiently mastered. Thus, a behaviorist-based app would not allow for flexible browsing of learning content, but rather would have a learner working on a fixed path.

In particular, these behaviorist strategies are useful when supporting learning at the lower levels of Bloom's taxonomy (see Anderson & Krathwohl, 2001, for an updated version; Bloom, 1984, for the original taxonomy), such as the learning of basic facts or concepts (Ally, 2008). However, they also can be used in support of learning at higher levels of the taxonomy, often integrated with strategies from other theories.

Cognitive Information Processing

Cognitive information processing theory focuses on memory, and is specifically concerned with how people store and retrieve information, passing it between short-term or working memory and long-term or storage memory. This theory in many ways mirrors how a computer functions, with random access memory providing a transient workspace that does not actually store anything, and storage memory that is stable but only effective if we have set up a logical file structure and used meaningful file names.

Theorists and researchers in this area have studied topics such as how much information people can effectively manage in their short-term memory and how we can best help people encode and retrieve information in their long-term memory. In the former case, relevant issues include cognitive load and the relative balance of germane and extraneous information that confronts people when they engage in learning. In the latter case, theorists have considered how learners might have information organized and stored in their long-term memory, with a focus on both how pieces of information are associated with each other and strategies that help learners make meaningful connections so that information is stored in a manner that will facilitate retrieval when the learner is confronted with relevant cues.

Feedback is also an important component of cognitive information processing theory. This theory elaborates on the behaviorist notion of feedback, adding the possibility that feedback might be instructive. In other words, a correct response may provide the opportunity to reinforce what a learner is thinking, and an incorrect response may provide the opportunity to either address a misconception or provide an explanation of the correct solution.

Most app designers must make decisions about how to divide up screen space and determine what content or buttons should be adjacent to other content or buttons. Additionally, they must focus on what is relevant to the learning experience and what might be distracting. Such decisions, globally common to all apps, reflect a concern with cognitive information processing. Common pedagogical applications of cognitive information processing to app-based learning include instructional multimedia; structured self-learning, such as e-books and how-to guides; and database-driven learning systems, which index and organize information for learners. These all have in common the reliance on information that has been carefully selected and presented to the learner in a manner that should optimize learning.

Cognitive information processing's implications for app designers include multiple communication channels, information chunking, and encoding strategies. The use of multiple communication channels (e.g., text, audio, and visual depiction) has been heavily researched by Mayer (2009; Mayer & Moreno, 2003) in a multimedia context. Mayer researched how combinations of different communication channels either enhance or inhibit learning. His findings include that words and pictures are better than words alone (multimedia principle); extraneous words, sounds, and pictures should be eliminated in a learning context (coherence principle); and when written text is added to a narrated animation, learning is inhibited (redundancy principle).

Chunking is important because it helps reduce cognitive load (Bransford, Brown, & Cocking, 2000; Schneiderman & Plaisant, 2005). In terms of information chunking, app designers must determine the best ways to group information so that it can be efficiently and effectively conveyed to learners. Classifying chunks of information under meaningful headings and showing the relationships between parts is one way of approaching this task. In practical terms it means that components such as tables of content and screen titles are very important. Mayer also has findings related to information chunking, specifically that shorter learner-controlled segments of content are preferable to a long continuous stream of multimedia.

Finally, encoding strategies are necessary to help learners create effective mental models from the information that they encounter. App designers can help learners by using devices such as mnemonics, metaphors, advance organizers, and organizational charts. These devices are meant to facilitate the process of connecting related concepts, thus facilitating both the retrieval of prior relevant knowledge and subsequent effective encoding of new knowledge. Further, Koole (2009) suggests that one of the strengths of mobile learning is the ability to help the learner create episodic, rather than semantic, connections between pieces of information. Although not every app will be used *in situ*, there are rich possibilities for the development of episodic memories that are enabled by iPads, iPhones, and iPods, particularly when information sources are being accessed on a just-in-time basis to support an activity that a learner is highly motivated to complete.

Constructivist Theories

Constructivist learning theories are concerned with how learners construct knowledge based on their interactions with both the environment and peers. There are two major types of constructivist learning theory: cognitive constructivism and social constructivism. They share many common beliefs, both encouraging learning that takes place in authentic settings or a reasonable facsimile and that involves real-world problem-solving skills. Thus, both take a highly contextualized approach to learning.

Cognitive Constructivism

In cognitive constructivism, the main focus is on providing a learning context that supports the learning in constructing experience-based knowledge. This is in contrast to a more didactic approach in which the learner is expected to simply receive knowledge. In this view, knowledge construction is an individual activity, but interaction with others often is a part of the learning process.

Learning is designed with clear goals and objectives, and the learner is guided toward meeting those objectives through carefully designed scenarios and interactions. Typically learning in this area involves problem solving and critical thinking set in an authentic environment or reasonable facsimile.

Cognitive constructivism's implications for app designers include situatedness, models, and scaffolds. Situatedness refers to the context in which learning experiences occur. Although learning may take place in classrooms, learners can be asked to solve problems that exist outside the classroom, using authentic tools and immersed in the culture and story surrounding the problem. iPods, iPhones, and iPads, due to their portability, readily lend themselves to use in an authentic or situated context, or they can provide tools that would help students solve situated problems.

Models and scaffolds, then, are used to support the learner in the problem-solving process. Models show students the processes or behaviors they might engage in during the problem-solving process. Essentially, they are examples of what to do. Scaffolds are pedagogical supports that make certain tasks easier, such as templates. They remove some of the extraneous cognitive load from the problem-solving process. Ideally, models and scaffolds are used to help the learner begin the learning process, and can later be faded or removed when the learner has progressed to a more advanced level. Apps often use models and/or scaffolds when initially presenting interactions that may occur at different levels. Examples may show the learner how to begin, and initial efforts may be supported by the initial removal of some challenges or simplification of tools.

Social Constructivism

In social constructivism, the peer role becomes of critical importance. Knowledge is viewed as the co-constructed artifact of peer interactions, ideally while engaged in some form of collaborative problem solving. A shared task orientation, which Vygotsky (1981; Wertsch, 1985) termed intersubjectivity, is a critical component of successful learning, as is the availability or development of shared norms and tools, including language (Wenger, 1998).

Additionally, learning interactions should occur in what is called the learner's zone of proximal development (ZPD), which is the range of learning activities that represents what the learner is ready to learn next with the assistance of a knowledgeable peer. In other words, the ZPD is a fluid zone (i.e. it moves as the learner engages with others and co-constructs knowledge) that is between what the learner already knows how to do alone and what is currently out of reach, even with assistance.

App-based learning that occurs via social constructivism requires that the app permit communication among a group of learners. Thus, it typically involves some type of social networking, sharing, discussion, or conferencing. Social constructivism's implications for app designers include collaboration, apprenticeship, and problem solving. Collaboration is the backbone of social constructivism, and may be contrasted with cooperation; those approaches respectively rely upon negotiating and completing a task together versus dividing labor and working individually. To facilitate sharing and negotiation processes, collaboration tools must enable rich discourse. Typically collaboration is in the service of problem solving. Much like in cognitive constructivism, authentic problems are the most appropriate ones. Finally, apprenticeship provides a means through which less experienced learners may gain the knowledge and guidance of their more experienced peers. To facilitate cognitive apprenticeship, a tool must help make the actions and thoughts of the more experienced learner visible to the less experienced one.

Designing for Different Paradigms of Use

As shown in Figure 2.1, each paradigm of app use has a primary relationship to a particular learning theory. However, each tends to draw upon and reflect tenets and strategies of other theories as well. Those secondary relationships are depicted as dashed

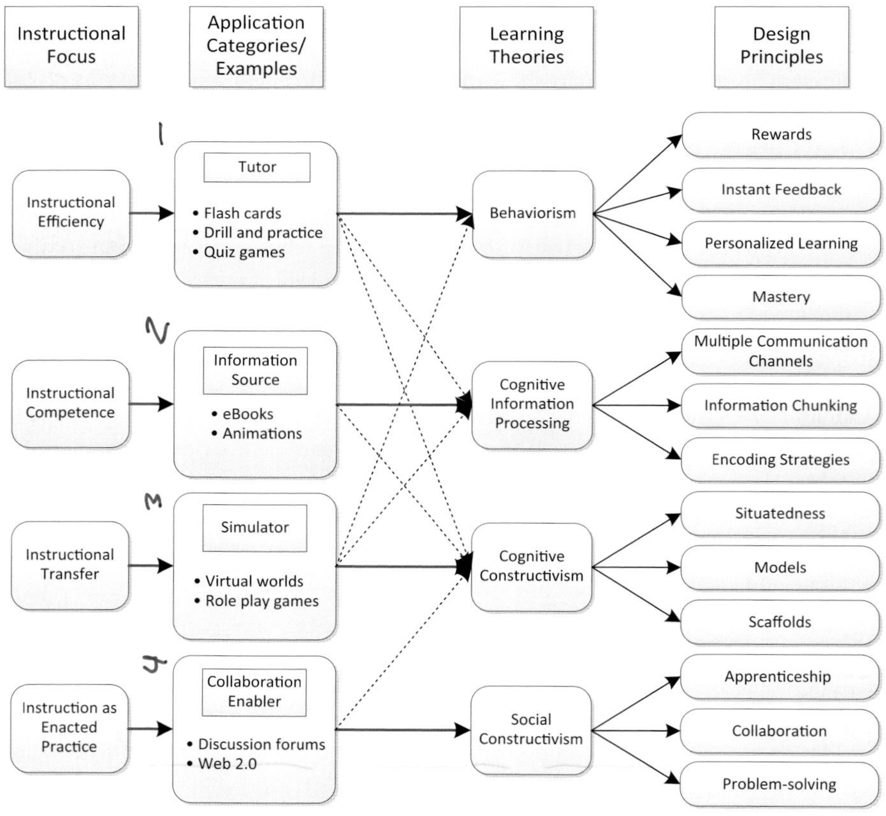

Figure 2.1
Relationship between paradigms and learning theories.

arrows in the figure. Much as Deubel (2003) concluded that no one theoretical or pedagogical approach unilaterally meets the design needs for all multimedia-based learning, we believe that no one approach will meet the needs for all app-based learning.

Throughout the remainder of this chapter, we share some of our own app prototypes and discuss how they both represent a particular pedagogical use and exhibit characteristics of different pedagogical strategies. Additionally we share apps that provide commercially available examples of the paradigms.

App as Tutor

A tutor, in the traditional sense of the word, is one who provides learning support, typically in an individualized (i.e. one-on-one) manner. The concept of tutor-based learning is reliant on constant interaction between the tutor—whether human or computer-based—and the learner. Apps that fit the tutor paradigm rely heavily on behaviorist principles.

In our example (see Figure 2.2), the learner is focused on spelling simple words. This example combines a behaviorist approach to learning with some elements of cognitive

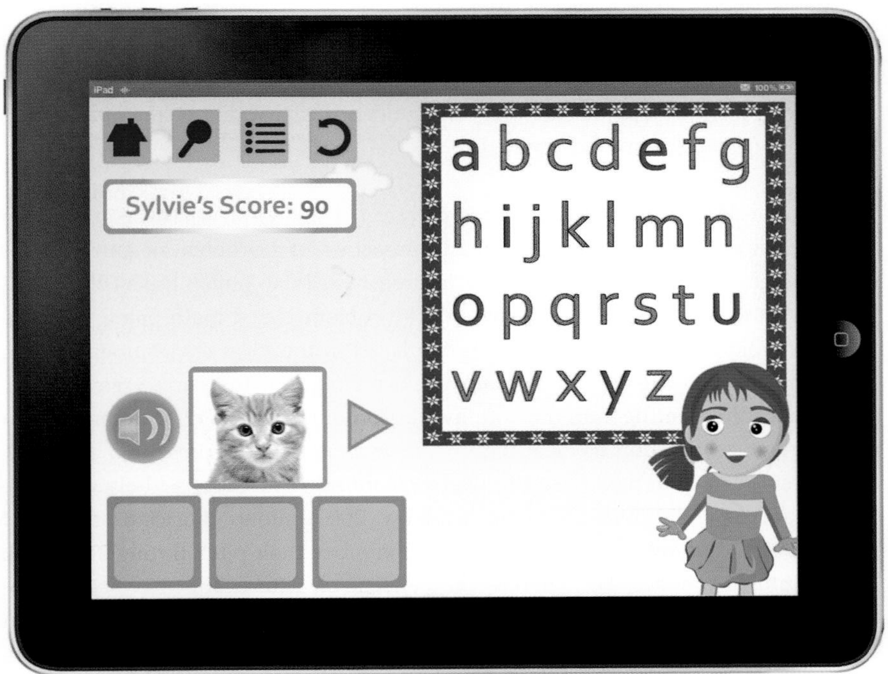

Figure 2.2
Sample tutor app.

information processing. The learner is presented with a well-defined task and all of the tools necessary to complete the task. Visual components of the screen include a picture of the word to be spelled, the letters of the alphabet, and entry blanks into which the learner will drag the correct letters. Auditory components include the ability to hear both the word and the letters pronounced. The learner has a score, which serves as a reward system. With each letter she selects, she receives instant feedback if it was correct (i.e. the letter remains in place) or incorrect (i.e. the letter snaps back to the alphabet). The learner must continue spelling three-letter words until the app has determined that she has mastered them, at which point she may move on to four-letter words. The app is personalized in two ways: The learner's name is presented on the screen and the learner may work individually, at her own speed.

Existing tutor apps are plentiful, in part because developers quickly recognized that people would want to use smartphones and tablets to practice and review content. Some of these apps focus on assessment only, but others teach a skill and walk learners through iterations of practice. For example, iWriteWords (dgiplus, 2012) shows children how to write different letters and spell basic words by providing letter templates with guides for swiping and then demonstrates how the groups of letters that the child wrote form words. The Living Language series of apps (Random House Digital, Inc., 2012) teach second language vocabulary and grammar and then tests the user via objective style games. In both instances, the content and assessment are chunked into developmentally appropriate units and guidance is provided by the app to keep the learner from being overwhelmed.

To be innovative in this area requires careful consideration of the content and learning context. Embedding the tutored interaction in a problem or game makes it more engaging than a context-neutral approach. FETCH: Lunch Rush (PBS KIDS, 2011) ties together augmented reality and a problem-based math game. The app uses printable game pieces, which can be placed in the local environment. When the animated character within the app makes a request, the correct game piece must be scanned. In the end, the core interaction of the app is no different from a multiple-choice question (i.e. learners choose from among the presented answers). Alternately, a tutor app can use the iPad's recording capabilities to help diagnose performance. Pitch Primer (Sibelius Academy, 2009) allows musicians to record themselves and then helps them analyze and improve their pitch through feedback and continued practice. So, whereas the concept of a tutor app may seem quite simple and the default interactions may seem largely template driven, creativity in content, interaction design, and tool use can help transform these apps from the standard (and oft overused) drill-and-practice format to one that will captivate and motivate learners.

App as Information Source

An information source does not support the entirety of the learning experience, but does provide the content. Learners may invoke self-instructional strategies in order to learn from these apps. Alternately, such apps may be used in a facilitated context, with teachers, or may be used as performance supports by individuals who are not seeking to learn the information, but rather who need to use it temporarily as a means to an end.

Often, learning-based apps combine use paradigms, and the information source paradigm is highly likely to be combined with others. For example, an app may have one component that is an information source and another that serves as a tutor. The learner may initially work through the learning content on her own, and then have the opportunity to practice and receive feedback. Or, a simulation app may present the learner with situations that indicate a lack of knowledge and the learner may then reference an information source, either built in or external, to help meet that need.

Our sample app (see Figure 2.3) provides nutrition information. It might be used for any number of learning or performance support purposes. The menu screen presents

Figure 2.3
Sample information source app.

an entree into chunked content; the content is organized by type of food (e.g., fruit, vegetable, dairy). These categories are familiar to most people and will not cause extraneous cognitive load issues. A person wanting information on peaches will know where to look within the app. Additionally, the menu has an option for a text list as opposed to visual icons, allowing learners to choose their preferred communication channel. The organization of the categories also has meaning, with grains, fruits, and vegetables next to each other; fish, meats, and dairy next to each other; and the less healthy fats and sweets next to each other.

Apps such as this one may be rather simple in terms of interactive and adaptive features, but they take full advantage of the mobile medium by bringing information directly to the situation in which it may be used. This nutrition app could readily have an instructional activity built around it; children could carry around devices with the app installed and use it to track the nutritional value of the foods that they choose to eat at each meal. The app could even have an interactive component in which users could photograph and then analyze their meals, perhaps even sharing them with others, or it could be embedded inside a game or simulation app, providing just-in-time access to knowledge needed to solve a problem or accomplish a task.

This category of app has proliferated, with programmers assimilating content on a chosen topic from sources such as books and Wikipedia into the app environment. Quality control, particularly with regard to content accuracy, remains an issue. The truly innovative learning apps in this category transcend simple content delivery. They embed interactive learning activities and provide meaningful news ways of interacting with or navigating the content. The Wordflex Touch Dictionary (Schematix, Inc., 2011) is not just a dictionary, but also a tool that facilitates visualizing and exploring word relationships. Geo Walk (Vito Technology Inc., 2012a) is an encyclopedia that can be explored by drilling down on a topic or spinning a globe, with quizzes that encourage exploration of content categories. Fancy Nancy Ballet School (Bean Creative, 2012) presents animated clips of different ballet clips and moves, and then rewards the learner with an opportunity to dance with the Fancy Nancy character using the camera and augmented reality.

App as Simulator

The key pedagogical elements of simulator apps are aligned with cognitive constructivism. They need to situate the learner in a particular environment or context and represent that setting to a reasonable degree. Although games set in virtual worlds have raised the bar in terms of expectations for graphics and animation, simulated learning environments need not be that sophisticated in order to be effective. Indeed, in some educational contexts there is a point at which there are diminishing rewards in terms of learning outcomes relative to development effort. Principles of cognitive information processing can be used to help determine the degree of detail that is necessary as well as what might be germane or extraneous detail given the learning objectives supported by the environment.

Typically, learners need support for interacting in a simulated environment. Thus, models, scaffolds, and instructive feedback are more prevalent in educational apps than in apps created for gaming or entertainment purposes. When a learner enters a simulation app, he may not know how to begin interacting with the environment. Trial and error may or may not yield satisfactory results, and can result in frustration or inefficiency. Thus, support should be focused on helping the learner identify and achieve the instructional objectives. For example, models can be provided, such as videos or animations showing the desired behavior. Scaffolds, such as virtual coaches, environment maps, task lists, and other organizers can be used to help keep the learner moving through the environment on a productive path. These forms of support provide some initial confidence upon entering the simulation (i.e. it's not just a random discovery experience, there will be help) and help ensure the learning experience will be a productive one.

Figure 2.4 shows a screen from Digital Ethics for Teachers (Dennen & Hao, 2012), a low-fidelity simulation app consisting of static graphics and text. This app was designed to teach digital ethics and places the learner in a school environment. The learner is placed in a variety of problem-solving situations and interacts with characters—such as the teacher shown in the screenshot. Along the way, she must make decisions that involve ethical judgment, and instructive feedback is provided. Apps such as this one often take on a game-like quality for learners, engaging them in role-play.

Simulation apps can bring together a wide range of learning experiences on one device. Virtual Manipulatives (ABCya.com, 2012) provides virtual tiles for practicing fractions, decimals, and percentages, and learners can save images of their screens for assessment purposes. Rat Dissection (Emantras, Inc., 2011), Frog Dissection (Emantras, Inc., 2012), and Virtual Human Body (QA International, 2012) enable biological exploration, and Chemist (THIX, 2012) provides a virtual chemistry lab. These apps emulate regular computer-based simulation software, with portability as the added feature offered by the mobile platform.

Other simulation learning apps have capitalized on the unique features of mobile devices, such as the ability to be in the field with a touchscreen, camera, geo-location tools, and motion sensors. Cookie Doodle (Shoe the Goose, 2012) is an app that capitalizes on the touchscreen and motion sensors. Users bake virtual cookies from scratch in this app, tilting and shaking the iPad and pinching and swiping the screen to put ingredients in the bowl. Although this app may not be explicitly educational, it demonstrates

Figure 2.4
Simulation app.

a range of inputs that mimic real-world actions and help app-based simulations both increase their realism and address psychomotor components of learning.

Cameras and geo-location tools may either be used while learners navigate an authentic environment or to insert learners into a fantasy or fictitious environment. The prototype depicted in Figure 2.5 is an example of an augmented reality app that supports learning in an authentic environment, combining elements of simulation with information source. In this example, the learner may take a photo of a plant and receive an overlay of information about it. The information may simply be declarative in nature, helping the learner understand artifacts in the environment as seen in the example, in which a description and information about cultivation and use may be accessed.

Leafsnap (Columbia University, University of Maryland, and the Smithsonian Institution, 2011) is an app that takes this concept a little further, integrating geo-location capabilities. A learner can take and upload a photo of a leaf specimen and not only receive

Figure 2.5
Prototype augmented reality app.

assistance identifying the specimen but also access information about other specimens that might be found in the local area. Other apps of this nature include LookBackMaps (LookBackMaps, 2010), which provides historical information about sights around the San Francisco area, and Star Walk (Vito Technology, Inc., 2012b), which provides a guide to navigating the local night sky by using the device's camera pointed at the stars.

Alternately, augmented reality may be used to help the learner perform tasks within the authentic environment by identifying relevant tools and providing just-in-time information about how they work. For example, an app might be used to help walk a learner through completing a specimen collection, indicating what tools are needed and how they should be positioned and used, or it might indicate the parts of a machine and how they function, bringing what would otherwise be a flat diagram to life.

The flip side of augmented reality, in which a learner is immersed into a simulated environment, may be more fun than functional at this point in time. Familiar non-education examples include Starbucks Cup Magic (Starbucks, 2011), which displays themed animations over the camera image when focused on a special cup, and Virtual Snow (www.UselessiPhoneStuff.com, 2011), which superimposes animated falling snow in front of the camera's image. In the education realm, apps such as ZooBurst (ZooBurst LLC, 2012), which allow teachers and learners to create their own 3D pop-up books and view themselves in the background of the book, are a bit clumsy at the moment, but nonetheless may be motivational for students to use and demonstrate the promise of this technology. The gaming world has presented more sophisticated and stable examples of the technology in action such as ARDefender (int13, 2012), which integrates a game environment (e.g., towers and weapons) within the user's local environment. The challenge for upcoming educational app developers will be to figure out how to focus this technology in ways that help learners achieve their objectives in a pedagogically sound manner. In other words, there are educational contexts in which this technology could truly be functional, and not just fun.

Layar Reality Browser (Layar, 2011), an augmented reality browser, puts the activity design and content controls in the hands of the end user. With this app, a teacher or learners might create their own augmented reality experience by setting target images and specifying what should appear or happen when the camera scans one of those images. The ability to engage learners as creators and potentially collaborators via this app pushes its use into the realm of constructivism.

App as Collaboration Enabler

The final paradigm of use is collaboration, which is closely aligned with social constructivism. When collaboration apps are used, the success of the learning experience is just as dependent on the users and their desired task as it is on the performance of the app. Although motivated users can sometimes compensate for what an app lacks, the app generally cannot compensate for unmotivated users. If the users lack intersubjectivity or elect to engage in cooperative rather than collaborative work, the learning outcomes are likely to be less satisfactory. That noted, it is quite possible for a collaboration app to scaffold the learning experience through the specific features and tools that it offers.

Our prototype collaboration app (see Figure 2.6) is designed for use in a science fair or problem-solving context. Learners are encouraged to contribute to their group's knowledge base by taking full advantage of the iPad's input capabilities; photo, video, and audio contributions are possible in addition to text, and learners also have tools to draw or concept map their ideas. Then, in the discussion tool, learners can work with each other to make sense of the various contributions to the group knowledge base. A teacher or other guest might enter the group space to provide guidance as needed or desired, essentially apprenticing the learners. This type of app is innovative because

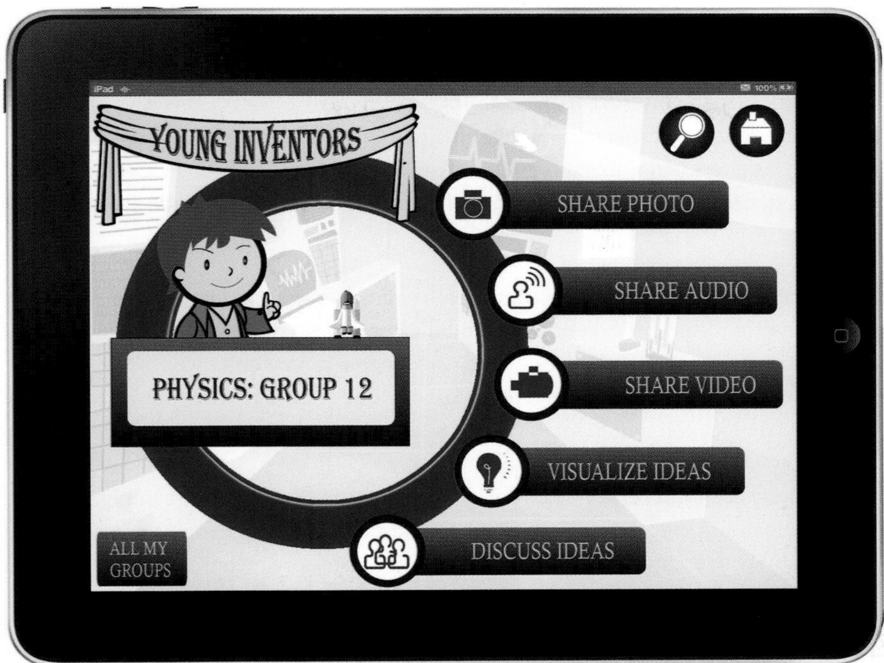

Figure 2.6
Prototype collaboration app.

it provides a multimodal connection among learners directly from the specific environments in which they may be doing inquiry or exploration-type work.

Educators may adopt any number of generic collaboration apps, mostly designed to support social or workplace interactions. Any app that facilitates contribution to a Web-based collaborative tool—e.g., Pearltrees (Broceliand SAS, 2012) or Edmodo (Edmodo, 2012)—via a mobile device would qualify in this category. Also in this category are general cloud computing apps such as Dropbox (2012) and collaborative writing and drawing apps such as SyncPad (Thirtynine LLC, 2012). Education-specific apps that are not off-shoots of a larger Web-based tool (e.g., StoryLines for Schools (Root-One, Inc., 2012), which emulates a vocabulary-based game of telephone) are less common at this time.

Not all collaboration apps need to be focused on fostering computer-mediated interactions. Stick Pick (Garwood, 2012) is an app designed to help teachers facilitate classroom collaboration. The app helps teachers randomly select students for questioning during class and suggests appropriate question stems based on the chosen level of

Bloom's Taxonomy. Each learner can be programmed to receive questions at a different level, and multiple-question stems are provided each time a learner's stick is selected.

App Design for Transformative Pedagogy

In order to create apps that support learning in a truly transformative manner, the challenge to designers is not to simply replicate existing tools for a mobile medium, but to take advantage of the affordances of a mobile device. In other words, designers should consider:

- Portability: the ability to access and record information from just about any location means that learning experiences can be extended beyond the classroom and that learning interactions in a variety of environments can be enhanced.
- Connectivity: the abilities to access just-in-time information either as needed or based on location and to interact with other people can make learning increasingly adaptive and relevant.
- Input devices and sensors: geo-location and motion-sensor data can help personalize learning experiences in certain situated contexts and content areas. Further, the ability to engage learners via authentic multisensory means (e.g., various finger movements, motion, visuals, audio) can increase a learner's sense of immersion within a mediated learning experience.
- Recording abilities: the ability to make, share, edit, and annotate audio and video recordings in just about any location from one integrated device can support learners as they collect data, practice skills, and document their achievements.

Designers should not strive to use these features in a "gimmicky" manner; pedagogy should always come first, and gratuitous use of features is likely to distract, increasing extraneous cognitive load. A good starting point for transformative learning app design is to consider first the learning objectives of a given app, and then explore the corresponding ways in which the iPad, iPhone, or iPod's unique features might help achieve that objective via a combination of content and interactions designed in a pedagogically sound manner.

Conclusion

In closing, educational app designers must have both a clear sense of how their app will be used to support learning as well as the related foundational learning theories. Although current research on learning apps is thin, research and theory completed on instructional multimedia can provide general guidance to app designers. App designers, in turn, should strive to use these principles not only to replicate earlier forms of multimedia-based instruction in an iPhone or iPad format, but to create new learning tools that take advantage of both the ability to carry these educational opportunities into a variety of environments and the unique features of mobile devices. It is through innovation that combines empirical design principles, pedagogical theory, and new technologies that apps will have the power to transform learning experiences.

References

ABCya.com. (2012). Virtual Manipulatives! (Version 1.2). [Mobile application software]. Retrieved June 5, 2012, from http://itunes.apple.com.

Ally, M. (2008). Foundations of educational theory for online learning. In T. Anderson (Ed.), *Theory and practice of online learning* (2nd edition). Edmonton, Canada: AU Press.

Anderson, L. W., & Krathwohl, D. R. (Eds.). (2001). *A taxonomy for learning, teaching and assessing: A revision of Bloom's Taxonomy of educational objectives*. New York: Longman.

Bean Creative (2012). Fancy Nancy Ballet School (Version 1.0). [Mobile application software]. Retrieved June 5, 2012, from http://itunes.apple.com.

Bloom, B. S. (1984). *Taxonomy of educational objectives book 1: Cognitive domain*. New York: Addison Wesley Publishing Company.

Bransford, J., Brown, A., & Cocking, R. (2000). *How people learn: Brain, mind, experience, and school*. Washington: National Academy of Sciences.

Broceliand SAS. (2012). Pearltrees (Version 0.9.4). [Mobile application software]. Retrieved June 5, 2012, from http://itunes.apple.com.

Columbia University, University of Maryland, and the Smithsonian Institution (2011). Leafsnap (Version 1.05). [Mobile application software]. Retrieved June 5, 2012, from http://itunes.apple.com.

Dennen, V. P. & Hao, S. (2012). Digital Ethics for Teachers. [Mobile application software in development].

Deubel, P. (2003). An investigation of behaviorist and cognitive approaches to instructional multimedia design. *Journal of Educational Multimedia and Hypermedia, 12*(1), 63–90.

dgiplus (2012). iWriteWords (Version 3.0.3). [Mobile application software]. Retrieved June 5, 2012, from http://itunes.apple.com.

Dropbox. (2012). Dropbox (Version 1.5.5). [Mobile application software]. Retrieved June 5, 2012, from http://itunes.apple.com.

Edmodo. (2012). Edmodo (Version 3.5.1). [Mobile application software]. Retrieved June 5, 2012, from http://itunes.apple.com.

Emantras, Inc. (2011). Rat Dissection (Version 1.1). [Mobile application software]. Retrieved June 5, 2012, from http://itunes.apple.com.

Emantras, Inc. (2012). Frog Dissection (Version 1.2). [Mobile application software]. Retrieved June 5, 2012, from http://itunes.apple.com.

Garwood, B. (2012). Stick Pick (Version 1.03). [Mobile application software]. Retrieved June 5, 2012, from http://itunes.apple.com.

int13. (2012). ARDefender (Version 1.5.7). [Mobile application software]. Retrieved June 5, 2012, from http://itunes.apple.com.

Keller, F. S. (1968). Goodbye teacher . . . *Journal of Applied Behavior Analysis, 1*, 79–89.

Koole, M. L. (2009). A model for framing mobile learning. In M. Ally (Ed.), *Mobile learning: Transforming the delivery of education and training* (pp. 25–47). Edmonton, Canada: AU Press.

Koschmann, T. (1996). Paradigm shifts and instructional technology: An introduction. In T. Koschmann (Ed.), *CSCL: Theory and practice of an emerging paradigm* (pp. 1–23). Mahwah, NJ: Lawrence Erlbaum.

Kukulska-Hulme, A. (2010). Learning cultures on the move: Where are we heading? *Educational Technology & Society, 13*(4), 4–10.

Kukulska-Hulme, A., Traxler, J., & Pettit, J. (2007). Designed and user-generated activity in the mobile age. *Journal of Learning Design, 2*(1), 52–65.
Layar, B. V. (2011). Layar Reality Browser (Version 7.0). [Mobile application software]. Retrieved June 5, 2012, from http://itunes.apple.com.
LookBackMaps. (2010). LookBackMaps (Version 1.0.1). [Mobile application software]. Retrieved June 5, 2012, from http://itunes.apple.com.
Mayer, R. E. (2009). *Multimedia learning*. Cambridge, UK: Cambridge University Press.
Mayer, R. E., & Moreno, R. (2003). Nine ways to reduce cognitive load in multimedia learning. *Educational Psychologist, 38*(1), 43–52.
Park, Y. (2011). A pedagogical framework for mobile learning: Categorizing educational applications of mobile technologies into four types. *International Review of Research in Open and Distance Learning, 12*(2), 78–102.
PBS KIDS. (2011). FETCH: Lunch Rush (Version 1.0.2). [Mobile application software]. Retrieved June 5, 2012, from http://itunes.apple.com.
QA International. (2012). Virtual Human Body (Version 1.3). [Mobile application software]. Retrieved June 5, 2012, from http://itunes.apple.com.
Quinn, C. N. (2011). *Designing mLearning: Tapping into the mobile revolution for organizational performance*. New York: Wiley
Random House Digital, Inc. (2012). Living Language—French for iPad (Version 1.1.4). [Mobile application software]. Retrieved June 5, 2012, from http://itunes.apple.com.
Root-One, Inc. (2012). StoryLines for Schools (Version 4.0.3). [Mobile application software]. Retrieved June 5, 2012, from http://itunes.apple.com.
Schematix, Inc. (2011). Wordflex Touch Dictionary (Version 1.1). [Mobile application software]. Retrieved June 5, 2012, from http://itunes.apple.com.
Schneiderman, B., & Plaisant, C. (2005). *Designing the user interface: Strategies for affective human-computer interaction* (4th edition). Toronto, Canada: Pearson Education.
Shoe the Goose. (2012). Cookie Doodle (Version 2.19). [Mobile application software]. Retrieved June 5, 2012, from http://itunes.apple.com.
Sibelius Academy. (2009). Pitch Primer (Version 1.0). [Mobile application software]. Retrieved June 5, 2012, from http://itunes.apple.com.
Starbucks. (2011). Starbucks Cup Magic. [Mobile application software]. Retrieved June 5, 2012, from http://www.starbucks.com/coffeehouse/mobile-apps/starbucks-cup-magic.
Taylor, R. P. (1980). *The computer in school: Tutor, tool, tutee*. New York: Teachers College Press.
Thirtynine LLC (2012). SyncPad (Version 1.5). [Mobile application software]. Retrieved June 5, 2012, from http://itunes.apple.com.
THIX. (2012). Chemist (Version 2.3.1). [Mobile application software]. Retrieved June 5, 2012, from http://itunes.apple.com.
Vito Technology, Inc. (2012a). Geo Walk (Version 2.4.1). [Mobile application software]. Retrieved June 5, 2012, from http://itunes.apple.com.
Vito Technology, Inc. (2012b). Star Walk (Version 6.0.1). [Mobile application software]. Retrieved June 5, 2012, from http://itunes.apple.com.
Vygotsky, L. S. (1981). The genesis of higher mental functions. In J. V. Wertsch (Ed.), *The concept of activity in Soviet psychology* (pp. 144–188). Armank, NY: Sharpe.
Wenger, E. (1998). *Communities of practice: Learning, meaning, and identity*. Cambridge, England: Cambridge University Press.
Wertsch, J. V. (1985). *Vygotsky and the social formation of mind*. Cambridge, MA: Harvard University Press.
www.UselessiPhoneStuff.com. (2011). Virtual Snow (Version 1.0). [Mobile application software]. Retrieved June 5, 2012, from http://itunes.apple.com.
ZooBurst LLC. (2012). ZooBurst (Version 1.1). [Mobile application software]. Retrieved June 5, 2012, from http://itunes.apple.com.

Chapter 3
Rich Remote Learning and Cognition
Analog Methods as Models for Newer Technology

Currently, applications for mobile learning devices are remarkably limited; while we can download the daily news, the latest video, or an augmented explanation of an environment, the richness of a remote learning experience is often lost through the delivery of electronic media. Applications for mobile learning with digital electronic devices can be guided by an examination of current and historical practices such as field notebooks, sketchbooks and commonplace books. Learning through analog mobile devices integrates cognitive effort into engaged activities enhanced by writing, thinking, reflection, drawing, diagramming, and editing. This chapter examines the use of notebooks, sketchbooks and commonplace books in the development of knowledge, and examines other forms of representation in the process of learning and as models for new applications for mobile learning.

For Designers

This chapter will help designers recognize and apply the inherent value of both analog and digital media. Designers need to work with the full spectrum of media to produce educational products and they must take advantage of a full ecology of active and integrated learning platforms. Designs that include both analog and digital activities and results will produce richer learning outcomes.

For Teachers

This chapter will help teachers recognize the values of working with various forms of media for active learning. Digital and mobile learning, when integrated with real life experience, can provide an exceptionally strong learning experience. The novelty of the new technology of mobile applications can also encourage increased use of analog, physical materials in active learning experiences.

For Researchers

This chapter will encourage researchers to examine other forms and methods of learning, particularly those that are experience- and active-based efforts. The value of problem-based learning, particularly as modeled by design and experimentation, can be significant if enhanced through the cognitive methods of mobile applications in digital and analog form.

The best mobile apps for learning will challenge the learner to do more and watch less, lessons learned from the best of paper and integrated into an ecology of media.

Dr. Brad Hokanson
Professor, Graphic Design, University of Minnesota;
Associate Dean for Research and Outreach,
College of Design, University of Minnesota

Brad Hokanson is a professor in Graphic Design at the University of Minnesota and serves as Associate Dean for Research and Outreach for the College of Design. He won the College of Design's award for Outstanding Teaching in 2008. He has a diverse academic record, including degrees in art, architecture, urban design, and received his Ph.D. in Instructional Technology. He has published his research in *Educational Technology Research and Development*, *Computers in Human Behavior*, *Interactions with Media*, *Educational Technology*, and the *Handbook of Visual Languages in Instructional Design*. He currently is researching the relationship between creativity and achievement in school children. He teaches in the areas of interactive media, critical thinking, and creative problem solving. His research focuses on creativity and design thinking. He is a registered architect with a number of award-winning projects, although no longer in active practice. Visits to Buenos Aires support his Argentine tango habit.

Dr. Brad Hokanson

Rich Remote Learning and Cognition: Analog Methods as Models for Newer Technology

Mobile devices are viewed as having great promise for learning. A growing number of schools, universities, and teachers are embracing mobile devices such as smartphones and tablets to advance education. As with the adaptation of any innovation, there are a number of rigorous challenges, and in this case, these challenges encourage us to examine the nature of mobile technologies and the nature of learning. We may be moving toward a flexible ecology of mobility, one which is less centered on specific devices or platforms, but which are accessible anywhere and which include analog paper artifacts.

As we well understand, electronic digital mobile learning devices have a set of capabilities and limits, which make their use promising and rapidly growing. Their novelty and their ease of individual engaged use have driven a substantial involvement in education (Alberta Education, 2011). These devices have a set of capabilities that have led to their wide use and application in education, and as the technology remains dynamic and expansive, we recognize its potential in many ways. What is outlined here is a brief for the development of what a mobile learning device could be, based on how we could use such devices to help teach and learn.

The promise of a new technology is one that we have seen; one of learning "anywhere and at any time" and includes education and learning. We understand the enthusiasm of the most recent innovation, one that can have the ubiquity of paper and the universal access of the digital cloud. The leading question we should ask is: how can we improve learning with the capabilities of this new(er) technology? We seek some of the same things we have pursued with previous technological innovations such as the personal computer, internet access for every school, and one computer for every child, each of which hopes to transform and broaden learning. We may, with this innovation, reach the point where the technology helps one learn at a higher level, and not just be used as a distribution system for standardized, low-level learning.

We also remember the shortfall of the previous advances; when one technology did not advance the cause of education to the same extent as productivity in other fields. If you examine the use of mobile learning devices, the first questions must be of how someone should approach learning: Examining or remembering the earlier caveats and lessons will help us move forward in the development of mobile education.

The goal of this chapter is to raise questions, arguments, and details that help guide the development of mobile learning objects, devices, and applications. And, subsequently, we can utilize innovation theory, as described by Rogers (2010), in reviewing technologies we continue to value and use on a day-to-day basis. Rogers' factors include relative advantage, compatibility, complexity/simplicity, trialability, and observability.

This chapter is about the nature of work and about the nature of learning, where it occurs and how it occurs, and then, subsequently, it is about the use of media and technology to improve learning and thinking.

Adoption of Educational Technology, Redux

The enthusiastic effort to engage and utilize mobile devices for learning is reminiscent of earlier efforts to adopt technology for education, and the same concerns are still applicable. Cuban recently echoed his technology concerns and challenges of decades earlier (1993, Cuban & Kirkpatrick, 1998):

> "There is very little evidence that kids learn more, faster or better by using these machines," said Larry Cuban, a professor emeritus of education at Stanford University, who believes that the money would be better spent to recruit, train and retain teachers. "IPads are marvelous tools to engage kids, but then the novelty wears off and you get into hard-core issues of teaching and learning."
>
> (Hu, 2011)

More significantly, Clark (1983, 1991, 1994) presented substantial evidence to argue delivering learning through different media would not change the educational outcome until the instructional method changed. Changing the instructional methods used in education as a whole is a substantial challenge and one that has slowly been evolving over the years, parallel with the introduction of digital technology. Instructional method, motivation, and learner engagement are all components of a successful learning experience. And all of these are changed with the introduction of new variables, new confounding principles, of mobility and individual technological experience. In his earlier writings, Clark explained much of the positive early effect of computer-supported learning through a novelty effect or temporarily enhanced engagement due to new technology. We may have a more evolved understanding of the need for motivation and engagement with this technological iteration.

As we begin to develop learning with mobile devices, we must examine our base understandings of learning, and reasons why learning should occur in diverse locations. In addition, we should not abandon the standards of active learning or well founded constructivist theory and we must recognize that learning can be enhanced through changes in teaching method and not, magically, through the use of any new technology or device.

One can read about the Arctic from the comfort of a living room or listen to a lecture while mowing the lawn. These are new examples of a didactic form of learning, a remote lecture. Using a mobile learning device in the field or context can be incredibly richer; recording events as they happen, gathering data on temperature, water quality, or taking pictures of one's experience are also rich and part of a more active learning pedagogy. However, even these examples fall short of more deeply engaged learning that, at present, is easily accomplished through the use of an analog device, the notebook.

The use of any mobile learning device is tied to its affordances; what it can do and what it is capable of doing. Why we adopt any innovation is tied to that new technology being able to complete a task better than other competing technologies. In simple terms, it is a choice we make as we choose any technology; for example, writing a telephone number on a cocktail napkin, on one's hand, or keying it into our phone is a conscious choice.

Innovation theory, as described by Rogers (2010), is highly pragmatic and direct; innovations are accepted for a number of valid reasons, primarily because the innovation offers a relative advantage to the user. The adoption of new *mobile* technologies is often tied to the benefits of ease and ubiquity of use. The *new* must be easy to adopt, quick to use, and have the other capabilities of our analog devices, and the ability to record and develop thoughts. It should build on the newness and cache of the technologies as well as the immediacy of use. And, beyond Rogers' factors, it must encourage and direct more complex and higher-order learning (when the newness wears off).

Mobile learning can be and is simplistically viewed as another education application for information delivery; properly structured and repeatedly applied, instruction can occur anywhere, including in the bathroom. A lecture can be heard in the car, on the beach, while mowing the lawn; and it will be almost as good as in the lecture hall.

We do absorb information constantly; we can be listening to learning materials at any time, asleep or behind the wheel or both. But as we seek higher-order thinking and learning, these means of passive absorption are less successful than engaged active learning and problem solving. People learn most effectively through engagement and action, whether by personal experience or by solving problems, and less effectively by simply receiving and viewing information.

This chapter is part critique and part an examination of the new territory of learning, learning outside the classroom, learning outside of school, learning in a true constructivist sense, in the environment, from an experience, and from one's specific context. If we are to develop our own understanding of an experience or context, learners must develop our own knowledge, not as directed by a teacher or in substitution, by a mobile device.

In some rare cases, technology may leap past existing use and media to present ideas that were not possible with previous media. In general, advances build or transform existing uses. Through the building or transformation, new functions develop and evolve, but for the most part, any innovation must improve on current practices to be fully adopted (Rogers, 2010). Therefore, examining current analog applications of mobile media can inform our search and development of new, digital applications.

The reason to explore the functions and value of analog uses of paper in a collection of writings concerned with electronic, digital mobile learning devices is to examine some possible applications that could be inspired by such earlier media. This writing, then, is an argument for the "applications" of paper books, and secondly, for those qualities identified with notebooks, to serve as a second generation of metaphor and as a brief for the advanced development of mobile learning devices.

Analog Models as Exemplars: Examining Affordances

Digital technology often uses modes or metaphors to engage and enhance the use of innovations. In the late twentieth century, the use of computers in society and in education adopted a generally common graphic user interface based on the desktop. "Desktop" remains a descriptive metaphor for the organization of accessible digital materials. We move information around in a way similar to the organization and movement of paper on a surface. That metaphor has helped shape the functions of database, spreadsheet, and word-processing programs for the first generations of the computer.

We know that there are numerous improvised memory devices such as Post-it® notes, slips of paper, cocktail napkins, and writing on one's hand. And for that matter, Post-it® notes, whiteboards, and chalkboards are often used in knowledge industries for the structuring and sorting of new ideas. Analog media are often used in the synthesis and development of knowledge.

Applications for mobile digital devices can be inspired by the use of analog, non-digital mobile media. We have learned the software (i.e. how to use a sketchbook, a field or lab notebook, and the commonplace book) and these methods of use can be applied to learning with mobile, digital devices. Presented here are three forms of analog media along a continuum of use.

Field Notebooks: Guided Observation in Remote Locations

> Put me in a room with a pad and a pencil and set me up against a hundred people with a hundred computers—I'll outcreate every goddamn sonofabitch in the room.
>
> (Ray Bradbury, in Geirland, 1998)

For this writing, notebooks are used for recording information in written form on paper. Notebooks are those types of user-generated record-keeping recorded information. They include field-, lab-, notebooks, and journals. Most information is in written form. They take advantage of simple paper for easy use and recording.

Affordances include cost, durability, ease of use, and flexibility; the same choices that evolved with the initial development of the technology of paper. The immediacy of paper to record an idea can be illustrated by the I HEART NY logo design process:

> "I can't get the damn problem out of my head," he says, "and then, about a week later the first concept was approved, I'm sitting in a car, stuck in traffic. I often carry spare pieces of paper in my pocket, and so I get the paper out and I start to draw. And I'm thinking and drawing and then I get it. I see the whole design in my head. I see the typewriter typeface and the big round red heart smack-dab in the middle. I know that this is how it should go."
>
> (Milton Glaser, in Lehrer, 2012, pp. 161–162)

Within the sciences, field notebooks are used to record observations in written and graphic form. Writing is cognitively valuable; we remember what we have physically noted much better than what we have merely recorded, and interpreted based on our personal presence.

With the lab or field notebook, the rigor and structure with which one records information is a learned practice, the software of the notebook or journal. The notebook is not of value because of the recorded information, but due to the translation of raw data of some form. Successful use of lab books, field notebooks, and journals require selection of information, recording of information, and reflection on what was written. These are strong indicators of learning in process, for learning does not come by accumulating information or data, but rather through the analysis and synthesis of information, and through the creation of new ideas or directions.

Some notebooks provide some scaffolding or support for the user, but it is often minimal. Lab or field notes often make use of a specific standardized format providing some scaffolding. Moleskine City notebooks also provide a structure to assist users in writing the "guide you build yourself."

Two attributes of notebook/journal use worth investigating for mobile devices are instant input to notation and learned habits and structures. Applications that could develop from these practices would remind users for input on a regular basis or in a scaffolded regular structure. Secondly, one of the main advantages of the physical notebook is the lesser cognitive load and effort required to begin use. As it is less mediated and less technologically advanced, the paper notebook allows the learner to quickly engage more working memory into writing and creating and less into management of the technology. Less is forgotten compared to a computer or tablet; you opening the computer, then the file, selecting a font, adjusting the margins and then the original thought is forgotten. Instant access buttons could be included on screen for note taking applications. Currently, while phone calls can be answered on a locked phone without logging in, all other applications remain inaccessible. This same access could be offered by note-taking software: the instant-on button.

Sketchbooks: Focused Cognition and Synthesis

> "When you draw an object, the mind becomes deeply, intensely attentive, and it is that act of attention that allows you to really grasp something, to become fully conscious of it. . . . drawing is really a kind of thinking."
>
> (Milton Glaser, in Lehrer, 2012, pp. 157–158)

Sketchbooks differ from notebooks as they seek to include a broader range of user input material; images, diagrams, and writing are all included. Sketchbooks may also include material samples, printouts from other sources, receipts and paper artifacts. Sketchbooks are very involved in the initial development of ideas and concepts for later finishing on a desktop (analog or digital) location.

We know learning occurs through the focused attention of the learner, and not solely through access to information. What we, as educators, would like to achieve, more than access to information, is the strong engagement of the learner . . . and this can happen most easily through the active use and manipulation of information or data.

Learning comes most effectively through efforts that engage the mind and encourage deeper thinking. Current theory holds that this frequently comes through active learning and problem solving, through writing more than reading, discovery rather than consumption, analysis more than recording, and as an example, through drawing more than photography.

Both photography and drawing have values of their own in terms of artistic creation and in the development of learned outcome. Drawing, due to its time frame and engagement with cognitive effort, adds significantly more to the cognitive outcome. Through history, scientists have drawn out their findings, as visual representation and as diagrammatic summaries. Botanists have learned through visually recording plant growth by drawing, not to develop their drawing skills, but rather to encourage reflection and more engaged perception. Architects and artists, in comparison, have made "grand tours" of the architecture of Europe in order to sketch and draw the aesthetic roots of Western culture. Drawing may improve through such experience, but more is learned through close observation and analysis in a visual form. Drawing forces attention and the time to sit and observe, to fully note and notate the new experience or artifact. One learns by thinking through drawing.

The value of a designer's sketchbooks is not in the information contained inside; while that has value and helps one to write, work and think, it is the effort of creating the books which has helped one learn and understand. This same set of values can be integrated into an educational tablet application.

There are limits to both the sketchbook and to the digital tablet. Building thoughts works well with paper, but not yet with mobile devices or digital media. Part of the challenge with any mobile device is that the representation of the ideas is small and remote. Small portable screens do not allow for the interchange of pieces with ease. Editing and the attendant synthesis of ideas can be done with a sketchbook or digital tablet, but the size and form also limit the ease of use. Mobility is in direct conflict with ease of editing.

Logically, more important than the artifact is the method and habit of recording, learning, and synthesizing ideas and information by the learner. Those tools that best support this practice will be the most valuable. If we utilize tools that de-skill and focus more on recording than on the meaning and content of the recording, then any technological innovation is not of value.

There are, of course, other limitations to the use of sketchbooks. They build in volume and must be stored in some manner for reference. Perhaps the most pressing problem occurs when searching and reflecting on current material. In a chronologically organized notebook, most information is included in a linear fashion and in a logical order that is historic and not thematic.

With a sketchbook or field notebook, material is not easily searched. Similarly, for that ill-structured, unnamed sprout of an idea, searching on a large digital hard drive is comparably difficult; the organizing and structuring of information do lead to learning and synthesizing of ideas and to the development of knowledge. This is a consistency in both digital and analog domains.

Commonplace Books: Long-term Collection and Synthesis of Information

A historical example of a long-term, portable data management system developed in early modern Europe. Commonplace books were a way to compile knowledge, usually in written form, but also with the inclusion of drawings, images, samples, recipes, and hand-transcribed quotations.

> Commonplacing is the act of selecting important phrases, lines, and/or passages from texts and writing them down; the commonplace book is the notebook in which a reader has collected quotations from works s/he has read. Commonplace books can also include comments and notes from the reader; they are frequently indexed so that the reader can classify important themes and locate quotations related to particular topics or authors.
>
> (Knowles, 2012)

Practitioners of commonplacing included W. H. Auden, Thomas Jefferson, and Charles Darwin:

> Commonplace books are one model for organizing and learning; in the 16th century, it was a method in which many were trained; to record, organize and integrate a broad range of ideas and quotations. Charles Darwin, Mark Twain, and Thomas Jefferson all maintained commonplace books. "The great minds of the period—Milton, Bacon, Locke—were zealous believers in the memory-enhancing powers of the commonplace book."
>
> (Johnson, 2010)

A commonplace book is comparable to a small personally authored encyclopedia with various topics of interest. Hand-transcribed quotations from readings are organized and connected with text; in many published versions, space is included for commentary and involvement by a reader. Commonplace structured books in analog form were also published to be used and completed by the owner; the application/software was an understanding of how to use the commonplace structure.

Commonplace books were not meant as a finished work, and were not meant to be generally presentable to the public as a linear structured argument. Nor should our work from mobile devices be the end of the learning process; they are the means to gather information and record information. Notebooks and sketchbooks are strong methodological processes that foreshadow the appropriate use of any mobile applications. They are not valuable in their use to record, but more valuable in their use to think; not to capture, but to learn through observation. Significantly, much work of editing and organization occurs in structuring the commonplace book.

The logic of the commonplace book can provide some insight into the use of mobile technologies, from the smartphone to the paper notebook. Information and experiences are gathered in the book, re-edited and synthesized, then organized to make sense of the experience.

One's own computer could be described as a commonplace book, with notations, data, reminders, and developing thoughts, and with everything saved in a series of large sock drawers. Better organization and file management are important to effective use, and applications beyond simple searching are available for most computers. These file, data, and information management applications are important components on all digital and analog devices, and they remain parallel to our own cognitive schemata. The flat filing system of the tablet computer could be like a true commonplace book, but they exist without user-developed structures and organization and most information is found, not created.

The act of organizing, structuring, and filing helps develop schema . . . memories and learning. Ironically, the fuzzy logic, artificial intelligence and content organization applications may limit the value to learning, and, in turn, user intelligence. Is the artificial intelligence used in database systems such as DevonThink de-skilling? Or does it lead to being aware of missed opportunities?

Challenges

> Machines are beneficial to the degree that they eliminate the need for labor, harmful to the degree that they eliminate the need for skill.
>
> (Auden, 1970, p. 257)

One major current assumption in the field of learning is that learning is more effective when education is active, engaged, and generative. The complex condition that is learning does not come from sitting passively and viewing presented information, but more effectively when the learners create the materials themselves, when the learner is active in a variety of ways such as writing, moving, or recording. The best learning activity is *exothermic;* i.e. it generates more energy than it consumes. A parallel argument exists in discussions of the use of tablets outside of education; whether tablets are capable of *creating* content versus solely *watching* content.

Most uses of mobile learning devices such as smartphones and tablets focus on information retrieval relating to the current context; descriptions are presented to the learner rather than developed by the learner. Even in best cases, more scaffolding is presented than is needed to justify the use of expensive technology. Sometimes, it's an over-explanation with all the libraries of the world in your hand, when what a learner should be doing is just going outside and being present.

Mobile technology devices also make it easy to record or capture data from remote locations. In some cases, this is part of a valuable investigation, but in many cases, this is a mechanical recording of the experience, not enhancing the learning. Remote sensing may have scientific value, but it often does not lead to improved learning on the part of the learner. The value is in the making and reframing. Being there, unmediated, brings with it a rich set of experiences that are invaluable even in the world of high technology.

Real media and materials also have a direct connection with learners; real paper, real mud, or real pancakes all react differently from digital versions. This immediacy makes understanding more grounded as well as each instance more unique. When one is learning, we need materials that are *less* finished and more transparent. Learners need to make their own meaning directly from the context or material. In other words, part of the problem with mobile devices is that the output and input are available as organized, finished graphics and texts, making things complete and the perfect, immutable truth. There is less challenge to understanding with perfectly packaged content.

One empirical opportunity for most in the modern age is to personally examine one's own use of new devices including smartphone- and tablet-based applications. The same limits we experience with these devices can guide our own designs for mobile learning including choice of platform: How do we choose to read serious articles? Where do we create and where do we edit our work? How do we best experience foreign travel? How do we personally learn?

Are cognitive uses completed on mobile devices instead of desktop or laptop computers, or do we selectively downscale our efforts to the simplest checking of time, email, calls, and playing a game? Our own experiences can provide us with a guide to the use of mobile devices in learning . . . as they are presently constituted. And supplemented: How we modify our mobile devices illustrates their weaknesses; keyboarding is better accomplished with a laptop or we purchase a remote keyboard. A stylus focuses our input; earphones improve the sound-out and a microphone the sound-in.

Conclusion

As users, we can think through ideas in almost any format, but the media we use to form our thoughts and communicate our ideas have radically changed. And more and more, the changes are not replacements, but additional choices to be used. Multiple media streams are used to develop learning and understanding as the new skill is working across the media ecology for effective use. "Intelligence is skill in multiple media" (Hokanson & Hooper, 2000). We move from paper to tablet to cloud to computer to paper; fluidly changing between media, with effective applications easing the moving between media channels.

In the end, the use of technology must be appropriate; and technology must be viewed as extending from the simple notebook to the most high-end and developed piece of electronic assistance. Use will vary with individuals; applications will be those that make the translations with ease and support an ecology of media use.

When will we put down our paper, our notebook, our journal, or our field notebooks and fully embrace a digital device? Perhaps when they can be fully replaced by something that includes and goes beyond their capabilities, by something that can help us understand and think about that which we have come to learn. And, perhaps, not at all. Hybrid use appears to be a valid means of use; using mobile devices to separately access data and capture materials in digital form. But paper still retains value, much like in the office, to quickly and rapidly record and archive information.

We are not going to stop paper notebooks or analog devices any more than non-mobile computers. Mobile apps must be the means to make connections between media, between ideas, and between the remote and the digital.

References

Alberta Education (2011). iPads: What are we learning? Summary report of provincial data gathering day. Retrieved July 28, 2012, from http://education.alberta.ca/admin/technology/research.aspx.

Auden, W. H., (1970). *SOMETHING: A commonplace book*. New York: Viking Press.

Clark, R. E. (1983). Reconsidering research on learning from media. *Review of Educational Research, 53*(4), 445–459.

Clark, R. E. (1991). When researchers swim upstream: Reflections on an unpopular argument about learning from media. *Educational Technology, 31*(2), 34–40.

Clark, R. E. (1994). Media will never influence learning. *Educational Technology Research and Development, 42*(2), 21–29.

Cuban, L. (1993). Computers meet classroom: Classroom wins. *The Teachers College Record, 95*(2), 185–210.

Cuban, L., & Kirkpatrick, H. (1998). Computers make kids smarter—right? *Technos, 7*(2), 26–31.

Geirland, J. (1998) Bradbury's Tomorrowland, *Wired* 6:10. Retrieved July 1, 2012, from http://www.wired.com/wired/archive/6.10/bradbury_pr.html.

Hokanson, B., & Hooper, S. (2000). Computers as cognitive media: Examining the potential of computers in education. *Computers in Human Behavior, 16*(5), 537–552.

Hu, W. (2011). Math that moves: Schools embrace the iPad, *New York Times*, 4 January 2011. Retrieved July 10, 2012, from http://www.nytimes.com/2011/01/05/education/05tablets.html.

Johnson, S. (2010). *Where good ideas come from: The natural history of innovation*. Riverhead Books: New York.

Knowles, L., (2012). Commonplace books. Retrieved July 16, 2012, from http://www1.assumption.edu/users/lknoles/commonplacebook.html.

Lehrer, J. (2012). *Imagine: How creativity works*. Boston: Houghton Mifflin Harcourt.

Rogers, E. M. (2010). *Diffusion of innovations*. New York: Free Press.

Chapter 4
The Logic of the "And"
The Nature of Collaboration

In this chapter we will address the nature of collaboration within the context of education. Specifically, we will focus on the lessons that the Montessori approach to education has to teach us about creating in a digital, mobile landscape.

For Designers

One of our greatest challenges was taking an existing design and practice, and implementing it within our current landscape. In this chapter, we'll highlight some of these design decisions, and elaborate the collaborative nature of the enterprise.

For Teachers

We live in an exciting and constantly changing educational paradigm. We're really excited to be a part of this conversation, and hope you can find value in some of the insights that we have gleaned while collaborating together.

For Researchers

We're on the cusp of some major changes in understanding the ways in which children learn. We're also on the frontiers of examining how educators and researchers can collaborate to prepare for this budding new landscape.

erested in developing a philosophy of life, one that is atte
tions of aesthetics and pedagogy.

eorge

ek Montessori,
South Dakota;

m (http://montessorium.com)

June George
Co-founder,
The Baan Dek Montessori,
Sioux Falls, South Dakota;
Co-founder,
Montessorium (http://montesso

rom Sioux Falls, South Dakota, Bobby George obtained hi
ersity and a Master's from the University of Warwick. Bob
a PhD student at the Center for Modern Research in Euro
e title of his dissertation is "I Love Arakawa and Gins: Forev
g with his wife, June, he founded The Baan Dek Montesso
app design firm. Bobby is interested in exploring the int
ics and pedagogy. Originally from Bangkok, Thailand, Jur
rom Chulalongkorn University and a Master's from the Ur
une George obtained her AMI Diploma from the Montesso

The Logic of the "And": The Nature of Collaboration

We would like to discuss collaboration within the context of education. "Since each of us was several, there was already quite a crowd" (Deleuze & Guattari, 1987, p. 3). You see, for us, it is our belief that collaborations are the modus operandi of the twenty-first century. We also think this model of thought can be applied to understanding education as a process, and not as a product. Of course, this mode of interaction probably extends much deeper and richer than any timeline could suggest. Collaborations are, in a turn of phrase, tied to this new digital and mobile educational landscape in rich and germinal ways.

Here, at Montessorium (http://www.montessorium.com), we have a unique but perhaps not uncharacteristically happenstance biography. One day, after school, two Montessori parents and two Montessori educators set up a time to meet to discuss the possibilities of developing a series of Montessori-inspired apps for children. From that moment on we started to think about which activities would translate best into this exciting and burgeoning new field of mobile learning.

For us, though, it wasn't about the product of translation, as if the materials and their intentions could be mapped out precisely the same way in another format, in this case mobile. Instead, it was about the processes of transformation, and exploring what new affects, activities, and methods could be invented on a new platform.

While our main intention was to expose an entirely new generation to the force of thought that Montessori enacted, we were also interested to address the possibilities that this new mobile medium afforded. In particular, we were keen to see what transformational learning opportunities could be presented, and, as a result, what interactions would be precipitated. The path we followed in the creation of Montessorium was one of collaboration.

With the Intro to Math and Intro to Letters iPad apps we've tried to enact a method of collaboration with our users, within the ecosystem of the apps. For instance, with our sandpaper letters exercises, while we were not able to replicate the actual, physical texture experienced in the classroom, we were able to duplicate the sound of the sandpaper, and generate a positive response to the user when they traced outside the lines. In addition, by being able to visually demarcate the tracing path the finger took, we're able to provide the user with helpful feedback on the form of the writing.

In traditional education, competition trumps collaboration. The system itself is set up to encourage contests. You need only think of homework, tests, and grades. The

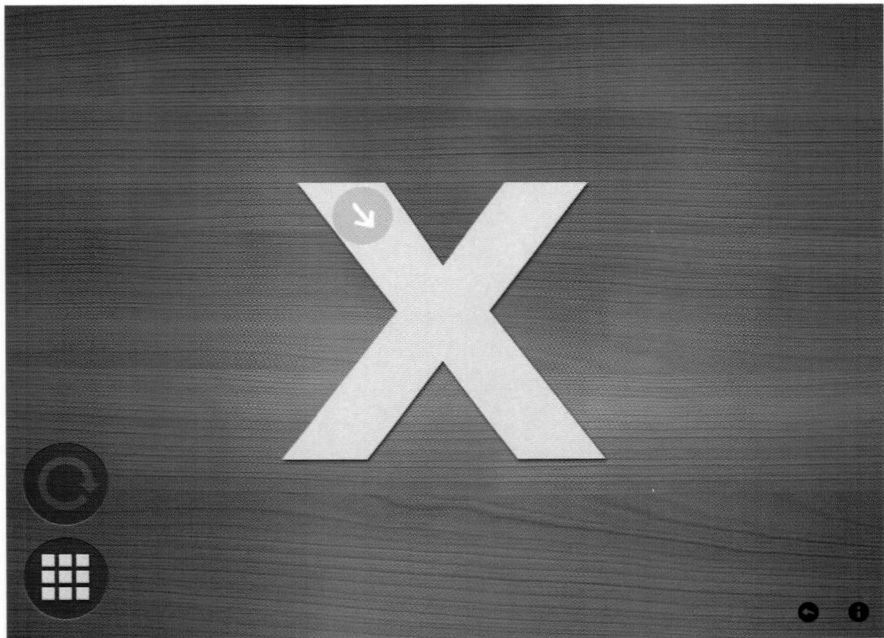

Figure 4.1
Intro to Letters iPad app by Montessorium.

conventional model is devised to foster and support characteristics and behaviors that accompany those who compete: manipulation and dissatisfaction are but two byproducts of this model. Of course, it could be argued that there are positive traits fostered in competition. We would argue, however, that it's much harder to compete with oneself.

Even the structure and architecture of the classroom are tied to modes of competition: opponents, rivalries, and adversaries. For example, you get a star if you complete the test within the allotted amount of time. Or, perhaps you receive a red checkmark if you missed a point on the exam. We all know the procedures of punishments and rewards. Whoever finishes first gets to head on out to recess, to enjoy the warm afternoon sun. In point of fact, our contemporary educational institutions are not set up to provide a foundation for collaboration.

Now, some of the promises of digital and mobile education are the abilities that are afforded by individualized education. For the first time, we have the opportunity to help children learn, based on their individual needs, and in accordance with their specific development. Never has this opportunity been more available or widespread. For once, education need not be geared towards a consensus. It can now be catered to the particular interests and challenges of the student.

As the architect Lars Spuybroek expresses, in a chapter of *The Sympathy of Things*, entitled, "The Digital Nature of the Gothic,"

> Growth never works when there is a lack of differentiation; it is absolutely impossible for a system to increase in scale without segmenting, because, as Galileo demonstrated, simply enlarging the same form leads to something that very quickly collapses under its own weight. No, growth is the redistribution of material, not blind excrescence; it is continual reorganization, not continual enlargement of the same form of organization.
>
> (2011, p. 33)

This is the foundation of Montessori: the only way to achieve the abstract is through the concrete. It's important to establish the foundations, to inspire the connections, before the leap is made. For instance, when we first start out with Intro to Math, the users

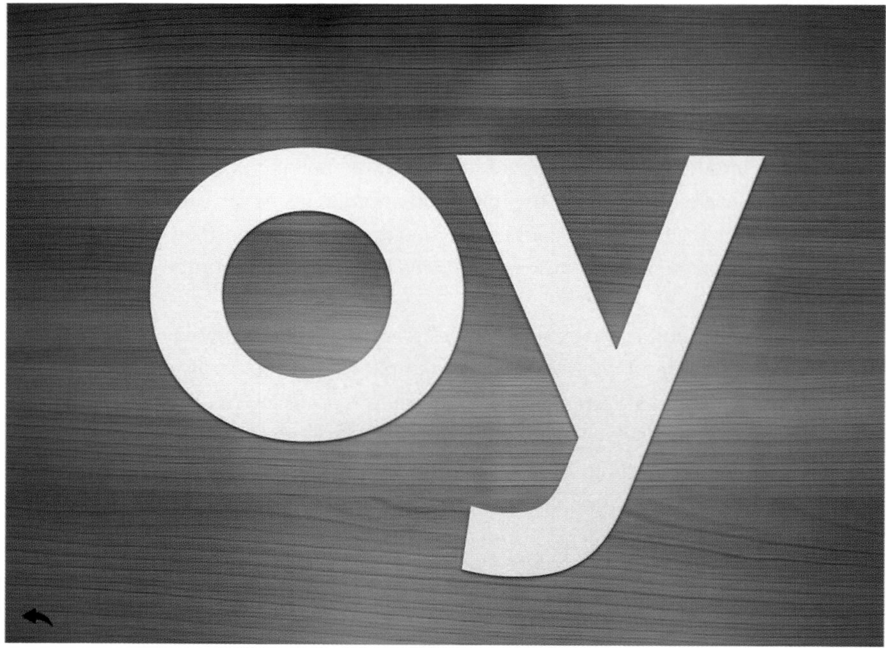

Figure 4.2
Intro to Letters iPad app by Montessorium.

Figure 4.3
Intro to Math iPad app by Montessorium.

learn to build the red rods. They come to understand and appreciate the quantity of the numbers, before they later, with the number rods, come to appreciate the numbers themselves. The abstract is only introduced after the concrete is understood. Of course, in traditional approaches, it's the exact opposite path that is followed.

Further, and with that in mind, instead of a generic curriculum that is applied to the entire class, a specialized set of activities can now be implemented and presented to a single student. Feedback loops are carefully put into place to help support and guide the student. The control of error, or the ability to regulate your own studies, is now a condition of the user. Growth inspires. In short, the onus is no longer placed on the teacher; it is now placed on the student. At long last, we can finally take education into our own hands.

Of course, the Montessori traditionalists would claim that this is not a new approach to education. It's been in existence for at least one hundred years. After all, this was Montessori's fundamental insight: each child is different, and each child learns at their own pace. We only need a system to accommodate their interests. What is new, however, is

Figure 4.4
Intro to Math iPad app by Montessorium.

the ability to disseminate these practices, methods and ideas, on a scale never before seen. How does collaboration fit into this new mobile landscape? Well, in our estimations, collaborations are the principal mode of education, not only philosophically, but also as it's put into practice, unfurling a novel dynamic.

Collaborations are open to change. They entice us to work with others. They can be detached and realigned. There is no linearity or homogeneity that cannot be infused with the non-linear and heterogeneous. More than anything, though, there is not just one way to approach collaboration, any more than there is just one way to create something new. Collaborations necessitate encounters. They open up possibilities, and by possibilities, we simply mean the activation of the new. Montessori classrooms are specifically designed with this in mind. In creating our apps, we also took this into consideration.

In this new landscape, then, it's not a question of subjects and objects. Instead, it's a question of relations and connections. Collaborations are, in principle, open and amorphous. They welcome the new and the unexpected. They are not fixed and predetermined.

The organizational structure is one of flexibility and spontaneity. There's an element in which collaborations are oriented towards improvisation and experimentation. Once more, it's about the process, not necessarily the product.

Does this mean that we promote disorganization, as opposed to organization? Nothing could be further from the truth. But, there is always an opportunity to disorganize the organization, to make it function in new and exciting ways. When you stop disorganizing, as Arakawa and Gins instruct, you end up in the kitchen, surrounded by bedroom doors and closets.

Imagine, for instance, a wrench in the line of a factory. Production instantly stops. A different team is called in to address the emergency of the situation. Time is lost. Production is thwarted. Now, imagine, the same process in collaboration. Throw in a wrench. Try it! See what happens. The element of the new, of the unexpected, it can spin the team in a new direction, offer a new insight and path for creation. Movement ensues, despite the wrench. Movement, of course, doesn't always mean progress, or productivity. It's a different landscape, where anexact terms are just as important as the STOP button on a conveyer belt.

As Deleuze and Guattari (1987) explain,

> in order to designate something exactly, anexact expressions are utterly unavoidable. Not at all because it is a necessary step, or because one can only advance by approximations: anexactitude is in no way an approximation; on the contrary, it is the exact passage of that which is underway.
>
> (p. 20)

Collaborations are, almost by definition, anexact. They don't always advance logically, or in terms that are easily measured and evaluated. They start in the middle. "The middle," as Deleuze and Guattari remind us, "is by no means an average; on the contrary, it is where things pick up speed" (p. 25). The processes of collaboration aren't linear, and that's part of what makes them so exciting. It's also what makes them, at times, so challenging.

Most evidently, then, this is why this model of working is not easily incorporated and adopted on a grand scale. A different logic is at work. You see, collaborations often commence in fits and starts. One portion of the collaboration works to support and strengthen the other. Sometimes you just don't have a role to play, but your involvement is still crucial. It's about pushing forward. It's about getting started. It's about finding your collective voice, en route. Collaborations follow the logic of the "and."

Collaborations are teams, but they're also more than that. They're singularities. They comprise, at one and the same time, individuals and collectivities. They need not be multiple, but of course, the multiple is already plural. Which is simply to say, collaborations are about expressions, not identities; about processes, not products. Often, collaborations work in opposition. They pursue multiple directions, simultaneously, and not always with a purpose apart from the collaborative. That doesn't mean, however, that they compete. Instead, they work to establish and foster new connections, often between disparate, unrelated fields, maximizing relations, and creating unexpected offshoots.

Collaborators are fierce competitors. As a matter of fact, we think that, in many respects, they're more healthy competitors than those they're often pitted against. Why? Because collaborators compete with themselves. They're not trying to measure up to their peers. They're trying to meet, and then exceed, their own expectations. Imagine, for instance, two students locked in a heated race to see who can achieve the results of an activity the fastest. The winner needs only to beat their opponent. They don't need to beat themselves. Collaborations will always trump competition. For us, this is the *new landscape* of mobile education: The "and."

References

Deleuze, G., & Guattari, F. (1987). *A thousand plateaus*. Minneapolis: University of Minnesota Press.
Spuybroek, L. (2011). *The sympathy of things*. Rotterdam: V2_Publishing.

Chapter 5
"Apping" its Way into the Future?
K–12 English Education

This chapter explores the invasion of iPads into K–12 education with a specific focus on English teaching and learning. A discussion of definitions and conceptualizations of literacy as well as the role of technology in encouraging literate practices follows an overview of iPads and apps. National standards and policy documents are identified and positioned as support for fostering contemporary literate practices through meaningful integration of technology tools such as the iPad. The chapter ends with two lists: (1) websites focused on meaningful technology integration, and (2) apps that support English teaching and learning.

For Designers

Designers will appreciate the exploration of historical and contemporary expectations and tensions inherent in technology-infused K–12 English education as well as the lists of valuable websites and apps for English educators that can help inspire new app ideas.

For Teachers

Teachers will appreciate an overview of the iPad's invasion into K–12 education, contemporary definitions of literacy, information on national standards, and valuable app and website resources.

For Researchers

Researchers will appreciate the historical overview of technology integration in K–12 contexts, definitions of literacy and literate practices, and the call to reframe technology integration efforts from tool centric to literacy centric.

ve years mobile learning will facilitate K–12 education from occurring e buildings to expanding outside into the real world.

Dr. Cassandra Scharber

Assistant Professor, Learning Technologies, University of Minnesota;
Co-Director, LT Media Lab, University of Minnesota

ndra Scharber is an assistant professor of Learning Technologies in the tment of Curriculum and Instruction within the College of Education and n Development (CEHD) as well as one of three co-directors of the new ng Technologies Media Lab (LTML) (http://lt.umn.edu) at the University nesota. Her research and teaching explore literacy within educational xts and the possibilities technology offers in aiding the transformation of ng and learning. Scharber served as co-editor of the Digital Literacies n for the *Journal of Adolescent and Adult Literacy* from 2008 to 2012 o date, she has published over twenty-five refereed journal articles and chapters. Scharber is also active in professional and community organi- s, including officer leadership within the American Educational Research ation and the Society for Information Technology and Teacher Education dem with her colleague Cynthia Lewis, she also provides local service and ship in the area of urban youth learning using digital media within school unity, and library settings. Cassie teaches courses both in online and assroom settings focused on technology integration, one-to-one laptop ad-based program implementation and practices; digital writing; online ng and learning practices; and doctoral seminars in learning technologies.

"Apping" its Way into the Future?: K–12 English Education

> A lot of technology in education looks like bolting an internal combustion engine on the back of a horse and buggy. We get something more exciting and noisy, but the rig can't go any faster. Information technology will transform education only when we unhitch the horse.
>
> (Spence, 2001, p. 18)

Since the introduction and incorporation of computers into K–12 schools during the mid-1970s, the field of education has been inundated with technological fixes for education, typically new tools (e.g., e-books, interactive whiteboards, clickers) that promise to solve one of education's many problems or new concepts (e.g., flipped classrooms, online learning) that claim to help students learn or teachers teach more effectively and efficiently. While Tyack and Cuban (1995) refer to these fads as "fireflies" due to how they appear so frequently, shine brightly for a few moments, and then disappear again, Spence's (2001) metaphor of technology being "an internal combustion engine on the back of a horse and buggy" more aptly captures the essence of the underlying issue with technology fads in education—many times technology fads simply encourage the same approaches to teaching and learning (i.e. the horse and buggy) that have been used for centuries rather than make possible and facilitate a re-imagination of what teaching and learning can be in the twenty-first century. The latest technology fad to enter the world of K–12 education is the iPad. Will the iPad help propel K–12 educators, students, administrators, school boards, and legislative officials to "unhitch the horse" or will the iPad remain an engine hitched onto the horse and buggy?

The iPad Invasion into Education

iPad Press

Chances are if you scan the news headlines at the local, state, or national level, you will encounter a story each week about the introduction of iPads into K–12 schools. Here are just a few sample headlines from the state of Minnesota: "Little Falls Schools to Give iPads to Students" (Minnesota Public Radio, 3/25/11); "High School Gives All Students iPads and Somehow It All Works Out [Gibbon-Fairfax-Winthrop High School]" (Marketplace, American Public Media, 9/5/11); "Farmington: An iPad for Every Student? That's the Plan" (*Pioneer Press*, 4/28/12); "Minnetonka Schools' iPad Program to Expand Next Fall" (*Star Tribune*, 5/5/12); "iPads for All, Western MN School District Says" (WCCO/CBS local, 8/17/12); "Hopkins 7th Graders Get iPads" (WCCO/CBS local, 8/23/12). To date, there is an iPad initiative or pilot program occurring in every state within the United States. Ready or not, the iPad is being thrust into the world of teaching and learning.

iPads as the Latest Technology to Invade Education

Similar to technological advances before them, iPads are being touted as the latest and greatest tool to be used in K–12 education. Amazingly, they have only been in existence for three years at the time of this writing. iPads were first released by Apple in January 2010 and were immediately heralded, questioned, and discussed by many as the next technology gadget to potentially "transform" education (cf. http://mediadecoder.blogs.nytimes.com/2010/03/31/and-an-ipad-in-every-backpack/, http://chronicle.com/blogs/profhacker/the-ipadhigher-education/22960). Indeed, iPads are the next chapter in the "this technology will transform education" saga. Historically, technology has always "promised" transformation of education, or rather, many people (including Thomas Edison in 1913 regarding the impact of film on the use of textbooks) have prophesied about the possibilities new technologies afford for teaching and learning, whether it was the overhead projector, TV, interactive white boards, or iPads.

As those of us who work in the area of educational technology integration understand and advocate for, the key concept to the (potentially) "transformational" nature of many technologies that is missing in most past and current conversations is the importance of *content* and *pedagogy* in synergy with technology. It is the synergy of these three "things" within educational contexts that can transform teaching and learning, not simply the technology itself (Mishra & Koehler, 2006; Mishra, Koehler, & Kereluik, 2009; Hughes & Scharber, 2008).

There is a powerful allure about incorporating iPads into K–12 education. Similar to laptop computers, iPads enable typical school-based activities such as note taking and annotating, Internet research, scheduling and organization, creating presentations as well as listening to, reading, and composing print-based and digital texts (including video). Compared to Apple's line of laptops, iPads are cheaper and offer features attractive to education. First, they are smaller and lighter than laptops (or textbooks), which makes them more portable. Next, iPads possess a flat screen that users can navigate with their fingertips. Battery length is typically superior to laptops, which is important in a typical K–12 school day. iPads also have built-in cameras allowing them to serve double duty as digital still and video cameras. Finally, there are thousands of educational apps available for use on iPads (many for free) that can aid in engaging most learners. Despite these cool and convenient technical affordances of iPads, the verdict is still out about the ways in which using iPads can positively impact teaching and learning.

What Exactly are Apps?

English educators understand that vocabulary acquisition is essential for empowerment. By extension, a big hurdle to integrating technology into teaching and learning is the understanding of educational technology's specialized vocabulary (e.g., cloud computing, servers, wikis, blogs). The term "apps" is simply short for "applications" (see Common Craft's video on a more detailed description: http://www.commoncraft.com/video/apps). Apps are software that can be downloaded quickly from the Internet onto mobile devices. With the introduction of smaller yet more powerful technologies (e.g., iPads, iPhones, iPods), apps became the avenue for downloading software, tools, and gadgets. Many apps are free or cost a few dollars. With millions of mobile devices and tablets in the world, software developers saw great educational, as well as entrepreneurial, opportunities. So, the "app" was born and its legacy ensued.

What Does This Invasion Mean for K–12 English Teachers and Students?

> The illiterate of the 21st century will not be those who cannot read and write, but those who cannot learn, unlearn, and relearn.
>
> (Alvin Toffler, in Swann, 1998)

Literacy Defined

The definition of literacy has changed dramatically in the United States over the course of its history, from being able to sign your name, to being familiar with certain canonical texts, to being able to read and write and make meaning from the written word, to being proficient in twenty-first-century skills (Kaestle et al., 1989; National Adolescent Literacy Coalition, 2007). Today, literacy is "no longer an end point to be achieved but rather a process of continuously learning how to be literate" (Leu, 2001, p. 568).

Historically, what "counted" as reading and writing, what it meant to be literate, slowly yet continually changed over time in tandem with societal realities and technological advances (Leu et al., 2004). What is different today, however, from ever before in history is the fusion of the speed-of-light pace of, mutable nature of, and new mechanisms for literate practices that have resulted in the "deictic" quality of literacy (Leu et al., 2011). For example, in only three years since its inception, the iPad has become the juggernaut icon for twenty-first-century education despite little to no research on the ways in which the affordances of iPads have positively impacted teaching, learning, or literacy. What research does suggest, however, is that "the Internet is reshaping reading, writing, and communication and sparking a transformation in the ways we teach and assess literacy and language arts" (Coiro & Castek, 2010, p. 314). The Internet began its foray into K–12 schools in the mid-1990s, and in the decades that have followed, the Internet continues to push the definitions and boundaries of education and communication, and therefore, what counts as reading, as writing, as literacy. Often overshadowed by the latest and greatest technology gadget, most recently the iPad, the Internet itself is actually the defining technology for literacy and learning (Coiro & Castek, 2010; Leu, 2001; Leu et al., 2004). Today, literacy is grounded in and stems from the Internet; the tools that harness it, including the iPad, are simply mechanisms for its distribution and connectivity.

Bringing Literacy Front and Center

Given this continually changing definition of literacy, what "counts" as reading in your classroom? What "counts" as writing? What does it mean to be literate in your classroom? What does it mean to be literate in the world today? How do you explain to parents, colleagues, administrators, and policy makers the motivation behind why and how you and your students are using iPads? The infusion of iPads into K–12 English classrooms should be grounded in the rationale of engaging in and encouraging literate practices. Unfortunately, the reality is that the iPad invasion is usually touted as a promotion of having the latest-and-greatest technological resources, which directly frames the rationale for the investment in iPads as one focused on technology itself rather than on the literacy practices it enables. While the difference in rhetoric is subtle, it is vastly important.

Currently, the discourse used by most educators to talk about, and ultimately understand, the role of technology in education needs to change as it reflects a "this tool is going to transform education" mindset rather than a "the world today demands multiple and continually changing literate practices" philosophy. It is imperative that educators embrace and articulate the literacy rationale rather than the omnipresent technology rationale. Consider this headline from the *Washington Post*: "My Teacher is an App" (2011) (http://online.wsj.com/article/SB10001424052970204358004577030600066250144.html?KEYWORDS=My+Teacher+is+an+App). While it may seem ludicrous that apps could actually replace K–12 teachers, many educational reform arguments and savvy business proposals, including the ideas presented in this article, imply the decreasing roles of teachers. For example,

> The growth of cybereducation is likely to affect school staffing, which accounts for about 80% of school budgets. A teacher in a traditional high school might handle 150 students. An online teacher can supervise more than 250, since he or she doesn't have to write lesson plans and most grading is done by computer.

Without apology, teachers are education's most expensive and valuable resource, and contrary to the efficiency rhetoric exemplified above, no technological tool will ever replace teachers.

English educators, by definition, skills, and passion, are in prime positions to more convincingly articulate the rationale motivating educational reform infused by technology to reflect one anchored in literacy. Will Richardson's plea to educators in his blog response to the "My Teacher is an App" story echoes this call to action:

> And it's time to raise our game, write comments and op-ed pieces and journal articles and books, have conversations with parents (or at least give them some reading to do), speak up at conferences and board meetings and elsewhere, not about the wonders of technology but about the changed landscape of literacies and skills and dispositions that the current [educational] system, online or off, is not able to provide to our kids in its current iteration. That schools can be places of wonder and exploration and inquiry and creation, not just force fed curriculum . . . That learning and reform as they are currently being defined are both nothing of the sort.
>
> (http://www.edutopia.org/blog/teacher-is-app-will-richardson)

As English educators, let us harness the power of our beloved language in all of its forms and media (i.e. written, verbal, pictorial, digital, multimodal) to redirect the perception of and dialogue around the importance of incorporating technology (including iPads) meaningfully into classrooms and schools: Technology can help teachers and students navigate and engage in the "changed landscape of literacies" while developing both current and yet unimagined literate practices that the world demands today.

Standards, Standards, Standards

English educators can harness the language of national English Language Arts standards, technology integration standards, and policy publications in support of fostering contemporary literate practices through meaningful integration of technology tools. Both the Common Core State Standards for English Language Arts & Literacy in History/Social Studies, Science, and Technical Subjects (2010) (http://www.corestandards.org/ELA-Literacy) and the National Standards for English Language Arts articulated jointly by the National Council of Teachers of Education and the International Reading Association (1996; reaffirmed in 2012) (http://www.ncte.org/standards/ncte-ira) are broad enough that they do not limit definitions of text to print-only thereby leaving room for expanded notions of reading and writing so that teachers and students can embrace, analyze, and construct digital texts. The International Society for Technology in Education's (ISTE) NETS standards (http://www.iste.org/standards) outline best practices for K–12 teaching, learning, and leading with technology in education for not only students (NETS•S), but for teachers (NETS•T), administrators (NETS•A), technology coaches/technology integration specialists (NETS•C), and computer science educators (NETS•CSE). These standards masterfully articulate the literate practices demanded in the world today as well as help provide direction for educational practices that better reflect the digital world (i.e. the changing role of teachers as co-learners). These standards are illustrative of the belief that "technology has forever changed not only what we need to learn, but the way we learn" (ISTE), and by extension, the ways in which we are literate.

In tandem with these standards, the National Education Technology Plan (NETP) (2010) (http://www.ed.gov/technology/netp-2010) also promotes the need for education to foster contemporary literacy skills, advocating for "applying the advanced technologies used in our daily personal and professional lives to our entire education system to improve student learning, accelerate and scale up the adoption of effective practices, and use data and information for continuous improvement." The five-year action plan comprises of goals for learning, assessment, teaching, infrastructure, and productivity. While NEPT's primary motivation for transforming the US education system is economic, "respond[ing] to an urgent national priority and a growing understanding of what the United States needs to do to remain competitive in a global economy," its language and vision in support of integrating iPads and other technologies into K–12 classrooms further support educators in enacting contemporary versions of teaching, learning, and literacy.

Where to Go? How to Move Forward?

It is difficult not to be excited about the influx of iPads into K–12 classrooms. iPads are beautiful, powerful, engaging tools. Like the technologies that have come before them, the iPad's status as an educational fad or revolution remains to be determined. However, the confluence of current political, social, educational, and technological timing may be perfectly ripe for enacting expanded concepts of teaching and learning. Is the iPad the technological tool that will finally be the conduit that spurs educators to continuously disrupt, re-imagine, and engage in contemporary definitions of reading and writing? Of teaching and learning?

The question posed at the beginning of this chapter asks, "Will the iPad help propel K–12 educators, students, administrators, school boards, and legislative officials to 'unhitch the horse' or will the iPad remain an engine hitched onto the horse and buggy?" While the unhitching has been and is currently under way in many educational contexts, in other contexts it has barely begun. Perhaps the horse and buggy analogy of our antiquated education system and its pedagogical practices is too dated, too linear for this conversation; rather, instead of a horse and buggy, let's conceive of education and its practices as the car in the film *Back to the Future* (1985). The car, a modified 1981 DeLorean, is actually a time-machine that can easily and quickly travel back and forth

Figure 5.1

between past, present, and future. Often times, the realities of the structures and expectations of twenty-first-century schooling require movement between and an honoring of traditional and contemporary teaching and learning practices, sometimes even in the space of one class period. Metaphorically, a DeLorean is therefore useful and more accurate in describing the maneuvering between these fluctuating expectations and blending both current and new conceptions of teaching and learning.

In our travels through time via DeLorean, technology tools (past, present, and future) must be understood for their impact on definitions of and expectations for literacy.

A literacy orientation and philosophy grounds historical, contemporary, and future understandings and reimaginings of education. Fostering literate practices is the reason for why we use technology in school—technology (re)defines how we communicate, interact, create, write, and read. And while our DeLorean time-machine enables us to move back and forth in time, if we keep our sights future oriented, then education's will be future oriented. As Doc says to Marty in the final scene of the film before they head off to the future, "Roads? Where we're going, we don't need roads."

Essential Blogs and Websites for Keeping Up with "Apps" in English Education

Dangerously Irrelevant

This is Scott McLeod's blog that examines technology and schools; his purpose is "trying to accommodate new realities within inappropriate existing institutions." Dr. McLeod is a prominent and respected academic expert on K–12 school technology leadership issues. http://dangerouslyirrelevant.org/

Edutopia's Blogs

Hosted by Edutopia, multiple educators share classroom strategies and tips as well as lesson ideas, personal stories, and innovative approaches to improving teaching. The "Technology Integration" blog is particularly interesting and useful, featuring posts about iPad initiatives around the country. A blog post in August 2012 highlighted an iPad launch at Burlington High School and the lessons learned, including the idea of a student-run "Genius Bar": "One of the best decisions we made before we deployed 1000+ iPads to our student body was to create a student-run genius bar. With this decision, we were putting a lot of trust in the hands of our students. However, it turned out to be a core component of the launch." http://www.edutopia.org/blogs

FreeTech4Teachers

The purpose of this website is to share information about free resources that teachers can use in their classrooms—including apps! In 2011 and 2012, this blog received the Edublogs Award for Best Ed Tech Blog. http://www.freetech4teachers.com

Learning with Literacy

Richard Beach and David O'Brien, two revered researchers and scholars in literacy, created this website as a companion to their e-book, *Using iPad Apps to Foster Literacy Learning Across the Curriculum* (2012) (available as a Kindle download) "in order to keep users up to date on how the rapidly changing world of apps for portable devices like iPads and phones can be used to support learning."Both the website and e-book are loaded with app resources as well as practical integration examples, but its true gift is in its tempered grounding in the rationale for using iPads and apps in education: fostering literate practices. http://www.appsforlearningliteracies.com/

Essential Apps for English Teaching and Learning

Comic Life

Simply the best comic creation app available. Extremely easy to use, smart designs with templates and panel layouts, multiple ways to share final comics, and loads of fun. Integrates the iPad 2's camera. Well worth the small price tag.

Evernote

Think of Evernote as "the organizational cloud" for both students and teachers. Free, aesthetically designed, and easy to use, this app allows users to take and share notes of all kinds (audio, text, image, docs, pdfs) via iPad, computer, and an app on your phone. Tags and bookmarks are used to index and organize notes while making them searchable. It is very difficult to lose or forget your materials with this app as it automatically synchs your notebooks wherever you are using Evernote—it may be time to get rid of the paper notebooks and planners. Check out Evernotes' videos (http://evernote.com/video/) for more ideas!

Free Books

English and language arts classrooms are not complete without books. This beautiful app contains 23,469 classic books under the public domain "to go" as well as highlights, dictionary support, and bookmark features as well as availability in multiple languages.

iAnnotate PDF

This app is a necessity for those of us who use PDF files. This app allows you and your students to annotate, manage, and share PDFs. You can also highlight, copy, and search.

iBooks

Similar to Free Books app, but in addition to accessing free books that are in the public domain, you can also access current books (usually for a small price) as well as textbooks.

iMovie

This app is a more simplistic version of iMovie that still makes possible digital storytelling but without the fancy features of iMovie for computers (remember, iPads are NOT computers). With this app and iPads' built-in cameras, students will easily compose and share digital texts.

Pages

There is no word-processing platform installed on iPads, and writing is a main component of English curricula. This app allows users to create and annotate Word and Mac documents. If you and your students also need a presentation tool or spreadsheet creator, consider purchasing the iWork mini-suite: Pages (word processor), Keynote (presentation tool), or Numbers (spreadsheet creator).

Penultimate

Do you and your students wish to use your iPad like a notebook and "write" on it? This handwriting app allows you to do just that as well as converting your handwritten notes into PDF files so you can share electronically via Evernote, Dropbox, etc. Easy to use and supports multiple languages.

Skitch

Another way to support digital text creation is with Skitch. With this app, students can annotate images (i.e. pictures, screenshots, maps, webpages), draw new compositions, and share compositions electronically. While the latest version (2.0) has received mixed reviews, most students find this app fun, creative, and engaging.

WritePad

Similar to the Penultimate app, WritePad allows students to take notes as if they are writing on their paper notebooks (with the bonus feature of a spell check). This app also enables copying, pasting, highlighting, and selecting texts. This app is handwriting recognition software for multiple languages, but there is also a virtual keyboard available. You can also email, tweet, Facebook, or connect to Evernote.

References

Coiro, J. & Castek, J. (2010). Assessment frameworks for teaching and learning English language arts in a digital age. In D. Lapp & D. Fisher (Eds.), *Handbook of research on teaching the English language arts* (3rd edition). Co-sponsored by the International Reading Association and the National Council of Teachers of English. New York: Routledge.

Hughes, J. E., & Scharber, C. (2008). Leveraging the development of English-technology pedagogical content knowledge within the deictic nature of literacy. In AACTE's Committee on Innovation and Technology (Eds.), *Handbook of technological pedagogical content knowledge for educators* (pp. 87–106). Mahwah, NJ: Routledge.

Kaestle, C., Damon-Moore, H., Stedman, L. C., & Tinsely, K. (1989). *Literacy in the United States: Readers and reading since 1880*. New Haven, CT: Yale.

Leu, D. (2001). Emerging literacy on the Internet. *The Reading Teacher, 54*(6), 568–572.

Leu, D. J., Jr., Kinzer, C. K., Coiro, J., & Cammack, D. W. (2004). Toward a theory of new literacies emerging from the Internet and other information and communication technologies. In R. B. Ruddell & N. Unrau (Eds.), *Theoretical models and processes of reading* (5th edition, pp. 1570–1613). Newark, DE: International Reading Association. Retrieved February 11, 2012, from http://www.readingonline.org/newliteracies/lit_index.asp?HREF=leu/.

Leu, D. J., McVerry, J. G., O'Byrne, W. I., Kiili, C., Zawlinski, L., Everett-Cacopardo, H., Kennedy, C., & Forzani, E. (2011, September). The new literacies of online reading comprehension: Expanding the literacy and learning curriculum. *Journal of Adolescent and Adult Literacy, 55*(1), 5–14.

Mishra, P., & Koehler, M. J. (2006). Technological pedagogical content knowledge: A framework for integrating technology in teacher knowledge. *Teachers College Record, 108*(6), 1017–1054.

Mishra, P., Koehler, M. J., & Kereluik, K. (2009). The song remains the same: Looking back to the future of educational technology. *Tech Trends, 53*(5), 48–53.

National Adolescent Literacy Coalition. (September, 2007). Foundational and emergent questions: Smart people talk about adolescent literacy. Retrieved December 11, 2012, from http://www.alinet.eu/index.php?option=com_docman&task=doc_download&gid=19&Itemid=47.

Spence, L. D. (2001). The case against teaching, *Change, 33*(6), 11–19.

Swann, Norman. (1998). Interview with Alvin Toffler, Australian Broadcasting Corporation Radio National,"Life Matters,"5 March.

Tyack, D., & Cuban, L. (1995). *Tinkering toward Utopia: A century of public school reform.* Cambridge, MA: Harvard University Press.

Section 2
Mobile Learning Design Guidelines and Frameworks

The design of online learning environments is historically regarded as a linear series of phases that constructs step-by-step models and processes "based on principles that are applied uniformly to all contexts," leading to the conclusion that explains why "instructional design is so seldom successful" (Jonassen, 2006, p. 26). A design process that is linear, constrained, and alienated from context is often limited in its potential, irrespective of the user domain. In contrast, current educational theory urges new teachers to be holistic and creatively adjust to classroom and societal change. Teachers are challenged to foster learning experiences that are authentic and innovative. Likewise, our instructional design processes should employ these same values: creativity, innovativeness, and authenticity, as well as an understanding of the contemporary research ideas and design frameworks of the field.

The design of learning environments, specifically in the context of mobile learning, is complex and is not well addressed by simple algorithmic processes or step-by-step models. Further, mobile designers often apply these same instructional design processes, merely to a smaller screen. We believe that mobile designers must harness the characteristics and opportunities of mobile technology that differ from traditional, desktop-based educational applications. To this end the following chapters present new frameworks and guidelines for the design and development of mobile learning applications in order to spark a discussion in our field, one of fostering transformation through design. The frameworks and guidelines presented in these chapters are not meant as recipes, but rather a foundation to adapt and evolve as we further explore the new and ever-changing mobile landscape.

Mr. Lecheler and Mr. Hosack begin this section by presenting seven considerations for educational software designers focused on creating transformative learning experiences for mobile platforms. These considerations represent what Lecheler and Hosack believe "are the most salient aspects of mobile technology, which, when thoughtfully considered, afford the best opportunities for mobile learning design." The authors conclude that a "deep understanding of how mobile applications differ in interaction mode, use context, scope, data management, access modes, design scale, and incentives is the first step toward thoughtful mobile learning design."

Next, Dr. Dikkers provides an overview of early iterations by educators "rethinking classrooms, museums, and civic engagement for learners and using mobile games to facilitate active participation in the world they are learning about." Based on these iterations that have "provided fertile ground for educational development of mobile," Dikkers continues with suggestions to advance mobile learning design and development through assumed access, production over consumption, amplification, and relevant practice via an authentic audience. The expanding number of students connecting and learning through mobile technologies, both inside and outside the formal classroom, is the driving force of Dikkers' research and suggestions for future design in this area.

Mr. Song concludes this section with an overview of research on mobile learning design and suggests the DCALE framework (Design Goal Setting, Context Analysis, Alignment with Platform, Learner Experience, and Enhancement of Performance) to guide future development. Song recommends, "development processes must not only consider operating systems and hardware device features, but must also address a more comprehensive set of project management issues." Contending that mobile learning is different than other forms of e-learning, Song suggests that future research will focus on the application of the DCALE framework, in addition to other mobile-specific frameworks, in authentic settings to remedy potential "dissatisfaction and frustration of both designers and learners" in the mobile realm.

Reference

Jonassen, D. H. (2006). *Modeling with technology: Mindtools for conceptual change*. Columbus, OH: Merill/Prentice Hall.

Shane Mielke
Interaction Designers,
Creative Director,
Graphic Designer

Educational design typically exists in clean, simple environments that accentuate, but do not overpower, the message. High-media corporate designs are often filled with large attention-grabbing visuals, trendy styles, and integrated social experiences that attempt to draw attention to the message. In both situations the process remains education, comprehension, retention, and action, but they are accomplished with drastically different design styles, strategies, environments, and results.

Design in education suffers from difficulty in initially capturing the interest and attention of students (i.e. tasks that marketing designers are very good at). High-media corporate design suffers from lack of retention in a sea of information overload (i.e. tasks that educators are really good at). Adapting techniques and experiences from one another to mend weaknesses and revolutionize their respective environments, then, may bridge this gap.

High-media corporate marketing has recently benefitted from long-standing educational design styles that are cleaner, less distracting, and more memorable in content and experience. In addition, traditional educational concepts like gamification are being used to great benefit. Achievement badges, levels, and virtual currency, techniques already revolutionizing marketing experiences, are methods now used in early education games to capture and retain student interest.

Comparably, education is advancing as it adapts to the ever-changing design trends, viewpoints, and lessons learned from aggressive media campaigns. Once oversimplified design styles are being rejuvenated to inspire students in new ways making learning more attractive, social, and engaging. Immersive concepts created in traditional media campaigns are inspiring concepts like adventure learning and collaborative online environments making learning more experiential and inquiry based.

Realizing that the goals of education (i.e. comprehension, retention, and action) are similar in both arenas is the key to bridging the gap. Within the realms of mobile learning and mobile marketing, we have a fresh beginning to compare and adapt styles, strategies, environments, and results for the benefit of all.

Dr. Som Naidu
Associate Professor and Director, Learning and Teaching Quality Enhancement and Evaluation Services, Charles Sturt University, NSW, Australia
Executive Editor, *Distance Education*

From goat herders in Southern India, to small business owners in Bangladesh, and small-scale crop farmers in Africa, mobile phones can be instrumental in improving the lives and livelihood of rural families and communities in the developing world. It is in these contexts where conventional technologies and infrastructures such as computers, terrestrial cables, and electricity are not available or their costs prohibitive that mobile technologies are and will be having the greatest impacts.

The developing world is experiencing exponential growth in the availability of mobile tools and technologies (see http://mobithinking.com/mobile-marketing-tools/latest-mobile-stats/). Much of this is driven by private-sector interests and initiatives which see in mobile technologies commercial opportunities that could not be realized with more established tools and infrastructure. Contemporary mobile devices are not dependent on sophisticated infrastructure or highly developed skill base for effective and efficient use. Users of all ages and literacy levels are able to use these devices in innovative ways and for a wide range of purposes including routine communication and business transactions.

Prominent instances of these are the use of mobile phones to support women goat farmers in Southern India with just-in-time information about best prices, weather conditions, feed management, and disease and health management of goats (see Balasubramanian et al., 2010); to support micro-financing in Bangladesh (http://en.wikipedia.org/wiki/Village_Phone); and to create financial transactions in Kenya (http://en.wikipedia.org/wiki/M-Pesa).

Access to information and education is crucial for social and economic development, and these are the ingredients that have stonewalled progress in developing societies. Today's mobile devices such as smartphones and tablets have the potential to provide essential information and education just-in-time to empower people and fundamentally transform their lives and livelihoods. They have the power of yesterday's computers and they are going to get even more powerful and affordable. The challenge and opportunity for developers of mobile applications is to stay independent of carrier service providers and device manufacturers, and focus their attention on simple text- and voice-based messaging applications which make most of the audio, video, and texting affordances of mobile devices (see http://www.col.org/blog/Lists/Posts/Post.aspx?ID=157).

Reference

Balasubramanian, K., Thamizoli, P., Umar, A., & Kanwar, A., (2010). Using mobile phones to promote lifelong learning among rural women in Southern India, *Distance Education, 31*(2), 193–209. DOI:10.1080/01587919.2010.502555. Retrieved January 26, 2012, from http://www.informaworld.com.

Chapter 6
Seven Design Considerations for Mobile Learning Applications

In this paper we present seven design considerations in the domain of mobile learning applications. More specifically, we point to ways in which designers can make use of the aspects of mobile technology that differ from traditional, desktop-based applications. In doing so, we also attempt to forward design principles that help educational software designers re-envision how to effectively create transformative learning experiences on mobile platforms.

For Designers

Designers will learn the characteristics that make mobile learning environments unique compared with traditional learning environments. These characteristics imply specific design considerations and principles.

For Teachers

Teachers will learn about the characteristics of mobile learning environments that directly impact pedagogical possibilities and how these characteristics affect the integration of technology into their classrooms.

For Researchers

Researchers will be able to identify the characteristics unique to mobile learning environments and the research-ability of those characteristics when evaluating learning outcomes.

As mobile technology advances, learners will expect innovation in mobile learning design. Designers will need to adapt to meet that demand.

Lucas Lecheler
Lead Developer, Learning Technologies Media Lab, University of Minnesota

Bradford Hosack
Lead Designer, Learning Technologies Media Lab, University of Minnesota

Lecheler and Hosack work as designers and developers in the Learning Technologies Media Lab at the University of Minnesota. Lecheler's interests include e-assessment, progress monitoring, and language learning. He is currently developing and researching Avenue, an innovative video capture and e-assessment platform for world language learning. Hosack's interests include user experience design, thoughtful information visualization design, and closing the experience gap between face-to-face and online learning classrooms. Both are pursuing research in how InfoViz can be designed to enhance learning.

Seven Design Considerations for Mobile Learning Applications

Only recently have mobile devices offered capabilities comparable with those of desktop computers. This increased capability makes for exciting times for those who believe mobile devices can greatly impact learning. This can be seen in current emphasis in the literature on the use of mobile technology to support learning, including a substantial increase in mobile learning research as well as conferences devoted specifically to how mobile technology can be used to support learning (Ting, 2012). Many researchers and practitioners are optimistic about the affordances of mobile technology, specifically a learner's ability to access information on the move as well as unique communication opportunities (Sharples, Taylor, & Vavoula, 2005). However, the use of mobile devices to support learning is not without issues. Mobile devices can create usability issues for learners (Ting, 2012). For example, limited screen sizes can inhibit user interaction. Beyond this, the mobility of these devices raises the concern of students interacting with learning material in contexts that they typically do not associate with learning (Kukulska-Hulme, 2009).

From a theoretical perspective, the literature ranges from frameworks that can simplify the design and development of mobile learning applications (Martin et al., 2011) to a number of theoretical models that can inform the analysis of mobile learning applications from a pedagogical perspective (Park, 2011). However, there has been little written from the perspective of designers of mobile learning environments and applications. As a result, designers of mobile learning environments and applications are often left without the theoretically grounded, yet pragmatic, example-based principles that help move projects forward. This chapter is written from the perspective of designers. We aim to fill the gap in the literature by referencing both scholarly articles as well as contemporary examples of well-designed learning applications in order to inform not only mobile design work but also the evaluation and integration of mobile learning applications. Ultimately, we do this by presenting mobile design considerations that lead to principles of effective mobile design.

Toward Principles for Mobile Learning Design

The following considerations for designers of mobile learning applications are not comprehensive, but rather are meant to spark discussion within the design community. They also represent what we feel are the most salient aspects of mobile technology, which, when thoughtfully considered, afford the best opportunities for mobile learning design. These considerations, in turn, highlight what we believe to be pragmatic principles for the effective development of meaningful mobile learning experiences. The seven considerations are the following:

- Mode of interaction
- Context of use
- Scope
- Data management
- Mode of access
- Design scale
- Incentives.

As we step through each item in the above list, we provide examples, both general and learning specific, that illustrate associated design principles.

Mode of Interaction

The most obvious difference between desktop and mobile applications is the mode of interaction. Unlike keyboard- and mouse-based interfaces, today's mobile devices use touch screens and gestures. Gesture-based applications have numerous benefits, especially for learners with disabilities. For examples, touch interfaces are often easier to navigate than mouse-based systems for learners lacking fine motor skills (Shah, 2011). iConverse (www.converseapp.com/), an augmentative alternative communication (AAC) application available on the iPad and iPhone, is designed for people with communication disorders (see Figure 6.1). The application uses large, simple, and clear icons that facilitate both the user's understanding of the application itself and his or her ability to interact with it (even when the user lacks fine motor skills).

However, while touch-based modes of interaction have benefits, these new interfaces also require design considerations that challenge existing frameworks. Additionally, rethinking modes of interaction goes beyond surface-level characteristics of the software. For example, with mouse-driven applications, designers can define feedback for when a user hovers the cursor over an element of the application (e.g., displaying detailed descriptions of interface items as tooltips). On a touch screen this particular state does not exist. Yet it is not enough for designers to simply acknowledge lack of roll-over states. Rather, they must find innovative ways to communicate the same information despite this limitation.

The example above illustrates the common mobile design challenge of working with relatively limited screen space. This limitation is especially important when considering minimum font sizes for text display. One way to effectively make use of screen space, especially in data- and feedback-intensive applications, is through information visualization, or InfoViz. InfoViz combines the use of pictures, colors, symbols and words to communicate complex information in a way that is clear, compelling, and convincing (Emerson, 2008). While many think of data display as static charts

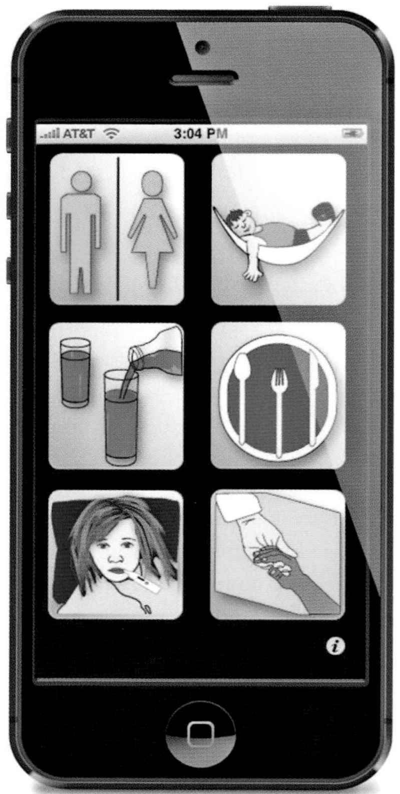

Figure 6.1
iConverse aids in communication for people with communication disorders.

and graphs, InfoViz also involves interactive online displays of information and an artistic design approach (Pousman, Stasko, & Mateas, 2007) that can foster engagement (Lau & Moere, 2007). Miller et al. (2012) further define InfoViz as the orchestration of data, design, and narrative, emphasizing thoughtful, data-driven design that moves beyond static representations of large datasets and toward informative, interactive, and salient learner experiences. InfoViz enables designers to turn lack of screen real estate from a design *issue* into a design *opportunity*. The confines of mobile devices may enforce more space restrictions, but these restrictions can be seen as an opportunity for a clear and compelling display of information that requires little text.

One such application that relies heavily on InfoViz is Roambi (www.roambi.com). Roambi allows a user to see various visualizations of large datasets, such as population data (see Figure 6.2). Additionally, the application affords user interaction, allowing users to drill down into a data set so as to find and display information that meets a specific need. This clear presentation of data is accomplished within the limited screen space of mobile devices.

Of course, data visualization is not a 'catch-all' solution for issues of limited screen real estate. However, an understanding of what constitutes effective InfoViz, and, more importantly, novel ways in which data display can solve design problems, opens up exciting possibilities for mobile learning.

Context of Use

Another important consideration of mobile applications is the context of use. Mobile technologies have dramatically changed the context in which users interact with

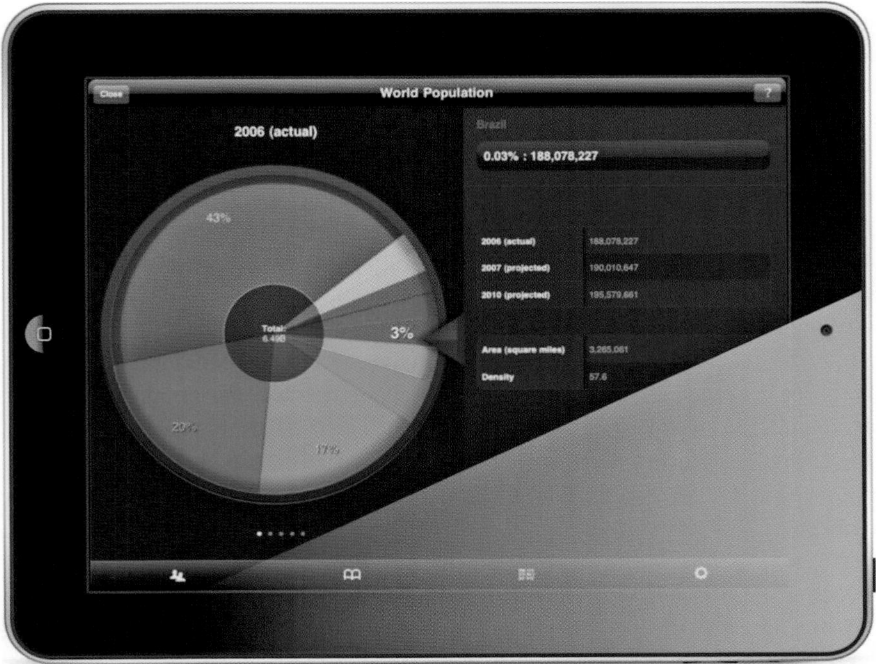

Figure 6.2
Roambi elegantly displays large, interactive datasets, such as world population data.

software. While traditional interaction with software at home or in a school is still common, mobile technologies are just that: mobile. Indeed, mobile technologies afford learning across space and time, and therefore require an understanding of the transfer of knowledge and skills across contexts (Sharples, Taylor, & Vavoula, 2005). Our interactions with software also occur more frequently and in less structured ways. Because of this, mobile learning is necessarily tied to self-directed and informal learning.

Marsick and Watkins (2001) describe formal learning as typically based in classrooms, sponsored by institutions, and highly structured. In contrast, informal learning is not highly structured and self directed (Bull et al., 2008). Hwang and Tsai (2011) argue that mobile devices "play an important role in the learning activities no matter whether the activities are conducted in the field or in the classroom" (p. 65). A study conducted by Clough et al. (2007) found that mobile device users engaged in informal learning through referential, location-aware, reflective, data-collection, constructive, and administrative activities. Their analysis shows that participants not only used mobile devices to support intentional informal learning, but also leveraged the power of mobile devices to "convert unforeseen events into informal learning occurrences" (p. 368). Thus, designers of mobile learning applications who consider use context have the twofold responsibility of understanding that learning can occur serendipitously, and that support for this type of learning requires contextual content.

Internet connectivity and location-aware devices have made contextual content possible almost to the level of augmented reality. The popular review site *Yelp* (www.yelp.com) provides an app that allows users to view reviews of nearby businesses (e.g., restaurants, bars, and coffee shops), filtered by a user's location. Additionally, the "monocle" feature, one of the first examples of augmented reality in mobile applications (Kirkpatrick, 2009), uses the device's camera to display an overlay of nearby establishments. The information presented is dynamic and situated within the context of a user's location at a given time. Furthermore, users typically call on an application like this at unforeseen times and in unforeseen places, supporting learning even in contexts that are not predefined. The technologies involved in this application have clear implications for informal learning, from contextual procedural information in the workplace (e.g., Godehardt, 2009) to authentic assessment opportunities.

Scope

Another aspect of software design and development that has been perpetuated by the influx of mobile technologies is modularity. Modular applications are ones that interface with existing technologies or applications in order to perform a specific function. For example, many applications leverage the power of other useful web technologies, such as Facebook, Twitter, or Google Maps. This is in contrast to robust desktop applications like Adobe's Photoshop or Microsoft's Word, which are stand-alone solutions for general tasks (photo editing and word processing, respectively). The design implications of the move towards modular applications are twofold. First, designers of modular applications must seamlessly integrate the various existing technologies necessary to accomplish a task. Second, designers of modular applications must focus on doing a specific job, and doing it well.

While integration of multiple technologies within a mobile application can be a complex process, the benefits are clear. Many applications offload management of user accounts through Facebook (i.e. the "log in with Facebook" buttons common on many sites in place of their own custom login form). For example, the streaming music service Spotify (www.spotify.com) lets its users log in through Facebook, and integrates other functionality such as automatically posting updates to their profiles with links to the songs they are currently listening to. Not only does Facebook integration minimize complex back-end development (e.g., managing user passwords and protecting sensitive account information), it also makes for scalable applications by implicitly adopting new features that the integrated application implements.

Effective mobile learning applications also perform a specific job well. This can be accomplished in two main ways. First, the designer of the application can limit functionality for the sake of simplicity. Second, the designer can create an auxiliary application that performs a single function within a larger system. The online performance assessment system Avenue (see lt.umn.edu/ave for more information) is a web-based tool for teachers and learners of world languages (Miller, Lecheler, & Rose, 2012). The system allows instructors to create tasks for students by using custom media, defining parameters for students to self-assess their performance, and providing numeric as well as textual feedback (see Figure 6.3).

Both desktop and iPad versions are meant for the complete lifecycle of a task (i.e. creating, managing, assigning, and completing). However, given that mobile phones have smaller screens and must often be held (limiting the ability of an American Sign Language learner, for example, to complete a task), the iPhone and iPod Touch versions of the application focus on task creation. However, these devices offer better portability and therefore increase the opportunities for creating media. Thus, instructors can take on-site pictures or video with their device, upload the media, and create and assign a task to students. This task then can be completed and assessed within the larger system. In this way, thinking of mobile applications in terms of modularity affords additional learning opportunities.

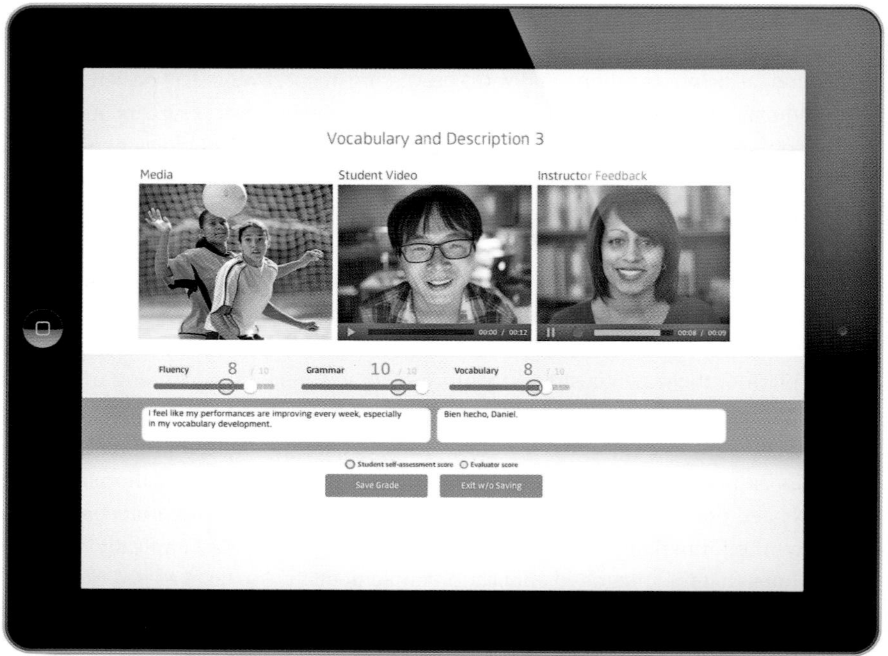

Figure 6.3
Using Avenue, learners complete language tasks, assess their performance, and receive feedback from instructors.

Data Management

Mobile learning does not necessarily require the storage and accessing of data. However, when the need to capture data in a mobile environment is necessary, there are a number of factors to consider. It is the responsibility of the designer to identify the types of data a learner will want (or need) to record, when and where they will be recording it, and how it will be accessed for later use. Will the learner be required to access an Internet connection? Are the tasks they are completing connected to other learners or their instructor(s) in any way? Are there media that may need to be captured and stored for later access? These are just a small sample of the questions a designer should be considering when designing and developing an environment for mobile learning. When the decision is made to capture data for the user there are two major ways this can be accomplished.

The first method is the utilization of storage space on the device the learner is using. This approach has the advantage of less latency (Mahmoud, Zanin, & Ngo, 2012) because it is not dependent on unknown variables such as Internet connection speed. It is also more manageable as the information being stored is user specific. One example of using localized data storage to track both a reader's progress and their user preferences are stand-alone applications of children's books (e.g., *You're Only Old Once* by Dr. Seuss). In applications like these it is common that the progress of the reader is stored locally so that as the application is opened and closed it can return the learner to the point at which they previously left off.

The second method is much more complicated to manage as a designer, but offers near limitless options for the learners' experience by allowing them the ability to connect with other learners' data. In addition, this functionality allows the designer the ability to provide richer feature sets for the learners by offloading computing power to the cloud (Bahl et al., 2012). That advantage comes at the expense of requiring Internet connectivity in order to utilize those features. This is demonstrated in numerous running/biking applications that use the devices' hardware to collect geo-location points and store them locally. Once a route is completed the app uploads that data to a server that can convert the information into detailed feedback about pace, elevation, speed, and even showing

Figure 6.4
Strava (www.strava.com) is an application for mapping your running or biking routes in addition to numerous other helpful pieces of data all assimilated online using data uploaded from the device.

a visual representation of the route on a map; all things difficult to process using just the device itself. An added advantage to this method is the availability of the information for further analysis on a desktop machine.

Mode of Access

A learner's expectation for the performance of a learning environment fluctuates considerably depending on the way they are accessing its content. Desktop applications are expected to be the most robust option, but mobile applications of those same environments should degrade as gracefully as possible. An environment's ability to be flexible largely depends on the device the learner uses when accessing its content. In order to plan for the best possible experience, the designer should fully understand their audience, and how they will be interacting with the environment being designed. If it is for a school that has implemented a one-to-one laptop program for example, the design considerations will be drastically different compared with the design considerations for an unknown population of users with the potential of them using any number of different

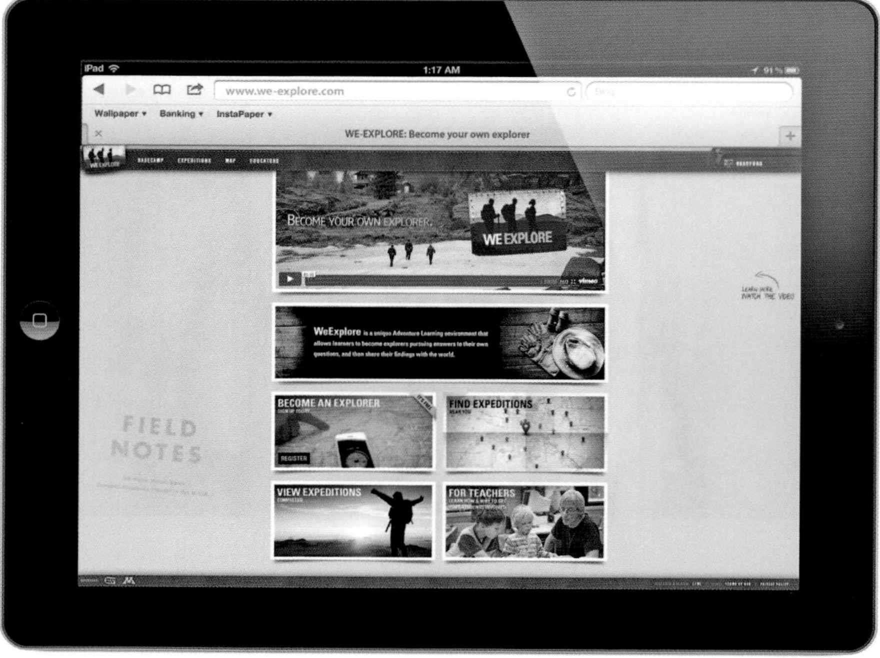

Figure 6.5
WeExplore is an online learning environment designed to work equally on any platform, regardless of the system or device.

devices. If the audience is unknown, a more generic design using HTML5, CSS3, and Javascript will help to ensure the learning environment can be accessed regardless of the learners' platform. This approach, however, limits functionality, in addition to hardware acceleration of graphics, on some devices by being forced to design for their respective mobile browsers.

Explore15 (see lt.umn.edu/projects/explore15 for more information) is a learning environment designed to allow the learners their chance to become explorers in their own community. Explore15 allows them to share and collect data in their own surroundings to share with the world in an educational context. The environment is designed to work on any browser and with any device, as described above. This flexibility can be seen in its conditional coding decisions that allow it to identify the device used and delivering the most efficient variation of the environment possible.

Design Scale

Learning environments are commonly accessed using mobile devices that are significantly underpowered when compared with modern desktop computers. As a result, learning environments must be designed in a way that will minimize the number of files (and file size) required to successfully deliver necessary content (Nichols, Zhigang, & Barton, 2008). One way to accomplish this is to remove unnecessary content areas not contextually relevant to the learner based on the specific device they use. This is closely related to the modular scope of mobile applications. An example of this is Geothentic.

Geothentic is an online scaffolded learning environment designed and developed to assist both teachers and students with integrating geospatial technologies in the classroom (Doering, Veletsianos, Scharber, & Miller, 2009). The Geothentic application for iOS (under development, 2012) is an example of a custom application that serves its own function rather than simply replicating content from the web-delivered learning environment. Rather than duplicating functionality, the application is designed to act as a supplementary tool allowing instructors to reflect on their own Technological, Pedagogical, and Content Knowledge (TPACK) in the application throughout the lesson plan while delivering the course material to students through the online learning environment (Doering, Scharber, Miller, & Veletsianos, 2009).

Designing applications in this way reduces content clutter on screen and reduces complexity of the navigational structure. Less navigation is important when designing for the smaller viewing area common to most mobile device screens. Additionally, layouts for applications on mobile devices can take on different forms based on the device's orientation and screen resolution. This maximizes the application's functionality while further reducing the inclusion of unnecessary content. Using OS-specific features can

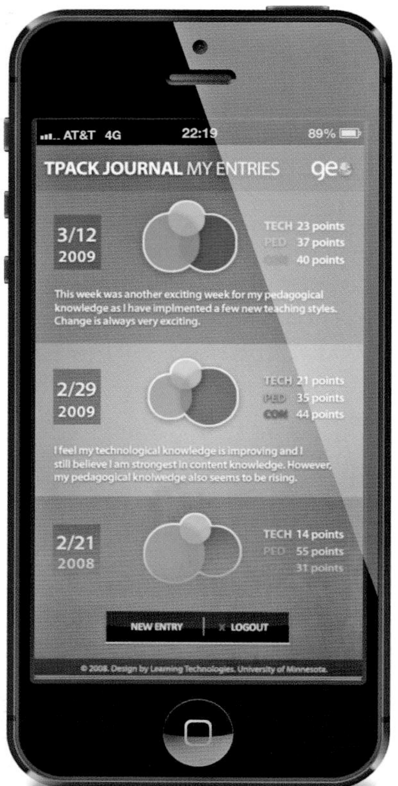

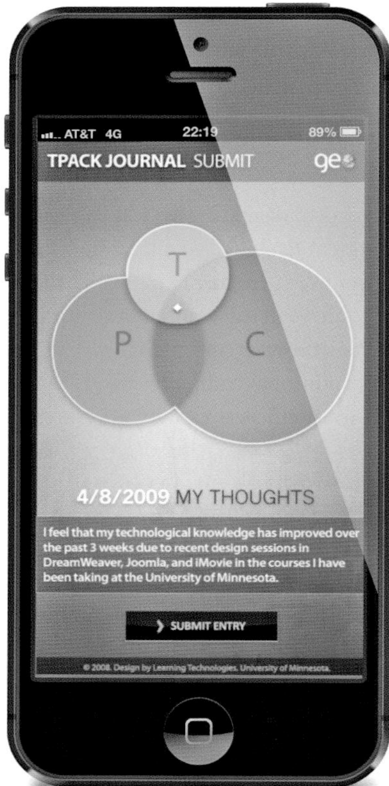

Figure 6.6
The iOS application Geothentic allows instructors the ability to reflect on their technology, pedagogy, and content knowledge over time and review their previous reflections.

further improve the experience for the learner by reducing time invested in getting familiarized with custom functionality or navigation. An added benefit is the performance gains seen when adapting OS-specific features that have been optimized for the devices' hardware.

Incentives

Learners are often responsible for completing assignments both in and out of the classroom. Intrinsic (i.e. self-satisfying) and extrinsic (i.e. motivated by rewards or punishment resulting in success or failure) incentives have historically played an important role in motivating learners to complete assigned tasks (Lin, McKeachie, & Kim, 2001). Sources of motivation in education vary greatly depending on an educator's teaching philosophy, but one of the more common learning theories used in mobile learning today is behaviorism. Trends in current application design draw heavily from the notion of using positive and negative reinforcement to apply or withhold stimuli in order to incite change in a learner's behavior (Watson, 1930).

Without a reason to open an application outside of class, it can easily be treated as out-of-sight out-of-mind. Designers can leverage a learner's behavior to their advantage by guiding them through key areas of content in order to complete specific activities. Accomplishing virtual achievements (e.g., collecting badges) to earn class points for completing these activities is one example of how mobile learners can be motivated to complete assignments and encourage their staying active in the application over time.

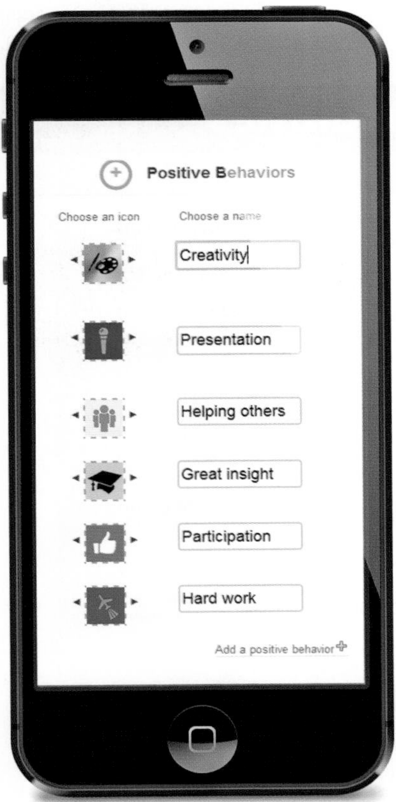

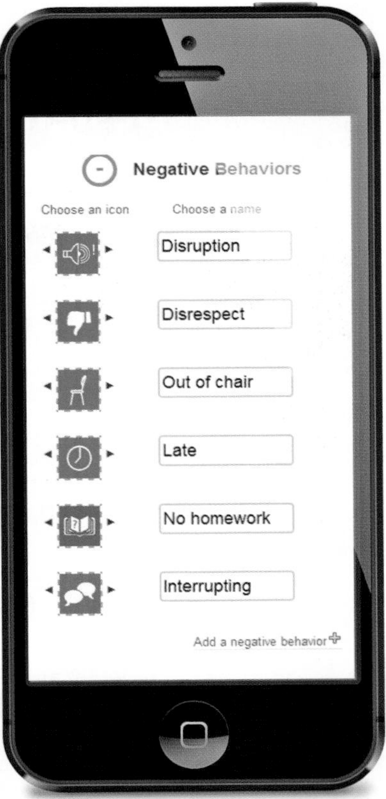

Figure 6.7
Class Dojo is an online tool and application that serves as a visual reminder used to guide student behavior by awarding custom achievements (positive or negative) to keep students on track.

The added encouragement of introducing the completion of these achievements as competition, like the first participant to collect every badge in a learning module for example, can further extend the desire for learners to return to an application. Utilizing the immediate feedback (e.g., push notifications) built into most mainstream mobile OS platforms is a way to further leverage features available to designers in order to draw learners back into the environment. This allows for sustainable motivation with regard to progress updates and other necessary information.

Conclusion

The above considerations provide a strong foundation for design based on the specific affordances of mobile devices within the context of learning. These considerations are particularly clear when compared with traditional learning software. A deep

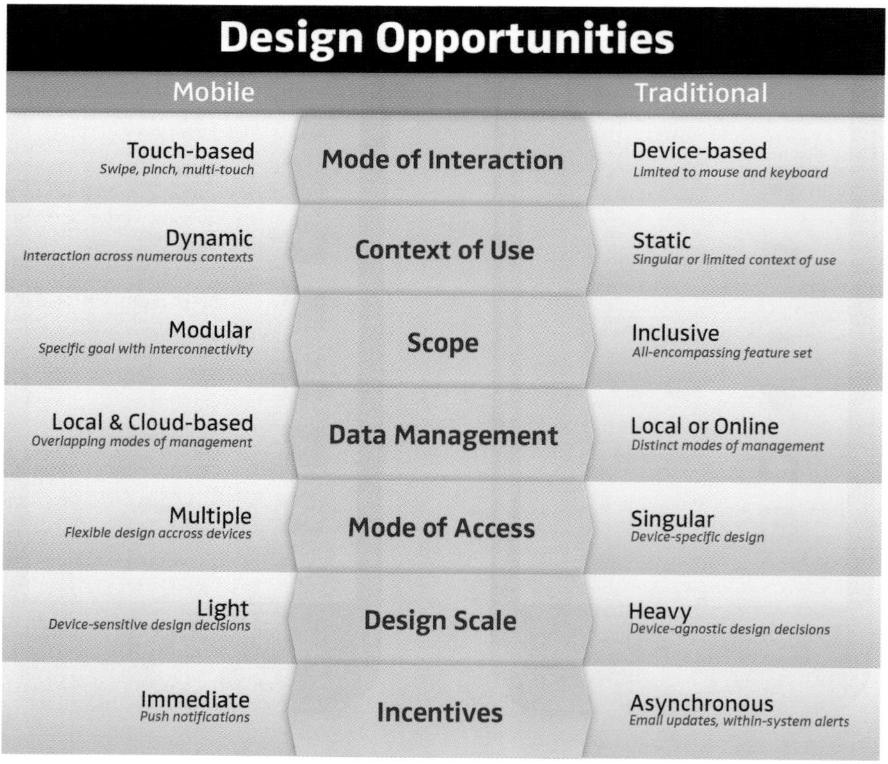

Design Opportunities

Mobile		Traditional
Touch-based *Swipe, pinch, multi-touch*	**Mode of Interaction**	Device-based *Limited to mouse and keyboard*
Dynamic *Interaction across numerous contexts*	**Context of Use**	Static *Singular or limited context of use*
Modular *Specific goal with interconnectivity*	**Scope**	Inclusive *All-encompassing feature set*
Local & Cloud-based *Overlapping modes of management*	**Data Management**	Local or Online *Distinct modes of management*
Multiple *Flexible design accross devices*	**Mode of Access**	Singular *Device-specific design*
Light *Device-sensitive design decisions*	**Design Scale**	Heavy *Device-agnostic design decisions*
Immediate *Push notifications*	**Incentives**	Asynchronous *Email updates, within-system alerts*

Figure 6.8
Seven design considerations for mobile learning applications.

understanding of how mobile applications differ in interaction mode, use context, scope, data management, access modes, design scale, and incentives is the first step toward thoughtful mobile learning design.

However, it is important to note that there are design considerations that transcend mobile and desktop technologies. For example, all learning applications should consider both a student and a teacher perspective to ensure a consistent experience for each. As new technologies are introduced, it becomes increasingly difficult for designers to effectively implement their ideas across all necessary platforms. Carefully considering how these technologies are similar to and different from existing technologies is a necessary first step in the development of meaningful learning experiences.

References

Bahl, P., Han, R., Li, L., & Satyanarayanan, M. (2012). Advancing the state of mobile cloud computing. In *Proceedings from MCS '12: The Third International Workshop on Mobile Cloud Computing and Services* (pp. 21–28). New York: ACM.

Bull, G., Thompson, A., Searson, M., Garofalo, J., Park, J., Young, C., & Lee, J. (2008). Connecting informal and formal learning experiences in the age of participatory media. *Contemporary Issues in Technology and Teacher Education, 8*(2), 100–107.

Clough, G., Jones, A. C., McAndrew, P., & Scanlon, E. (2007). Informal learning with PDAs and smartphones. *Journal of Computer Assisted Learning, 24,* 359–371.

Doering, A., Scharber, C., Miller, C., & Veletsianos, G. (2009). GeoThentic: Designing and assessing with technological pedagogical content knowledge. *Contemporary Issues in Technology and Teacher Education* [Online serial], *9*(3). Retrieved March 10, 2011, from http://www.citejournal.org/vol9/iss3/socialstudies/article1.cfm.

Doering, A., Veletsianos, G., Scharber, C., & Miller, C. (2009). Using the technological, pedagogical, and content knowledge framework to design online learning environments and professional development. *Journal of Educational Computing Research, 41*(3), 319–346.

Emerson, J. (2008). Visualizing information for advocacy. Retrieved April 4, 2009, from http://backspace.com/infodesign.pdf.

Godehardt, E. (2009). A framework for contextualized visualization supporting informal learning. *International Journal of Advanced Corporate Learning, 2*(3), 21–26.

Hwang, G., & Tsai, C. (2011). Research trends in mobile and ubiquitous learning: A review of publications in selected journals from 2001 to 2010. *British Journal of Educational Technology, 42*(4), 65–70.

Kirkpatrick, M. (2009). Yelp brings first US augmented reality app to iPhone store. *Read Write Web.* Retrieved September 10, 2011, from http://www.readwriteweb.com/archives/yelp_brings_first_us_augmented_reality_to_iphone_s.php.

Kukulska-Hulme, A. (2009). Will mobile learning change language learning? *ReCALL, 21*(2), 157–165.

Lau, A., & Moere, A. V. (2007). Towards a model of information aesthetics in information visualization. In *Proceedings of the 11th International Conference on Information Visualization* (pp. 87–92). Washington, DC.

Lin, Y., McKeachie, W., & Kim, Y. (2001). College student intrinsic and/or extrinsic motivation and learning. Retrieved June 7, 2012, from http://www.sciencedirect.com/science/article/pii/S1041608002000924.

Mahmoud, Q., Zanin, S., & Ngo, T. (2012). *Integrating mobile storage into database systems courses*. Unpublished paper presented at the 13th Annual Conference on Information Technology Education, Calgary, Alberta, Canada.

Martin, S., Diaz, G., Plaza, I., Ruiz, E., Castro, M., & Peire, J. (2011). State of the art of frameworks and middleware for facilitating mobile and ubiquitous learning development. *The Journal of Systems and Software, 84*(11), 1883–1891.

Marsick, V., & Watkins, K. (2001). Informal and incidental learning. *New Directions for Adult and Continuing Education, 89*, 25–34.

Miller, C., Lecheler, L., Hosack, B., Doering, A., & Hooper, S. (2012). Orchestrating data, design, and narrative: Information visualization for sense- and decision-making in online learning. *International Journal of Cyber Behavior, Psychology and Learning, 2*(2), 1–15.

Miller, C., Lecheler, L., & Rose, S. (2012). Avenue: Innovation and transformation in world language, reading, and writing e-assessment. In A. H. Duin, E. Nater, & F. Anklesaria (Eds.), *Cultivating change in the academy: 50+ stories from the digital frontlines at the University of Minnesota in 2012* (pp. 94–103). Minneapolis, MN: University of Minnesota.

Nichols, J., Zhigang, H., & Barton, J. (2008). Highlight: A system for creating and deploying mobile web applications. In *Proceedings of the 21st Annual ACM Symposium on User Interface Software and Technology* (pp. 249–258). New York: ACM.

Park, Y. (2011). A pedagogical framework for mobile learning: Categorizing educational applications of mobile technologies into four types. *International Review of Research in Open and Distance Learning, 12*(2), 78–102.

Pousman, Z., Stasko, J., & Mateas, M. (2007). Casual information visualization: Depictions of data in everyday life. *IEEE Transactions on Visualization and Computer Graphics, 13*(6), 1145–1152.

Shah, N. (2011). iPads become learning tools for students with disabilities. *Education Week Digital Directions*. Retrieved December 19, 2011, from http://www.edweek.org/dd/articles/2011/10/19/01speced.h05.html.

Sharples, M., Taylor, J., & Vavoula, G. (2005) Towards a theory of mobile learning. *Proceedings of mLearn 2005 Conference, 1*(1), 1–9.

Ting, Y. (2012). The pitfalls of mobile devices in learning: A different view and implications for pedagogical design. *Journal of Educational Computing Research, 46*(2), 119–134.

Watson, J. (1930). *Behaviorism* (revised edition). Chicago, IL: University of Chicago Press.

Chapter 7
The Future of Mobile Media for Learning

New and accessible tools for mobile learning are about to cause a proliferation of place-based experiences for both informal and formal learning. This chapter provides an overview of some of the early iterations of educators rethinking classrooms, museums, and civic engagement for learners and using mobile games to facilitate active participation in the world they are learning about. Therefore, educators have a central role in providing design guidance and demanding quality mobile experiences defined by access, production, amplification, and the relevance of activity, product, and audience for student productions.

For Designers

This chapter provides an overview of current and coming designs in the field and suggests principles for designs for learning in the future. This chapter highlights current designs that are forging the way for mobile media to be part of our everyday lives and create unique channels for civic participation, learning, and play. This chapter lays out pathway principles of design and seeds ideas for new designs that will transform the users' experience and encourage ubiquitous learning models.

For Teachers

This chapter presents a lens on education that uses the world as the classroom. This chapter shares examples of current and coming applications that are going to influence teaching and learning; then provides principles of design that serve as a guide for identifying mobile media applications that will have an impact on learners. Any teacher seeking to understand the coming changes for learning, rooted in powerful mobile media, should start with this chapter.

For Researchers

This chapter links the fields of both design and education for a compelling look at new pedagogical tools that shape the nature and context of learning outside of the classroom. Mobile media amplify information access, varied modes of data collection, and the ability to communicate instantly an affordable reality at scale and this chapter provides examples from practice and design-based research that are exploring the edges of how to think about transformative education.

Mobile learning will redefine who, what, where, when, and the nature of active, place-based, learning in the coming years—and this is a good thing.

Dr. Seann M. Dikkers

Assistant Professor, Educational Technology, Ohio University;
Director, Gaming Matter

Dr. Seann Dikkers is an assistant professor at Ohio University in the Educational Technology division of The Gladys W. and David H. Patton College of Education. Dikkers served fourteen years as a teacher, principal, and consultant in the public schools of Minnesota. Dikkers' research investigates new media integration strategies for educational leadership, teaching, and learning. His work bridges leadership and curriculum scholarship—including projects like CivWorld, ParkQuest, History in our Hands, Mobile Media Learning, Augmented Reality and Interactive Storytelling editor (ARIS), the Comprehensive Assessment for Leadership in Learning (CALL), Teacher's Toolbox, and books *Real-Time Research: Improvisational Game Scholarship* and *Mobile Media Learning*—published by ETC Press. Currently, Dikkers is the founder and director of Gaming Matter Labs and presents across the country on games and learning topics. Dikkers earned his doctorate in Educational Communications and Technology from the University of Wisconsin-Madison; his dissertation research examined teacher integration of technology.

The Future of Mobile Media for Learning

Mobile media is already ubiquitous, customizable, useful, increasingly connected, faster, and pleasantly fun. Really, the future is now. Have you seen the predictive image of Captain Kirk, of *Star Trek* fame, using a portable mobile pad for his work? On *Star Trek,* the pad and the communicator were different devices. So, in some delightful ways, we are already past that future. Consider that we can all have what used to be fantasy devices for productive, and not-so-productive, times during our day. If the future is now, what is next?

Futurist considerations are essential at this point in mobile media development to guide limited resources toward relevant mobile media learning opportunities. This chapter will review coming projects that are changing learning contexts, and finally provide guidance for how mobile media needs to be directed for effective use in the coming years.

After reading the last few chapters that cover the exciting present, why should we consider the future at all—when there is so much to take in now? Mobile is already everywhere; as of November 2011, worldwide cellular subscriptions reached six billion people with 1.2 billion broadband subscriptions (ICT, 2011). We find ourselves already flooded in more applications than can be navigated in a lifetime, and see our daily lives being transformed by increasingly potent access and tools we can hand pick for use.

Moreover, mobile media is not only a consumer resource; in only a few short years this technology has become a medium of *production*. Consumers are primarily entertained, where producers create new representations of knowledge and ideas. Ideas have always held value. In the same way that Shakespeare's pen or Hemingway's typewriter were technologies that we introduced to generations of young learner/producers, today, YouTube's portable cameras, Moveon.org's organization of information, or ImprovEverywhere's redefinition of space are tools of production that need to be part of any educational experience. These are just a few. Mobile media must be learned in the same way that we have taught kindergarteners to use a pencil—let me illustrate.

Recently, I was in a meeting where a team was pulling up cloud-based documents, contacting people for information, and pinging topical initiatives as we discussed them. It wasn't just the tools though; it was that almost everyone in the room knew how to use them well. There was a palatable rush to being hyper-efficient and getting work done *as we thought of it*—like being in the middle of a guild raid, a covert operation, or a snappy *West Wing* episode.

At one point "technology stuff" was for "techies"; today these mobile tools are so pervasive that to not know how to use them efficiently is a form of illiteracy that leaves the illiterate behind. The divide between those that can and cannot successfully use mobile media for communication, information, and production will be left sadly behind—or doomed to consumption, as some argue (Rushkoff, 2010).

When production tools shift from a hobby to a form of literacy, it's precisely the time that educators interested in opening doors for youth need to pay attention. Thankfully, this is happening. There are many that are paying attention to mobile media use in the future that I will only begin to share in this chapter.

Mobile Media for Learning: Examples of Ongoing Innovation

A growing community of scholars, educators, and developers are looking into the future of learning that increasingly involves mobile media learning. This chapter is thus indebted largely to the 300+ future-thinking colleagues that are paying attention to digital experiences as learning experiences. It is from these outstanding people that we can start to see what mobile for learning looks like. My own community at the University of Wisconsin–Madison likewise is seeking to see in what ways mobile media can be used for learning in the future. Our journey exemplifies the direction this kind of work is now taking.

Early in our work, we conceptualized a series of games that made use of enriched learning spaces like museums, the state capital, and cultural centers of Madison. But when we approached teachers, despite the potential, "technology stuff" didn't fare well versus competing demands that teachers experienced to cover curriculum, address learning gaps, and ensure basic literacies. Mobile media for learning had, and has, the design challenge of being relevant to the educators and students that may use it.

Together with Dr. Kurt Squire, we wanted to inform our designs with more information about how mobile devices were used "in the wild." We gave devices to a small sample of students ($n = 10$) aged eight to 18 to see what young learners would do with them without outside instruction (Squire & Dikkers, 2012). In short, we found that students were consistently amplifying their already existing learning interests because the devices facilitated easy access, usefulness, and flexible applications that could be used to learn about, participate in, and innovate for areas of interest. For instance, instead of simply babysitting, one youth used her device to search for craft ideas, take pictures, and send updates to the parents throughout the evening. When parents responded, her demand increased along with her hourly rate. It was then that we realized that *we* couldn't make the specific games teachers would use, but they could. We decided to make teachers a production tool for them to create their own mobile games. Teachers needed to be given the tools to use the devices in ways that amplified what they were already doing. This is when things got interesting.

With modest funding from MacArthur Foundation, institutional support from UW-Engage, the programmers at Engage were able to put together a free, open-source editor for developing more mobile games. This editor became a platform for hundreds of designers and thousands of users among which were more educators than we could have ever hoped to reach by making a consumable product. The accessible tool of production (see ARIS online) was UW's contribution to thinking about the future of mobile or"place-based"education (Squire, 2010)—but not the only one:

> Once the app is built, we'll extend the project to other parts of the city, gather more stories, and open it up to your contributions. We'll also share tools and code so that anyone can replicate our model in other cities.
>
> (Matt Blair, Know Your City Developer)

In addition, MIT's augmented reality editor, MITAR, is undergoing an overhaul and will soon be available as a simple editor (Sheldon, 2011):

> TaleBlazer is our next generation augmented reality suite, including a Web-based editor along with iOS and Android game-play clients. The TaleBlazer editor uses a visual blocks-based scripting environment to allow game creators to build rich interactivity into the AR experiences they design.
>
> (Josh Sheldon, MIT Scheller Teacher Education Program lab)

So, as the tools of production are now proliferating, what designs show promise for the future of mobile learning and why? To look into the near future of mobile, we can start by exploring what designers are building that could become a staple in mobile in years to come. In our recent book, *Mobile media learning: Amazing uses of mobile devices for learning* (Dikkers, Martin, & Coulter, 2012), Kurt Squire and Eric Klopfer recall a decade of work at MIT, Wisconsin, and Harvard to sort out how mobile media can be leveraged for learning. After gathering a collection of case examples for mobile learning design, this work complements this book by showing small glimpses of how mobile will be used in the coming years. These cases show both what is happening, and the current models being presented for massive implementation by local educators. The near future of mobile will be filled with applications like these five.

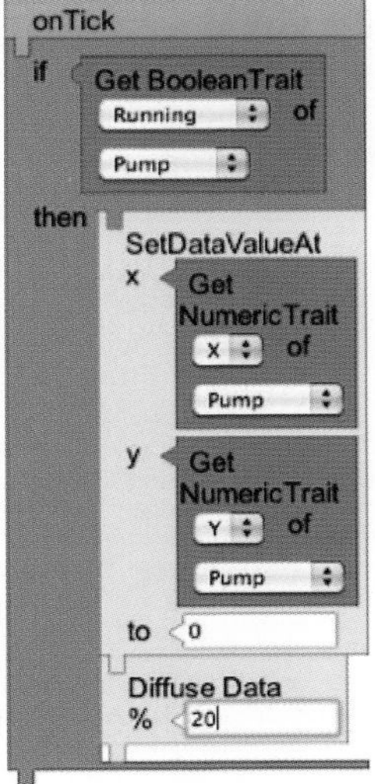

Figure 7.1
Color-coded, drag-and-drop mobile media editor coming soon from MIT STEP Lab. From http://education.mit.edu/blogs/jsheldon/2011/07/05.

Mentira

Mentira guides players in and out of a Spanish-speaking neighborhood. Designers wanted to have language learners actually experience neighborhoods where the language was spoken primarily and test their growing language skills in context. Within the classroom this is, at best, simulated; when students go mobile however, this is a real possibility.

DIY Democracy

Users can locate and share information about needed work and civic plans for their local communities. Designers provide a link between citizens and those making decisions for the community along with the tools to collect data that city planners find compelling.

Up River

Designers worked with local historians, scientists, and educators to build a quest-based ethnographic adventure for learners to encounter both digital and real people along the St. Louis River estuary. The design of the experience was to introduce players to topical issues, but also to integrate the tools of ethnographic research to players as game mechanics.

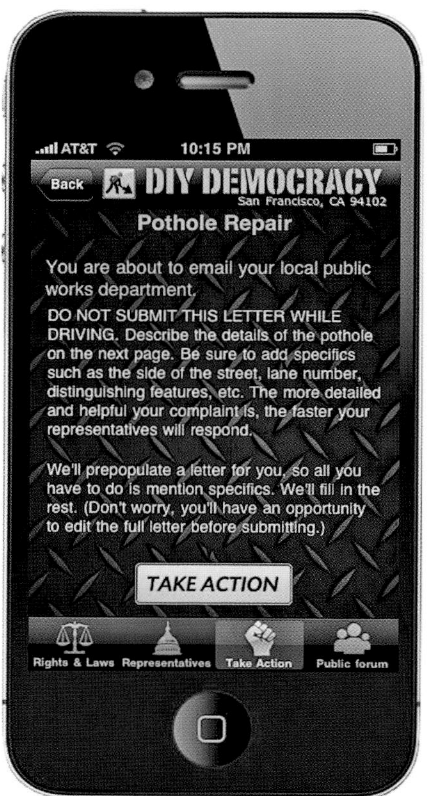

Figure 7.2
DIY Democracy.

Re:Activism

Using instant messaging, a map, and a grocery bag, designers worked out a mobile game that challenges players to visit the sites of a wide spectrum of activist events. Once there, students are given challenges to re-act, commemorate, and learn more about issues that were at contest in each space around a city.

Then, Now, Wow

Designers build a mobile adventure that transforms a museum space into a quest filled zone that allows players to experience narratives in context. In one sequence, players meet and eventually save iron miners by finding and "bringing" life-saving artifacts. The

Figure 7.3
Playing mobile games for learning: Then, Now, Wow at the Minnesota Historical Society.

relevance and personality of history can go back to the classroom as digital resources for projects, sharing, and a personalized library.

These are small examples of what is happening with mobile right now, but only the beginning. Once complete, all five of these models are readily available to anyone that wants to use the free tools and build their own—along with templates that can be"cut" and "pasted" in your location for modification and use.

The capacity to produce now has a remarkably low start-up cost, so it is easy to predict that neighborhoods, parks, cities, museums, and even schools will be transformed within the space of a few years to have an interactive mobile layer built onto them. Interestingly, as they connect life to learning, mobile experiences will also integrate nicely into more intimate aspects of life too:

JPray

Designers are designing mobile experiences that attempt to guide Jewish learners to explore the meaning behind traditional prayers and draw connections between faith-based values and the spaces in which young learners live.

Mobile media learning spans subject areas and will transform learning from subjects that are cloistered in the classroom to where they take place in the world. In fact, the traditional subject areas were chosen *because* they had relevance outside of the school. So when technologies to produce, track, guide, and record learning become available, it's only natural that expert educators will use them to take learning to its source: science in the river bed, ethnography in local settings, language learning where the language is spoken, activism on the streets, and even spiritual practice among people.

For instance, consider the very real potential of history being "kept" in the location events occurred. In fifty years, we can look forward to walking into a new city and looking at each building and park through the lens of a mobile infrastructure that lets us hear from the architects, city planners, civic leaders, storytellers, and youth that have made those spaces come alive over time. It's only a matter of time before the Dill Pickle Club gets funded for their KnowYour City 2.0 Project and we'll get a template for building city histories like this.

In the same way that Ebay opened the tools of *economy* up to the masses (and largely reduced prices), mobile media will open up the tools of data collection in the hard sciences, social sciences, and allow users to collect and organize ideas for writing, video production, and other arts. Mobile media will allow many more people to participate in what were once exclusive communities, or they will simply start their own.

At some point, the widespread use of mobile technology will produce products of excellence in various settings that are accepted as exemplars for future learners. This will only be after many, many efforts to perfect the medium for learning. Yet, these future mobile products should be sought out and included in a standard curriculum package along with great novels, calculators, and Bunsen burners.

For example, current applications like Pinterest or Instagram further mobile learning by allowing massive user-based collection and organization of interests and images. Using the "friending" structures mastered by Facebook, these applications take advantage of the mobile nature of learning in context and allow users to share instantly; incidentally, they also show the compound effect of API sharing. These applications are used first as consumable content, but progressively invite those in the community to produce and contribute more. The value of those contributions is then largely a meritocratic measure. Thus, tools that have a discrete purpose are already available, the future only requires for them to be used in innovative ways.

If these are the seeds of potential learning designs, organizations like KickStarter also allow independent developers to find funding from those that want to see their product developed. Not only can anyone share their ideas, but they can also simply, and quickly, offer them up as a funding target. This democratization of funding opens up a new future for mobile designs that are not dominated by corporate interests and agendas. If you want a better bike helmet, or a better mobile experience, find the project and fund it yourself—with a few thousand others. If you know how to make a better bike helmet or social history app, post it and get money to make it.

Moving Forward: Principles for Mobile Media Learning

If mobile media is already part of a literacy that we need schools to introduce youth to, then mobile media is ready to be used across disciplines, on location, and by everyone with a mobile device. What should we be asking about the future of mobile? More importantly, if these trends are a reality, what should educators be demanding as mobile develops?

First, in addition to a large network of mobile media experiences being locally designed, we can expect that corporate interests will grow wherever you find people. As more people enjoy learning and playing with mobile-facilitated space-based learning, expect the production quality to grow with larger investments and highly polished products. What remains to be seen is whether the availability of free production tools this early in the history of mobile learning will have established an educational community that produces competitive experiences; or, if the consumable services will outweigh the opportunities to produce and design as teachers and students.

New mobile media will work its way into the scope and sequence of schooling. For instance, we can already see that many simple tools, like restaurant guides, icon-filled maps, search engines, GPS trackers, mini-games, are available for mobile devices. These will continue to be refined by both the user bases and the companies that sell them. Their availability and use will eventually become an expected aspect of life for an "educated" citizen and it follows that the demand for schools to expose and teach students how to use them will increase. We all agree that students should learn to navigate their world with competence and the companies that sell these tools will, of course, willingly provide lesson plans.

As mobile media adds to learning opportunities, it will also make some learning irrelevant. For educators this presents another pedagogical challenge: Can we proactively continue to define teaching and learning as relevant? For instance, consider the need for massive amounts of memorized data—a staple in law and medical school. But, if a student can find information in less than thirty seconds, is it worth testing them on it? The answer is increasingly, no. Where pencils are good at making lists and taking notes for memorization, mobile tools are very good at accessing, guiding, recording, and sharing information and experiences. Fundamentally, mobile and the increased quality of mobile resources will challenge the purpose of having students memorize *information* and testing them on it later—but will increase the need for students to compose *meaning* from that information.

The personal nature of mobile, along with its capacity to be with a person in both formal and informal learning times, will expand the list of valid learning experiences beyond classroom and school certification. A degree has marked a "learned" person in years past; however, it only covers a limited range of learning experiences within an institution. Perhaps learning and schooling need to be considered separately (Collins & Halverson, 2009)?

For instance, mobile will accelerate the ability to record a visit to a museum, park, or to work with a blacksmith as learning experiences and then record them as part of the learner's record. Students will soon be able to collect a life history for future employers and present their cumulative life experiences (both inside and outside of traditional schools) to prospective employers. These digitized resumés can include courses and grades, but also gaming achievements, library visits, online learning, collective references, and hobbies—giving a much fuller picture (and accountability) to personal learning. As these systems are refined, learning and schooling will either marry or compete for relevant representations of student accomplishments. This will be influenced strongly by how educators respond to the rise of mobile media and tools of production.

Mobile media over the next few years looks to be a private interest domain; however, educators have much to gain from mobile platforms and applications too. Educators need to develop their own agenda for mobile media development that will avoid the interests of profit and capitalize social and academic proficiency in the most democratic way possible. I ask, what would such an agenda look like?

A Mobile Media Learning Agenda for Educators

Those that pioneer the use of mobile for learning are still shaping the future of mobile. It is for this reason that I close with suggestions for advancing the cause of learning for educators. Based on current trends that have provided fertile ground for educational development of mobile, there are some principles that will more quickly enable mobile education to move forward. I argue if these are part of every design initiative, the future of learning with mobile will be directed to more effective learning.

Educators should continue to support and encourage mobile media that fit these four principles of mobile media learning.

Assume Access

Schools have had some hesitation to open up wireless network access on their campuses. Information institutions that stop the flow of information should be suspect. The dangers of misuse should not dominate the educational dialogue, and usually haven't. As an analogy, the US has for decades supported an open, free, and accessible network of sidewalks in nearly every community. These sidewalks do become chipped and can cause physical injury to youth even when used innocently. Despite the dangers, we have not blocked sidewalk use. Our solution has been to teach youth the virtue of *caution*, and where our instruction isn't heeded, the sidewalks provide their own lessons. We do keep bandages in most schools. Educators need to start with an open, free, and accessible network infrastructure on all campuses to even start introducing youth to their future.

> *Example: Stillwater Public Schools. Stillwater, MN*
> School officials now allow students to bring their own devices (BYOD) to school. As long as students register with the district—they can address misuse of their wireless network easily without restricting the majority of students that use it responsibly. The result is a cost reduction for the district, less time policing devices and Internet access, and more time teaching with and how to use the tools for learning.

Production over Consumption

I worry when a project is designed to provide a consumable product to educators. Usually these projects waste valuable time and money developing a product that is, by design, only going to serve the local teacher consultants that helped develop the tool. Educators can and should ask for tools that enable their own production, editing, and customizing mobile applications for classroom use. That said, the future could be filled with consumables that are still worth exploring. However, these can be appreciated without seeing them as the end goal of educational mobile—the capacity to make things ourselves. Smarter mobile devices often have audio recorders, cameras, video recorders, note-taking applications, and other tools for collecting and producing content. These can be potent without a designed mobile experience built around them. Seek tools of production over tools of consumption—even for learning.

Example: ARIS Mobile Game Editor

The Augmented Reality for Interactive Storytelling (ARIS) Editor is free and relatively easy to build all types of mobile games from a simple scavenger hunt to a full-scale role-playing game. Expect an afternoon to learn the basics of editing your own games.

Amplification

Mobile media, like writing poetry, tends to be adapted to a person's existing interests. This means two things for educators: First, the need to introduce new subjects and interests is still a key consideration for educators. Mobile will simply speed up the process of students accessing and taking up new interests. Second, educators can and should expect that interests be pursued rigorously. Mobile media both facilitates access to expert practice like never before, but also allows for fourteen-year-olds to *become* experts (Lewis, 2001) in fields that require mobility.

Examples: Lots!

Any application that allows the user to expand or learn more about an area of interest serves amplifying that interest. For instance if you have or want students out taking pictures, consider introducing tools that build on the camera like Snapspeed, Pixlromatic, Instagram, or Pinterest.

Relevant Practice, Authentic Audience

We are now seeing that mobile media learning is potent because it blurs the line between simulation and real contact with places and people. Because learners can learn in the field, they *should* learn in the field. It shouldn't be at all surprising that the tolerance for traditional learning is waning. The idea that a single textbook is an authority over readily available tutorials and collective thinking communities available online is silly to those that activate those learning models in their lives—in much the same way that air travelers chuckle at those that insist on driving long distances. Also, the idea that a single teacher is the judge of work quality isn't always reflected in the current reality of the workplace. Authentic audiences for art, research, politics, and other venues for idea production are online and they number in the thousands. Going viral is the mark of success in a mobile world, but even having a hundred "likes" has more face validity than the opinion of a single person.

Examples: Again, lots!

Any application that has a community function or sharing capacity potentially allows for moving relevant practice to an authentic audience. Currently student work can be shared online via blogs, networks, websites, Twitter links, interest groups, and badge systems. If you have students actually designing applications, distribution channels like Apple's App Store, Google Play, and others make getting it out there easy.

These are progressively essential design principles for mobile learning. For instance, relevant learning without access is a nice hobby for a few, but not useful for large-scale learning. Access is foundational to all useful games for education. Conversely, games with "access" and the ability for users to "produce" something are welcomed, and worth exploring, even if they aren't developed so that they amplify the players existing interests or connect to an audience.

Consider math gaming—typically an easy target for cheap consumable "learning" products. Math games may make use of interstitial times and can be played without a network connection. As they remain a consumable product, they usually fail to amplify current interests, by providing problems derived by the designer. Math games can be good, of course, but the value of the mobile application roughly matches a set of paper

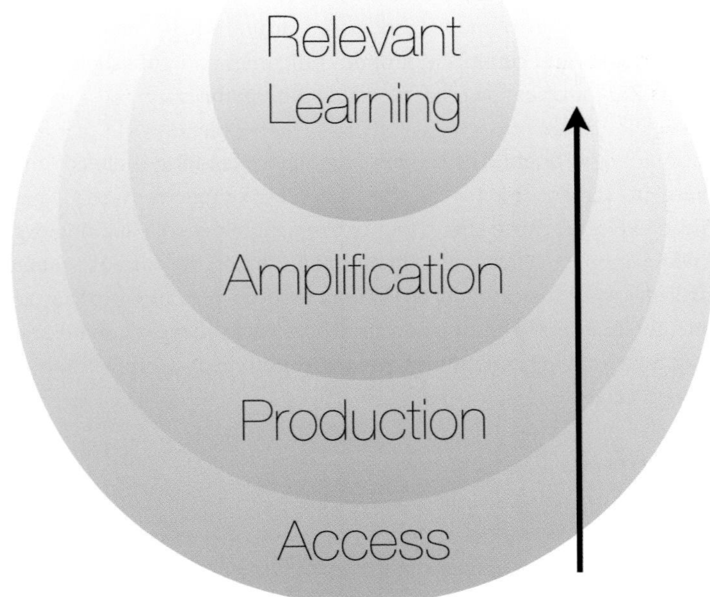

Figure 7.4
Elements of effective mobile media development for learning.

flash cards—so the advantages of the mobile medium are wasted along with time, money, and good intentions. You will still see comparative research that uses these types of poorly conceived products to "prove" whether mobile is valuable for learning. Good educators will be wary of this and look for designs that have students playing together (assume access), creating their own puzzles (production), tying the experience into their own interests (amplification), and sharing their work with experts in the field (relevant learning).

These four principles apply from the teacher's perspective too. If a mobile product meets some of these principles, but doesn't serve the learning goals you have for your students, then your interests aren't being amplified with the use of mobile media. Likewise if you are having students consume scavenger hunts without reflecting, adding to, or working to develop their own afterwards, then assets are being lost in the use of mobile.

Educators can, and should, continually be intentionally asking how to: (1) give others "access" to your lessons; (2) engage students to "produce" all types of media representations of what they learn; (3) encourage further creation that "amplifies" both your learning goals and student interests; and (4) seek out activities that are "relevant" on their own merit in the larger world of practice, then have students share them. These questions will earmark the future of learning, not just with mobile media, but relevant learning at large. The future of mobile media for learning will be directed and designed by individual teachers and curators alongside companies and publishers. These principles provide a filter for what you read, see, or do with mobile.

The future of mobile is bright. The future of mobile for learning is already moving forward with designs across subject areas, spaces, and exploring new ways to layer interactions with content as we move about. Out of these mobile media learning experiences, some will rise as more effective than others, and we are on the cusp of a renaissance of active, mobile, learning that introduces learners to ideas, histories, puzzles, and spaces layered with mobile access to information, and the capacity to record, share, and produce new learning for a growing community of learners both in and out of school settings.

Acknowledgements

This chapter largely reports on the amazing work of early developers and the future of learning they envision. A special thanks to the designers, programmers, and educators and their amazing cases noted above: Chris Blakesley, Tamara Donnefield, Philipo Dougherty, David Gagnon, Thomson Guster, Jacob Hanshaw, Leshell Hatley, Jesse Heineman, Chris Holden, Jeremiah Holden, Wendy Jones, Eric Klopfer, Breanne

Litts, Colleen Macklin, John Martin, James Mathews, Josh Sheldon, Jennifer Sly, Garrett Smith, Kurt Squire, Julie Sykes, and Mark Wagler.

References

Collins, A., & Halverson, R. (2009). *Rethinking education in the age of technology: The digital revolution and schooling in America.* New York: Teachers College Press.

Dikkers, S., Martin, J., & Coulter, R. (Eds.). (2012). *Mobile media learning: Amazing uses of mobile devices for learning*. Pittsburgh, PA: ETC Press.

ICT. (2011). *Key ICT indicators for developed and developing countries and the world (totals and penetration rates).* United Nations: International Telecommunications Union (ITU).

Lewis, M. (2001). *Next: The future just happened.* New York: W.W. Norton & Company, Inc.

Rushkoff, D. (2010). *Program or be programmed: Ten commands for a digital age.* OR Books. E-book ISBN 978–1-935928–16–4.

Sheldon, J. (2011). Just announced: TaleBlazer—Breaking new ground in location-based augmented reality gaming. [Online blog]. http://education.mit.edu/blogs/jsheldon/2011/07/05.

Squire, K. (2010). From information to experience: Place-based augmented reality games as a model for learning in a globally networked society. *Teachers College Record, 112*(10), 2565–2602.

Squire, K., & Dikkers, S. (2012). Amplifications of learning: Use of mobile media devices among youth. *Convergence: The International Journal of Research into New Media Technologies.* Retrieved November 18, 2012, from http://con.sagepub.com/content/early/2012/02/15/1354856511429646.full.pdf+html. doi:10.1177/1354856511429646.

Chapter 8
A Framework for Mobile Learning App Design: DCALE

This chapter reviews the research on mobile learning design and suggests a framework for mobile learning application software (app) design, DCALE (Design Goal Setting, Context Analysis, Alignment with Platform, Learner Experience, and Enhancement of Performance), in order to produce effective and efficient guidelines for instructional designers, teachers, and educators who are considering designing and adopting mobile technology in their educational setting. Limited research has been conducted to identify a framework for mobile learning design in the K–20+ context, and there are few design guidelines for developing mobile learning apps (especially for iPhone or iPad). This chapter explores the factors and design requirements that are crucial to the mobile learning environment, offers a framework with guidelines for application, and describes considerations for designing mobile learning apps (specifically iOS-based apps).

For Designers

This chapter focuses on a vision for a practical framework of mobile learning design principles for instructional designers. Design ideas and arguments are presented and a compelling guideline for expanding conventional wisdom about how a mobile technology can be utilized is offered. Drawing on my own experience of designing mobile learning, I tried to outline and introduce specific technological aspects of mobile learning design. In the near future I think designers will have a better appreciation for the nuances of designing in the mobile technology field.

For Teachers

This chapter articulates how to design mobile learning apps, and offers a cohesive road map for teachers to understand more about the capabilities of mobile technology applications. Using educational apps without any background knowledge can be a dangerous thing. As such, this chapter is an attempt to strike a balance between educational perspectives and technological viewpoints. I outline a framework for mobile learning app design in the hope that teachers will gain a better understanding of mobile learning context.

For Researchers

I present a synthesized practical view that has emerged as a mobile learning app design framework, and tried to envision a future in which mobile learning, whether acquired through formal learning or otherwise, can be designed validly. With the knowledge about a framework for mobile learning design, researchers can deal with diverse factors that include research design considerations as well as the values, attitudes, perceptions, and understandings that they want to conduct their research.

Mobile learning and its empowerment will enhance human development through personalized participation and augmented reality innovation.

Donggil Song

Doctoral student, Instructional Systems Technology Program,
Indiana University School of Education;
Educational Research Manager, Seeds of Empowerment;
Associate Instructor, Indiana University School of Education

Donggil Song is an educational research manager of Seeds of Empowerment and an associate instructor at Indiana University. He is currently pursuing a PhD in Instructional Systems Technology from the School of Education at Indiana University. He holds an MS in Computer Science and Engineering and a BA from Seoul National University (SNU), and also completed the master's program in Cognitive Science at SNU. He has conducted several research projects on measuring spatial intelligence and cognitive abilities of blind children in a mobile learning environment and has designed educational games for the subproject of Programmable Open Mobile Internet for Social Cause. He is a member of Stanford Mobile Inquiry-based Learning Environment research team led by Dr. Paul Kim, and has conducted several workshops and implementations using mobile devices. He is engaged in the mobile programming and system design/development of the Extreme Learning research project with Dr. Curtis Bonk. He is the author of an educational technology website (www.einbrain.com), which provides mobile learning apps and instructional technology resources.

A Framework for Mobile Learning App Design: DCALE

The emerging potential of mobile technologies has links directly to the learners' needs regardless of the amount of learning materials, or learning time and space (Peters, 2009). With mobile technology, exploring, practicing, building new knowledge, acquiring new skills, reflecting, and recording takes place in a seamless fashion (Kim et al., 2011). Learning happens instantly and everywhere, even as the learner leaves the classroom, travels home, or sits down to complete their homework (Bonk, 2009). Mobile technology can facilitate learning by making students experience a real situated context and make learning more appealing, motivating, and engaging. The variety of settings and diverse contexts that mobile technology affords can be conducive to more authentic learning (Motiwalla, 2007).

However, Peng et al. (2009) point out that the widespread and fuzzy characteristics of mobile learning technologies may cause problems. For instance, it may be difficult for designers, teachers, or researchers to monitor or control the progress of learners. Additionally, mobile technologies present specific limitations that prevent designers from applying common principles of e-learning (Parsons, Ryu, & Cranshaw, 2007). Due to the rapid advancement of mobile technology, neither a theoretical nor practical framework for mobile learning design has been established. In order to postulate a design framework for mobile learning application software (apps), we need to begin by identifying what uniquely distinguishes mobile learning from traditional e-learning.

What Makes the Mobile Learning Design Different?

By focusing on the unique characteristics of mobile learning we may understand better how knowledge and skills can be transferred across contexts and how mobile learning can be designed to support learners (Petrova, 2007; Sharples, Taylor, & Vavoula, 2010). The characteristics of mobile technology such as accessibility, mobility, collaboration, and the opening of the educational process for continuous and lifelong learning are significant advantages (Papanikolaou & Mavromoustakos, 2006). Mobile devices require less infrastructure and electricity, which makes mobile devices more widely distributable and easily employed than personal computers (Kim et al., 2011). However, these advantages refer to the technical/social aspects of the mobile learning and do not guarantee the success of mobile learning apps.

Mobile learning app design requires additional features that are less commonly found with the traditional design, including: (1) potential interaction with other applications; (2) sensor handling; (3) native or hybrid (i.e. mobile web) apps; (4) families of hardware and software platforms; (5) security; (6) user interfaces; (7) complexity of testing; and (8) power consumption (Wasserman, 2010). Mobile technology affords students opportunities to explore our physical world. This enables instructors to collect data unique to the learners' current location, environment, and time. Mobile devices are now equipped with geo-location receivers and other sensors. These can provide rich and interactive content about the learners' context. The mobility of learners augmented by mobile technology may contribute to the process of acquiring knowledge, skills, and experience (Sharples et al., 2009). Since mobile learning happens spontaneously in diverse contexts, mobile technology must enable people to acquire and share knowledge beyond the confines of a fixed location. Thus, we need to consider how mobile learning happens across locations, time, topics and technologies (Sharples et al., 2009). Keeping this in mind, I attempted to locate a framework capable of assisting mobile learning designers with practical knowledge of the design and development of iOS (e.g., iPhone, iPad, or iPod touch) apps.

Contemporary Guidelines/Frameworks for Mobile Learning Design

Table 8.1 summarizes the contemporary guidelines for mobile learning design. Taylor et al. (2006) suggest that theories of mobile learning must be tested against three criteria (see Table 8.1). Through these tests, the findings and results will feed back into the development and refinement of the task model. That is, the design and development shape learner behavior, and that behavior in turn affects the way that learners perceive technology.

In accordance with previous research (Sharples, Taylor, & Vavoula, 2005), Low and O'Connell (2006) apply a learner-centered activity model of mobile learning to their pedagogical underpinnings as a building block of mobile activity. Moreover, De Jong, Specht, and Koper (2008) have considered different classification schemes from the literature in order to apply the criteria for designing mobile learning. Additionally, Seong (2006) focuses on the usability aspects of the mobile learning design. Ayob, Hussin, and Dahlan (2009) propose a three-tier design model for mobile learning. Herrington, Herrington, and Mantei (2009) recommend design guidelines for the incorporation of mobile learning into a higher education learning environment. Finally, Vavoula and Sharples (2009) employed these developmental phases in their project.

There are a few frameworks that have been used in mobile learning research (e.g., Koole, 2009; Motiwalla, 2007). However, these frameworks are not designed for mobile learning designers or practitioners. Though there are some guidelines described in Table 8.1, the critical issue faced by mobile learning design is the lack of a practical

Table 8.1 Contemporary guidelines for mobile learning design.

Focus Area	Contents	Author(s)
Testing criteria for theories of mobile learning	1. Do they account for both formal and informal learning? 2. Do they analyze the dynamic context of learning? 3. Do they theorize learning as a constructive and social activity?	Taylor et al. (2006)
Learner-centered activity model	1. Record: The learner as a gatherer and builder of new knowledge 2. Reinterpret: The learner as an analyst of existing data to discover new knowledge 3. Recall: The learner as a user of existing information and resources 4. Relate: The learner as part of a social context and a network of knowledge	Low and O'Connell (2006)
Usability of mobile learning design	1. Usability theoretical framework: Learnability, efficiency, memorability, errors, and satisfaction 2. Considerations for achieving usability tailored learning a. Cognitive, perceptual, and motor capabilities and constraints of people in general b. Unique characteristics of the users' physical and social work environment c. Unique capabilities and constraints of the chosen software and/or hardware, and platform for the system/product 3. Unique properties a. Dynamicity: The interaction between the system/product and users is highly fluid b. Contextual awareness, adaptation and sensitivity: Apps designed are highly related to the contextual use, ability of adaptation and sensitivity to their surrounding	Seong (2006)

(*Continued*)

Table 8.1 *(Continued)*

Focus Area	Contents	Author(s)
Classification of mobile learning	1. Content: Describes applications based on the artifacts exchanged and shared by users 2. Context: Describes applications based on the context parameters taken into account for learning support 3. Purpose: Describes applications according to the goals and methods of the system for enabling learning 4. Information flow: Classifies applications according to the number of entities in the system's information flow 5. Pedagogical model: Pedagogical paradigms and instructional models	De Jong, Specht, & Koper (2008)
Design guideline	1. Analysis (context of use) a. Identify and document user's tasks b. Identify and document organizational environment c. Define the use of the system 2. Design (context of medium) a. Enable frequent users to use shortcuts b. Offer informative feedback c. Consistency d. Reversal of actions e. Error prevention and simple error handling f. Reduce short-term memory load g. Design for small devices h. Design for speed and recovery i. Design for top-down interaction	Ayob, Hussin, & Dahlan (2009)

	j. Allow for personalization k. Don't repeat the navigation on every page l. Clearly distinguish selected items 3. Testing (context of evaluation) a. Quick approach b. Usability testing c. Field studies d. Prediction evaluation	
Design guideline for the incorporation into higher education	1. Real-world relevance: Use mobile learning in authentic contexts 2. Mobile contexts: Use mobile learning in contexts where learners are mobile 3. Explore: Provide time for exploration of mobile technologies 4. Blended: Blend mobile and non-mobile technologies 5. Whenever: Use mobile learning spontaneously 6. Wherever: Use mobile learning in nontraditional learning spaces 7. Whomsoever: Use mobile learning both individually and collaboratively 8. Affordances: Exploit the affordances of mobile technologies 9. Personalize: Employ the learners' own mobile devices 10. Mediation: Use mobile learning to mediate knowledge construction 11. "Produse": Use mobile learning to produce and consume knowledge	Herrington, Herrington, and Mantei (2009)
Developmental phase	1. Requirements analysis, to establish the requirements for the socio-technical system (the users and their interactions with technology) and specify how it would work, through consultation with the different stakeholder groups 2. Design of the user experience and interface 3. Implementation of the service 4. Development of the service	Vavoula and Sharples (2009)

(Continued)

Table 8.1 *(Continued)*

Focus Area	Contents	Author(s)
Design guideline	1. Link people in real and virtual worlds 2. Create learning communities between people on the move 3. Provide expertise on demand 4. Support a lifetime of learning 5. Support learners to reach personal understanding through conversation and exploration 6. Support learners' collaboration in order to construct common knowledge 7. Use technology to enrich learners' collaborative knowledge building with other learners and teachers 8. Support learners' transitions across learning contexts	Sharples et al. (2009)

aspect and synthesized procedure that can lead us to effective instructional design for mobile learning. Thus, the following section introduces a framework for mobile learning app design, DCALE.

Mobile Learning App Design Framework: DCALE

Based on the literature review and personal experiences of mobile learning app design/development, a framework for mobile learning design, DCALE, is suggested. The framework comprises five broad phases: I Design Goal Setting; II Context Analysis; III Alignment with Platform; IV Learner Experience; and V Enhancement of Performance. Figure 8.1 further illustrates the framework.

I Design Goal Setting

Mobile learning apps should be designed based on the learners' needs and instructional purposes. When it comes to mobile learning itself, the learners' needs vary depending on sociocultural background, prior knowledge, skills, competences (Papanikolaou & Mavromoustakos, 2006), cognitive styles, and motivation (Seong, 2006).

The guidelines for mobile learning design are not much different from the learner analysis of traditional e-learning design. However, the significant difference is that we might

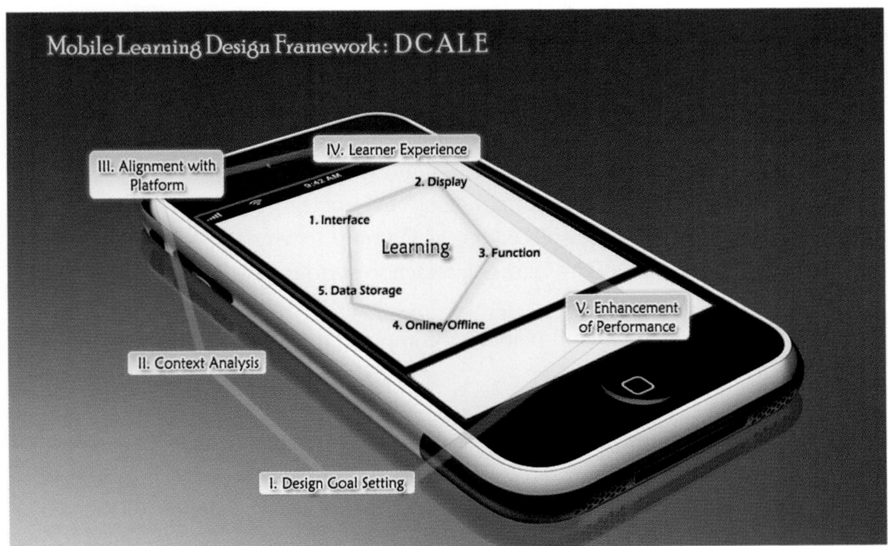

Figure 8.1
Mobile learning app design framework: DCALE.

not know how students use mobile devices in real situations because their use patterns could be different for each demographic type or learning location. Using a mobile device is quite different from studying with a personal computer. For instance, students are not always willing to use the virtual learning environment, due to the difficulty of using the mobile device, the non-intuitive nature of the environment, and the provision of reduced interactivity (Papanikolaou & Mavromoustakos, 2006). Since mobile learning technology adoption is rapid, seamless, and actively driven by the students rather than the teacher (Kim et al., 2011), long orientation guides may bore students. Instead of assuming a limited interaction model with mobile devices, designers must focus on the learners' skills, use patterns, and digital literacy.

II Context Analysis

Context is a crucial issue for mobile learning (Sharples et al., 2009; Uden, 2007; Vogel et al., 2010). The term context can be defined as "the combined physical, information and social setting of learning, which for mobile learning in particular is in continuous change" (Taylor et al., 2006). Context plays a significant role in the design and development of mobile learning apps. Mobile learning can provide authentic learning experiences that suit the specific context of learners (Jeng et al., 2010).

For analyzing the context for mobile learning, we can build upon this list provided by Uden (2007). The ten questions a designer must answer include:

1. Who are the learners involved?
2. What is the learner trying to achieve?
3. What is the purpose of the learning activities?
4. How are learning tasks organized towards learning goals?
5. How does learning get done in diverse contexts?
6. How do learners' activities fit into the objectives of learning?
7. What type of limitations is placed on the learning activity?
8. What is the structure of the learner interaction surrounding the learning activity?
9. Where do problems occur?
10. What tools do learners find helpful in completing the learning tasks in different contexts?

Designers need to identify how mobile learning takes place within a personal or school context by analyzing how the use of mobile learning practices or new ways of supporting learners can change the formal and informal learning experience (Vavoula & Sharples, 2009). Also, the indoor and outdoor integration of mobile learning or the combination of learning activities to be conducted across different educational contexts has expanded in importance (Vogel et al., 2010).

Technically, mobile learning apps are influenced by the contextual change and the learner interaction with their context. Although it may be difficult to track the progress of learning that occurs across multiple contexts, it is even more challenging to determine in advance where the learning may occur (Vavoula & Sharples, 2009). Nevertheless, mobile learning frameworks must support the learning that occurs outside the classroom. Mobile learning apps must be designed for varied learners' expectations and situations, such as learning time (e.g., daytime or nighttime), learners' status (e.g., standing, sitting, or even lying), behavior (e.g., standing still or in motion), situation (e.g., one or two hands free), and place (e.g., busy place or noisy place) (see Charland & Leroux, 2011).

Additionally, we must consider that many students who have mobile devices tend to use social networking services. These services allow for the contextualization of the learner's social and physical environment and enables new forms of learning support including: multimodal notification and messaging, content exchange and sharing, contextualization services or physical world tagging (De Jong, Specht, & Koper, 2008). Mobile learning needs to support a seamless flow of learning across contexts. Mobile learning is related to the lifestyle of the learner, who in the course of everyday life moves from one context to another, switching locations, social groups, technologies and topics (Vavoula & Sharples, 2009).

III Alignment with Platform

Another significant issue for mobile app design is to decide which platforms to support in the highly fragmented world of mobile development (cf. Wasserman, 2010). There are different operating systems (e.g., iOS, Android, BlackBerry, Windows, or Symbian), programming languages and supporting tools, and various devices with different capabilities for each platform. In the mobile app development field, the term platform typically refers to a mobile device's operating system or its software development kits. Each platform has its own user-interface conventions in its operating system and a closed architecture (especially iOS) that restricts the development of customized and integrated approaches.

However, since many educators have chosen the iOS platform for face-to-face and online classrooms, in this chapter the term platform can be used to refer to different aspects of the Apple iOS platform and its devices. The iOS platform has succeeded in retaining its lead since the iPhone AppStore opened in July, 2008 (Wasserman, 2010). When designing and developing iOS-based learning apps, there are several issues regarding platform alignment that must be addressed. For one, the iOS updates and changes its features frequently. Moreover, there are four types of devices that use iOS: iPad, iPhone, iPod touch, and Apple TV. Even the same type of devices may have different abilities (e.g., disk space, memory capacity, CPU power, or wireless networking method).

Mobile learning designers cannot rely upon sole support for just one version of iOS or one type of CPU power, memory capacity, or screen size/resolutions (e.g., there is a considerable difference between the screen size of iPhone and iPad), but rather, they need to support the other versions/types that users may use to access the app. Concurrently, iOS-based learning designers need to balance mobile web-based app and native apps based on the main purpose, development and environmental context, and the opportunities of the mobile web (Charland & Leroux, 2011). Thus, mobile learning app designers should consider these variations of the platforms.

IV Learner Experience

Now we need to consider practical aspects—the Learner Experience (LX) phase, named after User Experience (UX). A successful UX is crucial for successful app adoption. As Papanikolaou and Mavromoustakos (2006) suggested, designing the UX of mobile learning apps includes: architectural design, navigation design, interface design, content design, and production. However, this categorization can also be generally applied to e-learning design. Thus, for generating more specific guidelines that fit mobile learning, I suggest six components of LX: (1) interface; (2) display; (3) function; (4) online and offline; (5) data storage; and their overarching component (6) "learning."

1 Interface

Designing the learner interface is one of the main challenges for mobile apps. There are eleven elements in the interface component: (1) interface builder; (2) toolbar; (3) navigation; (4) keyboard input; (5) dismissing the keyboard; (6) accelerometer; (7) bluetooth; (8) screen orientation; (9) device rotations; (10) finger gestures: tapping, pinching, rotation, panning (dragging), swiping, long press; and (11) single/multi-touch.

For this sub-phase, the questions Uden (2007) suggested could be useful: (1) What resources are available to the learners involved in the design?; (2) What tools and materials are accessible?; (3) What rules, norms, and procedures are regulating the learner interaction and coordination?; (4) Is targeted technology integrated with other tools and materials?; and (5) What are the roles of existing technology?

Wasserman (2010) points out that the mobile user interface paradigm is based around widgets, touch, physical motion, and keyboards (physical and virtual) rather than the familiar WIMP (Windows, Icons, Menus, Pointer) interface style of operating systems for personal computers. He contends that the UX is also affected by other issues related to the device itself (e.g., weight and size). Given the different types of iOS-based devices, designers should consider physical aspects of each type of device when designing the interface of the mobile learning apps.

2 Display

Mobile learning app designers must consider how to display information within the small screen of mobile device. There are seven components for the display phase: (1) screen resolution; (2) screen aspect ratio; (3) screen rotations; (4) scrolling; (5) animation; (6) (auto) resizing; and (7) color depth. The input techniques for restricted display size and resolutions, and the increased cognitive load on learners when attempting to multi-task in this limited environment are major issues when designing mobile learning apps.

3 Function

The following is suggested for the function component of LX: (1) using media (e.g., image, audio, or video); (2) location; (3) background applications; (4) access to learners' personal data (e.g., contact list); (5) access to files; (6) control other hardware (e.g., speaker, microphone, or camera); and (7) capability (e.g., processing power, memory, or storage). A successful mobile learning app must explain the learner behaviors associated with these function components. In addition, wireless network and sensor technology provide new possibilities for learning activities utilizing augmented reality with real-time geo-positioned data and visualizations, which may increase students' engagement, enabling them to conduct scientific inquiries (Vogel et al., 2010) and intelligently interact with the learner-based knowledge of their environment (Seong, 2006).

4 Online and Offline

Learner experience can extend outside the mobile learning app. For example, we can use push notifications to wake up an app under certain conditions (e.g., location change) or to generate a new application to handle different application aspects (Charland & Leroux, 2011). However, when dealing with these data transactions, network status (i.e. online/offline) should be considered. There are several considerations for the online/offline component: (1) access to the Internet; (2) information retrieval; (3) push notifications; (4) connections to other web services; and (5) transferring method (e.g., using XML or JSON). All of these features should be working when mobile devices are in the online status considering its different speeds (e.g., Wi-Fi, 3G, or 4G LTE); at the same time, designers should consider when learners are in the offline status.

5 Data Storage

For evaluating the apps and its learners, learner data can be gathered and stored in the device or mobile web server. Thus, the following can be considered for the data storage component: (1) remembering the learner; (2) server- or client-side storage system; (3) file handling; (4) data handling software or system (e.g., SQLite or iCloud); and (5) saving and restoring the diverse state of learners.

6 Learning

As an umbrella component, "learning" should be centered in the Learner Experience phase. Obviously, the five components described above in the Learner Experience phase should interact with "learning." How to combine appropriate educational strategies for learning application is one of the most critical issues in mobile learning environment design (Jeng et al., 2010). Thus, mobile learning designers must consider what/how the five components and their sub-units should be designed in order to support students' learning.

V Enhancement of Performance

The success of any type of software application depends on a commitment to performance enhancement. Among the critical performance factors for mobile apps are efficiency/effectiveness (e.g., efficient use of device resources, responsiveness, and scalability), reliability (e.g., robustness, connectivity, and stability), quality (e.g., usability and installability), and security (Wasserman, 2010). There are some elements for the Enhancement of Performance phase:

1. Examining different app states
2. Multi-tasking support
3. Limited power of the device
4. Energy efficiency
5. Memory management
6. Observing low-memory warning.

Evaluation and Management

Since DCALE is a framework for designing mobile learning apps, the evaluation and management phases of mobile learning technologies are not included. Designing and development processes must not only consider operating systems and hardware device features, but must also address a more comprehensive set of project management issues.

Evaluation should be a continuous process starting with the initiation of a project and continuing on through design, development, and implementation (Sharples et al., 2009). In order to evaluate mobile learning in diverse contexts, Vavoula and Sharples

(2009) suggest that designers need to analyze: (1) the physical setting and the layout of the learning space; (2) the social setting; (3) the learning objectives and outcomes; (4) the learning methods and activities; (5) the learning progress and history; and (6) the learning tools. In addition, issues such as understandability, learnability, friendliness, playfulness, accuracy, suitability, compliance, interoperability, privacy, and ethics must be examined and evaluated carefully (Papanikolaou & Mavromoustakos, 2006).

Conclusion

Given that there is a short history of mobile learning apps, the lack of theoretical or practical frameworks is understandable. Although a few researchers (e.g., Sharples, Taylor, & Vavoula, 2005) have attempted to establish theory in this area, designers require additional practical evidence, research, guidelines, principles, and frameworks. As my effort to spark this continuing discussion, DCALE provides a framework that introduces mobile-specific considerations into the design and development of mobile learning apps.

The five phases of DCALE are not independent of one another. For example, because students may move around and interact with their peers in diverse environments,

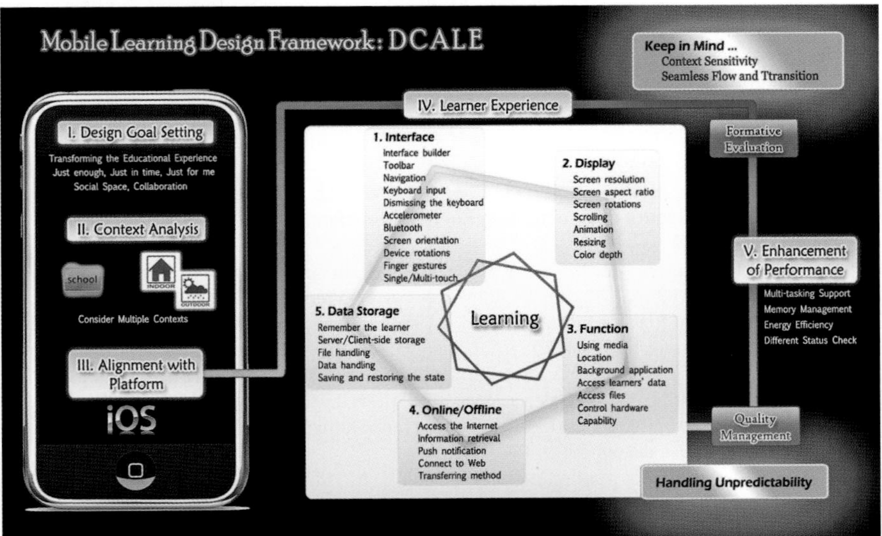

Figure 8.2
Mobile learning app design framework: DCALE.

context dependencies play a critical role in the learner experience. To provide learners with meaningful experiences, implementations must deliver designs that support the expectations established by their particular context. In utilizing the design process offered by DCALE, designers and researchers are able to consider context sensitivity and handle the unpredictability of mobile learning.

Future research will be oriented towards assessing this framework and identification of robust design principles. Future work will involve the application of the framework in authentic situations to enable the application of the framework in a diverse context and the subsequent design and development of a complete mobile learning app. Furthermore, educators must pay attention to the underlying sociocultural values that add to the formation of the learning activities (see Kim et al., 2011).

Mobile learning is "different" from other forms of e-learning. Moreover, traditional educational theory might not fit the characteristics of an ever-changing mobile learning environment. Well-organized guidelines, principles, and frameworks must support the future design of mobile learning; otherwise, we will see continued dissatisfaction and frustration of both designers and learners.

References

Ayob, N., Hussin, A. R. C., & Dahlan, H. M. (2009). Three layers design guideline for mobile application. Paper presented at the International Conference of Information Management and Engineering (ICIME 2009), Chengdu, China.

Bonk, C. (2009). *The world is open: How web technology is revolutionizing education*. San Francisco, CA: Wiley.

Charland, A., & Leroux, B. (2011). Mobile application development: Web vs. Native. *Communications of the ACM, 54*, 49–53.

De Jong, T., Specht, M., & Koper, R. (2008). A reference model for mobile social software for learning. *International Journal of Continuing Engineering Education and Life Long Learning, 18*(1), 118–138.

Herrington, A., Herrington, J., & Mantei, J. (2009). Design principles for mobile learning. In J. Herrington, A. Herrington, J. Mantei, I. Olney, & B. Ferry (Eds.), *New technologies, new pedagogies: Mobile learning in higher education* (pp. 129–138). Wollongong: University of Wollongong.

Jeng, Y. L., Wu, T. T., Huang, Y. M., Tan, Q., & Yang, S. J. H. (2010). The add-on impact of mobile applications in learning strategies: A review study. *Educational Technology and Society, 13*(3), 3–11.

Kim, P., Hagashi, T., Carillo, L., Gonzales, I., Makany, T., Lee, B., & Garate, A. (2011). Socioeconomic strata, mobile technology, and education: a comparative analysis. *Educational Technology Research and Development, 59*(4), 456–486.

Koole, M. (2009). A model for framing mobile learning. In M. Ally (Ed.), *Mobile learning: Transforming the delivery of education and training* (pp. 25–47). AB: Athabasca University Press.

Low, L., & O'Connell, M. (2006). Learner-centric design of digital mobile learning. Paper presented at Learning on the Move, Brisbane, Australia.

Motiwalla, L. F. (2007). Mobile learning: A framework and evaluation. *Computers and Education, 49*(3), 581–596.

Papanikolaou, K., & Mavromoustakos, S., (2006). Critical success factors for the development of mobile learning applications. In *Proceedings of the 24th IASTED International Multi-Conference—Internet and Multimedia Systems and Applications*, Innsbruck, Austria (pp. 10–24).

Parsons, D., Ryu, H., & Cranshaw, M. (2007). A design requirements framework for mobile learning environments. *Journal of Computers, 2*(4), 1–8.

Peng, H., Su, Y. J., Chou, C., & Tsai, C. C. (2009). Ubiquitous knowledge construction: Mobile learning re-defined and a conceptual framework. *Innovations in Education and Teaching International, 46*(2), 171–183.

Peters, K. (2009). m-Learning: Positioning educators for a mobile, connected future. *The International Review of Research in Open and Distance Learning, 8*(2), 113.

Petrova, K. (2007). Mobile learning as a mobile business application. *International Journal of Innovation and Learning, 4*(1), 1–13.

Seong, D. S. (2006). Usability guidelines for designing mobile learning portals. In *Proceedings of the 3rd International Conference on Mobile Technology, Applications and Systems*, Bangkok, Thailand.

Sharples, M., Arnedillo-Sánchez, I., Milrad, M., & Vavoula, G. (2009). Mobile learning: Small devices, big issues. In N. Balacheff, S. Ludvigsen, T. de Jong, A. Lazonder, S. Barnes, & L. Montandon (Eds.), *Technology enhanced learning: Principles and products* (pp. 233–249). Berlin: Springer.

Sharples, M., Taylor, J., & Vavoula, G. (2005). Towards a theory of mobile learning. Paper presented at the Mlearn 2005 Conference, Johannesburg, South Africa.

Sharples, M., Taylor, J., & Vavoula, G. (2010). A theory of learning for the mobile age. In R. Andrews & C. Haythornthwaite (Eds.), *The handbook of e-learning research* (pp. 221–247). London: Sage.

Taylor, J., Sharples, M., O'Malley, C., & Vavoula, G. (2006). Towards a task model for mobile learning: a dialectical approach. *International Journal of Learning Technology, 2*(2), 138–158.

Uden, L. (2007). Activity theory for designing mobile learning. *International Journal of Mobile Learning and Organisation, 1*(1), 81–102.

Vavoula, G. N., & Sharples, M. (2009). Meeting the challenges in evaluating mobile learning: A 3-level evaluation framework. *Mobile and Blended Learning, 1*(2), 54–75.

Vogel, B., Spikol, D., Kurti, A., & Milrad, M. (2010). Integrating mobile, web and sensory technologies to support inquiry-based science learning. Paper presented at the 6th IEEE WMUTE International Conference on Wireless, Mobile and Ubiquitous Technologies in Education, Kaohsiung, Taiwan.

Wasserman, T. (2010). Software engineering issues for mobile application development. Paper presented at the FSE/SDP workshop on Future of Software Engineering Research, Santa Fe, New Mexico.

Section 3
Mobile Learning Design and Development Narratives

In today's peer-reviewed academic research, particularly in the context of technology-mediated learning, the illuminating narratives of educational technology design and development teams are often lost (or, possibly, undervalued). Difficult to validate or generalize, these rich stories of creating and shaping tools that foster the learner experience through design represent the backbone of our field: the fusion of educational theories, pedagogical frameworks, interaction models, and research-based "ideas" for building transformational online and mobile learning opportunities. Design-based research, a methodology "premised on the notion that we can learn important things about the nature and conditions of learning by attempting to engineer and sustain educational innovation in everyday settings" (Bell, 2004), provides a foundation for sharing a glimpse into these intricate balances of pedagogy and design. However, the wider field of learning technologies has yet to embrace this paradigm within the realm of mobile learning environments. To this end, the following three chapters illustrate the challenges, complexities, and "a-ha" moments inherent within the mobile learning design process, focused through the lenses of the designers themselves.

Mr. and Mrs. George, co-founders of the Baan Dek Montessori school and Montessorium (an award-winning app design firm focused on building educational apps for children), begin this section by exploring the notion that "design is born at the interface of aesthetics and pedagogy." The authors share their "model of thought" in the design process behind two leading iPad apps, Intro to Letters and Intro to Numbers. Focused on the individual child's experience within each app, Mr. and Mrs. George outline several lessons learned from their designs and illuminate Montessori-based interactions as guidelines for all children's app designers. For this forward-thinking duo, consciously aware of their foundational nature of learning, "it's not so much that design can change the world, then, as attempt to imagine it otherwise."

Mr. Edwards and Mr. Nyquist continue this section with a chronicle of their shared design process in the development of HotSeat, a learner-centered exploration app based on geo-location and user-generated contextual questions. As students collaboratively developing their first mobile app, Edwards and Nyquist detail their journey by outlining core values, sketched visions, a parallel design process, and the scaffolded flow of user experience. Based on their belief that learning is the act of connecting, "the interlacing of experiential knowledge, collaboration, and social and cultural progression," the authors suggest that the"physical and digital space can dynamically be formed through the threading of personal connections."

Concluding this section is a narrative by Ms. Henrickson, a PhD student researcher and designer focused on instilling the exploratory essence of *adventure* as a core element in mobile learning. Henrickson begins by highlighting the concern of meaningfully integrating mobile apps into the K–12 classroom and argues, "educators and learning technologists should thus be concerned about, *as well as collaborators in*, the design and development of educational apps." Ultimately, Henrickson's adventure learning app design and development story is one intended to inspire and challenge others starting their own journeys into the complex and rewarding landscape of app design.

Reference

Bell, P. (2004). On the theoretical breadth of design-based research in education. *Educational Psychologist*, *39*(4), 243–253.

Dr. Jean Quam
Dean, College of Education and Human Development, University of Minnesota

How do you transform a college culture so everyone wants to use and integrate apps and tablets? What would happen if, as the Dean of a large college, I asked the entire teaching faculty to appear once a week to talk about how to improve our teaching and learning at a major research university? Some faculty members would say that they need to concentrate on conducting their research and writing grants. Others might say that teaching will happen when it needs to be done. Those who would come to such a session might easily drop out if the weekly discussions were not challenging, or did not offer important advice, or if they wasted their time. And yet, some of our faculty get together regularly and have impromptu discussions in the hallways and parking lots about their teaching and their learning. What makes the difference? Apps.

Two years ago, I was fascinated by a new tablet computer called an iPad. I speculated in the summer that it would be great to hand a tablet to an incoming freshman and say that everything that they needed for their first year in college could be found in their tablet. So, we tried an experiment. Two years ago, we gave 430 tablets to all incoming freshmen and all faculty who taught them. We challenged our faculty to have fun learning how to use it—play games, collect photos, check out Facebook, look at YouTube, Tweet, draw on it, write on it—and make it their own. Further, we gave each faculty member $100 credit in iTunes to purchase apps they wanted to try.

Last year, we continued and expanded the experiment—we gave another 440 iPads to freshmen and also gave iPads to more faculty, student advisers, administrators and development staff. Each year we have found new uses for the tablets and apps. Last year our development staff recorded my (the Dean's) sending individualized messages to potential donors and alumni. The reaction was powerful. Individuals felt cared about and the power of a visual movie was much stronger than a written note. For older alums, they marveled at the technology. Our education faculty taught student teachers to use the camera and an app that could annotate the recording of their work in the classroom. Student teachers had a peer or one of the students in the class record the teaching they were doing, the student teacher edited the piece on iMovie, and sent it off to their supervisor who was able to review it, add annotations of suggestions for change, and send it back to the student—all within hours rather than days.

Remember "the fence" in *The Adventures of Tom Sawyer*? "Thirty yards of board fence nine feet high . . . 800 square feet of fence to paint white." And,

Tom Sawyer made it look so much fun that every boy wanted a turn and some even were willing to pay him for the privilege of painting the fence.

For us, "the fence" is tablets and apps. As I walk down the halls, someone tells me, "I am on level 12 of Word Welder." Someone else tells me they just tried the latest new tablet and the resolution is amazing. I hear two other faculty members debating the merits of Notes versus Notability.

We give away tablets as door prizes at events, we take them to every meeting, we compare apps all the time, we established a website on the latest innovations in mobile teaching and learning, I author a Twitter account on technology, I give talks as iBooks, and I write a weekly column that includes the "app of the week." We installed televisions that can use presentations wirelessly from the iPad, and we offer professional development opportunities for two weeks out of the summer for faculty and staff who want help with using apps and tablets in their courses. In our summer camps, we feed them well, we teach them well, and we allow them to become excited about the possibility of apps in education.

I recently attended a meeting in which another dean said, "I would consider providing students with tablets but only if we turned off the apps we did not want them to use or were able to control what the students could load." Another faculty member added, "I don't want students looking at their tablets and trying different apps when they should be listening to me." These are *absolutely the wrong approaches to take.*

The tremendous number of apps available to be used and to be created is astonishing. It opens up the learner and teacher to a new world of creativity in learning. So, how do you transform a college culture? You encourage the use of apps on phones or tablets or any new device that is yet to be invented. You make it a part of everything you do, every part of your life, and you make it so engaging that everyone in the college will want to "paint the fence."

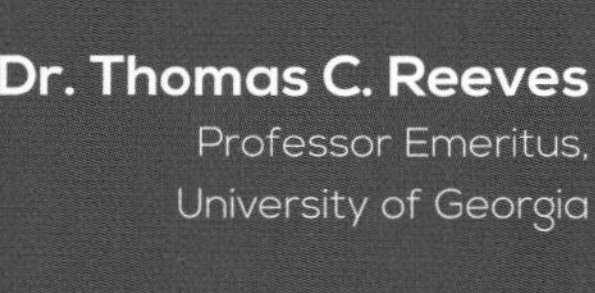

Dr. Thomas C. Reeves
Professor Emeritus,
University of Georgia

In Neal Stephenson's (1995) SciFi masterpiece, *The Diamond Age: Or, A Young Lady's Illustrated Primer*, a girl named Nell comes into possession of one of only three existing interactive mobile devices that provide unprecedented opportunities for learning and personal development. Nell senses that there is more behind the primer than mere programming, and a major theme of the book is the added value of human creativity over artificial intelligence. Another major theme relates to the purpose of education as instrumental (i.e. preparing one to play a productive role in society) or as transformative (i.e. preparing one to become a full-realized individual capable of dealing with life's inevitable challenges).

Much of what Stephenson forecasted in *The Diamond Age* is coming to realization in the numerous variants of mobile learning portrayed in *The New Landscape of Mobile Learning*. Inevitably, questions about the role of human creativity and the goal of education persist. I just asked Siri, the personal "intelligent" agent on my iPhone, "What is learning?" Siri responded, "OK, here you go," and displayed a screen of information about a periodical titled *Learning* (circulation, 150,000). Apple proclaims that Siri "can quickly understand what you're asking for, then quickly return a response." A response . . . yes, but an answer . . . no.

An answer to the question "What is learning?" clearly requires more than an app. It demands interaction with others, teachers and learners, as well as a real-world context and an authentic task. In *The Diamond Age*, Nell alone maximizes the potential of the Primer to lead "a more interesting life" by developing a subversive attitude toward the status quo. In the spirit of Postman and Weingartner's (1969) *Teaching as a Subversive Activity*, a more interesting life as an educator in the twenty-first century must be about more than creating mobile learning apps. We must engage our learners and ourselves in addressing profound questions such as "What is learning?" and "What is the purpose of education?" head on. This alone will "keep it interesting."

References

Postman, N., & Weingartner, C. (1969). *Teaching as a subversive activity*. New York: Delacorte Press.
Stephenson, N. (1995). *The Diamond Age: Or, a young lady's illustrated primer.* New York: Bantam.

Chapter 9
Playing with Gravity
On Designing for Children

In this chapter, we will examine the idea that, "Design is born at the interface of aesthetics and pedagogy." We will provide an overview of our current educational climate, with a focus on Steve Jobs and his vision for the future of education, and see how we can design for this new generation. Inspired by Deleuze and Guattari, we will also provide a new model or image of thought, which will help guide us through this emerging digital landscape. Lastly, we will describe our general thoughts on the process of design, and lay out some specifics of designing for children.

For Designers

Designing for children comes with a unique set of challenges. In this essay, we'll examine the conditions of both aesthetics and pedagogy. We'll provide practical considerations, and lay out a theoretical framework to keep in mind when designing for children.

For Teachers

There's a myth that persists in our current education landscape: that technology can solve all our problems. In this chapter, we'll chart a different path. Following Steve Jobs, we will discuss the importance that people play in the development of digital learning, and scope out a trajectory for thinking of education as self-education.

For Researchers

There's a secret no one wishes to discuss. Namely, that the advantages and disadvantages of digital education have yet to be fully scoped out, let alone incorporated. In this chapter, we hope to tackle some of the many misconceptions of education, and provide a framework for thinking through the challenges of learning in the twenty-first century.

We're interested in developing a philosophy of life, one that is attentive to the conditions of aesthetics and pedagogy.

Bobby George
Co-founder, The Baan Dek Montessori,
Sioux Falls, South Dakota;
Co-founder, Montessorium
(http://montessorium.com)

June George
Co-founder, The Baan Dek Montessori,
Sioux Falls, South Dakota;
Co-founder, Montessorium
(http://montessorium.com)

Originally from Sioux Falls, South Dakota, Bobby George obtained his BA from Lehigh University and a Master's from the University of Warwick. Bobby George is currently a PhD student at the Center for Modern Research in European Philosophy. The title of his dissertation is "I Love Arakawa and Gins: Forever, Always, Now." Along with his wife, June, he founded The Baan Dek Montessori & Montessorium. Bobby is interested in exploring the intersections of aesthetics and pedagogy. Originally from Bangkok, Thailand, June George has a BA from Chulalongkorn University and a Master's from the University of Warwick. June George obtained her AMI Diploma from the Montessori Training Organization in London, England. June George founded The Baan Dek Montessori & Montessorium, along with her husband, Bobby George.

Playing with Gravity: On Designing for Children

Our Culture and Climate

Design, it could be said, is born at the intersection of aesthetics and pedagogy. As the famous American graphic designer Paul Rand (2000) notes, "Design can be aesthetics." He also observes, in the following sentence, in a gesture of direction, "Design is so simple, that's why it is so complicated."While on the surface paradoxical, this statement resonates strongly, right to its core. Further down this path, then, and in keeping with Paul Rand's thinking, design, understood as an architecture of elements, can also impart an education.

In this spirit, design lives in the space of the "and," complete with the promise of the conjunction. In a way, design must always position itself for what comes next: anticipate happenings, believe intuitions, and relish opportunities. These are our coordinates. It's also a matter of understanding where to focus our attention. As will be conveyed in this chapter, when designing for children, the emphasis must be placed on two primary and complementary tasks: aesthetics and pedagogy. Steve Jobs might have named this process "Playing with Gravity."

On one hand, design must be oriented towards the construction of the "new." Of course, the "new" carries with it an element of the familiar, as there must be a reference point. But, that does not mean that design highlights the past. Paul Rand was a master at this balancing act: harnessing the forces of the prehistoric. This was also one of the major challenges that we faced at Montessorium (an app design firm that creates educational apps for children): how to take a one hundred-year-old way of learning and place it on a magical and revolutionary device. Understanding when to choose sides, knowing full well that you want to choose everything, is a difficult challenge, as well as an inspiring opportunity.

For us, the seeds of the future are planted, not in the present, but in the assurance of the future. The presentation of the "new," as such, affords a radical shift in perspective. It helps to wiggle us free from our determinations. We call this "aesthetics," following the Greek conception of aesthetics, as "sensation." Others might call it "architecture."

In either case, aesthetics is more than just a way of presenting or designing. It's also concerned to address the conditions of emergence. These are lessons that we've learned through our mistakes and experimentations. To elucidate: "the coming alive of sentience, as sentience," serves a vital function in understanding the role design plays in aesthetics. We hope to make this clear as we proceed.

On the other hand, then, design has the capacity to build an atmosphere for creative exploration. In our estimations, pedagogy has nothing to do with instruction. It's all about creation. This is a principle that we tried to remain faithful to, despite the temptations to the contrary. It's so easy to fall into traps, especially the ones you lay yourself. As we conceive it, pedagogy is committed to inspiration: it provides a context, fosters encounters, and supports discoveries. This endeavor of exploration—of searching—constitutes the processes of education. Which is to say, education is not a passive container for knowledge; it can't be prescribed or downloaded. It must be experienced. With our Intro to Letters and Intro to Math apps we attempted to provide just that: a milieu for self-discovery.

Ironically, these are the two main myths that are perpetuated in our current techno-cultural climate. Mainly, that we can instruct children, that they will learn and be evaluated by standardized tests. Also, and just as perplexing, that knowledge is something that can be digested and incorporated, acquired through the instance of a download. One click and you're done, to use a popular turn-of-phrase. The widespread dissemination of new technologies contributes to this discussion and subsequent confusion, but we would like to shift the focus towards education as experience. Experiencing thought: feeling it wrap its capaciousness and rigor around your passions and interests.

After all, education isn't just about technology. It's also about people. It's also about affects. You might be surprised by the following quote: "I used to think, when I was in my twenties, that technology was the solution to most of the world's problems. Unfortunately," says Steve Jobs (1995), "it ain't so." Why? Education takes people. Individuals have a unique ability to help guide and inspire other people. When people invest in other people, not only are they investing in themselves, they're also working to create new conditions of life. As Frank Chimero (2011) states, "The internet is people, all the way down."

In a wonderfully candid interview, conducted in 1995, Jobs was asked: "Some people say that . . . technology may be a way to bypass 'The problems of education.' Are you optimistic about that?" "I absolutely don't believe that," exclaims Jobs. "And as you pointed out, I've probably helped to put more computers in more schools than anybody else in the world . . . and I'm absolutely convinced that is by no means the most important thing." He continues, "The most important thing is another person. Another person that incites your curiosity, that guides your curiosity, that feeds your curiosity, and machines cannot do that in the same way people can" (Chimero, 2011).

Steve Jobs was very attuned to the general mischaracterizations of education, often levied by a misunderstanding of technology. Namely, and to reiterate, that knowledge is something that can be downloaded, and that education is something that can be acquired through transference. We've become remarkably accustomed to these generalized ways of speaking. Steve Jobs was seeking to overcome these determinations. The reductive model of learning has implications, both for thinking through systems of education, and for technological advances in the ways in which we learn.

For Steve Jobs, education is active, involved, and engaged. More than anything, though, it's about experimentation and discovery. The main criticism of education as technology is primarily concerned with users conceived of as passive receptacles of information. For Jobs, education is exploration, not reception. "What children need is something much more proactive, and they need a guide" (Chimero, 2011).

Enter the new mobile educational landscape, which has the power to combine aesthetics and pedagogy, in rich and unexpected ways. For example, this new field attempts to, and has the opportunity to, overcome the myth of education as a prescriptive enterprise. If traditional education is committed to the transmission of knowledge, of imparting lessons by a teacher, mobile education is committed to the exploration of collaborations. After Rousseau, no less than Nietzsche, education is about offering support and guidance so children can learn on their own: learning to overcome our own limitations. Make mistakes!

What is the fundamental tenet to this new landscape? Primarily, but not solely, it's scalability. Scalability is essential, chiefly because it changes the conversation. In short, it changes the architecture of education. No longer is education about teaching the same curriculum to the same class at the exact same time. Education is about offering a wide array of options to a plethora of different students. This might seem like a basic observation, but it provides the linchpin to the future of education. Each child is different and learns at their own pace: personalized education. Finally, then, we have the start of a system to assist and guide the student. Education has become individualized on an unprecedented level.

The very instant Steve Jobs introduced the iPad to the world, the educational universe was forever changed. It was our Neil Armstrong moment, "One small step for education; one giant leap for learning." Instead of the traditional model of education, as receptive and passive, education was instantly re-conceived as interactive and involved, committed to the exploration of the imagination.

For us, education is not about being taught, it's about discovering something new. Education is, first and foremost, the ability to educate oneself. As Maria Montessori (2012) imparts, "We must proceed, not on the basis of our own ideas or on our own prejudices,

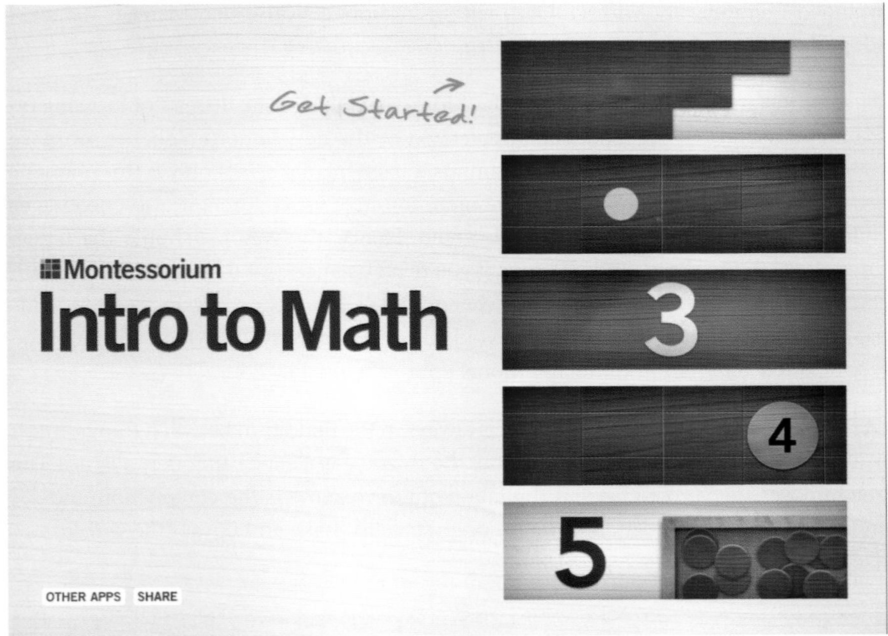

Figure 9.1
Intro to Math iPad app by Montessorium.

not on preconceived methods, but by observing the child" (p. 12). Follow the interests of the child. It's a theme not inapposite to our ambitions at Montessorium. It's on this basis that Montessorium was founded, as a new type of classroom, as a continuum of the education paradigm, focused on the interests of the child. Suddenly, the insights of a one-hundred-year way of learning are now accessible to a new generation, in this emerging digital educational landscape.

A New Model of Thought: Philosophy and Process

Deleuze and Guattari (1987) highlight a new model of thought, giving it an expression that runs counter to our conventional, arborescent model of thinking. They name it *rhizomatic*. As they explain, "We're tired of trees. We should stop believing in trees, roots, and radicles. They've made us suffer too much" (Deleuze & Guattari, 1987, p. 15). To this point, think of centers, points and hierarchies (i.e. the tree of knowledge). Let's picture a traditional classroom; it's predicated on this model. It's complete with a chalkboard, a teacher instructing in front of the class, and scores of carefully positioned desks, arranged methodically, with children sitting in alphabetical order. Instead, we must adopt the rhizomatic approach.

Take, for instance, Intro to Letters. In the Montessori classroom, instead of focusing on the memorization of the alphabet, popularized by the now famous alphabet song, we concentrate on the enunciation of the sounds the letters make. Not only is this phonetic approach to language considered to be more intuitive for children, it also encourages children not to memorize, but to understand. Hence, the way we shuffle the letters throughout the app is in random order. If you're off balance, you'll be more attentive. Of course, we also have a practice mode, wherein the user can choose to focus on individual letters at their own discretion. Unavoidably, and positively, the Montessori method is completely different from the traditional approach to education.

"A rhizome has no beginning or end; it is always in the middle, in between things, interbeing, intermezzo. The tree is filiation, but the rhizome is alliance, uniquely alliance. The tree imposes the verb 'to be,' but the fabric of the rhizome is the conjunction 'and . . . and . . . and.' This conjunction carries enough force to shake and uproot the verb 'to be'" (Deleuze & Guattari, 1987, p. 25).

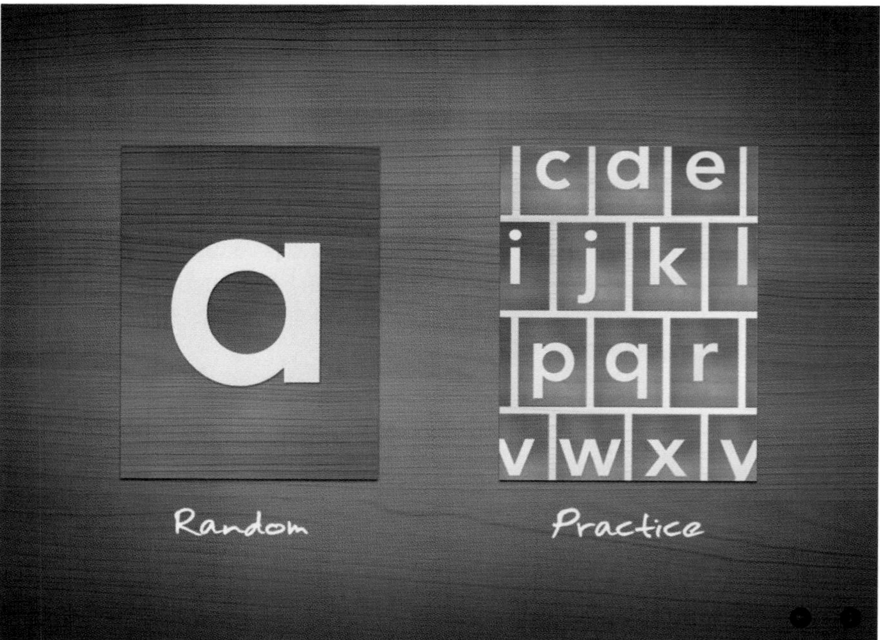

Figure 9.2
Intro to Letters iPad app by Montessorium.

Instead of setting expectations in relation to a pre-set curriculum, in which everyone must follow the same set of instructions, at the exact same time, in precisely the same manner, Deleuze and Guattari suggest a new type of pedagogy, a pedagogical aesthetics that is attentive to the conditions of the new. "Nothing is beautiful," elucidate Deleuze and Guattari, "or loving or political aside from underground stems and aerial roots, adventitious growths and rhizomes" (Deleuze & Guattari, 1987, p. 15). This is where design enters the conversation, growing between the cracks. It's also the space that Montessori attempts to present: a new type of education.

While the first material in the Montessori classroom is the foundation for the second material, (and in this specific sense, Montessori education is linear and progressive), we also provided multiple entrances and exits for students, dependent upon their abilities and interests. Sometimes it's just as important to make a new connection as it is to find a new point of departure. Keep your bearings, but don't be afraid to search for an errant line of flight.

In this respect, then, we return to some thoughtful insights by Steve Jobs. "The elements of discovery are around you. You don't need a computer to know . . . I mean, here . . .

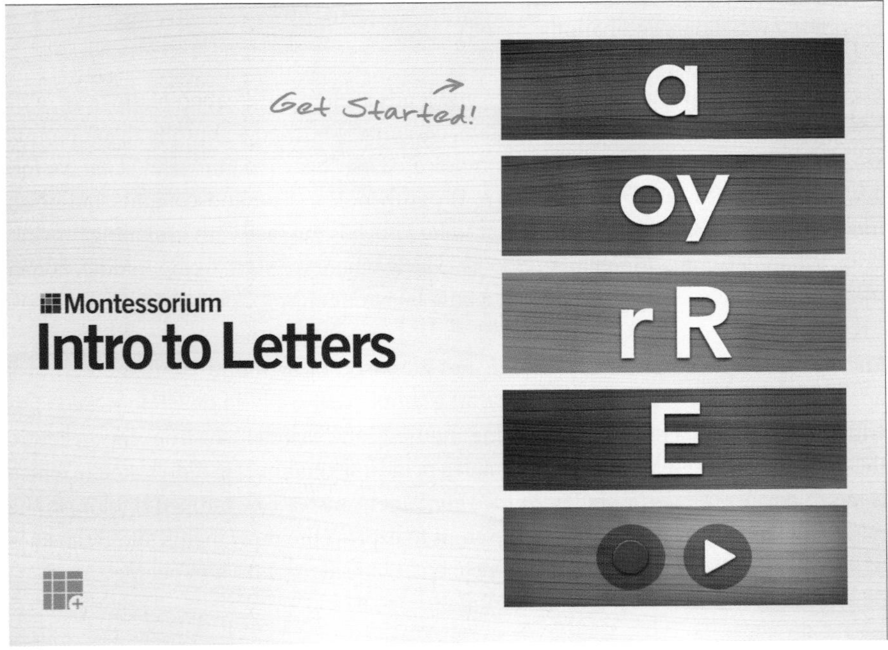

Figure 9.3
Intro to Letters iPad app by Montessorium.

(Steve Jobs picks up an object and let's it fall to the ground.) Why does that fall? You know why? Nobody knows why. Nobody in the entire world knows why that falls. We can describe it pretty accurately, but no one knows why. I don't need a computer to get a kid interested in that. To spend a week playing with gravity and trying to understand it, and coming up with reasons why . . . you do need a person."

Needless to say, this interview was conducted before the launch of the iPhone and iPad, and certainly, the landscape has changed since these initial statements. Nevertheless, this comment contains germinal ideas on the role education should serve in our society, and deserves rumination. Basically, Steve Jobs is assigning the task of creating questions to education. Education isn't about finding answers to readymade problems. Instead, it's about inventing new questions. It's about making your life a work of art. What does it mean to play with gravity?

In our estimations, this is precisely why aesthetics is so vital. Not the aesthetics of gravity, which would be a creative exercise and thought experiment, but the aesthetics of life. Aesthetics serves to entice, comfort, support, embrace, make strange, and ignite curiosity (Cadwell, 2007). When it's achieved, Paul Rand would remark that it makes things simpler. This is also a lesson from Montessori: design it with care. Display the beautiful, mysterious, and parlous!

Design has much to offer, as it conspires and lends itself to the creation of the new. At its best, though, design is not about the transmission of knowledge, but the inspiration of creation. If a motto exists, it is best communicated as, "Learn to innovate!" Lest we forget, however, as Ansell Pearson (1997, p. 1) rightly notes, "The 'and' conjoins, but never innocently or romantically. So much is at stake." Such is the case with designing for children. When designing for children, that is exactly where we start, in the middle. Forget the trees. Follow the trajectories. Now, a little bit about our process at Montessorium.

Lucian Freud, the great British painter, and grandson of Sigmund Freud, had a novel approach to the process of creation. It's an example that we hold dear. He would start with a simple blob. From there, working methodically, fastidiously, from the inside to the out, he would determine the coordinates of his imagination. He didn't sketch, which is to say, create outlines or predetermined containers. Instead, he jumped right in, in the middle of the process, in an effort to attempt to express the movements and intensities of his subject. It's a slight shift in approach, but a radical revolution in perspective. Gordon Bearn (2013) calls this "Life drawing."

In many respects, our work in the Montessori classroom, and our translation and transition of the prepared environment, complete with the activities and methods of

Montessori, to Montessorium, always happens in relationship to "and." It's not always about addition. Sometimes it's about subtraction. Most of the time, however, it's about finding the middle.

Freud noted, "A great deal of what is normally thought of as intelligence, is actually imagination'that is, an ability to see things as they truly are" (Gayford, 2010). On this model, then, imagination is active and engaged, as it participates in the world. It's not so much about creation ex nihilo, let alone the communication of ideas, but finding the process that allows us to search imagination. "It is essential for our new education that mental development be connected with movement and dependent on it" (Montessori, 1946, p. 52). Our role, in designing for children, is to create the opportunity for children to explore their imaginations. In order to accomplish this task, which is not always achieved, we must remove any unnecessary limitations, while still providing positive feedback.

Now, when we think about systemizing thought, laying out concepts, and creating new affects, it's not often that we think in such mosaic terms. As a result of this grandiose overture by Freud, starting in the middle, you can feel the swirls of intensity in his work. Radiant and ephemeral in their desire to reach out, his painting speaks to us, as if in a foreign language. It's understood, as if he placed himself in the mind of a child. That's exactly what we try to do: we become children.

Design and Action

Whereas apps for adults are more concerned with productivity and efficiency, finding a way to minimize tasks and maximize output, apps for children are primarily concerned with development. Slowing things down, instead of speeding things up.

We do not yet know what transpires in between: the interactions between new modes of aesthetics and new modes of pedagogy. Everything is possible. Which is to say, of course, that adults can learn on these new devices, but as we will see, creating apps for children requires an entirely different methodology and execution of techniques. How do we best create developmentally appropriate learning activities?

In many respects, creating apps for children is no different than creating apps for adults. However, there are a few key differences, elements that we would like to highlight in the discussion that follows. Here are some of our thoughts on creating, designing, and building apps for children.

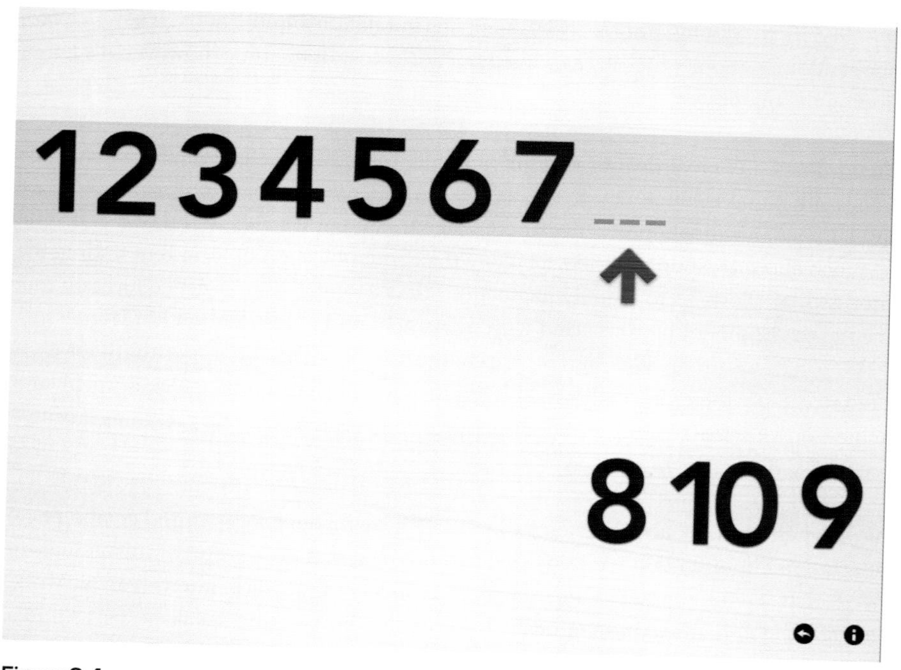

Figure 9.4
Intro to Math iPad app by Montessorium.

Lessons Learned from Intro to Math and Intro to Letters

1 Tempo is Essential

In our user tests, we discovered that tempo is absolutely fundamental to the way a child will interact with the activities. The pace can actually generate and sustain interest.

2 Size Matters

Adjusting the size of elements became crucial in a few instances. For example, when a child would select and drag an object, we had to keep that object visible under their finger.

3 Keep it Intuitive

Design should be intuitive with children. We watched for areas where it was unclear how to move forward, and integrated voiceover and visual demonstrations in order to avoid having directions. We don't want to teach; we want children to learn. In many respects, design itself should always be created with children in mind.

4 Margin of Error

a) How do we handle mistakes? b) How do we prevent unnecessary mistakes? We continue to see the need to make ongoing modifications to the margin of error for

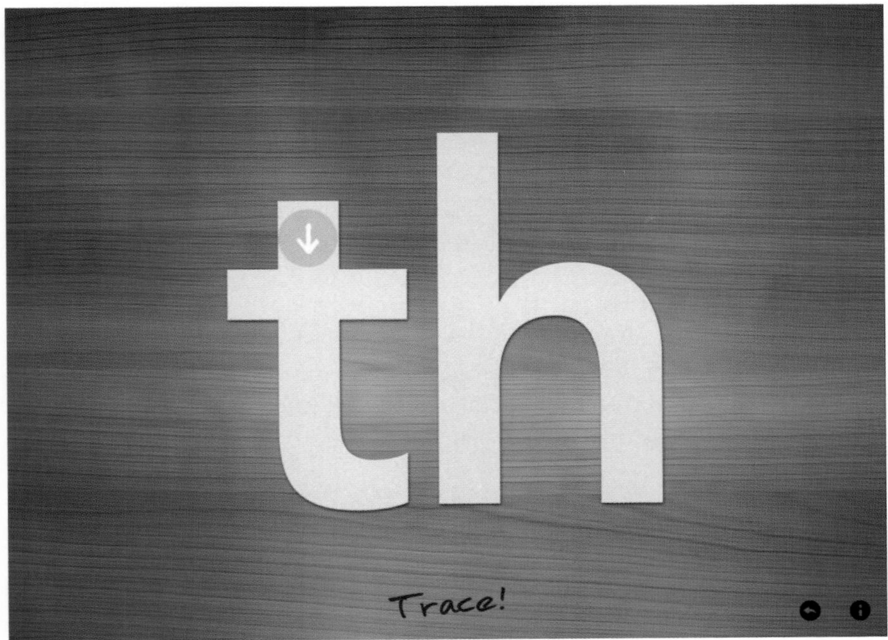

Figure 9.5
Intro to Letters iPad app by Montessorium.

the tracing portions. Montessori fosters a positive conception of mistakes. This is a key theme that we attempted to convey and employ by implementing a control of error.

Lessons Montessori Taught that are Carefully Implemented in our Apps

1 Movements

Movements must be slow, exaggerated, and precise. That said, it can't be too slow or deliberate either. Children may need multiple demonstrations, so our apps must be infinitely patient and understanding. They must support and maintain consistency. They must serve as guides.

2 Demonstrations

As in a traditional classroom setting, visual and auditory presentations are enhanced with precision, exaggeration, and independence. The app becomes the child's guide through the activities, with demonstrations anticipating when the child needs help.

3 Avoid Rewards and Punishments

Children learn on their own, with no rewards except the confidence acquired knowing that they accomplished the task. Otherwise they start to do activities, not for themselves, but for the praise of others. Think stars and stickers and loud noises and colors. Therefore, we had to avoid rewards, while allowing the child to discover the joy of learning on their own, through positive feedback systems.

4 Treat Children as they Wish to be Treated

This is one of our guiding principles. Children may need slower movements, and extra instructions, but they are extremely intelligent and wish to be treated accordingly. Let's not dumb things down. As Montessori says,"let's help them to help themselves."

5 Other Design Elements

In keeping with the aesthetics of Montessori schools, which are intended to feel like little homes for children, where children are not overwhelmed and over-stimulated, we tried to present muted colors and soothing tones (i.e. wood grains) and instructions. After all, no one likes screaming teachers!

Reflecting on Gravity

Our efforts are not so much movements of opposition, as catalysts for innovation and self-discovery. Children understand the nature of the "and," as that's precisely where they live, active and in the middle, searching for the new. It's not so much that design can change the world, then, as attempt to imagine it otherwise.

We'll leave you with Steve Jobs: "I'm a very big believer in equal opportunity, as opposed to equal outcome. Equal opportunity means to me, more than anything, means a great education" (1995).

References

Ansell Pearson, Keith (1997). *Deleuze and philosophy*. London: Routledge.
Bearn, G. (2013). *Life drawing: A Deleuzean aesthetics of existence*. New York: Fordham University Press.
Cadwell, M. (2007). *Strange details*. Cambridge: MIT Press.
Chimero, F. (2011). *"The space between you and me"*, in *The manual*. London: Manual Press.
Deleuze, G., & Guattari, F. (1987) *A thousand plateaus*. Minneapolis: University of Minnesota Press.
Gayford, M. (2010). *Man with a blue scarf*. London: Thames & Hudson.
Jobs, S. (1995). Interview, "The Steve Jobs 1995 Interview." Retrieved January 17, 2011, from: http://www.youtube.com/watch?v=121ofj_l6vM.
Montessori, M. (1946). *Education for a new world*. Madras: Kalakshetra Press.
Montessori, M. (2012). *The 1946 London lectures*. Amsterdam: Montessori-Pierson Publishing Company.
Rand, P. (2000). *A designer's art*. New Haven: Yale University Press.

Chapter 10
HotSeat: Learning and Designing on the Move

This chapter is a chronicle of our shared design process as ensued during a semester-long iPad app-based learning design and development course at the University of Minnesota. The goal of the narrative is to overview our design process, as students, and to provide a foundational understanding of how location-based development was carried through our collaborative learning. Topics range from the design process in a collaborative learning environment to balancing standard design patterns of the iOS platform with patterns conceptualized through our visioning and design process. Included in this student design perspective is our theoretical foundation and motivation for development, a review of our collaborative design process, techniques employed toward the achievement of design, and the development of key features and interfaces that embody the motivation and praxis of our work.

For Designers

Though the setting of this narrative is the classroom, and the participants students, the design process used in the development of HotSeat is very much in line with collaborative design practices used by today's user experience and interaction designers. Our fifteen-week journey challenged not only the process from which we derived our works, but also the ways in which we were able to charter new grounds in designing, developing, and collaborating.

For Teachers

Though the class consisted of deliverables and deadlines, and rightfully so, HotSeat was an entirely bottom-up enterprise that could only be possible in a student-centered classroom. Our visioning processing, collaborative core values development and interface production offer insight into the mobile design that are adaptable in designing curricula, lesson plans, and learning activities that are thoughtfully designed and learner centered.

For Researchers

From collaborative design in a parallel development environment to the crafting of meaningful user interventions, the design narrative of HotSeat showcases the creation of a learner-centered exploration platform through the coursework of two students in the Learning Technologies program at the University of Minnesota. Researchers and academics interested in examining knowledge creation through the collective process of design and construction will find interest in the design of HotSeat.

Mobile learning isn't something out there in some distant future. It is right here, among us, in a designable, higher potential, now.

Nathan Edwards
E-Assessment Designer,
Learning Technologies Media Lab,
University of Minnesota

Jason Nyquist
MEd student,
Learning Technologies,
University of Minnesota

Nate Edwards received his MEd in Learning Technologies from the University of Minnesota, where he researched, designed, and developed learning experiences rooted in the discovery of new paths of exploring and examining the connection between the digital and physical worlds. Nate also serves as an interaction designer for the Learning Technologies Media Lab, where he develops web and mobile applications dedicated to creating meaningful learning environments that inspire exploration and social connection.

Jason Nyquist had spent five years surveying each unique institution of English education in Japan until discovering the iPad, whereupon he returned to the U.S. to earn his Learning Technologies MEd from the University of Minnesota. His work focuses on the interaction and user experience design of digital artifacts so as to facilitate the experience of flow, especially in the contexts of complexity, productivity, and learning.

HotSeat: Learning and Designing on the Move

Learning in the Mobile Era

In the mobile era learning happens across space and time, not only in classrooms—physical or virtual—but also at work, at home, at the bar, on the bus, around the corner, and everywhere in between. Learning is local and afar; synchronous and asynchronous. Our learning sources are not only textbooks and teachers but also websites, apps, television programming, online videos, inscriptions on statues, our neighbors, peers, ourselves. Thus learning is also preeminently social and reflective (Brown, Collins, & Duguid, 1989).

As long as learning occurs in context, the object of that learning process shifts from the gathering and retention of hard facts to the development of soft knowledge. Assessments then become as flexible as the changing landscape in which they occur (Choi & Hannafin, 1995). Social proofs, such as Facebook Likes and Twitter retweets, act as methods of assessment, where the learner is rewarded based on contextual and shared knowledge. When this knowledge is flexed and new and varied interests, friends, and perspectives are embraced, the learner then becomes variously talented in even the most diverse of contexts, becoming, herself, a tapestry of local knowledge in exploratory praxis. When such a scenario is framed within the potentials of mobile learning the connection of people with places and experience do not seem to be such a stretch.

Within HotSeat, learning is the act of connecting—where the fabric of learning is the interlacing of experiential knowledge, collaboration, and social and cultural progression. The same holds true in the connective design of such spaces. Designing, in our realm of discovery, concentrated on the formation of narrative: the crafting of expositions, the building of metaphors, and the construction of identity, context, and place. The *designing* of HotSeat, thus, shares many commonalities with the core user-centered values we are attempting to establish within the application itself. In effect, our *process* of designing HotSeat reflexively informed the core foundation of the application, not only through line-by-line development, but also through the understanding of how we, as individuals within the human fabric, are able to connect with one another to form dynamic learning opportunities.

Becoming Explorers: The Journey of Core Values Creation

The first step in our design process corresponds with what Alan Cooper of VisualBasic fame refers to as the Framework Definition phase, wherein "designers create the overall product concept, defining the basic frameworks for the product's behavior," progressing from high-level ideation on through sketches and wireframes, to "visual design, and—if applicable—physical form" (Cooper et al., 2007).

To begin, we researched and collaboratively evaluated the application's potential audience and their goals by exploring the technical considerations of the iPad, examining methods from which context-based knowledge is created, conceptualizing the structural design of the application and its underlying environment, and considering the thoughtful elements of applications of like purpose. The reason behind this methodology was to begin to recognize how we, as both designers and developers, were to organize and prioritize the core values of the application prior to committing ourselves to any single task.

To capitalize on the technological affordance as physical augmentation of the iPad, what was to later become HotSeat began with the idea of an augmented reality photo application. In said application the user would be able to hold her iPad vertically as a window through time in any location to see that place as it used to appear and observe the shaping of the landscape through the movements and interactions of people. The user would be able to browse both by time and space and to also take or upload her own photos and record related reflections, effectively creating a semiotic layer connecting narrative to place.

Using this user-to-narrative-to-space interaction as the foundation of our application, we decided to focus entirely on facilitating and unlocking the conversations that may potentially occur in a space over time both asynchronously and in real time. So, instead of building connections from point A to B, we began crafting the user's journey. When the initial design process was framed in such a manner, it made it easier for us to envision the role of the application in the users' landscape. We began to seek out new perspectives with which to imagine our environment, essentially transitioning from architects of the environment to explorers. Shedding the role of builders allowed us to center on the dimensions of the application that we found to be of the greatest importance to user interaction and knowledge development.

When designing the application, we sought to ensure that it was fully able to support the users' activity—in this case, the movement from one location to another. When developing the experience of the application, we gathered experiential concepts and techniques we found best able to preserve the user's ability to develop a narrative within the context. What followed was a visualization process, where user interaction paths were designed and reviewed for inconsistencies in experience. Strategies were then devised to reduce dissonance while working towards the design of an immersive state. When faced with a design problem, such as user way finding or issues in content generation, functionality and interface alternatives were evaluated using process mapping and concept-based user interface construction. This allowed us to free ourselves from the extrinsic design problems,instead, focusing on divergent approaches to re-conceptualizing the user interaction flow and supportive interface models.

Sketching Vision: The Freedom of Pen and Pad

Sketching is one of the first and most important stages in the process of the externalization of one's ideas and is integral to the transition from vision to visual design. After our product vision, user goals, and interaction paths were formulated, they were "translated into design elements according to interaction principles and then organized, using patterns and principles, into design sketches and behavior" (Cooper et al., 2007).

There are many design principles and just as many libraries of design patterns, depending on the era and the targeted device. Principles and patterns both may target content layout and navigational schemes, the process of onboarding, the inclusion of social media functionality, etc. But what works for a desktop application may not for the web, while what works for either of those pointer-based interactive paradigms may not for a touch-based smartphone or a tablet. The particular principles and patterns we referenced, then, are Apple's iOS Human Interface Guidelines. Still, it is also beneficial

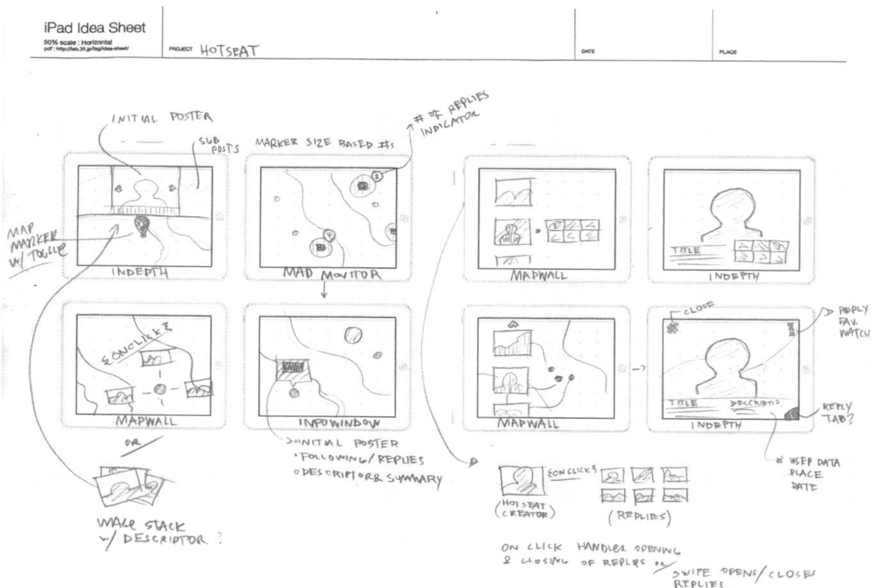

Figure 10.1

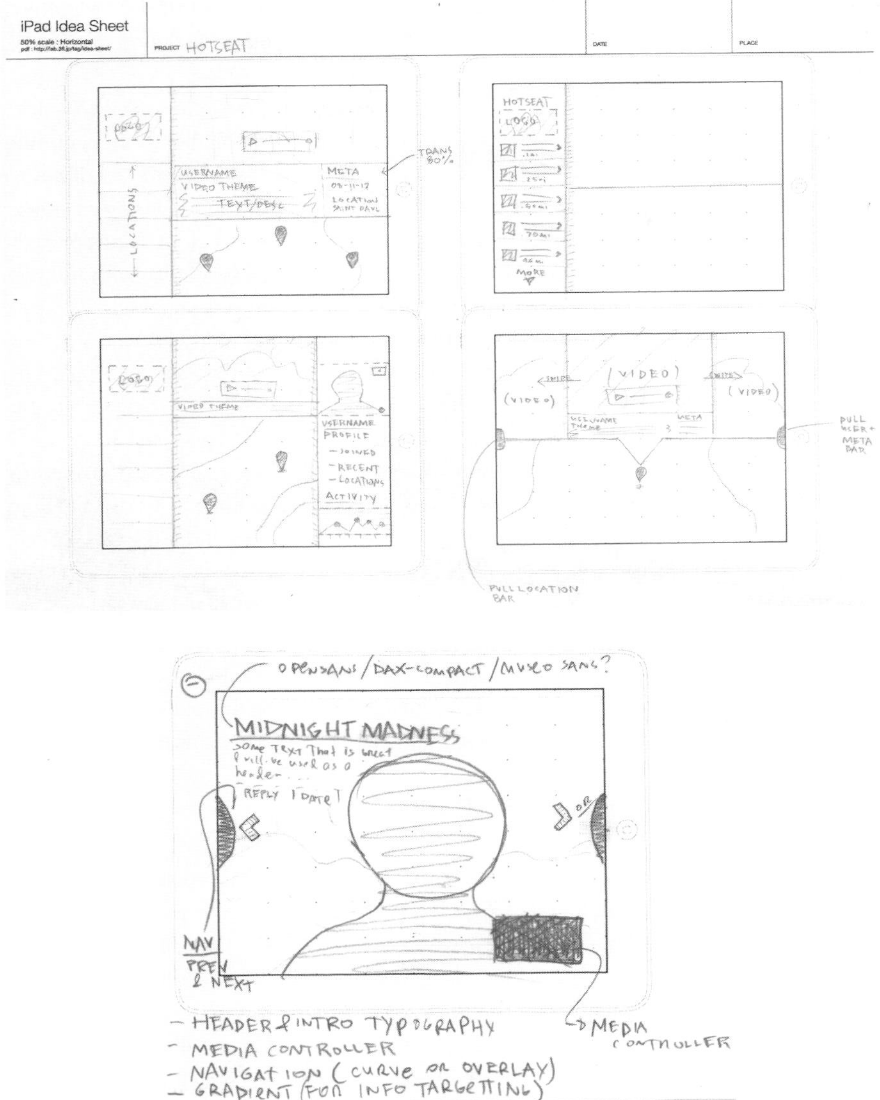

Figure 10.1 (Continued)

Early sketches were developed in small thumbnail templates to encourage rapid designing focused on key interface arrangements. The sketching of thumbnails allowed us a flexible design platform where we could quickly generate and compare interface elements. Many of the initial sketches seen above were combined and refined into a single developed interface.

Original image by Kevin Dooley, http://www.flickr.com/photos/pagedooley/6372227771/, under Creative Commons license.

to study other design pattern libraries like those as aggregated at http://j.mp/pattern-libraries and to compare them with current articles on device-specific good design.

Sketching user interfaces along those good design patterns, then, allowed us to quickly begin the process of iteration toward a final visual design. In collaboration, beginning with the sketch rather than jumping to wireframes or mockups "encouraged discourse about a proposed design, and also increased understanding of the renderings as representing work-in-progress" (Cooper et al., 2007), as sketching provides the designer the opportunity to imagine, break and re-imagine spontaneous design ideas without fixating on any one representation of an interaction. As such, it frees designers to construct and review large application concepts that are best developed holistically and without the need to concentrate on aesthetic design details as is often the case when working within visual design applications.

Sketching is also advantageous to collaborative design sessions as it provides opportunities to quickly and easily remedy key interfaces concerns, where early concepts and designs can easily be developed, explored, and re-worked rapidly and cooperatively. It provides a fast and versatile way of iteratively developing and testing shared ideas (Cerejo, 2010). Being able to see the interface, evaluate interface issues, and produce changes rapidly makes the process of design exploration much more efficient than on a computer. Using such a method in the early design stages also aided in the collaborative nature of our design team. Instead of making changes via laptop in isolation we were able to discuss and rationalize design decisions collaboratively prior to committing to designs.

Designing App Mockups: Parallel Design

The disciplined evolution from vision to visual design is a constant process of developing increased fidelity. Immediately following the shared understanding produced through sketching, interface mockups of HotSeat were then developed. We followed a parallel design process, wherein multiple distinct designs were created consecutively and subsequently evaluated based on core application values. We found numerous advantages to working under such a methodology. For one, it required us to carefully evaluate which features and components were of the highest importance and which design concepts should be eliminated or enabled at a lower, granular level of the interface. Secondly, the parallel design process provided us a flexible working environment, where poor designs could be identified and eliminated and successful alpha-stage designs merged into a working design (Nielsen & Faber, 1996). Parallel design also provides flexibility in designing under an unrestricted environment where creative design problem solving is encouraged. Instead of focusing on a single design, parallel design allowed us to rapidly design multiple interfaces, each of which could potentially solve key user experience issues. Once tasked with designing key interface solutions, we independently designed key interfaces based on application goals articulated in the planning stage. During face-to-face meetings, designs were presented, reviewed and evaluated independently based on our core application values. Design evaluations informed the revision process, allowing us to quickly re-craft designs based on concepts derived through the parallel design process.

Thoughtful design patterns as elicited through the review of other successful iPad applications and those significant of good design in general were used to aid in the grouping of progressive cognitive principles, functions, and layouts. Thus, emphasis is placed on the creation of an application that strikes a balance of implicit instructional direction and experience delivery.

Essential Interfaces: A User Experience that Flows with the Changing Environment

To craft a user experience that *flows* with the changing context of the locally situated user we must create interfaces that reflect the open-ended nature of exploration and inquisitive investigation. With that being said, great detail was paid in creating an environment that is focused but not directed. The hope is that when a user is allowed to captain the journey to their HotSeat of choice, they will then be less apprehensive to share. It also makes the user proactive in the process, which, in turn, emphasizes the user-focused design.

To accomplish this goal, we created interfaces that were exceedingly focused on the user's current point of interaction. If the current goal of the app were way finding the interface was entirely map-based with little to no visual elements focused on other interactions. Conversely, if the current objective of the app were to provide a platform for user-to-user interaction and feedback, the app would deliver an interface concentrated entirely on that point of interaction and nothing more. This allows us then to generate two interfaces, both orientated towards very different application objectives, which are especially focused and functionally simple.

While *simplistic interface design* may sound pejorative to some it should be understood that effective simplicity on the frontend requires, and is the result of, the effort to mitigate complexity through extensive planning, designing, and testing during earlier stages of the design process (Norman, 2010). Adding a depth of functional power to simplicity, then, yields an elegance of interaction (Löwgren & Stolterman, 2004, p. 135), where the user finds reward within the developed interaction. The founding of our design on this impression was based on the exploratory nature of the application and our intended audience.

We wanted to construct an environment, through our interfaces, that produces an emotion of boundless exploration while providing an undemanding platform that navigates the user from where they are to where they are compelled to be: a HotSeat. When HotSeat initially opens, the user is geo-located, and indicators of position of both the user and of HotSeats within proximity are dropped onto the HotSeat mapping environment. The process is to be that simple. No need to toggle functions or settings or require an unnecessary amount of effort or attention from the user.

The philosophy behind this approach is that, by default, users will want to search for HotSeats that are nearby. If this is to be the default user function it should be afforded without the need for user intervention. When faced with a map containing a set of points of interest and a geo-location indicator, the user cannot help but explore.

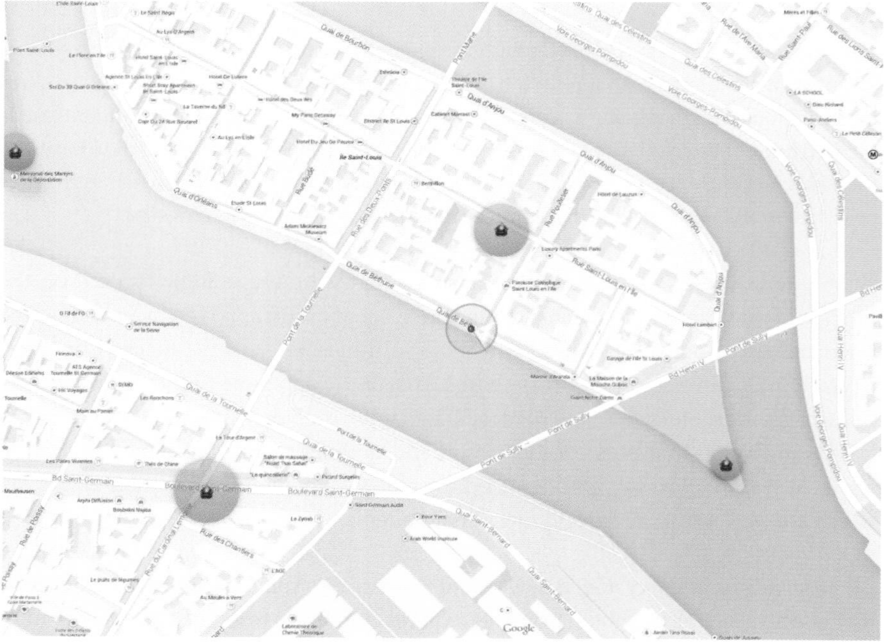

Figure 10.2

Initial map interface displaying user geo-location and HotSeat boundaries. HotSeat boundary range was to be determined by the overall activity of the HotSeat. The user is allowed to view and reply to the HotSeat conversation once they enter the HotSeat boundary.

Original image by Kevin Dooley, http://www.flickr.com/photos/pagedooley/6372227771/, under Creative Commons license.

There is also great power within an interface when the main structure is familiar to the user. Twitter and Facebook handle user login, while Google Maps provides navigation. Logins are only to be required if the user decides to interact and login information is, of course, stored for future use. Using these current and popular services provides a level of familiarity even in a new environment and allows users to leverage existing knowledge when dealing with ancillary application features such as login management and geo-location processing. Additionally, this simplistic approach allows the user to free up any cognitive load that may have existed and provides the user to focus on the application objective of *exploring*.

Where sketches reveal mere structure and, with accompanying verbiage, perhaps functionality, we hope that the ensuing mockups tell the story of the user experience.

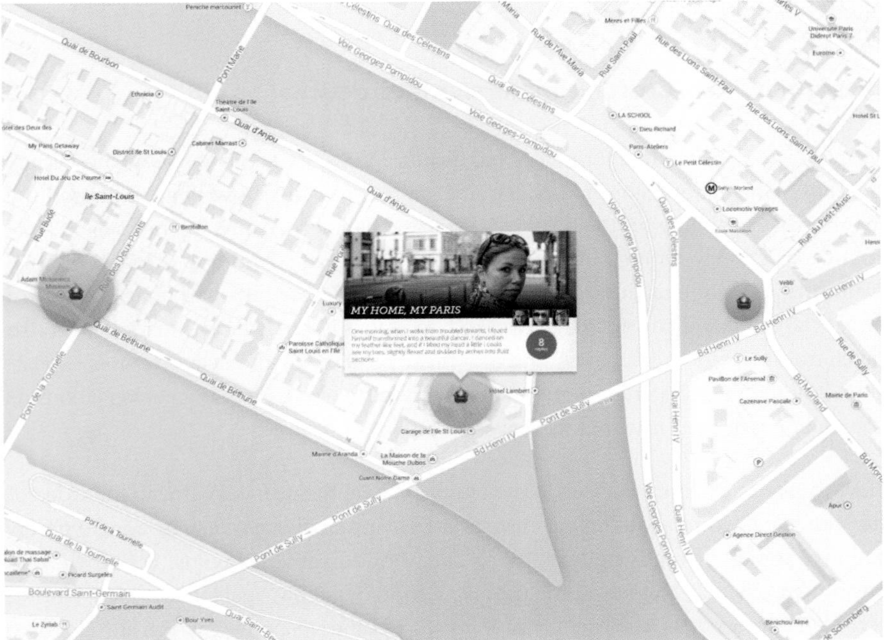

Figure 10.3

Map View with annotated HotSeat information bubble. The goal of the design is to provide the user a concise overview of the selected HotSeat conversation, metrics and navigation in an interface that does not obscure the map view.

Original image by Kevin Dooley, http://www.flickr.com/photos/pagedooley/6372227771/, under Creative Commons license.

More Than a Map: Scaffolding Exploration

When designing the application, we wanted the map view to hold precedence over all other elements on the iPad's screen to foster the sense of exploration. As opposed to presenting the user with the common UI elements of apps like Twitter and Facebook and forcing them to make multiple cognitive decisions on how to manipulate the interface just to extract information, the main decision presented to the HotSeat user is primarily physical: where to go to converse. Navigation is not of the UI but of the world. Any other UI elements or interactions can be seen as distracting from this goal and were excised.

The map displays conversational locations as HotSeats rather than pins. Tapping upon one expands an annotated view with the photo of the original conversation-fire starter and a short description of the conversation—that's it. To unlock further interactions, the user is compelled to make the journey. Upon entering the geographic boundary of a HotSeat, the user is then prompted to take a photo of herself in the HotSeat. Doing so unlocks our next view.

Dialog via Video: Crafting Immersive Interactions

To minimize the potential for emotional distance between any two users who occupy the same HotSeat asynchronously, we utilized the ever-increased bandwidth and the multimedia capabilities of today's smart devices. The interpersonal interactions of HotSeat occur entirely within video. Contrast this again with Twitter and Facebook, two platforms whose interactions center almost entirely on text, links, and images. Where a Tweet can be crafted and an image tweaked, a video is not only harder to fool but is also much truer to life, to interactions, and to context. By allowing the richest form of expression, it is the most accurate representation of a moment. Expressing conversations as compelling moments is what this view is all about.

Having taken a picture of herself in the HotSeat, then, the user is treated to the video of the individual who initiated the conversation. The original video may be a mere observation, a thought-provoking question, a dare, or alternative stimulus. Before viewing any other individual responses, the user is prompted to reply, again, with video. Having recorded her response, the user gains access to all other responses, which she can Like or Tweet about. She can then leave the conversation as is; respond to any number of individual users in kind, including herself; or respond to the conversation as a whole with any new thought that has come to mind.

Upon leaving the geographic boundary of the HotSeat, the background of the HotSeat pin changes color. In the future, if the user is to tap on the pin again, she will be

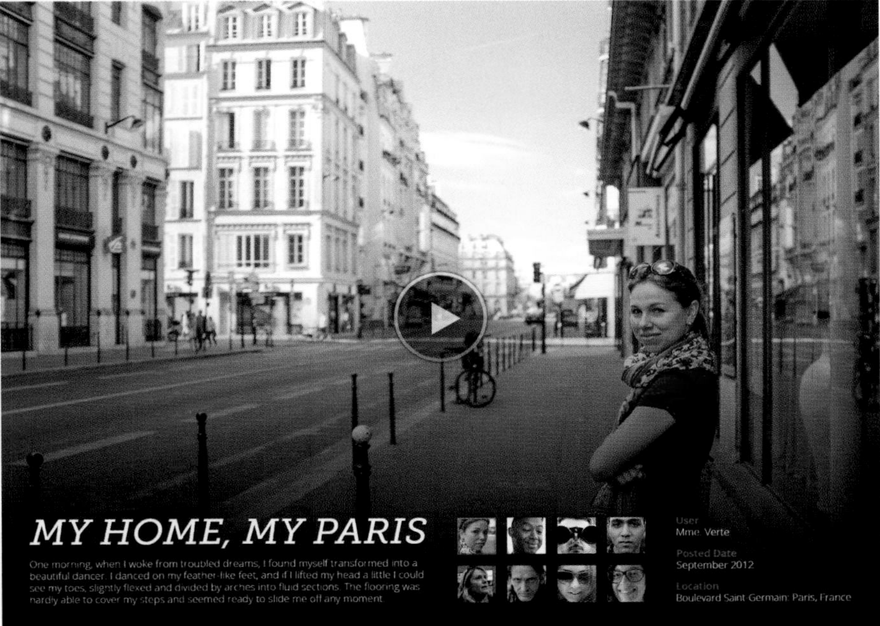

Figure 10.4

The DepthView is the centerpiece of HotSeat. This is where interactions between users and space occur. The significance of this interface, and subsequent user interactions, led us to craft an intimate interface that focused entirely on the user-generated conversations.

Original image by Kevin Dooley, http://www.flickr.com/photos/pagedooley/6372227771/, under Creative Commons license.

presented with an overview of any subsequent interactions to have taken place there. But in order to view or create any new content, that user will have to return to the HotSeat physically, thus drawing her into new patterns of local behavior.

Monitoring Change: Creating a Persistent Environment

The HotSeat Watcher provides users an opportunity to set boundaries from where they can watch for activity: HotSeat creations, updates, replies, and removals. The idea behind this feature and interface is to provide an additional avenue of connection with the users and space even if the visitor is no longer within the geo-boundaries of a particular place or set of HotSeats. This then allows the visitor to stay informed without being physically present.

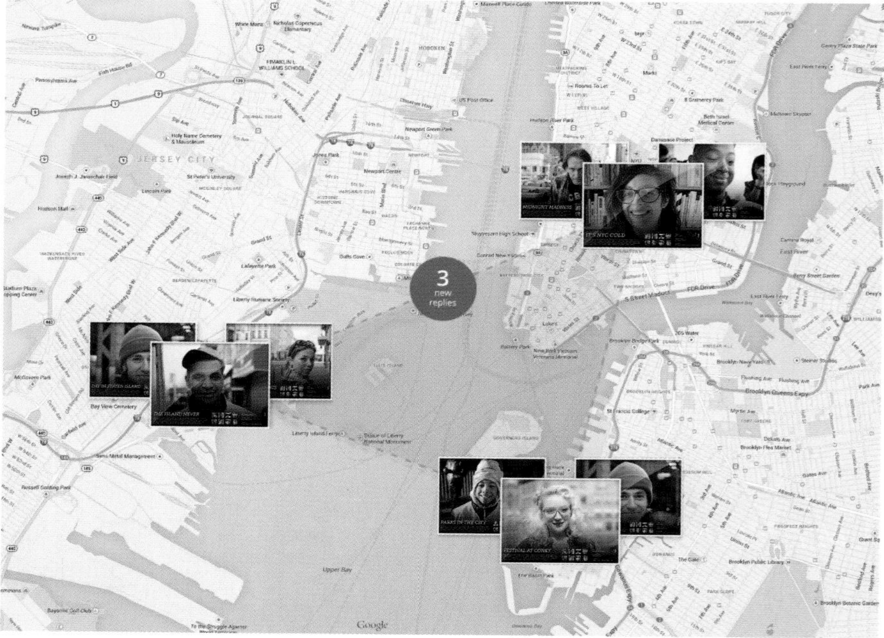

Figure 10.5

The Watcher View was developed to create an environment that visually notifies the user of changes at HotSeats of interest. User imagery, in the form of image stacks, was used to provide a sense of connectedness within the spaces.

Original image by Kevin Dooley, http://www.flickr.com/photos/pagedooley/6372227771/, under Creative Commons license.

As compared with the *Depth View*, the *Watcher* provides a level of interactivity from a macro perspective, whereas the *Depth View* creates a more intimate view of a single HotSeat. Consider it the difference between having a conversation with friends next to a campfire and revisiting a photo album of previous camping trips. As such, in this view the user can, with a slight flick, physically flip through stacks of thumbnail images of those conversations happening at a location.

Conclusion

At its core, HotSeat shares the same tenets of many other applications: connecting users. What makes HotSeat distinct is how users are connected to one another and how that connection is formed. The idea behind HotSeat is to leverage the affordances of smart devices to create virtual connections to physical beings and spaces—creating a synergistic environment where interactions are created and continued in a virtual space while being rooted in a physical one. This means that even if a space physically changes, or is no longer accessible in the same context, dialog—human connections to that space—can carry on. Equally as powerful is the ability to augment the physical space through web-based interaction, where both physical and digital space can dynamically be formed through the threading of personal connections. For us, this is the *new* landscape of mobile interaction.

We hope you enjoyed the journey.

References

Brown, J., Collins, A., & Duguid, P. (1989). Situated cognition and the culture of learning. *Educational Researcher, 18*(1), 32–42.

Cerejo, L. (2010, June 16). Design better and faster with rapid prototyping. *Smashing Magazine.* Retrieved February 27, 2012, from http://www.smashingmagazine.com/2010/06/16/design-better-faster-with-rapid-prototyping/.

Choi, J., & Hannafin, M. (1995). Situated cognition and learning environments: Roles, structures, and implications for design. *Educational Technology Research and Development, 43*(2), 53–69.

Cooper, A., Reimann, R., Cronin, D., & Cooper, A. (2007). *About face 3: The essentials of interaction design*. Indianapolis, IN: Wiley Pub.

Löwgren, J., & Stolterman, E. (2004). *Thoughtful interaction design: A design perspective on information technology*. Cambridge, MA: MIT Press.

Nielsen, J., & Faber, J. M. (1996). Improving system usability through parallel design. *IEEE Computer, 29*(2), 29–35. Retrieved February 23, 2012, from http://ieeexplore.ieee.org/xpls/abs_all.jsp?arnumber=485844.

Norman, D. A. (2010). *Living with complexity*. Cambridge, MA: MIT Press.

Chapter 11

The Conceptualization, Design, and Development of a K–12 Adventure Learning App

A central concern with the current rush to integrate mobile devices in the classroom is how prepared we are to do so, both from a teaching and a pedagogical standpoint. As has been shown by the worldwide one-to-one laptop initiative, the mass deployment of a technology in and of itself without proper teacher training or careful, contextual consideration of how that particular technology might be applicable and pedagogically integrated in a given learning environment is worth little. Educators and learning technologists should thus be concerned about, *as well as collaborators in*, the design and development of educational apps. In this chapter, I share a narrative centered on my personal process of conceptualization, design, and development of a K–12 adventure learning app, with the hope that my own experiences might be helpful to others starting their own journeys into the landscape of app design.

For Designers

Designers will learn about taking a specific pedagogical framework (in this case, adventure learning) and conceptualizing how a mobile app might be developed to support that framework in both formal and nonformal learning situations.

For Teachers

Educator input in app design is critical to ensure apps are being created that make sense in the classroom and in learning, and that fit the needs of teachers, curriculums, and most especially, learners. This narrative, through the eyes of a novice app designer, encourages educators to jump headfirst into the app development process, even if they have no background in coding and design.

For Researchers

There has been a multitude of studies of late focusing on the implementation and use of mobile devices and apps in the classroom. There are few research studies, however, that examine the app design and development process itself. Research into the process of conceptualizing and developing an educational app could benefit designers and educators alike, and could shed light into practices and theories that lend themselves to the creation of apps that have a meaningful place in learning environments.

tors and learning technologists should be collaborators in the
evelopment of educational apps.

enrickson

didate,
Technologies,
of Minnesota

nrickson is a PhD candidate in the Learning Technologies pro
ersity of Minnesota and a graduate research assistant for the
ogies Media Lab. Her focus is on researching and designing ac
environments, exploring the uses of mobile in both formal ar
cation, and getting kids outdoors, actively interacting with the
nent and their local communities. One of her most fun achiever
oulking across the Baffin Island in Canada as part of the North
60.co) expedition team. Along with being a phenomenal colla
endeavor, this experience has lent new insight into design co

Jeni Henrickson

The Conceptualization, Design, and Development of a K–12 Adventure Learning App

> Designing does not take place in a linear sequence and never did.
>
> (Roberts & Norman, 1999)

There are currently just shy of three-quarters of a million apps in Apple's App Store, and that number is growing steadily, with an average 700 to 900 new apps submitted per day. As of this writing, over 74,000 of the published apps are education based. These figures can be daunting. With so many apps already available, what's a novice app developer to think? What is there left to contribute to this burgeoning new area of cyberspace?

The wonderful thing about app development is that apps can fulfill a broad array of educational needs. That need can be small and specific—tied to an individual classroom, school, or subject matter—or large and universal, tied to learning across disciplines or across age groups. Apps also can be similar in focus but offer different features or user interfaces, engaging users in different types of learning experiences.

There have been a multitude of studies of late focusing on the implementation and use of mobile devices in the classroom (for a recent meta-analysis, see Wu et al., 2012), and only three years after the unveiling of the iPad, there are already more than 2,300 school districts implementing iPad programs. A central concern with this rush to integrate handheld devices into the classroom, however, is how prepared we are to do so, both from a teaching and a pedagogical standpoint. As has been shown by the worldwide one-to-one laptop initiative, the mass deployment of a technology in and of itself without proper teacher training or careful, contextual consideration of how that device or software or app might be applicable and pedagogically integrated in a given classroom or learning situation is worth little (for a recent report examining what is probably the world's most ambitious deployment of the one-to-one laptop initiative, in Peru, see Cristia et al., 2012).

I feel it's important to take a step back and consider not only these new devices and their place in education, but also the design and development of the apps that inhabit them and that are being put into play in classrooms worldwide. As educators and learning technologists, we should be concerned about, *as well as collaborators in*, the design and development of these apps, in order to ensure we are creating tools that make sense in the classroom and in learning, and that fit the needs of our teachers, our curriculums, and most especially, our learners. As such, I became interested in learning to design and develop apps, and was fortunate to have the resources to do so through my PhD program in Learning Technologies at the University of Minnesota. Now, with one published app under my belt and another in development, I'd like to share a narrative centered on my personal process of conceptualization, design, and development of a K–12 adventure learning app, with the hope that my own experiences might be helpful to others getting started in app design. To begin, I'll introduce the adventure learning framework, as it is seminal to understanding the conceptualization and design of my app.

Adventure Learning

In the early 1990s, explorers such as Will Steger, Dan Buettner, Robert Ballard, Lonnie Dupre, and Paul Pregont began experimenting with ways to use technology to connect classrooms with their adventures on the trail. These experiments led in 2004 to the development of Arctic Transect 2004—a 3,000-mile dogsled journey across Arctic Canada that was tied to a comprehensive curriculum and online learning environment—and the establishment of a new pedagogical framework known as adventure learning (Doering, 2006).

Adventure learning (AL) provides a framework for the design of learning experiences that allow learners to explore real-world issues through authentic, field-based narratives within an interactive online learning environment (Doering, 2006). AL blends experiential (Kolb, 1984), inquiry-based (Bransford, Brown, & Cocking, 1999), and authentic (Jonassen, 1991) learning, and synchs an online learning environment with teacher-led classroom activities. It is grounded in nine core principles: (1) a defined issue and place; (2) authentic narratives; (3) an element of adventure; (4) a sound curriculum grounded in inquiry; (5) collaboration and interaction opportunities between learners, experts, teachers, and content; (6) synched learning opportunities that tie together content with curriculum; (7) an online venue to deliver content; (8) multiple media that enhance the curriculum; and (9) scaffolding for teachers as well as learners (Doering, 2006; Doering & Miller, 2009; see Figure 11.1).

To illustrate, within an AL program, a team engages in an adventure-based expedition or exploration centered on a specific location and topic; for example, climate change in the Arctic. The team travels out into the field to capture authentic data and narratives that are synched with a predesigned inquiry-based curriculum tied to that expedition, issue, and location. The field experiences, data, media assets, and observations of the team are shared online in an environment in which learners are able to actively participate and collaborate with the explorers, their peers around the world, their teacher(s), and a variety of field experts. These online collaboration and interaction opportunities allow learners to form connections between what is happening in the real world and

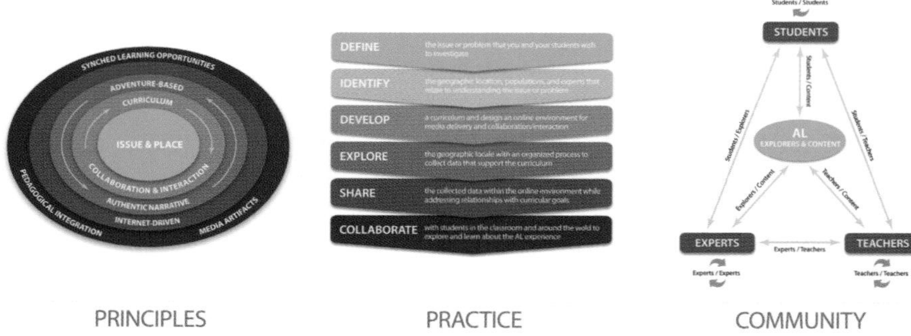

Figure 11.1
The principles, practice, and community models for adventure learning (Doering & Miller, 2009).

their studies. Learners complete activities related to the real-world events, engage in online and face-to-face discussions around them, and present potential solutions to issues that are raised.

In AL, field expeditions and authentic narrative play a key role. The field expeditions form the heart of the program. They bring excitement, engagement, and challenge to the learning and serve as journeys of discovery that are synched with the AL curriculum. These field expeditions also offer a means to gather authentic narrative, data, and media assets to be shared with learners. The narratives and media involve much more than simply capturing the voices of the explorers as they embark on the field expedition. The focus of the expedition is on capturing the narratives of people who live and/or work in the place where the expedition is taking place and/or who are connected to the real-world issue being explored.

Technology also plays an important role in adventure learning, from the collection of assets to the delivery of the AL program online. Expedition teams typically make use of laptops, GPS units, cameras, audio recorders, and satellite technologies, among other items, to collect and share data, media, and narratives from the field within the online learning environment. Participating classrooms have traditionally used desktop and laptop systems to access AL learning environments, along with multiple tools and software to, for example, engage in online chats with the project team and outside field experts; complete authentic activities to share online; and collaborate with other learners online.

AL has been shown to have a positive influence on student engagement levels, motivation, and learning outcomes across the curriculum (Doering et al., 2010; Doering &

Veletsianos, 2008; Henrickson, 2011; Koseoglu & Doering, 2011; Moos & Honkomp, 2011; Veletsianos, 2010). It is grounded in a strong curriculum and pedagogy, and focuses on transformative learning experiences.

The first adventure learning program supported by theory and long-term research was the GoNorth! Adventure Learning Series of circumpolar Arctic dogsledding expeditions (Veletsianos, 2010) (see chasingseals.com/gonorth). This program focused on climate change, sustainability, Arctic culture, and traditional knowledge, and engaged more than fifteen million learners worldwide. Other examples of AL projects include Earthducation (earthducation.com), the Jason Project (jason.org), the Quest series of bicycle treks (e.g., see www.teachervision.fen.com/tv/classroomconnect/maya/index.html), Eat Bike Grow (eatbikegrow.ning.com), AL@UI (alatuimainsalmon.wordpress.com), and World by Cycle (worldbycycle.info).

Though the best-known and -researched AL programs to date, such as the previously mentioned Arctic Transect 2004 or the GoNorth! Adventure Learning Series, have involved large-scale expeditions and remote locales, it's important to emphasize that AL programs can just as effectively focus on ordinary, everyday adventures with people familiar to us (Henrickson, 2011; Veletsianos et al., 2012). A new advancement in AL, in fact, is the creation of user-driven adventure learning environments (UDALE) in which learners create and share self-initiated AL projects online (Doering & Miller, 2009). Such environments have the potential to allow learners to act not only as explorers and expedition leaders seeking out answers to their own questions, but also as teachers and facilitators, strengthening their knowledge of a subject and a geographical area as they share their adventure with others. They also have the opportunity to practice their social networking skills as they interact with others online around a topic that is important to them. A prime example of a user-driven adventure learning environment is WeExplore (http://www.we-explore.com), a new and unique custom-designed environment that scaffolds learners through the process of creating their own AL project and sharing it online.

App Conceptualization

The age-old advice to "start with what you know" applies in app conceptualization as elsewhere in life. I have a strong interest in the natural world, and believe the best way to engage kids with nature is to get them outdoors, physically interacting with their local environment, be that a city neighborhood or park, a rural farm, or a remote wilderness area. Direct interaction with nature has been shown to have a positive impact on mental and physical health, lifelong curiosity about the natural world, and pro-environmental attitudes and behaviors (Louv, 2008; Zaradic & Pergams, 2007), among other things.

With its grounding in experiential, authentic, and inquiry-based pedagogies, adventure learning is a framework that aligns well with environmental education (EE) standards, including both the North American Association for Environmental Education (NAAEE; www.naaee.org) guidelines for quality EE, and the EE awareness to action model. The awareness to action model, established as part of the Tbilisi Declaration during the world's first intergovernmental conference on environmental education in 1977, provides a framework for EE that moves learners from awareness about and sensitivity toward the natural environment, through knowledge, attitude, and skill acquisition, with the ultimate goal of the learner actively participating in environmental stewardship, whether on an individual or larger group level. AL has been shown to move learners and teachers through a similar process, with similar transformative results (Doering & Veletsianos, 2008; Veletsianos, Doering, & Henrickson, 2012; Veletsianos & Kleanthous, 2009; Wilson & Parrish, 2011).

Mobile devices and apps have not specifically been integrated into AL programs to date, but they appear to be an ideal match for AL, both in large-scale AL projects, as well as in user-driven AL experiences. Because field expeditions, authentic narrative, and technology play such a key role in adventure learning, along with the need for multiple modes of data collection and sharing, it makes sense to employ mobile technologies for the collection and sharing of media artifacts, geographic data, and field notes tied to a given AL project, not to mention as an alternate means for learners, experts, and explorers to interact with each other from anywhere and anyplace.

My app conceptualization therefore began with my love for the natural world and my interest in adventure learning, along with a recognized need for a field-based education app grounded in a sound pedagogical framework that could scaffold learners in practicing observation, communication, and classification skills. The app would also allow for the creation of and presentation of field-based data in a narrative format tied to a specific issue, location, and curriculum. In other words, to scaffold learners in the creation of inquiry-based stories tied to real-world issues, supported by authentic data, and in which their peers, field experts, and others could collaborate.

Before digging into the design of this app, I explored existing field-based and nature-based apps to see what was available. I also began gathering screenshots of apps for which I liked the design or functionality, and taking notes on what types of features I thought might make sense in an AL app. While there are numerous apps in existence that concentrate on nature and environmental issues, many appeared focused on travel, trail information, crowdsourcing, species tracking, digital journaling, or gaming. I could not identify any existing inquiry-based apps that were grounded in a specific pedagogical framework or that scaffolded users in the creation of, for example, an AL project that might be usable in a classroom as part of a comprehensive curriculum. I decided, therefore, to concentrate my app design efforts in this area, using the framework provided by AL as a model for designing and developing such an app.

App Design

My initial idea was to design and develop an app that served as an AL tool that allowed learners to get outdoors and engage in fieldwork tied to an AL project, using mobile devices to (1) identify an AL expedition or exploration they would like to undertake and provide some background about the location and issue they were choosing to focus on; (2) go out into the field and collect, geo-locate, and organize photos, videos, audio files, maps, and field notes associated with that expedition; and (3) incorporate those assets into an AL project and share them with others through both the app environment and online. The online environment would be synched with the app and provide a platform for teachers to be able to, for example, pull up multiple AL class projects and discuss them in class, as well as a means for interested parties without mobile access to be able to explore others' AL projects.

I was fortunate at this time to be enrolled in the first app class taught anywhere that focused specifically on designing and developing apps for education. Taught by Drs. Charles Miller and Aaron Doering in the Learning Technologies program at the University of Minnesota, this course emphasized the importance of thoroughly thinking through the design and functionality of an app, as well as its purpose and role in education, before digging into its development. We discussed pedagogy, user experience, and what constitutes "good" design, in addition to technology components such as object oriented programming, Objective-C, model-view-controllers, variables, and functions.

The class was hands-on. After a period of time working on the design and conceptualization for our app ideas, we got to jump in and start building things in XCode, even though at least half the class had no prior programming experience whatsoever. Unbelievably, by the last day of class, every single student had created an app of their own design.

My original app idea, as described above, turned out to be too ambitious for my first app project, so what I chose to build for the class was an informational app about adventure learning that introduced the nine core principles of AL; showcased video clips from successful AL projects to date; and provided PDFs of current AL research. Thanks to the

Figure 11.2
The existing adventure learning app.

excellent structure and guidance provided by this class, I completed the app within the semester, was able to test it out on my own and some colleagues' devices, and went on to publish the app in the App Store within a month after the class concluded (see Figure 11.2).

The story doesn't end there, however. The class fueled my confidence in being able to design and develop a more complex app, and I was more determined than ever to build my original app. In the year following the class, I continued working on designs for the app, and they evolved slowly into something very different from how they had started.

App Design, Take 2

Design embodies much more than a visual interface. It embodies the whole of a project, from the structure to the flow to the visual layout, the typeface and colors used, the mood set, and the interactions invited. Design is about creating an experience (Hassenzahl, 2011) that engages multiple senses and emotions, as well as our intellects. It takes time and multiple iterations for most app designers to reach a point at which they are ready to jump into building what they have designed, and even then, the best designers continue to tinker with and refine their original designs.

I am admittedly not a patient designer. And while I know what I like and what I believe to be effective and engaging design, the artistic component of design is not my strength.

In the world of role-based design (Hokanson & Miller, 2009), I see myself most as an architect. I love envisioning the larger picture of what components need to be incorporated into a project and how those pieces will fit together and flow and how the artistic will be blended with the technical components to generate a seamless user experience. The mobile environment is the perfect environment for which to envision such things, with a small amount of real estate space and the opportunity to engage learners in a sensual journey as they pinch, slide, tap, and actively engage with and ideally *create* with your app.

I think deeply about what kinds of experiences I want to create for learners when they engage with the AL app. I then start to sketch out needed functionality and features, seeking out feedback from faculty and colleagues. I end up completely trashing the original designs that I started back in the app class and re-envision the look and flow of the app. Ultimately I begin to pull together a larger schematic of how the app might look and function (Figure 11.3).

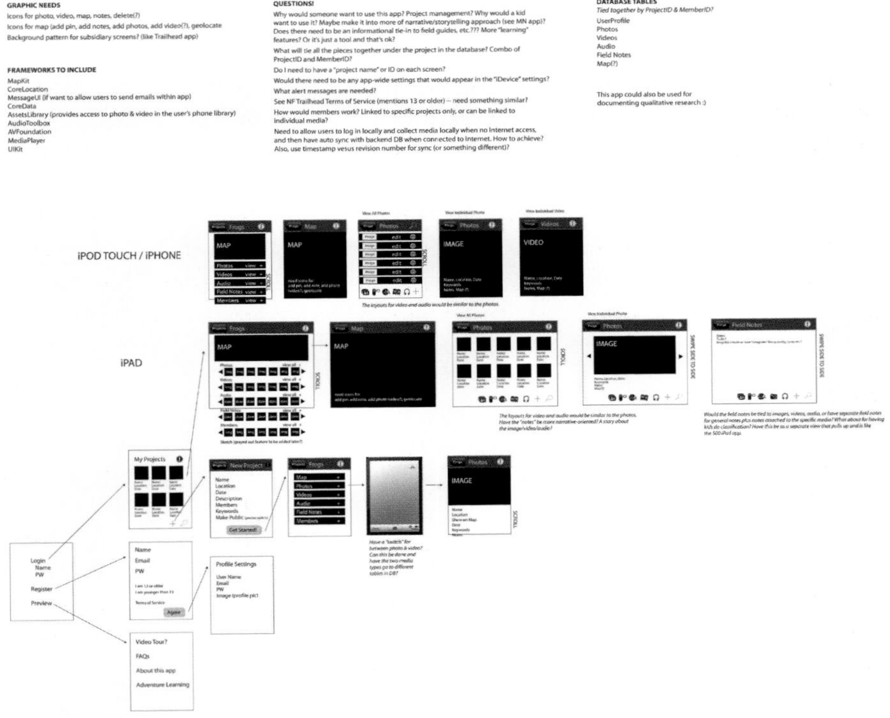

Figure 11.3
Sketching out the schematic for the new adventure learning tool.

After I have a schematic for the app sketched out, including thinking through database needs, iOS frameworks, graphics needs, wireframes, and lingering architecture questions to answer before I start to build the app, I turn to working on the visual designs for the individual screens. I plan to have versions of the app for both the iPod Touch/iPhone and the iPad, so separate designs need to be done for each, given the variance in screen size. My preferred software for doing layout work is Adobe Illustrator, though I switch back and forth between that and Adobe Photoshop, depending on the task I want to accomplish.

I struggle with this aspect of the design, working through and reworking the layouts, colors, fonts, images, and icons used. It is at once both a time of play and a time of frustration. As in writing or coding, there are small moments of "yes!" when I touch on something that I'm happy with or that appears to work. But there is never a moment of finality; it is a continual process of refinement and rework. I reach a point when I know I need to move into the development and continue to refine the design and layouts there, as things will look different in the actual device environments, and some interactions that I envision may not play out there as I hope. (See Figures 11.4 through 11.6 for sample screenshots from some of the screens at the time of initial development.)

Figure 11.4
The look of the new adventure learning tool, iPad version

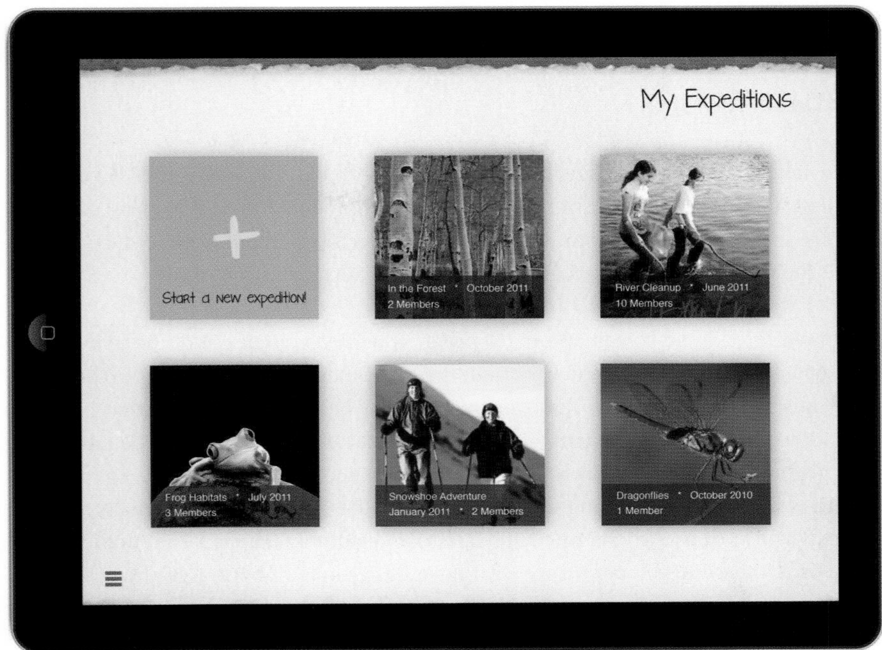

Figure 11.5
The look of the new adventure learning tool, iPad version.

Figure 11.6
The look of the new adventure learning tool, iPad version.

App Development

I then take the revised designs and move into the build. I discover the XCode environment has changed quite dramatically from the time I first used it in class, so time is spent re-exploring the environment and making decisions about how to start. I decide to use the new storyboarding feature to lay out my app there.

I begin with the login screen and try to progress with development of the app linearly, from where the user would enter through the steps they would take to set up and populate their AL project. I soon discover this isn't the best approach, however. I need to start somewhere toward the end, with the individual assets the user will be generating using the app, and work backward toward the login screen. I work on getting functionality to work locally first, using the Core Data on the device, and once that's working correctly will start trying to connect the app to an external database. I am not an expert coder or database developer; however, I have basic skills in both. I get frustrated and overwhelmed, but I don't want to give up. I do searches in online forums looking for answers. I don't always understand what I'm reading there.

So I talk with colleagues more experienced than I in coding, in app development, in database connections. A fellow PhD student (Shaomeng Zhang, I can't not mention your name here!) with phenomenal skills and understanding in these concepts helps me out. I begin to meet weekly with him to work through issues on the app's development.

And this is where I stand now, slowly working toward completion of the app's development, hoping to have a functioning model for testing by mid-2013. It has been from the start a collaborative, nonlinear process, and a valuable learning experience. It has taken far longer to work through than I originally thought it would, having been able to generate and publish my first app within a semester's time. I know I could simply abandon the project, give up, but will not. I thank the faculty, staff, and fellow students here at the LT Media Lab for serving as inspiration, resources, and exemplary models in all arenas: pedagogy, design, development, and real-world integration.

Conclusion

I share this narrative because I truly believe that anyone can build an app. If you have an idea and are willing to invest some research and time and effort into it, it is possible even for someone like me—a non-computer scientist without prior experience in Objective-C—to build and publish an app. You may need to begin with a basic app, however, and save the more complicated stuff for later builds.

I am fortunate to be in an academic program like the Learning Technologies program here at the University of Minnesota that not only emphasizes pedagogy and theory but that scaffolds students in the *practice* of design and development as well. As a take-away, I'd like to share my conceptualization of what the app design process might look like for a student or a novice developer (see below and Figure 11.7). Above all, I encourage novice app developers to be persistent and flexible, seek out help, and be willing to work in a nonlinear fashion, moving back and forth between conceptualization, design, and development, and willing to scrap ideas and restart on them when something doesn't work as planned.

The App Design Process for Novice Developers

- Explore existing apps, frameworks, designs, and functionality.
- Conceptualize an app based on your explorations and your passions, even if the functionality you envision doesn't currently exist (you can modify it as you design

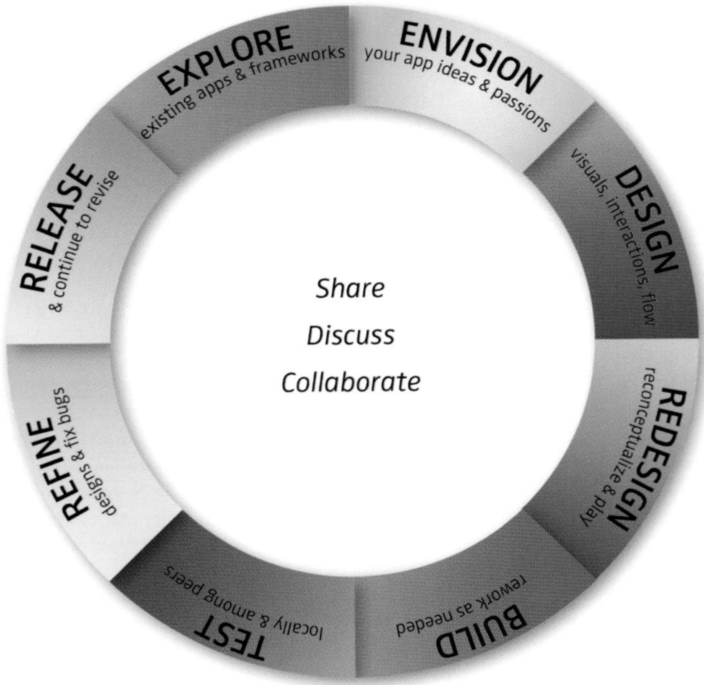

Figure 11.7
The app design process.

and build it, or with the rate of advance in the app world, it may be available by the time you move into your build).

- Discuss your ideas with colleagues, peers, and your target audience.
- Draw up initial designs that include the look, interactions, and potential flow of the user experience.
- Share your designs and get feedback.
- Redesign your concept, even if that means scrapping your original designs altogether.
- Build your app.
- Seek help as needed, from online forums and more experienced colleagues.
- Refine and modify the app's design as you build it.
- Test the app locally, and then share it with others to test before trying to publish it (you can share your app with up to 100 devices first using ad-hoc distribution!).
- Fix bugs and refine based on testing.
- Publish your app (it can be a daunting process, but there are lots of great online tutorials that walk you through the process).
- Continue to refine and update your app as needed.

References

Bransford, J., Brown, A., & Cocking, R. (Eds.). (1999). *How people learn: Brain, mind, experience, and school*. Washington, DC: National Academy Press.

Cristia, J., Cueto, S., Ibarraran, P., Santiago, A., & Severin, E. (2012). Technology and child development: Evidence from the One Laptop Per Child Program. Inter-American Development Bank. Retrieved November 11, 2012, from http://www.iadb.org/en/research-and-data/publication-details,3169.html?pub_id=IDB-WP-304.

Doering, A. (2006). Adventure learning: Transformative hybrid online education. *Distance Education, 27*(2), 197–215.

Doering, A., & Miller, C. (2009). Online learning revisited: Adventure learning 2.0. In C. Crawford et al. (Eds.), *Proceedings of Society for Information Technology and Teacher Education International Conference 2009* (pp. 3729–3735). Chesapeake, VA: AACE.

Doering, A., Scharber, C., Riedel, E., & Miller, C. (2010). "Timber for President": Adventure learning and motivation. *Journal of Interactive Learning Research, 21*(4), 483–513.

Doering, A., & Veletsianos, G. (2008). Hybrid online education: Identifying integration models using Adventure Learning. *Journal of Research on Technology in Education, 41*(1), 101–119.

Hassenzahl, Marc. (2011). User experience and experience design. In M. Soegaard and R. K. Dam (Eds.), *Encyclopedia of human-computer interaction*. Aarhus, Denmark: The Interaction-Design.org Foundation. Retrieved November 11, 2012, from http://www.interaction-design.org/encyclopedia/user_experience_and_experience_design.html.

Henrickson, J. (2011). Using the adventure learning framework to design for engagement and community building. In M. Koehler & P. Mishra (Eds.), *Proceedings of Society for Information Technology & Teacher Education International Conference 2011* (pp. 2502–2509). Chesapeake, VA: AACE.

Hokanson, B., & Miller. C. (2009). Role-based design: A contemporary framework for innovation and creativity in instructional design. *Educational Technology, 49*(2), 21–28.

Jonassen, D. (1991). Evaluating constructivistic learning. *Educational Technology, 31*(9), 28–33.

Kolb, D. A. (1984). *Experiential learning: Experience as the source of learning and development*. New Jersey: Prentice Hall.

Koseoglu, S., & Doering, A. (2011). Understanding complex ecologies: An investigation of student experiences in adventure learning programs. *Distance Education, 32*(3), 339–355.

Louv, R. (2008). *Last child in the woods: Saving our children from nature-deficit disorder.* Chapel Hill, NC: Algonquin Books.

Moos, D., and Honkomp, B. (2011). Adventure learning: Motivating students in a Minnesota middle school. *Journal of Research on Technology in Education, 43*(3), 231–252.

Roberts, P., & Norman, E. (1999). Models of design and technology and their significance for research and curriculum development. *The Journal of Design and Technology Education, 40*(2), 124–131.

Veletsianos, G. (2010). A small-scale adventure learning activity and its implications for higher education practice and research. *in education, 16*(1).

Veletsianos, G., Doering, A., & Henrickson, J. (2012). Field-based professional development of teachers engaged in distance education: Experiences from the Arctic. *Distance Education, 33*(1), 45–59.

Veletsianos, G., & Kleanthous, I. (2009). A review of adventure learning. *The International Review of Research in Open and Distance Learning, 10*(6), 84–105. Retrieved December 27, 2009, from http://www.irrodl.org/index.php/irrodl/article/view/755.

Veletsianos, G., Miller, B., Bradley Eitel, K., Eitel, J. U. H., & Hougham, R. J. (2012). Localizing adventure learning: Teachers and students as expedition leaders and members. In P. Resta (Ed.), *Proceedings of Society for Information Technology & Teacher Education International Conference 2012* (pp. 2164–2169). Chesapeake, VA: AACE.

Wilson, B. G., & Parrish, P. E. (2011). Transformative learning experience: Aim higher, gain more. *Educational Technology,* March–April: 10–15.

Wu, W., Jim Wu, Y., Chen, C., Kao, H., Lin, C., & Huang, S. (2012). Review of trends from mobile learning studies: A meta-analysis. *Computers & Education, 59*(2), 817–827.

Zaradic, P. A., & Pergams, O. R. W. (2007). Videophilia: Implications for childhood development and conservation. *Journal of Developmental Processes, 2*(1), 130–144.

Section 4
Mobile Learning Integration, Research, and Evaluation

If there is one area of learning technologies where quality research is needed, it is within the field of mobile learning. Although mobile learning, as we know it today, is quite new and changing rapidly, we all must rise to the occasion and deliver data that fuel the areas of design, research, evaluation, and integration. To this end, Chapters 12 to 20 move us steps closer to understanding a host of issues related to mobile learning ranging from how to teach within an iPad-centered classroom to how to evaluate apps for classroom integration. Chapters 12 to 14 focus on app evaluation while Chapters 15 to 17 look at the challenges of integrating apps into the classroom. Finally, Chapters 18 to 20 look at content-specific app integration.

App Integration

Dr. McLain begins the section by describing the need for new ways to think about and evaluate apps for education. He argues that apps are "pulling back the curtain on a new breed of individualized learning experiences that are increasingly integrated into our lives" and it's time to look at two broad categories of educational apps—Type 1 replicant apps and Type 2 extender apps. McLain describes these two categories and presents a new approach for evaluation that considers mobile learning through an experiential lens that has the potential to impact learner identity.

Our next authors, Ms. Kumar and Dr. Owston, discuss the need for apps to be evaluated through the lens of accessibility. They argue that we, as a field, must "ensure that all learners have an equitable opportunity to benefit from the app, regardless of ability, disability, or context of use." They note that although out-of-the-box apps are quite good in terms of accessibility, we, as designers, have a long road ahead of us. Accessibility, therefore, must be threaded throughout the beginning of the app development process to benefit all stakeholders.

Within Chapter 14, Ms. Rhodes focuses on a design-based research study where the research team collaborated with twelve intermediate school educators to design mobile data tools for teachers to integrate within their classroom. The research reveals that teachers collect and record data similarly while placing value on the ability to customize data collection tools. Designers learn about analyzing educators' needs and identifying design opportunities while teachers and researchers learn how to seek out and build relationships with research institutions while implementing a DBR approach to research.

Teacher Integration Challenges

Drs. Jahnke and Kumar provide us with a European lens on iPad integration by sharing insight into Danish schools and a Swedish university. They specifically look at how teachers use iPads in their classrooms and for what purposes. Based on the theoretical framework "iPad-didactics," they describe two ways in which the iPad can be used in classrooms that may be helpful to others engaged in implementing iPads or designing resources for teacher education.

Chapter 16 focuses on preservice teachers and their ability to integrate mobile apps within a special teacher education course. Drs. Baran and Khan provide a detailed examination of five mobile apps while giving recommendations to designers, teachers, and researchers for future development and integration. Numerous factors such as social interactivity and collectivity are discussed along with how teacher educators should design preservice teacher programs to assist with app integration.

Ms. Geurtz and Ms. Foote provide an insightful look into the challenges and celebrations when launching an iPad initiative from the perspective of the school librarian. Through a two-year investigation, using Puentedura's SAMR framework, they provide concrete examples of technology integration along with ten leadership behaviors recommended to support successful transformation within a school.

Content-specific Integration

The focus of Chapter 18 is a one-to-one iPad initiative described through the stories of Brett and Julie, two veteran high school English teachers, who are integrating iPads into their classroom. They are not ordinary teachers as these "risk-taking practitioners" discuss the many issues related to pedagogy, assessment, and new media literacies. Mr. Russell and Dr. Hughes conclude the chapter by sharing useful ways districts, schools, and practitioners can move into such an initiative and hopefully be successful.

In Chapter 19 Dr. Hagevik, Dr. Falls, and Ms. Lynn investigate ways in which a comprehensive teaching management system could provide factors known to be important to resilient individuals and successful teaching. They examined factors in resilient teaching and found that all twelve preservice teachers were able to use their iPads and the apps to manage themselves and their classrooms, to solve professional dilemmas, as a teaching tool, and as a means to relax and release stress.

Drs. Ramos and Devers close this section with insights into content-specific app integration as they research the use of iPads and apps in an introductory physics course. Although the course previously involved substantial laboratory equipment, the iPads and apps afforded students to automate repetitive and multiple tasks, enabled simplified interfaces, and promoted mobility of the experiments. The authors conclude with the benefits of this approach while promoting student engagement, enhancing measurement accuracy and consistency, and reducing student anxiety.

Chapter 12
Delineation of Evaluation Criteria for Educational Apps in STEM Education

Mobile apps are pulling back the curtain on a new breed of individualized learning experiences that are increasingly integrated into our lives. The mobile apps phenomenon demands new ways to think about and evaluate apps designed for education purposes. This chapter proposes two broad categories of educational apps: Type 1 replicant apps and Type 2 extender apps, along with a new approach for evaluation that considers mobile learning through an experiential lens that has the potential to impact learner identity.

For Designers

Designers will explore implications for the design of innovative apps through experiential learning theory to generate deeper user app experiences.

For Teachers

Teachers will view the integration of apps within learning environments as technology-enhanced learning experiences that can contribute to science identity construction, and explore the notion of teachers and students becoming apps themselves as designers utilizing agile software development methods.

For Researchers

Researchers will expand their range of evaluative considerations to a more holistic model for assessing the educational value of mobile apps as vehicles for experiential learning.

Mobile learning will increasingly place the locus of control within the learner and individualize learning experiences that are fully integrated within our lives.

Dr. Brad McLain
Director,
XSci: Experiential Science Education Research Collaborative,
University of Colorado, Denver

McLain's research focus is on science identity construction and the role of narrative (storytelling) in content understanding and personal meaning making. He is also an accomplished documentary filmmaker and multimedia designer, having been the lead for several NSF and NASA projects over the past ten years. Prior to joining the faculty at UCD, McLain was an educational researcher at the Space Science Institute, a multimedia instructional designer in the online learning industry, a NASA educational lead, and a social science researcher at the National Center for Atmospheric Research (NCAR).

McLain's NASA experience began in 2001 as an education lead for space shuttle mission STS 107, Columbia's final flight which ended in tragedy. Following his stint on the human space flight side of NASA, he became involved in several educational efforts in space science and astrobiology through the NASA Astrobiology Institute.

Delineation of Evaluation Criteria for Educational Apps in STEM Education

Three Questions for Educational Apps

What makes one "educational app" better than the next one? How shall we evaluate the pedagogical validity of educational apps? By what outcome criteria should apps be assessed for their educational value? Respectively, our answers to these three questions are: Who cares? Don't try, and; Are you sure you want to go there?

These quippy answers are not to imply that mobile apps hold no educational value. Quite to the contrary, in many cases mobile apps represent a new mode of personalized individual and social learning. But as a new mode of learning, many of our methods of looking at traditional educational tools simply do not apply. So let us take a closer look at those questions posed above and our seemingly dismissive answers to gain some perspective on evaluation criteria for educational apps, particularly in STEM education.

First, who cares? To ask what makes one educational app better than the next is to beg the obvious critical question: To whom? When we began seriously thinking about this question and discussing it with educators and software developers, it was universally assumed that such a determination was best made by educational experts, professional evaluators, researchers . . . people like us. But after chasing our tails through the usual paces of evaluating any other educational tool, we began to realize that with mobile apps we were missing the point. To impose an external, top-down, or *objective* point of view is to precisely fail to recognize what makes mobile apps so compelling and revolutionary to so many. And that is the personalized *subjective* experience they can provide.

Mobile apps are hardly distinguishable from the mobile devices they run on—interactive technology that people wear like clothing (in some cases literally as fashion accessories). This is especially true for the young. According to a recent study by the Kaiser Family Foundation, there has been "an explosion of media consumption in American youth" (aged eight to eighteen) in the last five years through the use of mobile devices, and the proportion of eight- to eighteeen-year-olds who own their own cell phones has increased from 39 percent to 66 percent. As cell phones have evolved into smartphones and with the appearance of iPods and iPads, the study found that children are increasingly using applications on these devices rather than just voice or text communication, and are increasing their use of mobile devices as they age (Rideout, Foehr, & Roberts, 2010). Naturally, there is great interest on the part of educators to somehow harness this veritable flood of media use for learning. And clearly there is a growing need for a better-informed community of apps-savvy educators as well as some kind of framework for assessing apps for educational use. So the obvious part of the answer to "Who cares?" is that educators care. However, given the very personal nature of mobile apps, it is essential to understand that educators are not the most important answer to "Who cares?" about what makes one educational app better than the next. Users are.

The experiences apps provide are now seamlessly blended into our lives, whether we are texting our friends while riding the bus, navigating to the hotel in a strange city, or reading an interactive comic with our kids. Apps are even more intimately woven into the tapestry of today's youth culture through social networking, a wide variety of related games, activities, and virtual environments, as well as online video sharing—all examples that are markedly skewed to younger audiences. However, even this fact is changing as we observe older people tapping into the apps craze and as we see yesterday's apps-fed youth emerge as the young adults of today. In a very real way, mobile apps have become cultural prostheses through which, in part at least, we experience and share the events of our lives. The point is, when thinking about educational apps, we need to recognize that the user is the first and last answer to the question "Who cares?" And in this way, mobile apps are unlike other educational "tools." In fact, to view them merely as tools is to limit them in many ways and ignore their strengths as subjective conduits for interaction and experience. At their best, educational mobile apps can be seen as the digital epitome of learner-centered, learner-directed education.

To proceed from this premise then, the second question is: How shall we evaluate the pedagogical validity of educational apps? In the cases of the most creative apps—the ones that successfully harness the user-centered learning potential of mobile apps technology—we shouldn't. The normal rules simply do not apply. New learning approaches, such as those that apps present us with demand new perspectives of analysis and forms of evaluation. That is not to say we couldn't, however. We could apply to all apps a wide variety of pedagogical and content assessments to examine them for effective instructional methods and strategies. And for some apps, that may in fact be most appropriate. If, for example, a given app is replicating a Montessori reading exercise or channeling a multi-lingual math tutor, then such standard instructional approaches fit standard assessment methods. In those cases, let's go ahead and examine the learning goals and objectives. Let's analyze the designed learning cycle and sequence at work. Let's consider such apps as "interventions" and assess outcome gains. But this chapter is not about standard educational assessments of standard educational approaches—even if they happen to flicker across the screen of a mobile device.

We are suggesting that to examine mobile apps in that way—or to narrowly design educational apps simply as digital versions of classroom exercises, workbooks, or virtual surrogates for educators—is to miss the paradigm shift that is occurring right under our noses and often in spite of the best laid plans of rutted instructional designers. The power of mobile apps for education is not to be found in viewing them as tools for the delivery of more of the same educational pedagogies we currently use, but rather as vehicles for new kinds of learning experiences.

This leads us to the third question: By what criteria should apps be assessed for their educational value? And our answer; are you sure you want to go there? Precisely because of their nature as extensions of our personal and social lives, educational apps offer the potential to more acutely operate within the realm of our everyday lived experiences wherein we make meaning from experience, wherein our knowledge transitions to understanding, and wherein the personal relevance of our learning is established. In this light, any attempt at evaluation of educational apps must then consider value in terms of the user experience and the integration of apps use into users' lives. Such a holistic approach is more complex and decidedly messy when compared with the relatively cut-and-dried examination of learning goals and learning outcomes, which are the stock in trade of traditional educational evaluation. Therefore, here we need to make an immediate distinction between two broad categories of educational apps . . . Type 1 and Type 2.

Type 1 apps we may call the "replicants" (*Blade Runner* fans, we salute you). Replicant apps are those that seek to replicate learning activities or interactions that can and do take place in other domains. Such apps include apps versions of storybooks, apps math flash cards, or even an app-based chemistry tutor. They also include traditional educational tools such as app calculators, app reference materials, or app-based maps. These apps will feature varying degrees of interactivity and varying degrees of fidelity to the reference system, or original (non-app) version of the activity or tool. But broadly speaking these replicant apps would be appropriately assessed using any number of traditional evaluative methods as equally applied to their reference system counterparts.

In contrast, Type 2 apps we may call the "extenders." Extender apps are those that enhance the learning experience in ways not otherwise possible except through apps technology. In other words, these are apps that engage users in learning experiences that do not replicate counterpart activities that can be done in classrooms, for example, but rather extend and deepen the learning experience precisely *because* it is facilitated through a mobile app. Hallmarks of these apps, especially where STEM learning is concerned, include a heavy emphasis on such things as critical thinking, problem solving, personal expression and communication, data handling and interpretation, and enhancements of actual experiences. Examples include apps that feature: augmented reality; virtual or simulated environments; role-playing games; exploration and inquiry; social construction, communication, and collaboration; opportunities for reflection and individual meaning making; as well as higher degrees of creativity and self-expression. Examples include Star Walk, Theodolite, Musical Me HD, Facebook, and Tonic's DoGood, to name a few.

Notably, among the apps in this category are those for which instructional design holds little or no meaning. These are the "toy apps"—apps that are meant to be played with as toys rather than played in the sense that games are played, or in the sense that designed experiences lead users through a learning sequence. These digital toys, like their real-world counterparts, support unstructured play and invoke the closely related psychologies of learning and creative play behavior.

Extender apps are the kind of apps that require us to both broaden and deepen our ideas of educational value and evaluation. These are the game-changers. When looking at the educational use of extender apps, we need to consider a more holistic and personal assessment perspective that can capture not only their educational impacts, but also the "how" and the "why" behind their use and value to users. This involves examining their use as components within a broader learning experience. That is to say, we

Figure 12.1
Theodolite app.

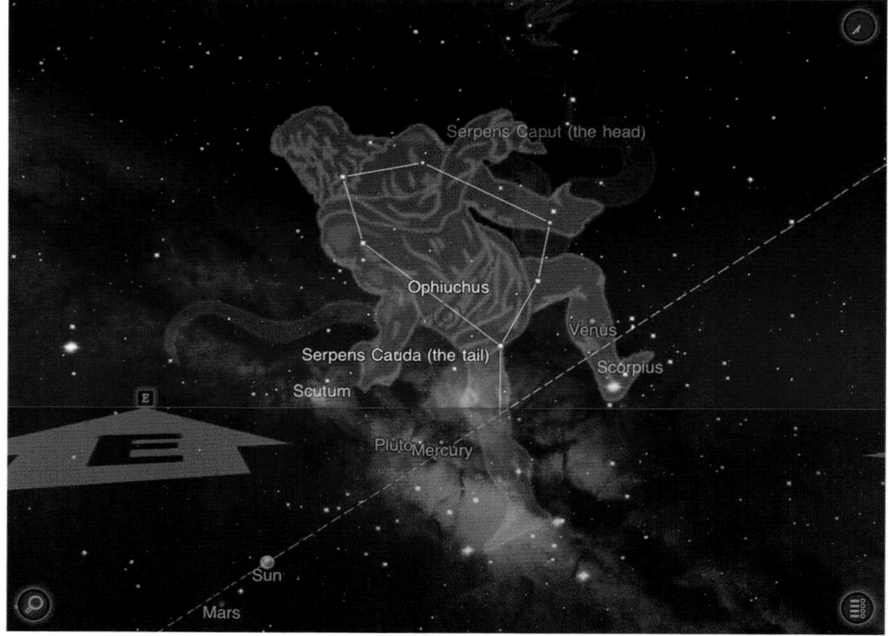

Figure 12.2
Star Walk app.

are suggesting an experiential learning perspective where the app is a component of an experiential learning process that is learner centered and learner directed or controlled to varying degrees. Therefore, evaluation for their educational validity and utility must reach beyond content- and process-based learning goals and objectives, to assess the holistic experience that extender apps provide and were, in most cases, designed for. In order to do so, we need to briefly examine experiential learning theory and how it applies to mobile apps.

Experiential Learning Theory: The Secret Sauce of Extender Apps

When developers of so-called "extender apps" sit down to design app form and functionality, they are thinking about the relationship between the app and the user. That is, they are focused on not just designing an app, but an experience. Viewing apps design and use in this way is important because it ushers in a wealth of informed perspectives from the field of experiential learning. Experiential learning theory is concerned with learning from direct first-person experiences and a holistic perspective that goes beyond content to include the construction of knowledge, attitudes, beliefs, and transfer of learning (Itin, 1997). By definition, experiential learning places the locus of control and focus of the process directly within the learner. We suggest that the development and use of extender apps, by design or accident, falls in perfectly with this view of learning.

One of the best-known models for experiential learning theory was put forth by David Kolb in the early 1980s. Kolb asserted, "learning is the process whereby knowledge is created through the transformation of experience" (1984, p. 38). In his formulation, Kolb deliberately invoked John Dewey's general philosophy on experiential learning in this regard. In Kolb's model, there is a transition from concreteness to abstractness, or what is often interpreted as the linkage of specific experiences to more general principles that may be applied in other and new situations. Transition from the specific to the general occurs through processes of observation and reflection.

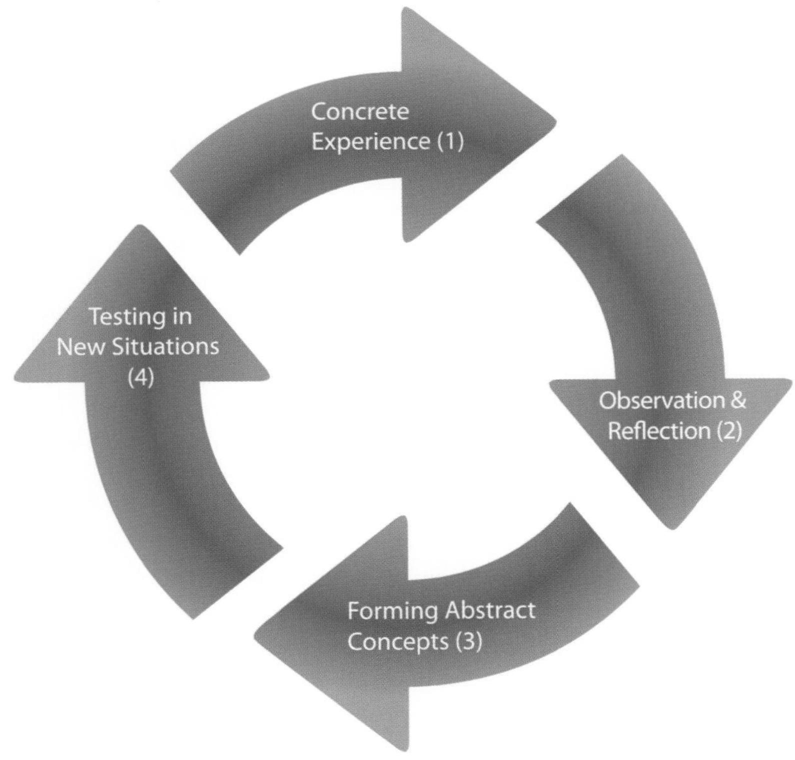

Figure 12.3
Kolb's experiential learning model.

This element of reflection is a keystone component of many experiential learning models, for it provides pathways to individual meaning making and linkages of current experiences to prior learning as well as projections into possible futures. John Dewey, in his seminal book *How We Think* (1933), laid down a foundational process of five stages of reflection on and during experiences:

1. Suggestions, in which the mind leaps forward to a possible solution.
2. An intellectualization of the difficulty or perplexity that has been felt (directly experienced) into a problem to be solved.
3. The use of one suggestion after another as a leading idea, or hypothesis, to initiate and guide observation and other operations in collection of factual material.
4. The mental elaboration of the idea, or supposition as an idea (reasoning, in the sense in which reasoning is a part, not the whole, of inference).
5. Testing the hypothesis by overt, or imaginative action (pp. 199–209).

In many cases, the use of extender apps as learning experiences includes opportunities for just such reflection. When a learner is *experiencing* extender apps or interacting with such apps as a component of a larger learning goal, we see these stages playing out.

Take for example one of the many excellent astronomy apps that utilize augmented reality. Upon pointing your mobile device at the night sky, using GPS and internal accelerometers, these apps generate real-time data overlays of the skyscape before you, including star names, constellations, planets, even the orbital tracks of satellites and the International Space Station. With these kinds of apps, users can explore the night sky over their corner of the world in great detail. Point the mobile device at the ground and users can immediately see the night sky as observed on the other side of the world. Not only do such apps provide extraordinary experiences of ordinary things (the night sky in this case), they become powerful windows for reflective learning. Consider the use of such apps with students to discover for themselves the astronomical orientation of the Earth, or to predict and track the retrograde motion of different planets, or determine the launch windows for spacecraft missions to Mars.

If an educational evaluation of such apps only considered the content programmed into them or even went so far as to examine the learning outcomes in terms of student content gains, and ignored the psychological processes of discovery-based and inquiry-based learning *experienced* when using them, then we would have failed to see the deeper educational value in terms of learner experience.

Given this perspective and the notion of viewing extender apps within the context of experiential learning, what does this mean for evaluation and how we should go about it? First, as stated above, we must broaden our view to consider the app as a component of a learning experience and begin by focusing on that experience. This takes the focus away from the app as a stand-alone entity, and suggests we need to consider the relationship between the learner and the experience of using the app and how this relationship manifests in complex ways. These include impacts on the learner's conceptual understanding, capacity to apply that understanding, individual attitudes and self-efficacy regarding the learning (astronomy, in the example above), and future choices.

These impact or outcome categories are decidedly holistic in that they embed both intellectual as well as emotional and in some cases physical elements. But one thing they all have in common is that they deal extensively in the realm of learner self-concept with the idea that experiences can change the way we see things. In the most compelling cases, experiences can change the way we see ourselves and thus influence our lives and future choices in meaningful ways. In our work researching many different kinds of learning experiences, we look at such impacts through the lens of identity theory and believe it to be uniquely informative when examining extender-type apps. In particular, when thinking about the evaluation of mobile apps for STEM education, we wish to focus on the experiences facilitated by such apps in terms of their impact on learners' sense of science identity.

Science Identity Construction through Mobile Apps

Briefly, within the sociological field of identity theory, the *self* is systematically unpacked into *identities* as dynamic mental constructs that emerge, grow, compete, disappear or evolve over time and are directly related to agency, behavior, choices, and performance (Burke & Stets, 2009). Through the lens of identity theory, the learning of new things can go beyond their incorporation into internal schema for understanding (Piaget, 1926; Zemelman, Daniels & Hyde, 1993), to actually inform, modify, and become integrated into a person's identity or identities. Identity learning theory incorporates the *self* via the relationship of the knower to the known as essential to meaning making, personal relevance, and life choices.

Science identity can loosely be thought of as one's relationship to science—whether with science content, processes, or the culture of science itself and its members (Falk & Dierking, 2000; Hull & Greeno, 2006; Roth & Li, 2005). In our work, it describes personal ownership and integration of STEM into an individual's sense of self through personal interpretation and meaning making via experience. The concept of science identity incorporates the relationship of the whole individual to STEM in order to make personal meaning and relevancy. If the relationship is positive, it may take the form of STEM literacy resulting in STEM-related pursuits, a scientifically informed worldview, or a STEM-related career choice. If the relationship is negative, it may take the form of STEM avoidance or even repulsion resulting in the all-too-familiar refrain, "I'm no good at science or math," often echoed as a badge of honor among children and adults alike.

Identity learning theory allows us to examine the experience of using extender-type apps to draw direct linkages from apps experiences to factors known to affect and predict future STEM academic and career choices. The identity "construction zone" model shown here is based on identity research through experiential STEM learning programs and serves to link different dimensions of science identity construction to associated indicators. With this model, we are suggesting that the focus of educational apps evaluation efforts be on the users (shown in the middle of Figure 12.4) and their experiences with apps.

Users will experience different kinds of personal growth and learning, which are considered *science identity construction zones* and include agency, content confidence, emotional connection, and personal relevance. Prior work has described these elements as precursors to learner outcome areas (see below) (Brickhouse, Lowery, & Schultz, 2000;

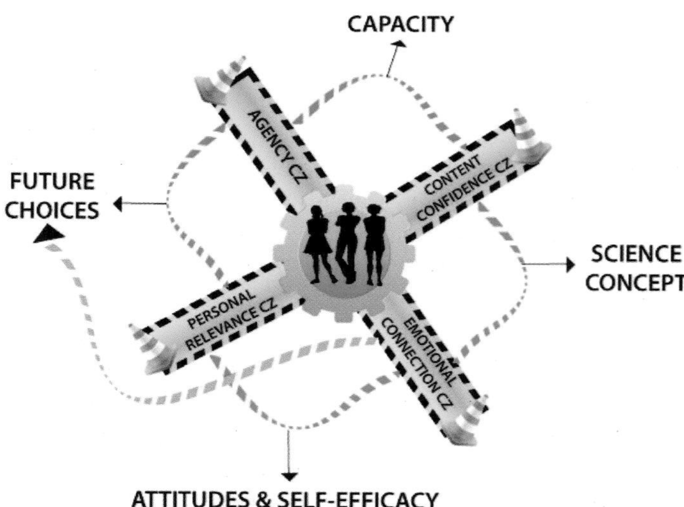

Figure 12.4
Science identity construction zones and outcomes.

Hunter, Laursen, & Seymour, 2006; van Driel, Beijaard, & Verloop, 2001; Vogt, 2008; Weinberg et al., 2007). Therefore, these construction zones represent the general "experience areas" for evaluating the experience of using an extender app. The categories around the perimeter represent the "learner outcome areas" for examining the results of those experiences. This model, then, suggests a framework for evaluating the educational value of Type 2 extender apps that goes well beyond traditional evaluation approaches. Our intent is to reveal value in deeper, broader, and more holistic experiential terms in keeping with the very personal nature of mobile app technology.

One Final Pot of Gold: Designing Apps

An area of the educational use of apps for STEM learning that bears special mention here is the emerging potential for teachers and students to become designers of apps themselves, rather than only consumers. We whole-heartedly endorse such efforts and have even begun to develop our own mobile apps development program as part of a teacher technology certificate. Why is this a pot of gold? The answer lies in the *process* of apps development much more so than in the products.

Mobile apps development presents a unique opportunity to leverage an exciting new trend in technology innovation *as it is occurring* and that also holds tremendous potential for STEM education and the early incitement of young minds to become interested in STEM careers. Beyond the value of mobile apps for everything from work utilities and communication, to entertainment, art, and even research . . . there is another key component to the mobile apps craze that makes it fertile ground for the development of fundamental twenty-first-century attitudes and skills necessary for STEM work environments and careers—and that is the *accessibility* of apps design. Today, one need not be a consummate programmer with expertise in the intricacies of programming languages to enter the arena of mobile apps design. This is especially true of the Apple iOS Software Development Kit (SDK) and the XCode environment, which one can learn in very short order. With more than twenty million Apple iPads and in excess of a hundred million iPhone and iPod Touch devices currently in use, exponentially rising numbers of universities, K–12 schools, and institutions are selecting the iPad and iPod Touch as the platforms of choice for both face-to-face and distance education classrooms (Bradshaw, 2011). However, a disparity exists between the individuals responsible for creating the apps (i.e. development companies with little to no instructional experience, masked behind the business-minded protection of the iTunes App Store) and the ultimate consumers in the classroom (educators and students). The classroom teacher can no longer be viewed as simply the end user or content expert; they must serve an important role in apps design to create transformative change.

Further, the design of apps presents the opportunity for educators to understand and present to their students the cutting-edge realities of how software is produced today. Contemporary apps development is based on *agile* software design methods: frequent and rapid delivery of useful software; working software is the measure of progress; face-to-face conversation is the best communication; projects are built around motivated individuals who should be trusted; continuous attention to technical excellence; simplicity; self-organizing teams; and regular adaptation to changing circumstances (Agile Manifesto, 2011). Companies employing agile methodologies (e.g., Zynga and Google) share important characteristics: (1) the iteration cycle for testing and feedback is two weeks or less; (2) developers and testers meet every day to discuss progress; (3) they deal well with constant change. Agile design is used to gain competitive advantages in both creativity and efficiency and is particularly relevant for mobile apps design because it allows for rapid deployment of working software and provides a structure for continuing to evolve existing software.

Certainly, introductory educator and student apps designers will not be engaged in this level of development as they generate their very first apps. Even so, using modern design methods is extremely important. First, agile methodology describes the realities in today's cutting-edge tech work environment. If we are intending to better prepare educators to reach their students with the exciting and dynamic world of mobile apps as a gateway to STEM career paths, then they must experience it themselves.

Secondly, frequent design team meetings that include iterative feedback from end users is a variation on the concept in educational research of *participatory design*. It is a goal of participatory design to give members of the target audience a seat at the development table for educational products to help ensure the viability of those products. This is critical for the development of twenty-first-century skills, which include: critical thinking and problem solving; communication; collaboration; and creativity and innovation.

In this light, apps can and should be viewed both as software products resulting from a software design process and as educational products resulting from an instructional design process. Therefore, we suggest innovative approaches to apps design training for educators that also welcome their students to the table as critical members of the target audience for which the resulting apps will presumably be designed. Such approaches may even provide additional and much-needed support for teachers as they attempt to integrate apps design and use in the classroom by having knowledgeable students helping in the effort. As school districts across the country increasingly strive to meet the needs of STEM education through the creation of designated STEM schools or the deeper integration of STEM concepts within their traditional schools, apps design represents a strong type of engineering activity not normally found within such initiatives. Teachers need all the help they can get for this kind of innovation.

Lastly, the experience of designing apps stands to be much deeper and potentially beneficial than merely using apps. This is true even if the apps under development by educators and students are Type 1 replicant apps, which most first-time developers would likely create. Given the richness of the experience of developing apps, the construction zone evaluation framework presented above takes on even more meaning in terms of the development of agency, content confidence, emotional connection, and personal relevance in relation to apps as a software design experience and as exposure to twenty-first-century work modes. Experientially based methods require experientially based evaluation approaches.

Summary

It used to be that most people could open the hood of their car and go to work on the engines with a working knowledge of its form and function. Nowadays,

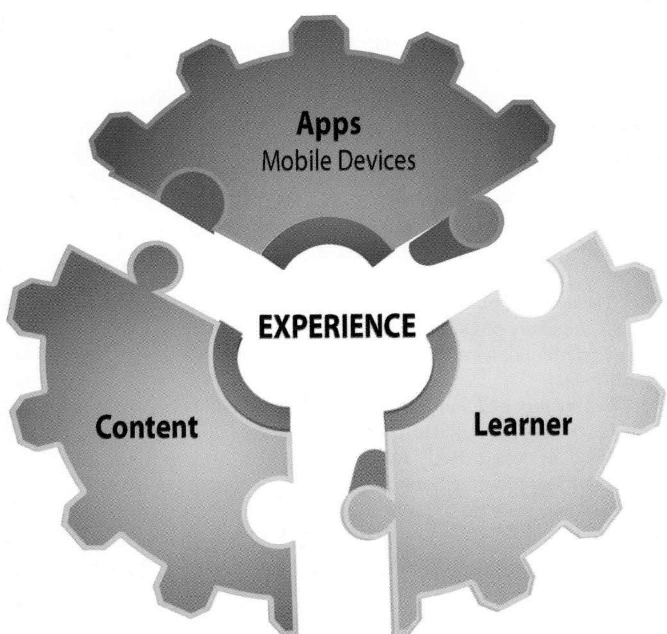

Figure 12.5
Evaluating apps for STEM education.

most people don't even bother to open the hood and gaze upon an utterly complex and baffling arrangement of components that do indeed make the car go. The same has been increasingly true of technology over the past twenty-five years. However, mobile apps present us with an opportunity to change that. Both for the ubiquity and integration of mobile devices in our lives and for the accessibility of designing apps, this new technology is a gateway that can open the fast-moving world of technology and STEM in general to student and educator alike. By their very nature, mobile apps invite us to consider their use holistically, as the nexus between learners, content, and the apps themselves—all resulting in a unique and powerfully individualized learning experience. So let's look under that hood and get busy!

References

Agile Manifesto. (2011). Retrieved May 14, 2011, from http://agilemanifesto.org/principles.html.

Bradshaw, T. (2011, March). Tablet devices: iPad takes over as the lecture hall aid of choice. Retrieved April 5, 2011, from http://www.ft.com/cms/s/2/d776cbf6-4b71-11e0-89d800144feab49a.html?ftcamp=traffic/email/content/BizEd/March/memmkt#axzz1Ggg0W3AB.

Brickhouse, N., Lowery, P., & Schultz, K. (2000). What kind of girl does science? The construction of school science identities. *Journal of Research in Science Teaching, 37*(5), 441–458.

Burke, P., & Stets, J. (2009). *Identity theory*. New York: Oxford University.

Dewey, J. (1933) *How we think. A restatement of the relation of reflective thinking to the educative process* (revised edition). Boston: D.C. Heath.

Falk, J., & Dierking, L. (2000). *Learning from museums: Visitor experiences and the making of meaning*. Lanham, MD: Admiral Press.

Hull, G., & Greeno, J. G. (2006). Identity and agency in nonschool and school worlds. In Z. Bekerman, N. Burbules, & D. Silberman-Keller (Eds.), *Learning in places: The informal education reader* (pp. 77–98). New York: Peter Lang.

Hunter, A., Laursen, S., & Seymour, E. (2006). Becoming a scientist: The role of undergraduate research in students' cognitive, personal, and professional development. *Science Education, 91*, 36–74.

Itin, C. M. (1997). *The orientation of social work faculty to the philosophy of experiential education in the classroom*. University of Denver, Denver, CO.

Kolb, D. A. (1984). Experiential learning: *Experience as the source of learning and development*. New Jersey: Prentice-Hall.

Piaget, J. (1926). *The language and thought of the child*. New York: Harcourt, Brace, Jovanovich.

Rideout, V., Foehr, U., & Roberts, D. (2010). Generation M2: Media in the lives of 8- to 18-year-olds. A Kaiser Family Foundation Study. Retrieved March 3, 2013, from www.kff.org.

Roth, E., & Li, E. (2005) Mapping the boundaries of science identity in ISME's first year. Paper presented at the annual meeting of the American Educational Research Association, Montreal, Canada.

Van Driel, J., Beijaard, D., & Verloop, N. (2001). Professional development and reform in science education: The role of teachers' practical knowledge. *Journal of Research in Science Teaching, 38*, 137–158. doi: 10.1002/1098–2736(200102)38:2<137::AID-TEA1001>3.0.CO;2-U.

Vogt, C. (2008). Faculty as a critical junction in student retention and performance in engineering programs. *Journal of Engineering Education, 1*, 27–36.

Weinberg, J., Pettibone, J., Thomas, S., Stephen, M., & Stein, C. (2007). RSS-2007 Workshop: Research in Robots for Education. Institute for Personal Robots in Education. Retrieved November 18, 2011, from http:// www.roboteducation.org/rss-2007/.

Zemelman, S., Daniels, H., & Hyde, A. (1993). *Best practice: New standards for teaching and learning in America's schools*. Portsmouth, NH: Heinemann.

Chapter 13
Accessibility Evaluation of iOS Apps for Education

The evaluation of apps used in educational contexts must include accessibility evaluation. This is essential to ensure that all learners have an equitable opportunity to benefit from the app, regardless of ability, disability, or context of use. iOS devices are exemplary with respect to out-of-the-box accessibility, including a wide array of built-in features that allow learners to customize the way that they interact with their devices and apps. In addition, there are iOS app-specific, mobile app-specific, and general learning technology accessibility guidelines that developers can refer to when developing an app to ensure maximal accessibility. However, our survey of several popular educational apps reveals that accessibility is not always proactively incorporated into the app development process or considered by educators when recommending apps for educational use. It is crucial to not only place a priority on accessibility during the app development process, but also on classroom implementation and evaluation of educational apps. An approach that includes multiple stakeholders, from app developers, to learners, teachers, researchers, and parents is required in order to work towards a truly accessible mobile learning experience.

For Designers

Designers of educational apps will gain an appreciation of the importance of proactive accessible design, as well as relevant design approaches and guidelines.

For Teachers

Teachers who wish to incorporate educational apps into the classroom will gain an appreciation of the importance of selecting apps that are maximally accessible to meet the needs of all learners, as well as general methods of examining an app for accessible features.

For Researchers

Researchers will gain an appreciation of the importance of learner-centered methods of accessibility evaluation of educational apps, as well as insight into how to conduct research on app accessibility.

Accessible iOS apps designed for education can increase the flexibility of mobile learning and meet the needs of all learners.

Kari Kumar
Lecturer,
Faculty of Health Sciences,
University of Ontario Institute
of Technology

Dr. Ron Owston
Director,
Institute for Research on Learning
Technologies, York University, Canada;
Professor, Education, York University, Canada

Kari Kumar is a lecturer in the Faculty of Health Sciences, UOIT, Oshawa, Canada; and a doctoral candidate in the Faculty of Education at York University, Toronto, Canada. Her current research is directed towards examining methods of evaluating the accessibility of learning technologies. Her interest in accessibility and inclusive learning environments stems from her background in life sciences and experience teaching post-secondary science.

Dr. Ron Owston is the founding Director of the Institute for Research on Learning Technologies and University Professor of Education at York University, Toronto, Canada. His specialty is the evaluation of technology-based learning. His latest project, the Open Virtual Usability Lab (OpenVULab), focuses on researching the accessibility of websites for users with disabilities. Current research efforts are being directed towards development of an accessible OpenVULab app that may be used to evaluate the accessibility of educational apps.

Accessibility Evaluation of iOS Apps for Education

Accessibility is an essential evaluation criterion for iOS apps that are intended for educational use. Apps that are not maximally accessible may exclude some learners, particularly students with disabilities, from using and benefitting from them. This is significant in light of a growing trend towards inclusion of students with exceptionalities in mainstream K–12 classrooms, and the concomitant increase in students with disabilities who pursue higher education. In the United States, for example, recent estimates suggest that 11 percent of the student population in higher education may have a disability (U.S. Government Accountability Office, 2009), compared with estimates of 3 percent from 1978 (National Council on Disability, 2003).

Accessibility is a somewhat subjective variable because what is accessible to one learner may not be accessible to another. To better understand how we might define accessibility in the context of e-learning, consider these statements by the IMS Global Learning Consortium:

> Accessibility . . . is the ability of the learning environment to adjust to the needs of all learners . . . The needs and preferences of a user may arise from the context or environment the user is in, the tools available . . ., their background, or a disability in the traditional sense. Accessible systems adjust the user interface of the learning environment, locate needed resources and adjust the properties of the resources to match the needs and preferences of the user.
>
> (IMS Global Learning Consortium, 2004)

These statements suggest that an accessible e-learning environment is flexible and that learner needs may be shaped by their ability or disability, as well as the learning context. In other words, accessibility is important for all learners—not just learners with disabilities. An accessible iOS device should therefore be adaptable by allowing all users to customize the way that they interact with the device, and the same applies to iOS apps that should allow learners to use the app in a manner that suits their learning needs in a variety of learning contexts.

It is not only simply good practice to ensure that apps are designed and implemented in a manner that makes them accessible to diverse learner populations; there is also emerging legal motivation in several jurisdictions to ensure that all learning technologies are accessible. For example, in the United States, the Americans with Disabilities Act (ADA) and the Rehabilitation Act make it unlawful for schools that are state- or locally funded or federally funded, respectively, to provide electronic or information technology that is inaccessible to learners with disabilities. The United States Department of Education has explicitly stated that Section 504 of the Rehabilitation Act applies to all e-learning infrastructure including emerging technologies, even when selected for pilot testing (Joint Department of Justice and Department of Education, 2011). This clarification arose following a lawsuit in which the National Federation of the Blind and American Council for the Blind sued Princeton and Arizona State universities for violation of the ADA and Rehabilitation Act for launching pilot programs using the Kindle DX, an e-book reader that is not accessible for students with visual impairments (U.S. Department of Justice, 2010a, 2010b). Indeed, United States case law includes several examples of legal action against educational institutes for implementation of inaccessible learning technologies (refer to Kincaid, 2009 for more examples). Additional examples of anti-discriminatory legislation applicable to education in other countries include the Special Education Needs and Disability Act (SENDA) and the Equality Act of the United Kingdom (Her Majesty's Stationery Office 2001, 2010), and the Accessibility for Ontarians with Disabilities Act (AODA) that is in effect in the province of Ontario, Canada (AODA, 2011).

Given the moral and legal imperatives to ensure that learning technologies are accessible to all learners, it is essential to ensure that accessibility evaluation is proactively incorporated into the development of iOS apps. In this chapter, we describe built-in accessibility features of iOS devices that may assist learners in customizing the way that they interact with their devices and apps, and steps that developers may take to develop accessible iOS apps. This is followed by a discussion of accessibility of selected apps designed for educational purposes, and methods that educators and researchers may take to evaluate app accessibility.

Built-in iOS Accessibility Features

With many built-in accessibility features, iOS devices exhibit exemplary out-of-the-box accessibility. Figure 13.1 is a screenshot of the accessibility menu of a third-generation iPad, which shows that there are several options for user customization of the user interface that are categorized according to vision, hearing, and physical and motor needs.

Users with disabilities may find these built-in features particularly helpful when working with apps on iOS devices. Table 13.1 presents a brief description of the functionality of these features as they work in the third-generation iPad. More detailed descriptions about the accessibility features built-in to the various iOS devices are available from the Apple website (http://www.apple.com/accessibility/).

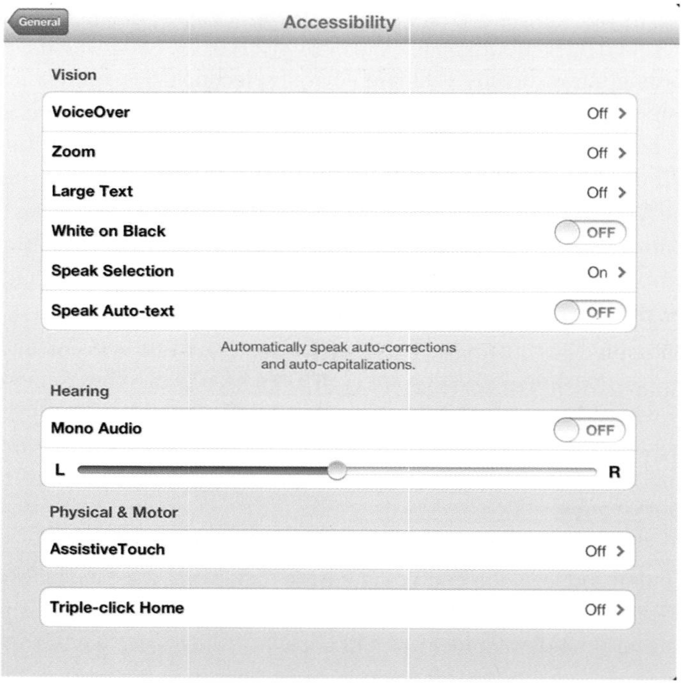

Figure 13.1
Screenshot of the accessibility menu of the third-generation iPad.

A device with these built-in accessibility features can be quite advantageous. Their presence can represent both a convenience and cost savings, as users may not need to purchase and install additional assistive software. Moreover, if a single iOS device meets several needs of a user, the same device can be used for many different purposes and can also reduce the need for users to carry with them multiple devices and/or external assistive technologies.

There are several positive attributes of the built-in iOS accessibility features. Firstly, the accessibility features work well with built-in device apps that were designed to be compatible with the features. Secondly, many of the features are quite easy to use. In particular, the Zoom, Large Text, White on Black, Speak Auto-text, and Triple-click Home features are simple to use with a very small learning curve. Thirdly, several accessibility features may be useful for users who do not identify as persons with disabilities but who would also like to customize the way that they interact with their device and apps. For example, the Zoom feature may be useful for a learner with a visual impairment who wishes to enlarge the size of a button or image displayed on an app. At the same time,

Table 13.1 Description of built-in third-generation iPad accessibility features categorized by user needs.

Accessibility Feature	Function
Vision	
VoiceOver[a]	Converts text to speech
Zoom[a]	Magnifies the screen
Large Text	Magnifies the text in selected built-in apps (Calendar, Contacts, Mail, Messages, and Notes)
White on Black	Inverts the screen colors
Speak Selection	Converts text selected by the user to speech
Speak Auto-text	Speaks autocorrections while the user types
Hearing	
Mono Audio	Merges sound intended for the left and right ears
Physical and motor	
Assistive Touch	Activates additional gestures to reduce physical demand of device use; allows users to create custom gestures
Triple-click Home	Short-cut function allowing users to return to the homescreen; users can customize the triple-click to perform a different task

[a] VoiceOver and Zoom cannot be used simultaneously.

a learner working in an area with low light may also wish to enlarge the display of an app in order to view the display better, as may an adult learner who does not have his or her reading glasses handy.

There are also limitations associated with the built-in iOS accessibility features. While they work well with built-in apps, they do not function with all apps. For example, the VoiceOver function will not convert the text associated with an app button to speech if the button and text are an image, for which the app developer has not also included alternative text that VoiceOver may access and read. Additional specific examples of partial functionality of accessibility features will be discussed further in the "Accessibility Evaluation of Apps" section of this chapter.

Even when the accessibility features are compatible with a particular app, a second limitation is that they may be awkward to use. For example, some users may find a significant learning curve associated with using the VoiceOver function. This is because the touch-screen gestures change and it is necessary for users to learn new gestures in order to navigate not only within a particular app but within other areas of the device (including navigating back to the accessibility menu to turn the feature off). The Zoom feature is easy to use, though if a user requires a substantial magnification increase when working with a particular app, navigation can be inefficient and physically demanding if substantial scrolling is required to move within the app.

A third limitation is that learners cannot use the VoiceOver and Zoom features simultaneously. This could be problematic for learners with low vision who may benefit from the VoiceOver text-to-speech function but would also like to view the display with the magnification enhanced. Similarly, learners with cognitive or learning disabilities often benefit from both text-to-speech and screen magnifying assistive software, and may wish to make use of both features simultaneously.

Finally, a fourth limitation is that even if all of the built-in accessibility features were fully functional and easy to use with a particular app, they may not wholly address the needs of learners with cognitive or learning disabilities. For example, such learners may benefit from simple language and intuitive navigation of an app, which are attributes that are not adjustable with the assistive features. Therefore, in order for an app to be maximally accessible for a diverse population of learners, app developers must not only ensure that the app is designed to be compatible with the built-in iOS accessibility features, but must also consult other best practices that promote designing for users with needs not addressed by the built-in features.

Developing Accessible iOS Apps

There are several accessibility guidelines that app developers may consult prior to submitting an app to be published. Those developing apps for iOS devices may refer to Apple's accessibility guidelines, which include a number of useful suggestions for the development of accessible iOS apps (Apple Inc., 2011a). These suggestions include making the app compatible with assistive software, avoiding the use of color alone to convey information, providing output in multiple modalities so that information may be received by more than one of the senses (e.g., sound effects could also be represented by a visual effect), allowing users to customize response times (e.g., so that users with physical disabilities may take additional time to complete a task), and avoiding the use of blinking objects on the screen in frequencies that are known to cause seizures in people with photosensitive epilepsy. Apple also recommends using the Accessibility Inspector and Accessibility Verifier tools during the development process for formative evaluation of app accessibility (Apple Inc., 2011b), and even offers iBooks Author software (http://www.apple.com/ibooks-author/) that is intended to make it simple for developers to create accessible iBooks.

In addition to Apple iOS accessibility guidelines and tools, there are other more general accessibility guidelines that developers may consult when developing an iOS app. The One Voice for Accessible ICT Coalition (with members representing academia; IT professionals; research groups and consultants; and charitable organizations) has also put forth accessibility guidelines intended for mobile app development. The One Voice suggestions are general steps to improve app accessibility, and are applicable to development of apps for any platform (One Voice, 2012a). The recommended first seven steps are for developers to:

1. learn about accessibility by becoming aware of the needs of users with various disabilities;
2. conduct a quick accessibility check, including a visual inspection of the app and testing for understandability with a screen reader;
3. publish an accessibility statement, including mention of steps taken to enhance accessibility and known limitations;
4. provide a Contact Us function, so that users may provide feedback on app accessibility;
5. ensure reading sequence is logical and comprehensible, so that output from screen readers and other assistive technologies make sense to the user;
6. create a user interface that is easy to understand and operate, including a simple layout, intuitive navigation, and tolerance for error (e.g., include "back" buttons and "delete confirmation" buttons); and
7. ensure text formatting can be altered, so that users can adjust text style and size as needed (One Voice, 2012a).

One Voice cautions that the first seven steps are just that—the first steps that developers should take to create an accessible app—as continued evolution of app platforms may lead to new challenges or opportunities related to accessibility.

In addition to these iOS- and app-specific guidelines, the well established and internationally influential Web Content Accessibility Guidelines (WCAG) (W3C, 2008) may also be useful in this context. To this end, Derek Featherstone, of the accessibility consulting company Simply Accessible Inc., has stated that "Even though WCAG 2.0 isn't designed to be used beyond web content, its technology agnostic nature and foundation in user needs means that we can use it as a tool for assessing iPhone/iPad apps, desktop apps and more" (Featherstone, 2010). Indeed, several of the Apple iOS accessibility guidelines closely resemble WCAG 2.0 guidance.

While there is a substantial amount of guidance available for developers wishing to create an accessible app, it is important to recognize that apps will not be accessible by default—developers must be aware of and must make efforts to meet accessibility best practices. Moreover, while Apple does recommend that developers conduct user testing prior to sending an app for publishing, apps need not meet accessibility criteria in order to be published. These observations are highly relevant to the increasing popularity of apps as educational tools. At a recent webinar hosted by EDUCAUSE, MIT accessibility and usability experts Stephani Roberts and Katherine Wahl were asked about how they, as consultants for the university, deal with the growth in apps. To this question, Wahl replied,

> We have not had to deal with that much at all. I think that that's something that we'll probably start to see a lot more of in the future. And, again, I think the only reason is that there's a lack of awareness and so people are choosing tools and downloading them and just using them . . . I think people just, at this point, are kind of the wild, wild west, in a way. They're kind of doing what they want, and I think that more guidelines will need to be structured and somehow handed down for people to follow. But they're not there yet.
>
> (Wahl, 2012)

Key questions that arise are therefore whether accessibility has been on the agenda of developers of educational apps and educators that promote the use of apps in the classroom, and how educational researchers may conduct app accessibility evaluation. In the next section of this chapter, we briefly explore the accessibility of several popular educational apps and discuss methods of app accessibility testing that researchers may engage in.

Accessibility Evaluation of Apps

Accessibility of Educational Apps

To select iOS apps with educational applications to examine, we compared lists of popular apps categorized under Education in the iTunes Store with online recommendations by educators. Interestingly, at the time of this comparison, we did not find a correlation between iTunes popularity and recommendations by the education community. We therefore chose apps to examine that we found to be frequently recommended by educators, including the Texas Computer Education Association (TCEA; http://www.tcea.org/), teachers of the Expert Knowledge Academy (http://www.ekacademy.org/), Adam Coccari of the InterAction Education blog (http://interactioneducation.com/), and recommendations submitted by educators to Appolicious (http://www.appolicious.com/); and which represent diversity both in terms of their intended learning outcomes and age of audience. Table 13.2 presents an overview of three apps that we selected for examination.

Table 13.2 Description of iOS apps selected for accessibility evaluation.

App	Description	Learning Outcomes	Age Group	Developer
BrainPOP (version 2.0.1)	Learners watch an animated video and then take a multiple-choice quiz	Promotes learning in a wide array of subjects	Suitable for Grade 3 and up	BrainPOP (creates animated educational content, including teachers, animators, writers, and parents in the process)
Math Drills Lite (version 4.1)	Learners practice math drills in addition, subtraction, multiplication, and division	Promotes development of math skills	Suitable for Grades 1 and up	Instant Interactive (software development company with focus on software for Mac and iOS devices)
Toontastic (version 1.71)	Learners create animated cartoons	Promotes development of creativity	Suitable for kindergarten and up	Launchpad Toys (multimedia experts that create digital tools for kids)

Note: All apps selected are available to download for free.

To gain an idea of whether the app developers had considered accessibility when creating the apps, we first tested all relevant built-in accessibility features with each app while working on the third-generation iPad. The results of this testing were consistent across all three of the apps: the Zoom, White-on-black, and Triple-click Home features were fully functional, however VoiceOver and Assistive Touch gestures were only partially functional. With BrainPOP and Toontastic, buttons lacked maximally helpful descriptive text for VoiceOver to read. Rather than reading a description of what a button is intended to do, either the file name of the button was read or there was no text associated with a button at all (and therefore no corresponding VoiceOver speech output). With Math Drills Lite (see Figure 13.2), the button names (followed by the label

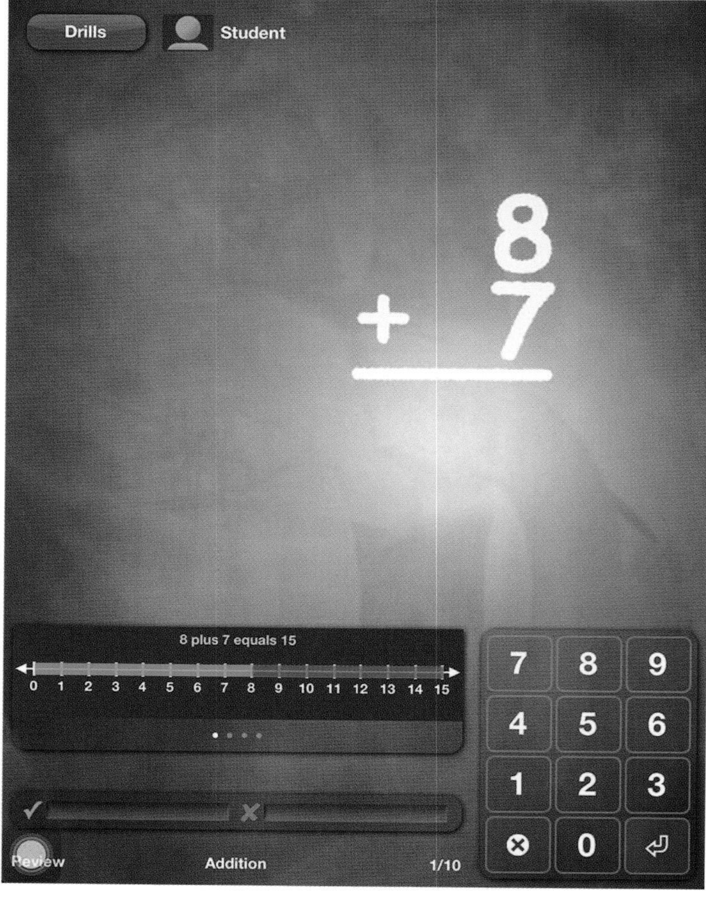

Figure 13.2
Screenshot of Math Drills Lite on a third-generation iPad.

"button") and keypad numbers are read by VoiceOver; however, the math problems themselves and a numerical scale that learners may use to help them solve the problem are ignored. Finally, with all three of the apps, only some of the Assistive Touch gestures were functional. This could be problematic for some learners with physical or motor disabilities who may find the apps physically demanding to use without specific assistive gestures.

This cursory examination of compatibility of built-in iOS accessibility features with apps that have been developed by multimedia software development companies and endorsed by educators is somewhat alarming. It is clear that the apps would not be accessible to learners who require some types of assistive technology (though it is possible that the apps may work better with additional external assistive tools). To explore the accessibility of the apps further, we referred to the One Voice recommendations described in the preceding section, and also conducted a visual inspection of the apps and applied our knowledge of needs of users with disabilities to gauge other accessible or inaccessible features of the apps.

This inspection revealed that both BrainPOP and Toontastic also exhibit exemplary accessibility features. For example, BrainPOP videos are all captioned (refer to Figure 13.3), which is a helpful feature for learners with hearing impairments, learners who are studying in a quiet place who prefer to turn off the sound, and learners for whom English is not their native language. Toontastic provides simple, step-by-step instructions to guide learners along the process of creating a cartoon, which is useful for any user first learning to use the app and is also well-suited for the young age group that the app is intended for.

It is more difficult to determine by inspection whether the apps would be fully understandable and easy-to-use by all learners of the intended age group. For example, attributes such as ease of navigation and simplicity of the user interface (which may be highly valued by learners with learning disabilities and cognitive disabilities) are difficult to objectively quantify in the absence of feedback from users. To give a specific example, the homepage for the Toontastic app (refer to Figure 13.4) is perhaps cluttered and includes moving flashing lights which could be problematic for learners who are easily distracted. However, it is difficult to discern how accessible or inaccessible an app is without soliciting feedback from actual intended users of the app. In the following section, we describe methods of accessibility evaluation that include learners as participants and which would allow researchers to better gauge overall accessibility of an app.

Learner-centered Methods of App Accessibility Evaluation

It is generally accepted in the e-learning accessibility literature that user testing is required in addition to expert testing when evaluating accessibility of learning

Figure 13.3
Screenshot of a BrainPOP video playing on a third-generation iPad.

technologies (for example, refer to Power et al., 2010). It therefore stands to reason that student users could also provide additional useful insight into app accessibility to complement accessible design efforts made by developers. An exemplary example of a learner-centered approach is the iterative development of the MyChoicePad app (http://mychoicepad.com). The app is an assistive tool for learners with learning and/or communication difficulties who wish to use signs and symbols to aid in their communication. MyChoicePad was developed in consultation with parents, students, and teachers at a United Kingdom school for students with learning disabilities. The One Voice coalition spoke to developers of the app, who described the value of feedback from learners and suggestions from parents. For example, upon observing learners working with the app, it was found that they were getting distracted with some of the touch-screen gestures that were included with app, and it was helpful to simplify the interface so that learners could focus on the function of the app (One Voice, 2012b). This example highlights the fact that sometimes "less is more" and that it is difficult to

Figure 13.4
Screenshot of the start page of the Toontastic app on a third-generation iPad.

discern how learners will actually use an app without actually observing them engage with it.

Observing and working with learners and documenting their use of an app is a method of user-centered app accessibility evaluation. This method is aligned with traditional methods of usability testing, where a user works with technology while being observed and recorded by recording software being run on a computer (if a computer-based application is being tested), and/or with a video camera (Rubin & Chisnell, 2008). Traditional usability testing methods are now frequently adapted to conduct accessibility testing by including a diverse collection of users as testers. In the context of accessibility testing of educational software, including iOS apps, this would include students with disabilities as testers.

Accessibility testing may be moderated (where the learner and researcher interact in real time) or unmoderated (such as in remote testing which takes place over the Internet, where there is no real-time learner–researcher interaction) (Bolt & Tulathimutte,

2010). Both the stage of app development and the age of the learners are factors for researchers to consider when planning app accessibility testing sessions. For example, the majority of post-secondary students that we have worked with for e-learning accessibility testing sessions have indicated that they would prefer to work with technology independently, without a researcher watching them or video camera recording them. Students have told us that they are more accustomed to working independently and feel uncomfortable knowing that someone is watching them (Owston & Kumar, 2012), which may be a common preference of adult learners in contrast to younger learners who may prefer or need more interaction with a researcher.

There are a variety of screen recording tools that can be employed on desktop computers to facilitate recording of learners' on-screen interactions and verbalizations as they work with desktop applications (e.g., Techsmith's Morae and Camtasia; http://techsmith.com). However, there is currently a need for new screen recording tools that are compatible on mobile devices to facilitate screen recording during accessibility testing sessions. To this end, we are currently developing an iOS app version of our open-source web-based accessibility testing tool OpenVULab (http://openvulab.org). Our goal is to develop an accessible app-based version of this accessibility testing tool, to facilitate moderated and unmoderated app accessibility testing.

Concluding Remarks

This is an exciting time for mobile learning from the vantage point of teaching and learning possibilities as well as new avenues for educational research. There are now so many possibilities for learners with respect to the variety of mobile learning technologies and devices from which to access the technologies. iOS devices offer exemplary out-of-the-box accessibility, as well as several highly accessible built-in apps. The ability for learners to customize the way that they interact with their iOS devices and specific apps will further enhance the value of apps for education as there is the potential for mobile learning to be highly adaptable and thus accessible for individual learners.

At the same time, with the increasing interest in and demand for mobile learning, it is paramount that app accessibility is a key priority for developers and educators. Maximal accessibility is not likely to be default feature of any app, and a multi-layered approach to proactively building accessibility into the app development and implementation process is essential. As illustrated in Figure 13.5, an approach that includes multiple stakeholders, from app developers, to learners, teachers, researchers, and parents is required in order to work towards a truly accessible mobile learning experience.

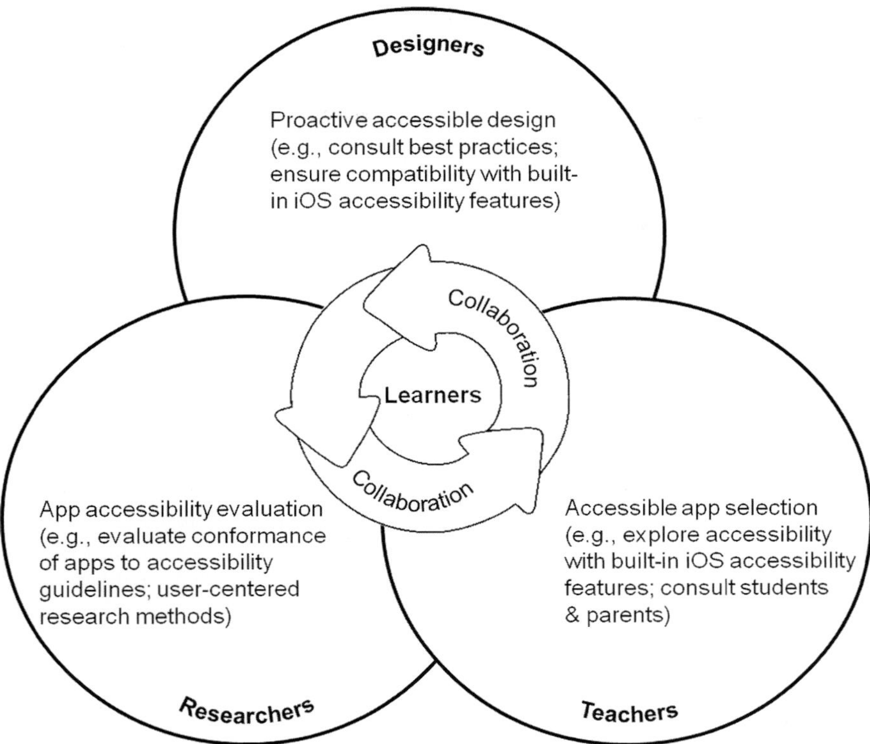

Figure 13.5
Designers, teachers, and researchers must work together and include learner-centered approaches towards ensuring that educational apps are maximally accessible for all.

References

AODA. (2011). Integrated accessibility standards. Retrieved November 12, 2012, from http://www.e-laws.gov.on.ca/html/source/regs/english/2011/elaws_src_regs_r11191_e.htm#BK15.

Apple Inc. (2011a). Accessibility overview: Developing an accessible application. Retrieved April 8, 2012, from https://developer.apple.com/library/mac/#documentation/Accessibility/Conceptual/AccessibilityMacOSX/OSXAXDeveloping/OSXAXDeveloping.html.

Apple Inc. (2011b). Accessibility overview: Testing for accessibility. Retrieved April 12, 2012, from https://developer.apple.com/library/mac/#documentation/Accessibility/Conceptual/AccessibilityMacOSX/OSXAXTesting/OSXAXTestingApps.html.

Bolt, N., & Tulathimutte, T. (2010). *Remote research*. Brooklyn, NY: Rosenfeld Media.

Featherstone, D. (2010, November 9). WCAG 2.0: Beyond web content [Web log post]. Retrieved November 12, 2012, from http://simplyaccessible.com/article/wcag2-beyond-web-content/.

Her Majesty's Stationery Office. (2001). The Special Educational Needs and Disability Act 2001, London. Retrieved November 12, 2012, from http://www.legislation.gov.uk/ukpga/2001/10/contents.

Her Majesty's Stationery Office. (2010). Equality Act 2010, London. Retrieved from http://www.legislation.gov.uk/ukpga/2010/15/section/92.

IMS Global Learning Consortium. (2004). IMS access for all metadata overview. Retrieved April 8, 2012, from http://www.imsglobal.org/accessibility/accmdv1p0/imsaccmd_oviewv1p0.html.

Joint Department of Justice and Department of Education. (2011). Frequently asked questions about the June 29, 2010, Dear Colleagues letter. Retrieved November 12, 2012, from http://www2.ed.gov/about/offices/list/ocr/docs/dcl-ebook-faq-201105.html.

Kincaid, J. M. (2009). Highlights of ADA/Section 504 decisions as applied to institutions of higher education. Retrieved March 23, 2012, from http://www.ahead.org/affiliates/utah/past-conferences/spring-2009.

National Council on Disability. (2003). People with disabilities and postsecondary education—position paper. Retrieved February 29, 2012, from http://www.ncd.gov/publications/2003/Sept152003.

OneVoice. (2012a). First seven steps to accessible mobile apps. Retrieved April 8, 2012, from http://www.onevoiceict.org/first-seven-steps-accessible-mobile-apps.

One Voice. (2012b). Moving together: Mobile apps for inclusion and assistance. Retrieved April 8, 2012, from http://www.onevoiceict.org/news/moving-together-mobile-apps-inclusion-and-assistance.

Owston, R., & Kumar. K. (2012). [E-learning in higher education: Designing for diversity]. Unpublished raw data.

Power, C., Petrie, H., Sakharov, V., & Swallow, D. (2010). Virtual learning environments: Another barrier to blended and e-learning. In *Proceedings of the 12th International Conference on Computers Helping People with Special Needs: Part I* (pp. 519–526). Berlin and Heidelberg: Springer-Verlag.

Rubin, J., & Chisnell, D. (2008). *Handbook of usability testing*. Indianapolis, IN: Wiley.

U.S. Department of Justice. (2010a). Letter of Resolution, D.J. No. 202–48–213 Princeton University. Retrieved August 11, 2011, from http://www.ada.gov/princeton.htm.

U.S. Department of Justice. (2010b). Settlement agreement between the United States of America, the National Federation of the Blind, Inc. ("NFB"), and the American Council of the Blind ("ACB"), and the Arizona Board of Regents ("ABOR"), for and on behalf of Arizona State University ("ASU"). Retrieved August 11, 2011, from http://www.ada.gov/arizona_state_university.htm.

U.S. Government Accountability Office. (2009). Higher education and disability: Education needs a coordinated approach to improve its assistance to schools in supporting students (No. GAO-10–33). Retrieved November 12, 2012, from http://161.203.16.70/products/GAO-10-33.

W3C. (2008). Web Content Accessibility Guidelines 2.0: W3C Recommendation 11 December 2008. Retrieved November 12, 2012, from http://www.w3.org/TR/WCAG20/.

Wahl, K. (2012, April 4). Accessibility and usability at MIT [Webinar transcript]. Retrieved November 12, 2012, from http://www.educause.edu/Resources/AccessibilityandUsabilityWorki/249577.

Extended Bibliography

Apple Inc. (2012). Accessibility programming guide for iOS. Available from http://developer.apple.com/library/ios/#documentation/UserExperience/Conceptual/iPhoneAccessibility/Introduction/Introduction.html.

AppleVis. (n.d.). AppleVis for vision impaired iOS users. Available from http://applevis.com/.

The Centre for Internet & Society. (2011). Making mobile phones and services accessible for persons with disabilities. Available from http://g3ict.org/resource_center/publications_and_reports/p/productCategory_books/subCat_1/id_191.

W3C. (2010). Mobile web application best practices. W3C recommendation 14 December 2010. Available from http://www.w3.org/TR/2010/REC-mwabp-20101214/.

WebAIM. (n.d.). Using VoiceOver to evaluate web accessibility. Available from http://webaim.org/articles/voiceover/.

Chapter 14
Mobile Data Tools for Teachers
A Design-based Research Pilot Study

While data use within formative feedback systems has been shown to improve teaching and learning in schools, the Data-Driven Instructional Systems (DDIS) research revealed that school data systems have at least two levels: a district-level, technologically complex summative system and a distributed, fragmented teacher-driven formative system (Halverson et al., 2007). Information was rarely exchanged across these levels and there was a lack of assessment data tools for teachers. Building upon the DDIS work, via a design-based research approach, the KidGrid iOS app research and development team collaborated with twelve intermediate school educators to design mobile data tools for teachers to use in the classroom. We found structural similarities in how teachers collected and recorded data. We also found that teachers valued the ability to customize their data collection tools. The design process highlighted the tension between district-level standardization and teacher-level customization requirements; the KidGrid app database and interface design mitigates this tension.

For Designers
Designers will learn about one method of analyzing educators' needs and identifying design opportunities in order to articulate and illustrate a rationale for the alignment of mobile learning product design decisions on structural and functional authentic tools and practices.

For Teachers
Teachers will learn about one way to seek out and forge relationships with research institutions project teams that will help support teaching and learning at the grassroots level.

For Researchers
Researchers will learn about, and hopefully improve upon, a successful implementation of design-based research. We hope this case inspires researchers to forge tighter links between academic institutions, schools, and industry via start-up business models and product-based companies.

In the next five years, mobile learning tools will haptically, visually, and aurally engineer raw student data into useful, real-time information.

Suzanne Rhodes
PhD student,
Department of Educational Psychology,
University of Wisconsin–Madison

Suzanne is a graduate student in the Educational Psychology department, Learning Sciences specialization at the University of Madison–Wisconsin. She studies how data collection and information visualization mobile tools support and influence teachers' decision making and local school data systems to improve teaching and learning in the classroom. Prior to attending UW–Madison she managed two IT development and awards programs for faculty at the University of Texas at Austin's Division of Instructional Innovation and Assessment (now Center for Teaching and Learning). Prior to UT Austin, she worked as a senior instructional designer, content strategist, project manager for Human Code, an Austin game development company, and Sapient, Inc. She holds a BS in English with a teaching certification, an MA in Curriculum and Instruction Instructional Technology, and an MS in Educational Psychology specializing in Learning Sciences.

Suzanne Rhodes

Mobile Data Tools for Teachers: A Design-based Research Pilot Study

Federal initiatives such as No Child Left Behind (NCLB) leave schools drowning in summative data, which is decontextualized from the environment where learning actually occurs. The NSF-funded Data-Driven Instructional Systems (DDIS) study investigated how schools use data to improve student learning in response to these initiatives. While data use has been shown to improve teaching and learning in schools, the DDIS researchers found that K–12 data systems have two levels: a district-sponsored, technologically complex summative system and distributed, fragmented, teacher-driven formative systems. Information was rarely exchanged between these two levels largely because

1. of a lack of attention paid to the teacher-driven formative level;
2. tools that provide teachers the kinds of formative information necessary for student learning are often left out of holistic data system designs; and
3. formative data tools that do exist are usually low-tech paper-and-pencil designs which result in data fragmentation.

These results initially encouraged us to expand the initial DDIS study and experiment with building data tools that could connect classroom-based formative systems to school and district summative systems in order to reduce data fragmentation. Our primary research question was: How do teachers collect, track, make sense of, and reflect on student classroom data and instruction? We focused on data *tools* because such technologies can support action and reflection as an integrated component of work culture (Cole, 1996; Wenger, 1998). The benefits of *networked handheld* tools, exemplified by research on handheld assessment tools in the science classroom (Roschelle et al., 2004; Roschelle, Patton, & Tatar, 2007), encouraged us to focus on formative assessment software for handheld devices. In this chapter we report on an analysis of the teacher-level formative data artifacts and strategies used by teachers in an intermediate school and the iOS app design-based research (DBR) approach for the first KidGrid pilot study user interface design.

Design-based Research

We selected a design-based research (DBR) approach for our study as "Design is central in efforts to foster learning, create usable knowledge, and advance theories of learning and teaching in complex settings . . . and for understanding how, when, and why educational innovations work in practice" (Design-Based Research Collective, 2003, p. 1). In summary, DBR is a flexible, systematic methodology applied to a real-world learning environment to develop innovative artifacts, theories, and practices via iterative, collaborative processes based on researcher–practitioner collaboration (Barab & Squire, 2004; Wang & Hannafin, 2005). Key elements of DBR include a high sensitivity to context, a formative, iterative series of approaches, and tight collaboration between practitioner and researcher teams (Barab & Squire, 2004; Brown, 1992; Collins, 1992).

Using DBR to build tools for and with teachers encourages an exchange of knowledge to refine the design over time: researchers test theories of action against practitioner experience and tool affordances; practitioners make their theories of action explicit in tool design and learn from reflecting on their practice; designers understand the environment within which practitioners work. This approach promoted the rapid assimilation of perspectives between all stakeholders in our pilot study as design-based methods surface the constraints and affordances that shape what professionals see as possible and provide an authentic opportunity for testing the effects of mobile data tools in practice.

Pilot Study Team Members

Our team was made up of a principal investigator, two graduate students, an undergraduate student programmer, the district technology coordinator, the principal, the instructional coach, two teachers from each of the three intermediate school grade levels (3 to 5), the reading specialist, the physical education teacher, and the art teacher. We selected the pilot school because of its reputation for effective data use to inform student learning and its established record of improving student test scores as discovered through the prior DDIS study. Perhaps more importantly, this school expressed a strong interest in working on a data tool design project with us because of its culture of thoughtfulness and innovation in learning environment design. We worked with the school principal and instructional coach and via purposive sampling, recruited experienced educators who had taught between ten and twenty years and were knowledgeable about both school-wide and classroom-centric data and assessment programs and processes. Many of our teacher participants served on school-wide committees such as the technology and building committees and all were keen to integrate mobile assessment technologies into their practice. Because this study was an exploratory design pilot with one goal of producing a highly usable formative data tool, we found this type of recruitment to be very advantageous since we needed practitioner expertise to drive the app design.

Data Collection and Creation

We collected data and, collaboratively with the teachers, created requirements, concepts, and design data documentation from Fall 2008 through Spring 2009.

First, we reviewed the district data systems with the instructional coach in a meeting in the school's conference room. These systems primarily consisted of summative data and testing information for students' reading, writing, and math knowledge and skills. The district systems also included the open-source student management system that contained curricula, student, and summative grading information.

We then interviewed the teachers individually (except in one case where we interviewed two team teachers at the same time) about their assessment and data practices pre- and post-app use. Teachers would often refer to and explain their assessment documents during the interviews, which helped us link teachers' reflections on data use to artifacts used in actual practice and to focus our classroom observations.

We assembled forty paper-based assessment and data collection tools and artifacts used and developed by teachers while we were observing classrooms and during the interviews. These documents included grade sheets, report cards, teacher–student meeting forms, student self-assessments, observation checklists, rubrics, and test forms. By collecting these paper-based artifacts we intended to develop a detailed typology of local assessment practices and tools in order to identify the critical junctures for which our app, KidGrid, might be used in practice and to inform the tool interface design in a way that would integrate with as well as support, stretch, and reveal data collection practices.

We observed teachers' classrooms prior to and during KidGrid use at various times during the day and week and our efforts on teachers' use of assessments and data in the classroom and wrote up detailed field notes. While observing KidGrid use, we often provided technical support and collected ideas on app improvements.

We also engaged in collaborative design meetings to determine project requirements and teachers' formative assessment needs. From all the design and research data we developed a requirements document and then a concept document, which included, initially, eight possible digital tool designs for teachers. We regularly posted all information and designs on PBWorks, an online team collaboration wiki. We reviewed this content in five design meetings to check assumptions and elicit feedback; the teachers also reviewed postings and submitted comments asynchronously. The content from the three design iterations and documents included narrative and graphical use cases, information architecture diagrams, and several versions of user interface designs.

During the design phase, our team selected the iOS platform, and the iPod Touch specifically, because of its mobile and multimedia affordances, the fact that a data plan was not required (which the grant could not fund), and because the iOS software development kit had just been released. We fully intended to take advantage of the device's anticipated audio and video capture capabilities in future iterations of our app. We, the researchers, purchased iPod Touches for the participating teachers in 2008 so they could familiarize themselves with the device, the operating system interface, and use other commercial productivity and learning apps before using KidGrid in the classroom. We distributed KidGrid mid-spring 2009 to nine of the teachers who participated in the design process.

Data Analysis

DBR analysis was an organic, collaborative, iterative part of the DBR process. We relied on the field notes, meetings, and interviews to inform initial tool requirements and identify opportunities for KidGrid use in the classroom with students. Use cases, system architecture, and interface designs were part of the collaborative design process and reviewed by all team members to check theories, assumptions, and usability. We analyzed teachers' assessment documents for functional and structural similarities and differences because we wanted to fully detail teachers' current formative feedback tool designs in order to map the technological system onto the authentic world of practice: "The system should speak the users' language, with words, phrases and concepts familiar to the user, rather than system-oriented terms" (Nielsen, 1994). Therefore, we conducted a document analysis, which is the systematic examination of documents in order to describe an instructional and assessment activity and identify needs and challenges, on the teacher-level assessment artifacts surveyed (Division of Instructional Innovation and Assessment, 2007). We initiated the analysis with Bazeley's (2007) questions of "who, what, when, why, how, how much, what for, what if, or with what results?" to determine the kinds of assessments tools teachers use and create. We then asked more detailed questions to create both structural/attribute and thematic codes such as:

- Who sponsors this document (single teacher, curriculum team, curriculum program)?
- Who uses this artifact: student, teacher(s), both?
- What are the structural features of the artifact?
- What processes and actions do the features afford and constrain functionally?
- In what ways does the teacher customize or augment the tool and the data?
- In what context is this assessment used: whole-class instruction, student–teacher conference, small-group instruction/assessment?

The document analysis yielded a richly detailed account of teachers' assessment instrument designs and practices that informed KidGrid's features and functionality and provided us with default content that we could pull from the district data systems.

Data Analysis Results

Like the initial DDIS study determined, the school was drowning in summative student performance data. We counted five different summative data sources that leaders, teachers, and staff already had to juggle. The split between school formative and summative data systems documented in prior research by Halverson, Prichett, and Watson (2007) was reflected in daily teacher practice. Teachers rarely used the summative district data tools to initiate formative classroom action. Teachers that did access these district tools (and then usually via the instructional coach who reformatted the reports "to make them easier for teachers to use") used them to acquire diagnostic information about student performance, although how that information directly influenced interventions and assessments in the classroom was unclear from the data. Nearly all the teachers stated that their assessments and instructional interventions were driven first by the curriculum and then by the needs of individual students. Teachers were thinking in terms of the curriculum, but they used student-centric data, especially behavioral, soft-skills observational data of students to change classroom instruction as part of their local formative data models. Teachers primarily "had conversations [with students]", listened to them, took notes about them on seating charts, and "checked off" students over the course of a lesson. These data would then enable them to pursue "individualized" instruction over time.

The document analysis revealed data collection practices, assessment tool, student performance symbol (e.g., grades, scores) consistencies, and variances across teachers and disciplines. The formative type of assessments were mainly locally generated and stored, and most were idiosyncratic to particular teachers. Teachers created their own assessments, like rubrics and worksheets, and would write notes about student achievement on summative assessment tools like gradesheets. Table 14.1, for example, illustrates a content sample from three teachers' gradesheets for math and literacy.

While there were surface differences in teachers' annotated information styles, there were deep content similarities: teachers chunked, contextualized, re-presented, and transformed student data. For example, teachers often use the numerical values of "3,"

Table 14.1 Sample teacher gradesheet assessment symbols

Teacher	Math	Literacy—Reading Comprehension
1	5, 4, 3, 2, 1, blank, absent	3, 2, 1
2	A, N, A/N, N/A, ½, ⅔, ¾	4/☺, 3, 2, 1/☹
3	+, √, –, blank, abs, LATE	3, 2, 1, blank, abs, –, ◤, ◥

"2," or "1" to represent levels of student understanding and performance in literacy per the district curriculum assessment model. However, they would all add annotations, expand the numerical grading scale, and layer new symbols (e.g., emoticons, hash marks) to represent contextual, personalized information on top of raw standardized score data. In this way, summative-type documents, such as whole-class grading spreadsheets, provided a default design structure and the data content was also transformed in similar structures for the functional purposes of contextual information sense making. Teachers used the assessment data symbols and tools in common district-level subject-matter curricula but they found great utility in the flexibility of their personal formative systems.

During the design process, underlying assumptions on formative data use surfaced while the team discussed needs and practices and identified common and individual goals. The teachers strongly preferred to not adopt tools, however interesting the possible functionality, that would require them to add yet another layer of data collection. However, the formative data records were not systematic *between* teachers, and the idiosyncrasies of individuals reflected the fragmentation that we, the researchers, had assumed must be overcome in order to provide a systemic organization for formative data collection. However, teachers pushed back on this approach and during one mid-design phase meeting we re-documented our mutual goals as:

- Make data collection, informal assessment of students, data analysis, and data sharing easier, faster, and better for teachers.
- Learn about and inform possible changes in teaching, learning, and the local data context.
- Provide seamless integration with current instructional practices, learning programs, and technologies.
- Standardize data categories within primary academic instructional programs.
- Allow for generic and flexible yet individualized use across multiple teaching and learning contexts.

These shared goals served to align researchers' and teachers' perspectives to better focus the design of KidGrid's content, features, and functionality for teacher adoption.

Design Results: The KidGrid App

Features and Functionality

Norman (1988) recommends that designs should follow real-world conventions. Not only does KidGrid map on to and integrate with teachers' assessment document and formative data collection system designs structurally and functionally, the interface also maps onto features and functionality found in the iPhone/iPod Touch operating system UI to minimize teachers' KidGrid learning curve and student programming time. Figure 14.1 illustrates the main menu screen for KidGrid, which is a grid of icons that represent all students in a class, akin to the structure of the iOS UI and a teacher's grid-based whole class gradesheet.

The student icons on the grid are designed to contain pictures of students. KidGrid syncs with the district's curriculum and student management system, and via wifi, downloads class lists and the district-level curriculum assessment information and grade contents on initial login. Once the information is downloaded to KidGrid the teachers can then view a graphic grid or text list view of all the students in the class(es) she teaches according to her daily schedule. In addition, teachers' can also create groups of students within each class. This class grid and assessment information is updated each time KidGrid is synced via wifi to the district system.

To enter student performance data, such as a grade for a lesson, teachers tap on a student icon on the main menu grid to view the individual student information screen (Figure 14.2), which was inspired by teachers' table-based individual student assessment tool structures. At this point, teachers can access the assessment data entry screen (Figure 14.3), enter text annotations connected to a new or previous record, and view

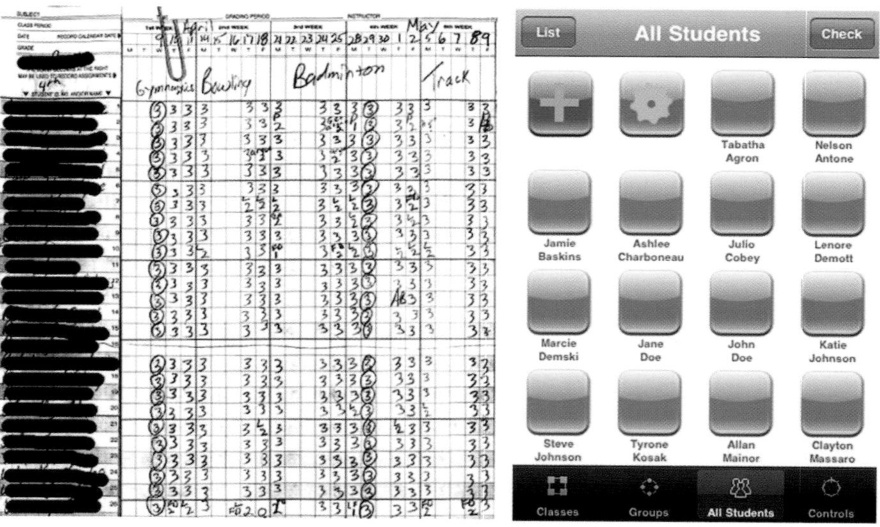

Figure 14.1
KidGrid class grid view of students.

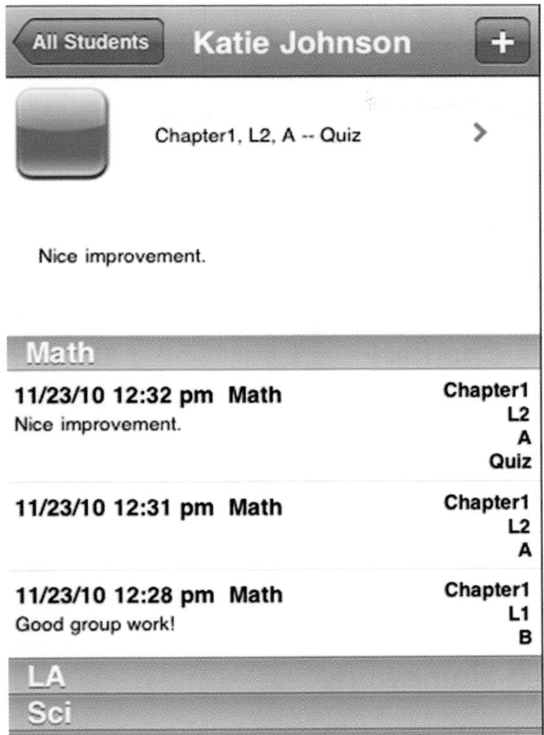

Figure 14.2
KidGrid individual student information screen.

and edit past records information in a list format. If teachers tap the screen to access the assessment data entry screen they can quickly select data from the wheels by swiping them. The top wheels typically contain curriculum benchmarks, learning unit and objectives, and codes such as grades. The bottom wheel is intended to contain common instructional feedback. After teachers select performance and feedback data or enter text annotations, the data are time-stamped and saved in list format for each student by class and subject for tracking student progress. The saved data can be edited any time. Teachers can also quickly check off and batch assess students in the class or group grid view by using the "check off" feature (Figure 14.4), tapping on multiple student icons to select them, then selecting wheel assessment data. Teachers remove checkmarks from the icons by shaking the iPod Touch or tapping on the icons individually.

When teachers sync KidGrid, all collected data uploads securely to a database on a local device and district server. They may also email all or the most recent data entered about

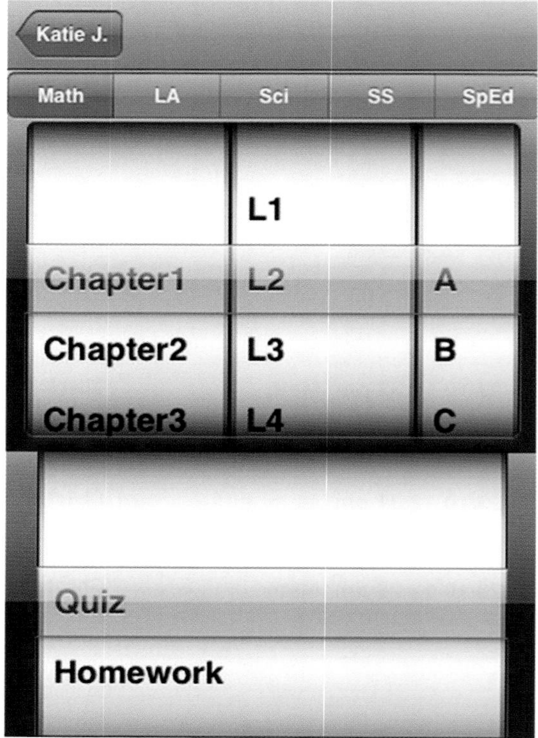

Figure 14.3
KidGrid assessment data entry screen.

students in a basic tab-delimited text format report to themselves, other teachers, and parents.

The wheel data are curriculum-driven per the district and school instructional programs. However, these wheels can be customized by each teacher individually (Figure 14.5). Teachers can add and delete any number of lesson and assessment information including symbols and numerical values that they use to record student performance on this screen.

Narrative Use Case

Ms. Jansen is teaching a reading unit focused on students' "Making connections." She rotates to each student during reading time for individual assessment and consultations and asks them to describe connections between themes of the story to their own lives.

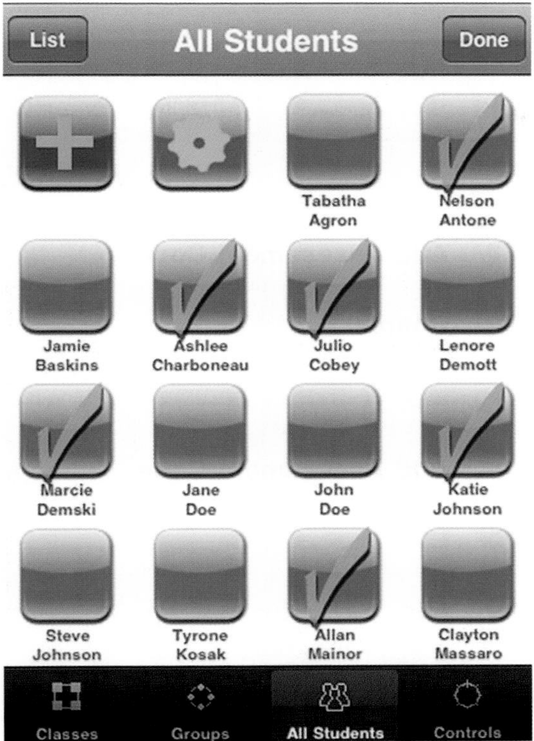

Figure 14.4
KidGrid check feature for batch data collection.

Using KidGrid, Ms. Jansen selects the "Making connections" benchmark item from the top, first column wheel and then a performance code of "2" in the top right column wheel if the student described a moderately linked connection. Ms. Jansen then selects "Suggestion" from the bottom formative feedback wheel to track that she provided a suggestion as to how the student might make a stronger connection following up by adding text annotations about questions she asked as well as student responses. Thus, Ms. Jansen has collected data about a formative teacher–student interaction, a concrete teaching–learning experience beyond a mere grade, and that data is saved to a database using no more than three taps of her finger to navigate. Ms. Jansen reviews the data she entered for the student and the instructional feedback she provided and compares that data with other information she entered previously to reflect on the student's learning, her instructional practices, and her instruction over time. She then applies the data

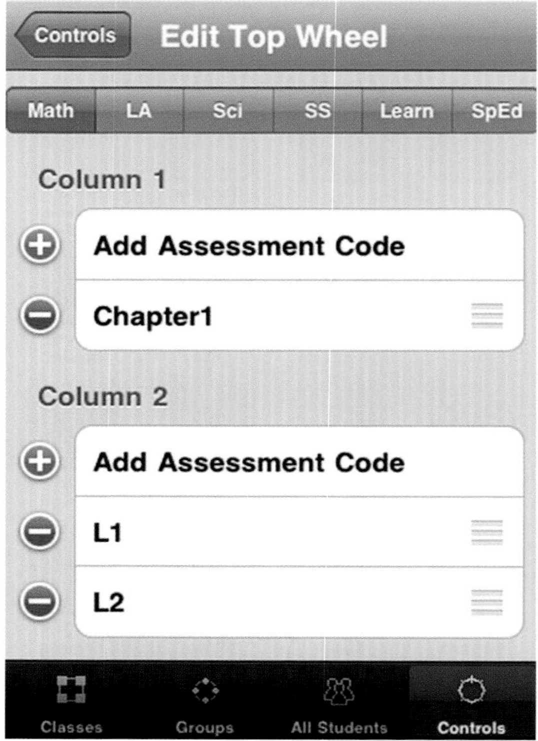

Figure 14.5
KidGrid assessment data editing screen.

to plan her next lesson and future individual consultation sessions with the student. Ms. Jansen can also bring a KidGrid-generated report to a meeting with the student's parent or other educators in her local school community to collaboratively plan and reflect on practice, student learning, and curricula.

Conclusions

The fragmentation of the teacher-level data within a school can be interpreted as an important feature of the environment rather than a bug; data tools should not necessarily reduce the fragmentation at the classroom level but rather integrate individual practices structurally and functionally within the holistic organizational data system of the larger school and district community. Therefore, a primary challenge for educators' mobile data app designers is to address the tension between standardization and

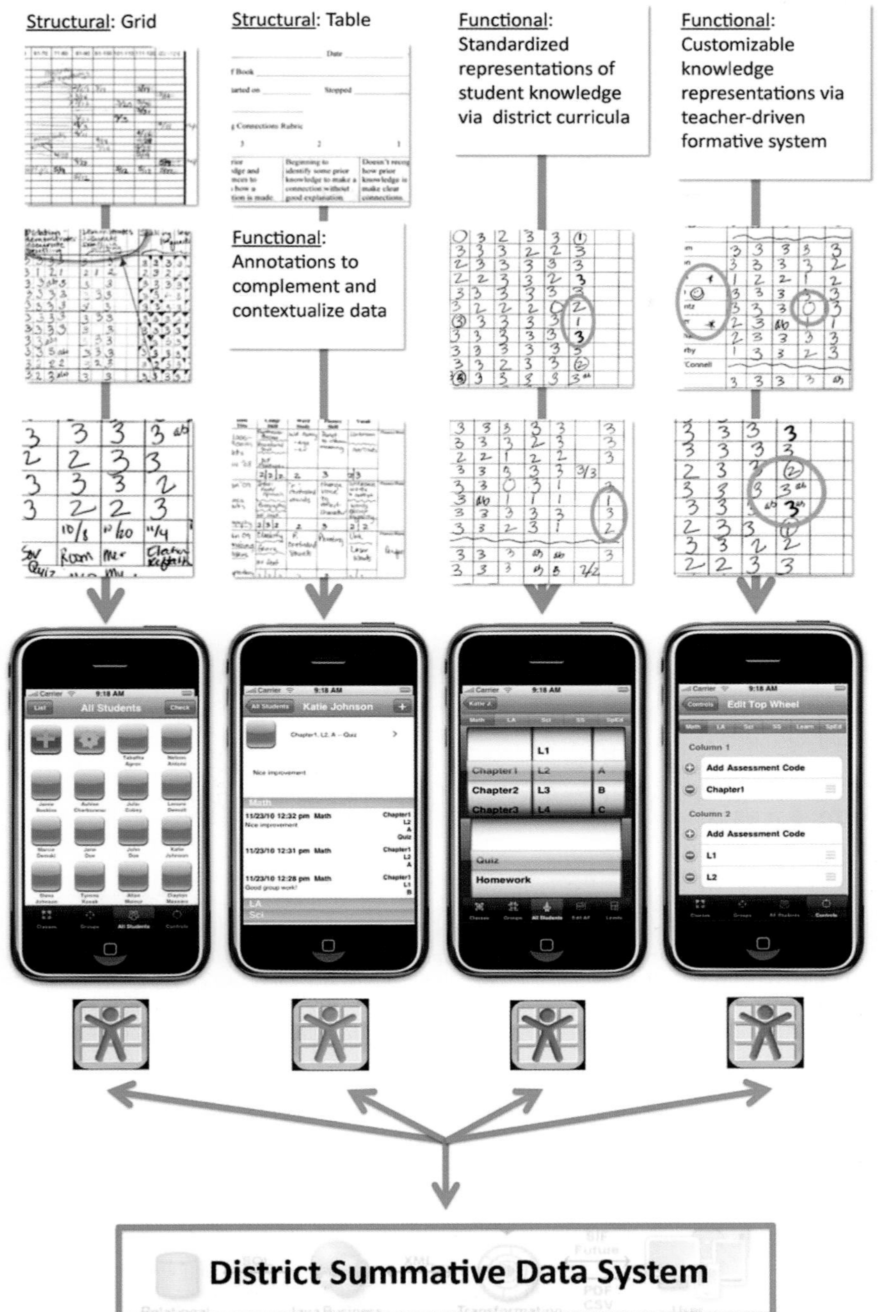

Figure 14.6

The holistic system design and the structural and functional mapping of KidGrid's design onto teachers' formative data systems.

customization of tools to support educators' formative activities in practice. This first pilot study resulted in three formative data systems app design conclusions:

1. While teachers' personal formative feedback systems are often paper based, idiosyncratic, and removed from district systems, they are situated vertically in the district curricula. So,
2. Teachers' data tools should be connected to district systems, to push and pull data vertically, and aggregate it, to afford data actuation for teachers and reporting to district and parent stakeholders. However,
3. Data collection apps should support the deep structural and functional similarities that are present across teachers' personalized systems.

A stand-alone version of KidGrid, without the backend components that hook into district databases, is available on Apple's iTunes App Store.

Acknowledgments

Dr. Richard Halverson, DDIS and KidGrid Principal Investigator, University of Wisconsin–Madison; National Science Foundation Grant #0347030; Wisconsin Center for Educational Research.

References

Barab, S. & Squire, K. (Eds.). (2004). Design-based research: Putting a stake in the ground. *The Journal of the Learning Sciences, 13*(1), 1–14.

Bazeley, P. (2007). *Qualitative data analysis with NVIVO*. Thousand Oaks, CA: Sage.

Brown, A. L. (1992). Design experiments: Theoretical and methodological challenges in creating complex interventions in classroom settings. *The Journal of the Learning Sciences, 2*(2), 141–178.

Cole, M. (1996). *Cultural psychology: A once and future discipline*. Boston: The Belknap Press of Harvard University Press.

Collins, A. (1992). Towards a design science of education. In E. Scanlon & T. O'Shea (Eds.), *New directions in educational technology* (pp. 15–22). Berlin: Springer.

Design-Based Research Collective. (2003). Design-based research: An emerging paradigm for educational inquiry. *Educational Researcher*, 32, 5–8.

Division of Instructional Innovation and Assessment. (2007). Document analysis. *IAR: Instructional Assessment Resources*. Retrieved September, 2008, from http://www.utexas.edu/academic/diia/assessment/iar/teaching/plan/method/doc-analysis.php.

Halverson, R., Grigg, J., Prichett, R., & Thomas, C. (2007). The new instructional leadership: Creating data-driven instructional systems in schools. *Journal of School Leadership, 17*(2), 159–194.

Halverson, R., Prichett, R., & Watson, J., (2007). Formative feedback systems and the new instructional leadership (WCER Working Paper No. 2007–7). Madison: University of Wisconsin–Madison, Wisconsin Center for Education Research. Retrieved July, 2010, from http://ddis.wceruw.org/resources.htm.

Nielsen, J. (1994). Heuristic evaluation. In J. Nielsen and R. L. Mack (Eds.), *Usability inspection methods* (pp. 25–62). New York: John Wiley & Sons.

Norman, D. N. (1988). *The design of everyday things.* New York: Doubleday.

Roschelle, J., Patton, C., & Tatar, D. (2007). Designing networked handheld devices to enhance school learning. In M. Zelkowitz (Ed.), *Advances in computers, 70* (pp. 1–60). Burlington, MA: Academic Press.

Roschelle, J., Penuel, W. R., Yarnall, L., & Tatar, D. (2004). Handheld tools that "informate" assessment of student learning in science: A requirements analysis. In *Proceedings of the 2nd IEEE International Workshop on Wireless and Mobile Technologies in Education,* Washington, DC, March 23–25 (p. 149). WMTE: IEEE Computer Society.

Wang, F., & Hannafin, M. J. (2005). Design-based research and technology-enhanced learning environments. *Educational Technology Research and Development, 53*(4), 5–23.

Wenger, E. (1998). *Communities of practice: Learning, meaning, and identity*. Cambridge, UK: Cambridge University Press.

Chapter 15
iPad-Didactics—Didactical Designs for iPad-classrooms
Experiences from Danish Schools and a Swedish University

The iPad device came to the European market as recently as March 2010 but schools in Scandinavia have already implemented these devices and teachers are very enthusiastic to use iPads. This research explores teaching in iPad-classrooms. Specifically, how do teachers in Danish schools use iPads in their classrooms and for what purposes? For example, is the iPad only a textbook substitute or do the teachers create new didactical approaches, and if so, which ones? Classroom observations and qualitative data were collected in Odder municipality (Denmark) where 200 teachers and 2,000 students aged six to sixteen use iPads in classrooms. Based on the theoretical framework "iPad-Didactics," we describe two ways in which the iPad can be used in classrooms that could be helpful to others engaged in implementing iPads, in designing teaching and learning in teacher education, and in the use of mobile devices and educational apps in classrooms. In addition, the results show new forms of pedagogical concepts for education like transformative learning and complex learning supported by mobile ICT and interactive media and learning (IML).

For Designers

Designers will learn how to implement iPads into didactical designs to foster student learning. There is no single solution but there are several possibilities. The examples of personalized and peer-reflective learning illustrate what a useful design might be. The designs by the teachers stress a shift (a) from information consumption to a focus on action, and (b) in the social relations to foster reflections by using different apps. iPad-Didactics provides a framework for designing iPad-classrooms.

For Teachers

Teachers will learn how to design "learning to be creative" focused on action in which the students produce something. The examples of personalized and peer-reflective learning illustrate how the iPads can be used for teaching and learning beyond reproducing existing knowledge. Such an approach enables the learner to expand her thinking beyond a consumption behavior to an active agent of creating new knowledge.

For Researchers

Researchers will learn that iPads can facilitate meaningful learning. The examples of personalized and peer-reflective learning illustrate useful designs for teaching and learning. The central factors are (a) the changes made by the teachers from information consumption to knowledge co-construction, and (b) the newly designed collaborative reflections between student–student as well as teacher–student by using iPads. iPad-Didactics provides a framework for studying further iPad-classrooms.

In five years, the majority won't have iPad-Didactics; two sides of a coin: creative teaching increased; big data analytics used to control students?

Dr. Isa Jahnke
Professor,
Department of Applied Educational Science,
Umea University, Sweden

Dr. Swapna Kumar
Clinical Assistant Professor,
College of Education,
University of Florida

Dr. Isa Jahnke is a professor in ICT, Media and Learning at the Department of Applied Educational Sciences, Umea University, Sweden. She studied social sciences, was a PhD student at Informatics & Society, Dortmund University, Germany; worked as post-doctoral student at the Department of Information and Technology Management, University of Bochum. In 2007, she visited the Center for Lifelong Learning, University of Colorado at Boulder. She was an assistant professor at the Center for Research on Higher Education and

Faculty Development. She studies sociotechnical approaches focused on creativity and didactical designs.

Dr. Swapna Kumar is a clinical assistant professor in the School of Teaching and Learning, University of Florida, USA. She coordinates the online Ed.D. in Educational Technology and her current teaching and research focus on blended learning, online pedagogy, emerging technologies/mobile devices in education, and online communities. Her prior experiences include technology integration, teacher professional development, faculty development and training evaluation.

iPad-Didactics—Didactical Designs for iPad-classrooms: Experiences from Danish Schools and a Swedish University

The omnipresence of digital devices in our environment has led to an increased interest in ubiquitous computing in education in the last decade. Educational institutions have invested in one-to-one laptop programs and programs that integrate handheld devices such as PDAs, the iPod Touch, MP3 players and cell phones. For example, the magazine Computersweden.idg.se Sweden reported that Kungsbacka bought 1800 iPads (http://computersweden.idg.se/2.2683/1.425430/ipadvag-i-skolan, Jan. 2012) and Härryda in Sweden around 500 devices.

Small screen size, a challenge that often prevented educators from using handheld devices (Song, 2008), was resolved with the advent of the iPad, released in 2010 by Apple Inc. The iPad integrates several features of both laptops and handheld devices and unleashed a multitude of applications on the market, opening up unforeseen opportunities for teaching and learning. Prior research in different subject areas such as math, science and social studies about previous handheld devices in K–12 education (Dixon, 2007; Lary, 2004; Roschelle et al., 2005; Royer & Royer, 2004; Vess, 2006) and reports of their potential for improving student engagement (Ng & Nicholas, 2009) and achievement (Clements & Sarama, 2003; Naismith et al., 2005; Staudt, 2005) have led to huge investments in iPads for schools, despite a scarcity of empirical research about their potential for teaching and learning.

This research is an attempt to study the potential of these devices for teaching and learning by exploring how teachers are using their new iPads in classrooms. We present the initial results of classroom observations and interviews in thirteen iPad classrooms in Danish schools with an aim to provide empirical evidence for how iPads can be integrated in teaching. The didactical designs and teaching strategies reported here will be of use to all educators and administrators engaged in the use of iPads for teaching and learning.

Context of the Research

In 2011, researchers at the IML (Interactive Media and Learning) group at Umeå University, Sweden bought iPads for approximately twenty-five instructors and researchers in teacher education with the aim of exploring the benefits and limitations of iPads for teaching and learning. Simultaneously, the Department of Applied Educational Science (Tillämpad utbildningsvetenskap, TUV) decided to equip preschool university teachers (early childhood teacher education professors in the United States) and student teachers (in early childhood education) with iPads by September 2012. The teachers and student teachers were to receive professional development in using iPads from the IML group. In the context of these two projects, the IML group met with Apple Northern Europe and learned during this meeting of the Odder project in Denmark. The Odder municipality in Denmark, which has a population of around 20,000, decided to implement iPads in all of their seven schools in 2011. All the teachers (approximately 200) received iPads in October 2011, followed by all the students (c. 2,000) in January 2012. Following several Skype conferences, the IML group decided to visit Odder for five days to understand how teachers there were using iPads in their classrooms.

Initial use of the iPad at the Swedish university had already led to some preliminary reflections on the use of iPads. In addition to the capabilities and applications available, new mobile devices like iPhones or iPads[1] created a new quality of online presence that we call "omnipresent online presence" (Jahnke et al., 2012, p. 152). The access to knowledge has changed, as has students' ability to communicate anytime and at any place. With the iPad this change has become visible. For example, when students use iPads, there is a change in the discussion cultures of daily-life groups: when facts are discussed at least one person takes her smartphone and "Googles" the information. New communication patterns emerge. These aspects of iPads, while presenting tremendous potential for teaching and learning, also pose several challenges to the ways in which teachers can integrate them into current didactical situations. Another important insight was that iPad use depends on the teacher and his/her understanding of technology and iPads.

Theoretical Framework: Digital Didactical Designs

Knowledge construction and collaborative learning are defined as a form of co-creation of new knowledge among a group of people that is "an active process of constructing rather than acquiring knowledge" (Duffy & Cunningham, 1996, p. 171). These areas of focus for teachers and researchers in education represent a shift from teaching to learning (Barr & Tagg, 1995). International communities on instructions and excellence in teaching and learning (e.g., POD/USA http://www.podnetwork.org and SEDA/UK http://www.seda.ac.uk, two professional organizations for academic workers in HE and K12) confirm that active learning is one of the best ways to learn; those learners develop a deeper understanding and through reflection several other skills like critical thinking.

1 iPads are just one form of mobile devices also known as small multi-touchpads. For example, Android devices are also available. We focus here on iPads, and do not mix different devices, only with the aim to reduce the complexity of the study design. Different devices may cause different technical problems for schools. The pros and cons of Androids and iPads are discussed elsewhere.

"Active" refers to the need for learners to become active agents within the learning process, e.g., "prosumers" (not consumers only). The goal is for didactical designs to integrate those possibilities and opportunities to enable collaborative learning (Stahl, 2006). Active learners expand their thinking beyond consumptive behavior at schools and beyond the traditional reproduction of existing knowledge. Laurillard (2007) specifically discusses different pedagogical forms of mobile learning from Kolb's learning cycle (1984), wherein learning includes concrete experience, reflective observation, abstract conceptualization, and active experimentation by learners.

The term "didactical design" follows from the German concept of *Didaktik* by Klafki (1963, 1997) and is inspired by Hudson (2008) and Fink (2003) who stress the differences of teaching concepts and learning activities and call them designs for teaching and designs for learning. From that point of view, a didactical design includes teaching objectives, the *plan how to* achieve those objectives in such a way that the learners are able to develop competencies and skills that the teachers have in mind, and different forms of feedback and assessment to assess the learning progress of the students (Biggs & Tang, 2007). According to Bergström (2012), process-based assessment is the most effective method to foster learning. The difference from an instructional design is that didactical designs also include the design of the social relations like teacher–student and student–student (Bergström, 2012).

The *digital* didactical design is the advanced model that integrates educational technology and educational apps. To each of the four design levels the design question is, how

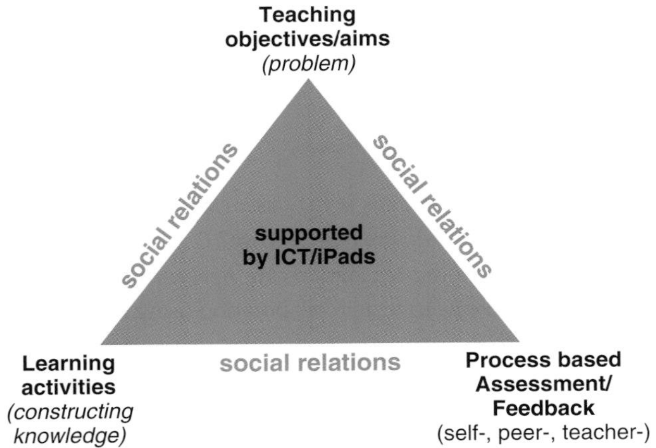

Figure 15.1
Digital didactical design.

can the iPad support such an activity? The implementation of new technology in education means to rethink the existing underlying didactical concepts and communication patterns (Jahnke, 2010, 2011). ICT (information and communication technologies) can play an important role in making learning visible. In two case studies, Mårell-Olsson and Hudson (2008) illustrate different types of digital portfolios (traditional online applications for stationary computers or laptops) in which students develop the ability to "collect, organize, interpret and reflect on their own individual learning and practice and become more active and creative in the development of knowledge" (p. 73).

This research assumes that the iPad by itself does not lead to a change of teaching or learning experiences in the classroom. It is possible (a) that traditional teaching patterns will be reinforced using the new technology (Song, 2007); (b) that the classroom will be changed into a creative learning experience; or (c) that the teacher applies new forms of five-minute-didactics or other types of microlearning (Bruck & Lindner, 2008); or (d) that something else happens. A qualitative approach was used to explore how teachers used the iPads in classrooms in Odder, Denmark. The overall aim of this study was to examine how the teachers use iPads in their classrooms, and to what extent the teachers design an active and collaborative learning experience for their students. The results contribute to the research on teaching practices enhanced by mobile devices. The goal is the development of a theoretical framework titled "iPad-Didactics"—closely connected to the work of teachers and adapted for the use of mobile devices in schools that can even function as scientific input for rethinking the teacher education programs at universities, to develop appropriate didactical workshops for teachers and to implement mobile devices in the classrooms of tomorrow.

Research Questions

RQ 1: *For what purpose* do the teachers use the iPads? What are their didactical designs (what do they have in mind)? What do they expect regarding the learning outcomes of their students?

RQ 2: How do the teachers *use the iPads in the classrooms*? For example, is the iPad only a textbook substitute? What apps do the teachers use? Do the teachers apply traditional communication patterns or do the teachers create new forms of communication and sociotechnical–didactical designs to foster collaboration using iPads?

Methods

The research questions were studied using qualitative methods, namely, classroom observations and teacher interviews, as part of a larger study of iPads in Danish schools and a Swedish university. In April 2012, thirteen classroom observations (forty-five to ninety minutes each) and ten interviews (c. sixty minutes each) were conducted in five schools in Odder municipality in Denmark. The teaching subjects ranged from language/Danish, math and English, art to physics. The classes ranged from preschool to ninth grade with class sizes of fourteen to twenty-five students. Classroom observations were conducted in the morning and the interviews after lunch.

The classroom observations were based on the didactical triangle design teaching aims, learning activities, different forms of feedback/ assessment; and the role of the iPads (see Figure 15.1). The observation sheet included: (1) a description of the classroom; (2) how the iPads are used/applied in the classroom; (3) communication patterns; (4) collaboration and/or forms of cooperative learning; (5) feedback and assessment (e.g., process based, when, how); (6) whether the observer can see creative learning activities; (7) special skills of the teacher; (8) what seems to be good/bad in relation to what; (9) anything else. The classroom observations were conducted by two to five researchers who took notes, photos, and video recordings with teacher permission.

The interview guide was divided into five parts and contained twelve questions in the following areas: (1) background (age, gender, years as teacher, teaching subjects; first "thought" about implementing iPads); (2) designs for teaching and designs for learning when using iPads; (3) creativity and collaboration using iPads; (4) skills and support; and (5) magic wizard offers three wishes (what would you wish for?). The interviews were conducted by a total of three researchers and recorded.

Data from the observations and interviews were first analyzed according to each classroom taught by a teacher (i.e. the observations and interviews for each case were combined) and then open coded (Bryman, 2008; Strauss & Corbin, 1990). This paper presents a preliminary analysis from two classrooms that serve as initial insight into how two teachers used iPads in their classrooms.

Results

The results of classroom observations in two classrooms and interviews with teachers in those two classrooms are presented here as examples of peer-reflective learning and personalized learning using an iPad.

Peer-reflective Learning

The first classroom described here was a seventh grade with twenty-one students (nine female, twelve male) about fourteen years old and a female teacher. The class took place from 8:45 until 9:30am. The subject was Danish and the objective was to improve writing skills in Danish, the mother tongue of the students. The learning activity required students to write about something from their childhood and to conduct peer reviews of their writing skills. The following learning activities occurred in the class:

- Individual assignment: The students used their iPads (each student had one) to write a story about something that happened in their childhood using the application Pages in their iPads and parts of it were copied into Facebook to get feedback from their peers as well as the teacher.
- Peer feedback: Students commented on the stories of the others by using the functionality of the "comment" button in Facebook and by using items from a "guide" provided for the reviews by the teacher. In the interview, the teacher asserted that such a list is helpful for students to reflect on their own story and how it is written, as well as on the stories of their peers. She showed the students the guided list and the plan for the assignments at the beginning so that students understood how to respond to their peers' texts.
- In the next phase, the teacher used the Smartboard to present some of the stories that were in Facebook and peer reviews were also shared face to face in the classroom.
- As a last step, the students revised their first draft in the Pages app based on the comments of the others and uploaded their final version into an account at Dropbox using the Dropbox app (http://dropbox.com).

In this example of a peer-reflective learning approach, the Pages app was used to write the stories, and the Facebook app was used to form groups and to give peer feedback online within small groups. Classroom observations reported that the "learning environment was relaxed and very informal." The learning outcomes that were assessed in this case are the stories created by the students that were viewed as products of the student learning process. The final products were uploaded into folders in the students' Intranet. Such a student Intranet is part of a broader personal learning environment where the students collect all their learning products to document their learning progress. This is a process of "pedagogical documentation" that is part of all schools in Scandinavia.

In terms of what motivated the didactical design in this case, the teacher stated during the interview that "it is important to challenge the pupils"; however, she provided scaffolding throughout the learning process. She provided students with a guided list for reviews and gave online feedback in Facebook as well as face to face during the lesson. The process-based assessment was both asynchronous and synchronous to support the learners. The assessment activities were also part of the scaffolding of the learning process.

This example showed that traditional teacher–student communication, which can be summarized as "teacher asks, student answers, teacher says correct or not correct," can blur with the use of the iPad in the classroom. Although the teacher acted as a mentor to the students in the writing process, she also understood that students can be experts in certain fields. The classroom observations revealed that the teacher asked her students if she had issues with Facebook or with iPads. She explained during the interview, "I ask my pupils when it comes to technical issues or Facebook problems; they know it better than me."

Personalized Learning

The second case was a ninth-grade physics classroom with a male teacher and fifteen students (eight female, seven male) from 8:00 to 9:30am. The main learning activity for the students was to design new experiments based on the prior knowledge the students gained from previous classes. The objective was to apply the recently learned knowledge and to show the teacher the learning outcome in the field of sound, light, magnetism, electricity and chemistry. The teacher's instruction to the students was: "Please, show me something essential about sound or light, and create a new experiment." He also asked them to document their process of planning and conducting the experiment.

While some students gathered and built groups and started to work on the assignment, one group of two students were not sure how to start. The teacher thus created a new assignment for their personal needs but asking them to create a joint mindmap using the app Popplet. They brainstormed to collect their knowledge into one mindmap to identify their personal gaps in knowledge. That gap then served as the starting point to plan the experiment.

The other groups had some ideas already and started with the experiment without making a mindmap. In one group there were up to seven students who worked together, in other groups there were three students. As part of their experiment, the students used the camera and video recording features in the iPad, and took photos and made podcasts. They also podcast the preparation of the experiment in case the experiment failed, to show the teacher what they had done up to that point and to analyze why the experiment failed. iPads were thus used by the students to document the process of creating the experiment, in addition to the following ways in which they used them:

- information searches (in Google/Bing, YouTube, etc.)
- the Textbook app (an app that has a lot of textbooks)
- Pro Tuner (a tuning app)
- uploading documentation (Dropbox app).

In this case, the students got the opportunity to reflect on their existing knowledge and to create new knowledge. The assessment was process based and part of the learning process because the teacher could gauge how much the students had understood from previous lessons. The teacher said in the interview that followed, "How do I know when the students have learnt something? When they can apply it to the real world." The teacher also immediately checked the results of the experiment in the class and gave feedback. Students then shared the results in Dropbox and got feedback from their peers.

One classroom observer described the feeling in the classroom "somewhat chaotic, but in a good way." He stated that, "some teachers would not have liked the informal way of doing teaching." However, the observers noted that all students were engaged in the task and looked genuinely interested in their experiments. The main communication in this classroom was among the students. This corresponded to the teacher's statement during the interview that he strongly focused on "informal teaching," where he would rather be in the background and let the students experiment. He liked to foster a role change, where students become the person who teaches other students, and he acts like a process mentor who supports the personal learning needs of the students instead of telling them the facts. One example of this during classroom observations: the teacher asked the students to first present their idea for a new experiment on a blank sheet of paper and, so, the students themselves got a "aha" effect; they suddenly saw that the idea was not clear enough and why the experiment went wrong.

The teacher also stated that this assignment was based on his philosophy of students "learning by mistakes." He said his designs for learning are based on the idea that students "test their theories through experiments within a given field (e.g., sound, light) and translate it, to learn how it works in reality." He believed that the iPad is a good tool for teaching and learning:

> Before the iPads were launched, there was a lack of access to knowledge. Before, those students who had a computer were in front; now all have the same access to knowledge; now, everyone is equal; everybody has the same resources.

Discussion–iPad-Didactics

This chapter reports on an initial analysis of two cases from a larger study on the use of iPads by teachers in K–9 classrooms in Odder, Denmark. While the small sample limits the generalizability of our findings, the data provide useful insight into the ways in which iPads can be used for learner-centered, collaborative learning in a classroom. The two teachers depicted here were chosen because they were classified as "early adopters" (Rogers, 2003) and were likely to be implementers of digital didactical designs in their classrooms. Their strategies might be useful to others beginning to use iPads and researchers or educators engaged in studying iPad integration in classrooms. The cases reported here are one component of a pilot study and further interviews and classroom observations are planned with teachers who belong to the other groups identified by Rogers (2003).

Both the cases presented here represent active learning where there was a focus on action and a focus on students "to produce something." The teachers' design for teaching and their design for learning included active student participation, student engagement, and student motivation by "doing" something. The students produced something and while doing so, they reflected and learned, reflection research that points to a positive relationship between being active and a deeper learning outcome (Chapman, 2003).

The didactical designs by the two teachers were process oriented rather than product oriented. The teachers did not focus only on outcomes or exams/test and did not expect students to reproduce the facts. Both the teachers had a learner-centered approach—they allowed their students to learn by making mistakes, they wanted to challenge their students, and yet they scaffolded the learning process by providing feedback and personalizing the learning experience for students who struggled. In both examples the iPad served as a "booster" to foster learning as a *process*. In both the cases, the iPad was integrated into a digital didactical design because in addition to active learning and a process orientation, the didactical design included both teacher–student and student–student interaction and feedback.

An analysis of the other cases in the larger study will provide more insight into the ways in which teachers used the iPad and whether these were also digital didactical designs. Given that the teachers in these two cases were early adopters of the iPad as a classroom technology, a further area of research is whether they previously used similar designs with other technologies or whether the iPad was used differently from other technologies. One challenge, a teacher told us, within the iPad project is "to know when to shut off the iPad; when not to use the iPad". This raises the question—for what purposes is each kind of method or tool appropriate, and more importantly, how do the teachers decide (and why) what to use when?

Conclusion

According to this study, the digital didactical design perspective reflects the following:

- Using the iPad, the design for teaching is shifting to more "informal teaching" where the teacher is in the background and challenges the students; s/he catches them if they fall, for instance, when they make mistakes or are not satisfied with themselves.

- Adopting the iPad, the design for learning is shifting to a "focus on action" where the social relations among the peers as well as the teacher–student relation is integrated in the designs for a situation that is "unknown" (Bergström, 2012).
- Interesting here was that the teacher used the apps in ways other than originally intended. A characteristic of an iPad-Didactics teacher is that s/he is able to adopt the technology in an advanced way.

When we began this research we raised the question of whether the iPad serves as a textbook substitute. The examples showed that that was not the case. Instead, the teachers created new didactical approaches where they transformed their traditional classrooms into a complex learning experience for their students; that can be summarized as approaches for "learning to be creative" (Figure 15.2). The iPads were used for a learning experience beyond reproducing existing knowledge. Such an approach enables the learner to expand her thinking beyond a consumption behavior to an active co-construction of knowledge. There is no single solution but there are some clues. The explicit designs made by the teachers stress (a) a shift from information consumption to a focus on action; (b) a shift to use the iPads as booster to intensify learning as a process; and (c) a shift of designing social relations to foster collaborative reflections between

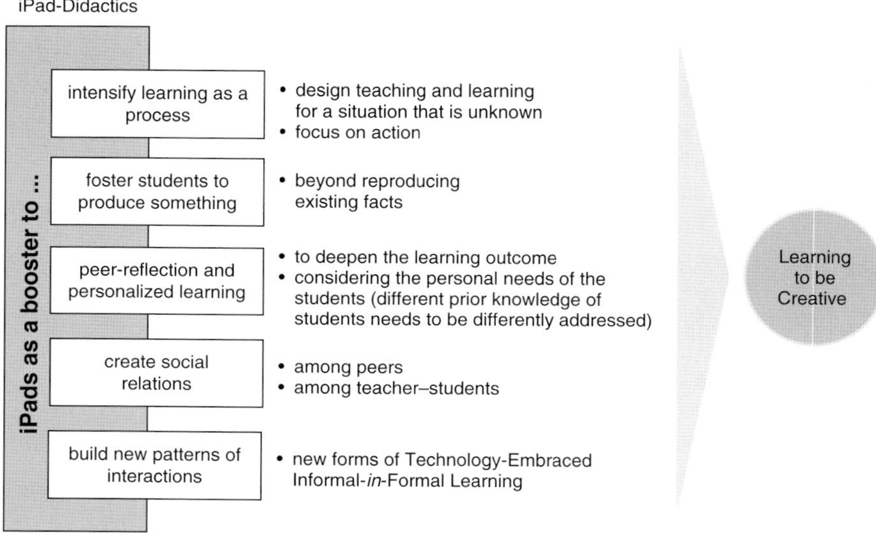

Figure 15.2
iPad-Didactics.

student–student as well as teacher–student by using different apps. We will use the iPad-Didactics as a framework for studying further iPad-classrooms.

Acknowledgements

We thank Lise Gammelby very much, the schools, the school leaders, head teachers as well as all teachers in Odder municipality (Denmark), who do an amazing teaching job, for supporting the research project. We would also like to thank Lars Norqvist, Andreas Olsson, Krister Lindwall, and Peter Vinnervik at Umeå University for their participation and work in the Odder project as well as their very wonderful hints, questions, comments, and ideas.

References

Barr, R. B., & Tagg, J. (1995). From teaching to learning: A new paradigm for undergraduate education. *Change Magazine, 27*(6), 12–25.

Bergström, P. (2012). *Designing for the unknown: Didactical design for process-based assessment in technology-rich learning environments*. Umeå University Press.

Biggs, J., & Tang, C. (2007). *Teaching for quality learning at university* (3rd edition). New York: Auflage.

Bruck, P., & Lindner, M. (Eds.). (2008). *Microlearning and capacity building: Proceedings of the 4th International Microlearning 2008 Conference*. Innsbruck: Innsbruck University Press.

Bryman, A. (2008). *Social research methods* (3rd edition). New York: Oxford University Press.

Chapman, E. (2003). Alternative approaches to assessing student engagement rates. *Practical Assessment, Research & Evaluation, 8*(13). Retrieved October 22, 2012, from http://PAREonline.net/getvn.asp?v=8&n=13.

Clements, D. H., & Sarama, J. (2003). Young children and technology: What does the research say? *Young Children, 58*, 34–40.

Dixon, A. (2007). Finding your way: GPS and geocaching. *Learning and Leading with Technology, 34*(8), 29–31.

Duffy, T. M., & Cunningham, D. J. (1996). Constructivism: Implications for the design and delivery of instruction. In D. H. Jonassen (Ed.), *Handbook of research for educational communications and technology* (pp. 170–198). New York: Simon & Schuster Macmillan.

Fink, D. L. (2003). Integrated course design. Idea paper #42. Idea Center, Kansas.

Hudson, B. (2008). A didactical design perspective on teacher presence in an international online learning community. *Journal of Research in Teacher Education, 15*(3–4), 93–112.

Jahnke, I. (2010). Dynamics of social roles in a knowledge management community. In *Computers in Human Behavior, 26*(4), 533–546.

Jahnke, I. (2011). How to foster creativity in technology enhanced learning. In B. White, I. King, & Ph. Tsang (Eds.), *Social media tools and platforms in learning environments* (pp. 95–116). New York: Springer.

Jahnke, I., Bergström, P., Lindwall, L., Mårell-Olsson, E., Olsson, A., Paulsson, F., & Vinnervik, P. (2012). Understanding, reflecting and designing learning spaces of tomorrow. In I. Arnedillo Sánchez & P. Isaías (Eds.), *Proceedings of IADIS Mobile Learning 2012*, Berlin (pp. 147–156).

Klafki, W. (1963). *Studien zur Bildungstheorie und Didaktik*. Weinheim: Beltz.

Klafki W. (1997). Critical-constructive didactics. In M. Uljens (Ed.), *Didaktik* (pp. 215–228). Lund, Sweden: Studentlitteratur.

Kolb, D. A. (1984). *Experiential learning experience as a source of learning and development.* New Jersey: Prentice Hall.

Lary, L. M. (2004). A baker's dozen: 13 Palm applications for mathematics (and math related!) instruction. *Learning and Leading with Technology, 39*(9), 22–27.

Laurillard, D. (2007). Pedagogical forms for mobile learning: Framing research questions. In N. Pachler (Ed.), *Mobile learning: Towards a research agenda* (pp. 153–175). London: WLE Centre, IoE.

Mårell-Olsson, E., & Hudson, A. (2008). To make learning visible: In what way can ICT and multimedia contribute? *Journal of Research in Teacher Education, 15*(3–4), 73–90.

Naismith, L., Lonsdale, P., Vavoula, G., & Sharples, M. (2005) Literature review in mobile technologies and learning. A report for NESTA Futurelab.

Ng, W., & Nichols, H. (2009). Introducing pocket PCs in schools: Attitudes and beliefs in the first year. *Computers & Education*, 52, 470–480.

Rogers, E. (2003). *Diffusion of innovations* (5th edition). New York: Free Press.

Roschelle, J., Penuel, W. R., Yarnall, L., Shechtman, N., & Tatar, D. (2005). Handheld tools that "informate" assessment of student learning in science: A requirements analysis. *Journal of Computer Assisted Learning, 21*(3), 190–203.

Royer, R., & Royer, J. (2004). What a concept! Using concept mapping on handheld computers. *Learning and Leading with Technology, 31*(5), 12–16.

Song, Y. (2007). Educational uses of handheld devices: What are the consequences? *TechTrends: Linking Research and Practice to Improve Learning, 51*(5), 38–45.

Stahl, G. (2006). *Group cognition: Computer support for building collaborative knowledge.* Cambridge: MIT Press.

Staudt, C. (2005). *Changing how we teach and learn with handheld computers.* Thousand Oaks, CA: Corwin Press.

Strauss, A., & Corbin, J. (1990). *Basics of qualitative research: Grounded theory procedures and techniques.* Newbury Park, CA: Sage.

Vess, D. L. (2006). History to go: Why iTeach with iPods. *The History Teacher, 39*(4), 479–492.

Chapter 16
Going Mobile in Science Teacher Education

With a more widespread adoption of mobile technologies in society and particularly by youth, educators are now looking for opportunities to integrate mobile apps into their teaching environments. There remains, however, an emergent need to develop methods and resources to support teachers in their classroom use. This study explores how mobile apps were employed by preservice science teachers in a special teacher education course where they evaluated their affordances for teaching and learning science. Observations of the preservice teachers in a series of five hands-on mobile app activities were analyzed. The teacher educator and preservice teachers' experiences are synthesized into suggestions on taking advantage of the capabilities of mobile apps for teaching science and on designing mobile apps for educational purposes.

For Designers

Over one hundred mobile apps available in 2011 were reviewed for this study. The review highlighted three critical features scarce in many apps that could be employed to promote science education, including social interactivity, collectivity, and use of the mobility feature. This chapter draws attention to these features for designers interested in producing usable mobile apps.

For Teachers

The findings of this research also present a number of recommendations to teacher educators who plan to integrate mobile apps into their own teacher education courses. We recommend teacher educators design individual, peer, and group activities to allow for individual and collaborative explorations as well as helping preservice teachers to compare and evaluate these apps and different types of activity structures. This chapter, further, presents teacher educators with a number of resources where they may locate information on educational apps and mobile apps suitable for use in their courses.

For Researchers

In order to begin the process of translating evidence into guidance and resources for student learning, this chapter recommends that in addition to research on teachers' use of these technologies, researchers establish criterion-referenced assessments to judge the educational value of apps and investigate how the unique affordances of mobile apps and mobile devices impact learners' cognition and understanding of science. Researchers are also encouraged to analyze findings from the early years to assist interested educators in generating practice guidelines that include this age group in technology across the lifespan of learning.

New advances in mobile devices will support inquiry-based mobile learning across multiple physical, conceptual, and social spaces.

Dr. Evrim Baran
Assistant Professor,
Curriculum and Instruction,
Middle East Technical University

Dr. Samia Khan
Associate Professor,
Science Education,
University of British Columbia

Evrim Baran is an assistant professor of Curriculum and Instruction at Middle East Technical University, Turkey. From 2011 to 2012, Dr. Baran worked as a postdoctoral fellow with Dr. Samia Khan who is an associate professor of Science Education at the University of British Columbia, Canada. Dr. Baran and Dr. Khan's collaborative research focused on preservice teachers' development and mobilization of model-based teaching with (and) technology in different teacher education contexts. Dr. Baran and Dr. Khan's interest in mobile technologies stems from their study that explored how preservice science teachers used them in a science teacher education course where they evaluated their affordances for teaching and learning science. Dr. Baran and Dr. Khan's study aims at contributing to the research base on mobile learning and suggesting guidelines for teacher educators and designers.

Going Mobile in Science Teacher Education

Going Mobile—Preservice Science Teachers Evaluating Mobile Apps

Mobile apps have been reported as the fastest growing feature of mobile devices and as one of the most important technologies for the near future in education (Johnson, Adams, & Cummins, 2012). With recent advances in mobile devices (e.g., embedded sensors, cameras, motion detection, location awareness, social networks, web search), mobile apps have begun to lend themselves to a variety of applications in education. For example, in terms of science education, mobile apps have been employed to support inquiry-based learning across multiple physical, conceptual, and social spaces. As educators further explore the potential of mobile apps for learning and teaching science, the role of teachers in "orchestrat[ing] the affordances and constraints" (Kennewell, 2001, p. 107) of mobile apps becomes essential to appropriately address students' learning needs in science.

Recent research has emphasized teachers' understanding of the affordances and constraints of technologies for the representation of certain concepts areas, pedagogical approaches to teach that content, and how technology can address students' prior understandings, conceptions, and misconceptions in particular contexts (Khan, 2011; Koehler et al., 2011; Voogt et al., 2011). Within the teacher education courses, varied hands-on activities have reportedly fostered preservice teachers' knowledge and practices of technology integration, such as: learning technology by design activities (Chien et al., 2012; Koehler & Mishra, 2005), developing lesson plans and curriculum materials with technologies (Agyei & Voogt, 2012; Bos, 2011; Haciomeroglu et al., 2011), and critiquing technological resources (Hardy, 2010). Among these, technology evaluation activities have been employed by teacher educators to engage preservice teachers in the examination of making relational connections among the affordances of technologies, pedagogy, and content (Angeli & Valanides, 2005, 2009). The investigation of the affordances and constraints of technologies has the potential to help preservice teachers develop an understanding of the "complex web of relationships between users, technologies, practices, and tools" (Koehler & Mishra, 2005, p. 132). Building on this previous research on technology integration in teacher education, we recognized the timely importance of preparing our future teachers for the effective integration of mobile app technology. To begin to explore methods of integrating mobile apps into their future inquiry-based teaching practices, we presented them with learning environments within a teacher education course so they could begin to analyze the affordances and limitations of mobile apps for teaching and learning science. We hypothesized that by engaging in hands-on activities, preservice teachers may begin to develop essential skills to make informed decisions about the curricular uses of mobile apps in their future classrooms. Various pedagogical questions arise as the curriculum for this teacher education course was being developed. For example, how can teachers themselves become "learners" of mobile app technology? Given the large number of mobile apps available, how do teachers best select which mobile apps to integrate into their learning environments? Our study of future teachers aims to contribute to these questions on integration and evaluation of mobile apps in and for teacher education.

Gauging the Affordances of Mobile Apps for Science Education

The number of science mobile apps available—some free and some not—continues to grow, of which a number are relevant for topics in school. Compendia of mobile apps reviewed by communities of educators have begun to shed light on the potential and limitations of these apps for science education. For instance, Education Apps Review (IEAR.org) encourages collaboration among classroom teachers, administrators, and app developers who are interested in examining apps marketed in educational or game categories to determine their values and impact in education. At the time of this review, Education Apps Review brought together over 500 educators and over thirty volunteer educator app reviewers in its professional network. Other informal user reviews can be found in mobile apps downloading sites such as iTunes. While such compendia are certainly helpful, the reviews are not reported using standardized criteria for assessing the use of mobile apps for teaching science (these have not been developed yet).

The potential for mobile devices to support science education arguably lies in their special affordances (qualities) of portability and social interactivity (Roschelle & Pea, 2002; Squire & Klopfer, 2007, p. 95) subsumed within a single digital device. The portability feature, in particular, is conducive to moving to learn and the anytime, anywhere mobilization of information, both relevant to scientific inquiry. In science education, mobile devices, such as compasses, ph probes, and meters have long been the tools for conducting fieldwork where learners can record observations (via text, voice, photo) and measure their environment. With the recent advances in mobile devices (e.g., context-aware systems, real-time connection, collaboration, and social networking), mobile apps in particular hold the additional affordance of being able to convey multimedia information, engage in a multi-way exchange of information in real time, perform computation, and guide student inquiry with search, selection, and feedback. For example, mobile apps have the capacity to support collaboration through access to interactive databases, help students run what-if scenarios and take advantage of mobility and visualize macro-level experiments, all processes associated with scientific inquiry. The ways these mobile apps support inquiry-based learning can be further explored by teachers, teacher educators, and researchers who are willing to design off- and online activities.

There remain currently few suggested curricular methods of how these apps should be used to teach science.

Science teachers, by engaging in the implementation and evaluation activities, as well as collaborative and social investigative tasks, may develop effective teaching practices with mobile app technologies. This approach may support them in their own future instructional environments with learners. In order to translate evidence and practice into guidance and resources, we involved preservice science teachers in exploring mobile apps as learners, implementers, and evaluators.

Context of the Study

This investigation was conducted within the context of a new teacher education course entitled "Computers for Science Education and Community" that was offered to preservice science teachers enrolled in a one-year teacher education program at a major public university in North America. The teacher educator of this course intended to help preservice teachers investigate the potential of mobile apps for teaching science by evaluating the affordances of various mobile apps developed within the science content domain.

Selecting the Mobile Apps to Explore with Preservice Teachers

The mobile apps selected to showcase in the course were obtained from an extensive search of available mobile apps in 2011, followed by the application of criteria to select those suitable for the teaching of secondary science topics. The extensive search included the following initial criteria: (1) free mobile apps that (2) cover different science content domains such as biology, physics, and chemistry. The reason for limiting ourselves to free mobile apps was because of the limited budgets of teachers and students available in school districts for the purchase of these technologies to personal devices. The search strategy for these mobile apps was applied to the Google search engine, iTunes Library, and social bookmarking sites such as Diigo and Delicious. In addition, websites that reported lists of educational apps were also reviewed. From this search process, a compilation of over a hundred free science and math mobile apps emerged and was categorized (Biology, Physics, Math, Chemistry, Sensors, Everyday Apps, Foundational Science, Science Ethics, and General Science Teacher Apps containing two calculators and a units conversion app). The apps were showcased in a freely available Glogster webpage as a resource for preservice teachers, accessible at the time of this study at tinyurl.com/freemobilescienceapps. Out of a hundred mobile apps, ten of them were selected for further investigation within the course (see Table 16.1).

Table 16.1 The ten free apps employed in the course, their compatibilities, and contextual landscapes

		Mobile Players (Hardware)				
Mobile Application	**Discipline**	**iPod Touch**	**iPad**	**iPhone**	**Android**	**Class Activity**
Project Noah (http://www.projectnoah.org)	Biology	✓	×	✓	✓	Outdoors
Orbits HD (http://web.me.com/rschluetsoftware/rSchluet_Software/Orbits.html)	Physics	✓	✓	✓	×	Classroom station
Exoplanet (http://exoplanet.hanno-rein.de)	Physics	✓	✓	✓	✓	Classroom station
Distant Suns (http://www.distantsuns.com)	Physics	✓	×	✓	×	Group discovery
Element Match (http://www.slate-tablets.com)	Chemistry	✓	×	✓	×	Classroom station
Chemical Touch (Lite) (http://openscience.org/~chrisfen/Pages/Programs/theChemicalTouch.html)	Chemistry	✓	×	✓	✓	Classroom station
MolSim (http://molsim.info/mobsci/)	Chemistry	✓	×	✓	×	Classroom station
AcceleroGauge (http://sites.google.com/site/limbumjong/accelerogauge)	Physics	✓	×	✓	×	Indoors
Experimenter (http://cramzy.com/apps/experimenter)	Chemistry	✓	×	✓	×	Classroom station
Mitosis (http://www.mitosisapp.com)	Biology	✓	✓	✓	×	Classroom station

These apps were finally selected because they were free, were judged by the teacher educators to have some degree of interactivity, required some conceptualization and computation rather than just information retrieval, and were applicable to common North American K–12 curricular concepts in the categories of biology, physics, and chemistry sciences.

Engaging Preservice Teachers in Hands-on Mobile Apps Activities

The Mobility and Mobile Apps activities in the course involved several hands-on investigations by preservice teachers to engage them in the theory and practice of a teaching science with models and inquiry. In general, preservice teachers were introduced in brief to the mobile apps through a handout and discussion, permitted to explore it in a structured way and asked to respond to embedded questions about how they might be used to help students' inquiry learning processes.

In order to help preservice teachers prepare to use the mobile apps, an informational brochure on the ten free mobile apps selected for the course was distributed. The brochure included definitions of mobile apps, compatibility of the mobile apps across different platforms, and step-by-step instructions on: installing iTunes (downloading the software and creating an account); searching, downloading, and installing apps on various mobile devices; and running apps on a desktop computer (if this option was available). One week was provided to review the definitions and install the apps on their personal mobile devices (preservice teachers who did not own a mobile device were encouraged to borrow one). In addition, teacher educators acquired three mobile devices to lend preservice teachers, including an iPad.

During the mobile apps activity, preservice teachers were provided with a brief overview on the use of mobile apps in science education, including any relevant research on this new topic. Preservice teachers were introduced to the activities involving mobile apps. A specially created mobile apps handout that included instructions on how to use individual mobile apps, the location of the activities and the times allocated for each activity, as well as questions for the preservice teachers, was distributed. For each mobile app, the mobile apps handout provided questions aimed at using specific features of the app first as a learner, exploring the potential of the app as a teacher and evaluating the affordances for science learning.

To take advantage of the mobile nature of the devices, the mobile apps activities were situated within four teaching landscapes or geographies that placed the future teachers in the roles both of a teacher and a learner of science: (1) learning science outdoors with mobile devices and apps; (2) exploring mobile apps in a classroom stations activity; (3) using mobile devices and apps within built environments, and (4) looking high and low in groups to explore the Sun and constellations (see Table 16.1). The preservice teachers naturally formed into pairs or groups even though they had the option, for some of the activities, to work independently.

Observing Preservice Teachers' Use of Mobile Devices

Observations were conducted by four individuals to learn about preservice teachers' engagement with the learning activities. These individuals included a technology teacher, a graduate student in education, the teacher educator (and second author of this paper) and a researcher (the first author of the paper). Preliminary observational data included photos taken during activities and notes recorded about what preservice teachers did during the activities as well as their perceived levels of engagement. High levels of engagement were coded as when preservice teachers performed on-task behavior, pointed or gestured towards the digital technologies or artifacts that were relevant to the task, expressed surprise (verbally such as "Wow!" or with facial expressions), and expressed interest (eye gaze or verbally such as "That's neat!"). Conversely, low levels of engagement were coded when off-task behavior was present, no gestures were made towards the interface, or limited expressions of surprise or interest were generated. Debriefs were conducted among the observers after each class to discuss observation notes and compare activities. In the following sections, each mobile apps activity is shared along with observations of high levels of engagement of preservice teachers' use of particular apps. Finally, the evaluation criteria developed by the preservice teachers are presented.

Learning Science Outdoors and with Mobile Devices: Project Noah

The first activity involved Project Noah. Project Noah is an interactive outdoor mobile app to explore, share, and document local wildlife and Earth's biodiversity. Launched by New York University's Interactive Telecommunications Program (ITP), Project Noah aims to collect large-scale, ecological data through the help of mobile users who document their encounters with nature. Project Noah allows users to upload a spotting by entering the information under categories in the app—the biota's common name, scientific name, description, habitat, category, satellite tracked location, date, tags, and videos.

A special outdoor activity was designed that allowed preservice teachers to explore and catalogue local flora and fauna using their mobile devices, the Project Noah app, and a digital camera (some preservice teachers used their iPhones, while arrangements were made to lend cameras to the other preservice teachers). To explore Project Noah's affordances, preservice teachers were provided with directions to locate plants in a preselected outdoor area, choose species similar to what they wanted to photograph in field that day (such as moss, horsetails, native ferns), and determine if any species mapping had been archived on the Project Noah database near their locations. The preservice teachers were then guided to explore the garden area as a group and take a photo of their respective species using a digital camera or a mobile device. Once they returned to the classroom, they uploaded their photos to the Project Noah Website for our local ecological region (see Figure 16.1).

Figure 16.1
Preservice teachers uploaded a spotting on Project Noah website.

Preservice teachers noted the information and their picture of the species on the Project Noah website. They were then invited to generate criteria and evaluate this mobile app. Engagement level was deemed high for this activity, and also compared with the other course activities, as represented by observations of on-task behavior, limited guidance sought, and pointing and gesturing towards the plants as well as the mobile device, computer, and digital photo cameras utilized for this activity.

Exploring a Series of Mobile Apps in a Classroom Stations Activity

For this activity, a "stations" model was employed to explore science with seven different mobile apps. Preservice teachers were provided with information about the content and features of the apps and then asked to work in pairs to explore at least two of these free science apps at a station. After every app explored, preservice teachers were asked to evaluate them based on criteria they developed. The stations apps are described below.

Exploring Thermodynamics within MolSim

MolSim demonstrates how molecules interact and provides an interactive space for users to control the numbers of molecules (density) and temperature, while observing phase changes at a molecular level. While exploring the MolSim app, preservice teachers were asked about the meaning of the graphical representations within the app and to generate new graphs by changing these parameters and predicting the results with their peers.

Presenting Science-based Experiments: Experimenter

Experimenter includes the videos of science-based experiments, safety tips, required ingredients, step-by-step instructions, and how and why sections. To explore the Experimenter app, preservice teachers were asked to select and view the videos of different experiments (i.e. Pepsi and Mentos), investigate its how and why sections, and review the safety tips for chemistry and physics.

A Periodic Table: Chemical Touch

This app consists of a periodic table with multiple layers for referencing elements and relationships such as mass, density, melting point, boiling point, etc. To explore this color-coded periodic table, preservice teachers were asked to reorder the periodic table by changing its parameters (i.e. selecting "mass"), and making predictions, such as how might the periodic table look different if ordered by density.

Exploring Elements: Elements Matching

This is a chemistry app that contains three layers that represent three sets of digital mobile flash cards for learning symbols, charges, and Bohr models of the first thirty elements in the periodic table. The app also includes timed versions of three different games in which users are challenged to match all of the elements. To explore the Element Matching app, preservice teachers were asked to work with their peers to match the elements with their symbols, and then choose the correct atomic orbitals and charges.

A Reference App on Discovered Extrasolar Planets: Exoplanet

This is an app that includes reference databases of discovered extrasolar planets linked to over 50,000 scientific publications, interactive visualizations, animations, a 3D plot of the Milky Way, and multi-touch correlation plots. The app is based on an open-source project called the Open Exoplanet Catalogue that contains the physical parameters of exoplanets; the database is reportedly updated on a daily basis. To explore the Exoplanet, preservice teachers were first asked to locate the Milky Way, choose a random planet, check the database for the planet for detailed information (planet's name, host start, transit depth, and duration), compare the size and orbit of the planet with Earth, and finally plot the path of the planet.

An Interactive Virtual Solar System: Orbits HD

This is an interactive science app that features a virtual solar system in which the user has full control over the Sun and the planets. Newton's Laws, physics of forces, and sustainability and human footprint are some of the potential concepts to be approached through this app. To explore the Orbits HD app, preservice teachers were asked to examine the virtual solar system by changing the behavior of the planets, modifying the Sun's mass and observing the results, and manipulating the time scale to see solar changes faster.

Interactive Exploration of Mitosis: Mitosis

This app includes the interactive exploration of mitosis accompanied with actual light-microscope photographs of cells and associated video content. The app includes access to a glossary and resources. Preservice teachers were asked to explore the app, such as definitions, audio, glossary, and images.

Mobile Apps in the Stairwell: AcceleroGauge

This app was explored in the built environment. Preservice teachers moved from the stations activity within the classroom to a stairwell. AcceleroGauge is an interactive app that uses the built-in accelerometer of Apple mobile technology. Accelerometers are used to detect impacts, deploy automobile airbags, and retract the hard disk's read/write heads when a laptop is dropped. AcceleroGauge senses real-time 3D acceleration and gravity-related values and then records those max–min values in an x, y, z log.

In order to get familiar with the app, preservice teachers were asked to explore the four aspects of the app interface. Preservice teachers were then asked to press "Start" and walk quickly downstairs to exceed the alert sound value, and press "Stop" at the bottom of the stairs. Preservice teachers then observed a saved log of their x, y, z max/min values. Later, we asked them to repeat the steps in an elevator, and compare the differences between values in the stairwell and elevator experiments.

The engagement level was notably high for AcceleroGauge, similarly to Project Noah, and less high for the other apps, such as those in the stations, as represented by observations of on-task behavior, limited guidance sought, expressions of surprise and interest, and time to complete tasks.

A Discovery of Distant Suns: Social Collaboration with Distant Suns

Distant Suns is an app that focuses on astronomy. Reference layers support a database of thousands of stars, nebula, and galaxies. Constructions of the Milky Way relate lessons on astronomy to geography, eco-tracking, and navigation. All eighty-eight constellations are also linked to articles on their Greek mythology. If connected to the Internet, the GPS-aware feature provides opportunities for users to examine their actual environment.

In order to explore this mobile app, a projector was mounted on the ceiling of a meeting room to show the app above the preservice teachers. While navigating on a tablet that was projected onto the ceiling, preservice teachers were asked to hold the mobile devices in front of their faces and bend ninety degrees backwards so they faced the sky above, and select the Distant Suns interface that located their spots in relation to the stars right above their head considering the exact time and field details. Preservice teachers were invited to explore the constellations, details of stars, telescopic locations, closest "deep-sky wonder" to their current locations, and the distance of the Sun and Moon to their telescopic locations.

Apparent high engagement with this mobile apps activity was observed, as preservice teachers, in groups, shared information, consulted with each other, pointed to the ceiling and the interface, and exhibited expressions of surprise and interest.

Preservice Teachers Favorably Rated Several Mobile Apps

The purpose of the evaluation component of the mobile apps activities was to encourage preservice teachers to take an active role in developing criteria for gauging the affordances of these emerging technologies, in light of none being readily accessible in curricula or on the Internet. We asked the preservice science teachers to develop criteria and rate apps of their own choosing. The criteria were posted on a SMART Board (an interactive whiteboard designed to help improve learning outcomes). They did not consistently record responses to the questions embedded in the tasks; however, individually, they appeared keen to evaluate their apps. We observed preservice teachers both creating criteria and evaluating the app based on their criteria.

The preservice teachers were able to evaluate seven out of the ten apps in the time allotted (Project Noah, MolSim, Experimenter, Element Matching, Mitosis, Exoplanet, and AcceleroGauge). While Project Noah was evaluated by all five preservice teachers and

Table 16.2 Preservice teachers' self-generated evaluation criteria

Criteria
Usability (ease of use, appropriate level of difficulty)
Integration to curriculum (relevance and application with learning outcomes)
Entertaining
Engaging
Usefulness for outdoors
Clarity
Relevance to real world
Compatibility
Content (repertoire)
Extras

AcceleroGauge by four preservice teachers. Not all of the apps were evaluated because preservice teachers had the choice to visit some of the apps in the stations activity.

The list of criteria generated by preservice teachers is shown in Table 16.2. As can be noted, preservice teachers generated criteria that were more general and more specific in some cases, warranting a discussion about the standardization of criteria and rating scales as a future lesson for teachers on developing methods of evaluation. For accessibility, some of the specific criteria were relabeled into their major categories, such as "usability."

Coupled with an analysis of our observations, as well as the evaluation criteria and ratings generated by the preservice teachers, Project Noah, AcceleroGauge, Element Matching, and Mitosis were most favorably reviewed by the preservice teachers as the top apps for teaching and learning science. Experimenter, Exoplanet, and MolSim, on the other hand, received the lowest ratings by the preservice teachers in this study. Although the teacher evaluation could be better supported by activities that helped to create common criteria, and standardized tests for rating, their preliminary self-generated criteria and ratings suggested preservice teachers' initial choices for mobile apps and point to the potential use of those ones in their classrooms.

Conclusion

Because we are deeply interested in supporting future teachers in their endeavors to incorporate emerging technologies into their teaching practice, we designed a special course for preservice science teachers on technology that included a mobile devices and apps component. The purpose of these curricular activities in teacher education was to help preservice science teachers develop the skills and knowledge regarding the use and critical evaluation of mobile apps including the examination of these technologies' affordances for learning and teaching science. The observational data suggested that interactive out-of-classroom experiences, that appeared to capitalize on the mobile aspect of learning, were of the highest level of engagement and interest by the preservice teachers, compared with activities involving seat work with the mobile apps, such as the stations activity. Secondly, preservice teachers produced ten possible criteria with which to evaluate mobile apps. Their criteria supported the future use of four mobile apps in particular that spanned the fields of biology, chemistry, and physics.

The integration of mobile apps into the activities within a teacher education course led us to develop a number of recommendations for teacher educators, researchers, and designers who are interested in the integration of mobile apps into the learning and teaching of science. These recommendations are presented in Figure 16.2.

The review of existing mobile apps revealed that designers need to further incorporate the critical features such as interactivity, collectivity, and mobility into the design of

Figure 16.2
Going mobile in science teacher education: recommendations.

mobile apps that target learning and teaching science. Researchers may also establish criterion-referenced assessments to evaluate the educational value of apps for learning and teaching science. Collaborations between teacher educators, researchers, and designers are encouraged to develop resources and generate practice guidelines. We present recommendations to interested teacher educators who plan to implement similar activities for future teachers in the following sections. As well, these findings can serve to guide mobile app developers and researchers who are interested in engaging teachers and preservice teachers in the use of mobile apps in classrooms.

Involving Preservice Teachers in Generating Content and Resources

Our initial search to select mobile apps revealed that very few online reviews and databases were available to support educators to integrate mobile apps into their teaching and learning environments. For instance, while Education Apps Review (http://www.iear.org/) included an extensive list of apps reviewed by students and teachers and the iTunes store website allowed "customers" to give an overall rating and comment, these descriptive reviews did not follow standard sets of criteria or community generated norms to rate these apps. Moreover, other online resources (e.g., blogs) included a brief description of these apps, yet lacked a critical review on these apps as well as suggestions for lesson integration. Given the interest in using mobile apps within the classrooms, preservice teachers may be involved in activities within their teacher education programs by (1) developing criteria for the evaluation of mobile apps for educational use; (2) suggesting criteria for evaluation in specific content areas (e.g., science); and (3) participating in efforts to standardize the criteria. By engaging in conversation regarding the integration of mobile apps into various educational settings and contributing to a database or collection of resources with their reviews of mobile apps, preservice teachers may provide ideas for new mobile apps that could potentially help produce more standardized criteria and usable applications.

Investigate the Affordances of Mobile Apps for Social Interactivity, Assessment, and Inquiry-based Learning

Preservice science teachers should be encouraged to investigate the affordances of mobile apps for mobile learning. As more socially engaging mobile apps for science become available, preservice teachers should consider how the social, interactive, and collaborative features of mobile platforms can be utilized in lesson plans, activities, handouts, and for student assessment. Particular apps to support inquiry-based learning would be especially useful for fieldwork. Additionally, teachers may find mobile apps that could support assessment (e.g., personal assessment of learning, feedback to students on their apparent changes in learning or perceptions) especially useful in environments where the teacher would like to be mobile as well (e.g., stations activities, lab experiments, bell ringers, field experiments).

Teacher Educators Preparing for Mobile App Integration into the Curricula

The nature of the activities, evaluation component, and support material were vital to the success of the mobile apps component of the course. First, the activity structures may have been related to the level of preservice teacher engagement observed with these apps and subsequently influence their future use of them. Teacher educators may design individual, peer, and group activities to allow for individual and collaborative explorations as well as helping preservice teachers to compare activity structures, and where applicable, to take advantage of the social, mobile, and collective features of the mobile apps. Those mobile apps activities that generated the highest engagement among preservice teachers appeared to be ones that incorporated some aspect of mobility and collective cooperation to find out, discover, or explore. Secondly, a critical examination of educational resources is an important skill for new teachers. Interested teacher educators may wish to begin a similar mobile apps activity by establishing a common set of evaluation criteria, such as those suggested by our preservice teachers on usability, engagement, entertainment, usefulness for outdoor activities, clarity, relevance to real world, compatibility, and content repertoire for an initial review. Additional criteria could be built on these based on the context of implementation. Finally, the use of handouts within class to guide preservice teacher use and prompt thinking as they use the app, as well as the information brochure beforehand, was vital in our opinion to the success of the lesson. Teacher educators may wish to create or contribute to an online platform whereby preservice teachers could share their reviews of mobile apps and which could serve as a reference site which preservice teachers could continue to contribute to in the future. Finally, it would be appropriate to discuss the implications of mobile apps within the classrooms with potential emerging issues such as school policies, accessibility, security, and as a potential solution to limited computer resources available to teachers.

References

Agyei, D. D., & Voogt, J. (2012). Developing technological pedagogical content knowledge in pre-service mathematics teachers through collaborative design. *Australasian Journal of Educational Technology, 28*(4), 547–564.

Angeli, C., & Valanides, N. (2005). Preservice elementary teachers as information and communication technology designers: An instructional systems design model based on an expanded view of pedagogical content knowledge. *Journal of Computer Assisted Learning, 21*, 292–302.

Angeli, C., & Valanides, N. (2009). Epistemological and methodological issues for the conceptualization, development, and assessment of ICT-TPCK: Advances in technological pedagogical content knowledge (TPCK). *Computers and Education, 52*(1), 154–168.

Bos, B. (2011). Professional development for elementary teachers using TPACK. *Contemporary Issues in Technology and Teacher Education, 11*(2). Retrieved October 10, 2012, from http://www.citejournal.org/vol11/iss2/mathematics/article1.cfm.

Chien, Y., Chang, C., Yeh, T., & Chang, K. (2012). Engaging pre-service science teachers to act as active designers of technology integration: A MAGDAIRE framework. *Teaching and Teacher Education, 28*(4), 578–588.

Johnson, L., Adams, S., & Cummins, M. (2012). *The NMC horizon report: 2012 higher education edition.* Austin, Texas: The New Media Consortium.

Haciomeroglu, E. S., Bu, L., Schoen, R. C., & Hohenwarter, M. (2011). Prospective teachers' experiences in developing lessons with dynamic mathematics software. *International Journal for Technology in Mathematics Education, 18*(2), 71–82.

Kennewell, S. (2001). Using affordances and constraints to evaluate the use of information and communications technology in teaching and learning, *Journal of Information Technology for Teacher Education, 10,* 101–116.

Khan, S. (2011). New pedagogies on teaching science with computer simulations. *Journal of Science Education and Technology, 20*(3), 215–232.

Koehler, M. J., & Mishra, P. (2005). What happens when teachers design educational technology? The development of technological pedagogical content knowledge. *Journal of Educational Computing Research, 32,* 131–152.

Koehler, M. J., Mishra, P., Bouck, E. C., DeSchryver, M., Kereluik, K., Shin, T. S., & Wolf, L. G. (2011). Deep play: Developing TPACK for 21st century teachers. *International Journal of Learning Technology, 6*(2), 146–163.

Roschelle, J., & Pea, R. (2002). A walk on the WILD side: How wireless handheld may change computer-supported collaborative learning. *International Journal of Cognition and Technology, 1*(1), 145–168.

Squire, K., & Klopfer, E. (2007). Augmented reality simulations on handheld computers. *Journal of the Learning Sciences, 16*(3), 371–413.

Voogt, J., Westbroek, H., Handelzalts, A., Walraven, A., Pieters, J., & De Vries, B. (2011). Teacher learning in collaborative curriculum design. *Teaching and Teacher Education, 27,* 1235–1244.

Chapter 17
Librarian Technology Leadership in the Adoption of iPads in a High School

This chapter describes a district librarian's experience and leadership role in a high school when iPad tablet technology becomes ubiquitous. The goal of the iPad initiative was to change the culture of teaching and learning to reflect twenty-first-century learning goals centered on the 4Cs of communication, collaboration, creativity, and critical thinking.

Writing from the perspective of the librarian, we organize this case as a series of vignettes, starting in April, 2010 through May, 2012. Throughout the two years, the librarian served as a leader, researcher, collaborator, mentor and day-to-day trouble-shooter. Using Puentedura's SAMR framework (2010), we provide concrete examples of technology integration. Furthermore, we provide a list of ten leadership behaviors that we believe support successful transformations. We conclude that the twenty-first-century school librarian is a vital leader in ubiquitous computing initiatives.

For Designers

Following a detailed chronology of events and a text-rich description, designers will be able to identify opportunities for new apps and app redesign. The apps integration examples will reinforce the need for apps that are linked to educational outcomes and academic standards required in today's school climate. In the conclusion, the librarian describes her vision of ubiquitous computing in schools and school libraries, specifically.

For Teachers

The authors identify a broad variety of iPad apps which are successfully used in a high school setting. The authors describe numerous detailed examples of iPad and app integration in a variety of academic content areas, including science, math, English, foreign languages, and special education. The chapter concludes with advice on leadership behaviors that are encouraging to technology integration initiatives.

For Researchers

Researchers will be provided with a personal narrative of a large-scale one-to-one technology integration project. The chapter will inspire researchers to consider: (1) relative ıdvantages of various apps; (2) ways to improve implementation strategies amonį school constituents or academic content areas; (3) the impact of ubiquitous access tc tudent academic and social development; and (4) this narrative as a comparison tc other school technology integration efforts.

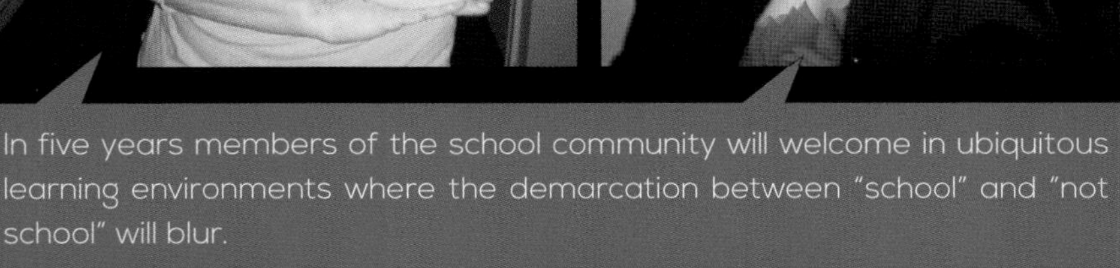

In five years members of the school community will welcome in ubiquitous learning environments where the demarcation between "school" and "not school" will blur.

Renata Geurtz
PhD candidate,
Department of Curriculum and Instruction,
University of Texas, Austin

Carolyn Foote
"Techno" Librarian,
Westlake High School,
Austin, Texas

Renata Geurtz is a twenty-year veteran teacher of computer information system education. She has taught at private professional development firms, university, community college, and high schools. She is a doctoral student at the University of Texas, Austin in Instructional Technology. Ms. Geurtz earned he Master of International Management from Thunderbird Graduate School o Management and a BA from the University of Southern California. Her researc interests in the field of instructional technology center on the K-12 experience specifically how are American public schools preparing students to participate in a technology-rich society.

Carolyn Foote is a "techno" librarian at Westlake High School in Austin, Texas, as well as the District Librarian for Eanes ISD. Formerly an English teacher, she uses both her library background and teaching experience to lead and collaborate with classroom teachers on her campus. A Master's graduate of the University of Texas with a specialty in Curriculum and Instruction and libraries, and a BA in Liberal Arts, she participated in the Hill Country Writing Project as well as being part of a jointly funded project between Eanes ISD and the University of Texas to study the impact of technology infusion into the classroom.

Librarian Technology Leadership in the Adoption of iPads in a High School

Some schools are embracing the digital age through adoption of digital devices to create a ubiquitous computing culture for teaching and learning. These school-centered trends reflect overall societal trends where the vast majority of Americans have access to digital devices. School librarians have an opportunity to facilitate the integration of technology for both students and teachers.

The *NMC Horizon Project Preview, 2012 K–12 Edition* (New Media Consortium [NMC], 2012) predicts that for K–12 schools, the time-to-adoption of tablets is one year and less. "As these new devices have become more used and understood, it is clear that they are independent and distinct from other mobile devices such as smartphones, e-readers, or tablet PCs. With significantly larger screens and richer gesture-based interfaces than their smartphone predecessors, they are ideal tools for sharing content, videos, images, and presentations because they are easy for anyone to use, visually compelling, and highly portable (NMC, 2012, p. 1)."

Friedman (2007) eloquently described and statistically supported the broad distribution of digital media that have radically transformed business, politics, government, journalism, and medicine. Reflecting society's focus on digital media, many schools have initiated technology infusion efforts (U.S. Dept. of Education, 2010). Professional and advocacy organizations such as ISTE, the American Association for School Librarians (AASL), and the Partnership for 21st Century Skills have developed technology standards for schools that motivate leaders, teachers, and students to move towards digital literacy (AASL, 2009; Partnership for 21st Century Skills, 2009). Bringing technology into the classroom is a complex process dependent on organizational vision, institutional infrastructures, professional development, and personal pedagogical constructs (Zhao & Frank, 2003).

In many schools, the library is the primary place for access to technology devices and tools and to obtain technology help and guidance for both teachers and students (Massey, 2009). Professional librarian standards (AASL, 2009) recognize that librarians should be technology leaders within the learning environment positioning learners to develop the skills and knowledge they will need to be active participants in the digital world. Librarians regularly collaborate with teachers as they plan instruction which meets the needs of twenty-first-century learners (Kuhlthau, 2010). For most librarians, working collaboratively with teachers takes many forms including one-on-one with teachers, formal professional development sessions, or guest teaching classes as the embedded librarian.

Librarians also work directly with students to develop the information literacies they need to be successful in school and work. The American Library Association (1989) defines information literacy as "recognize when information is needed and have the ability to locate, evaluate, and use effectively the needed information." Information literacy is a foundational skill, common to all academic disciplines and all educational levels. With ubiquitous Internet access, students must be taught how to safely and ethically access, evaluate, analyze, and utilize information (Livingstone, 2008). As part of their work, librarians are expected to fulfill many responsibilities, including supporting the development of twenty-first-century digital literacy for both students and teachers. The meeting these responsibilities changes continuously as digital media develops.

Even though there is a body of literature documenting the affordances and processes of ubiquitous learning, empirical examples of the librarian's role as both a leader and collaborator are limited (Johnstone, 2012). This chapter documents and describes the experiences of a high school librarian as her school adopted iPads and worked towards creating a ubiquitous learning campus.

Contexts

The District and School.

Westlake High School (WHS) is located in a suburb of Austin, Texas and is the only high school in the Eanes Independent School District. Eanes has nine schools serving 7,700 students. WHS serves 2,500 students (74 percent White, 11 percent Hispanic, 10 percent Asian, 4 percent multi-race, 1 percent African-American; 3 percent economically disadvantaged; 2 percent limited English proficiency). WHS typically earns an "Exemplary" annual yearly progress rating, and 96 percent of graduates attend college. Using local technology bond funds, in Fall, 2011, the district purchased and distributed 1,600 iPads to all junior and senior students and all high school teachers.

The School Librarian

Today's library professionals are experts in technology integration, information literacy and curriculum alignment rather than the limited view as storytellers and information resource providers (Bishop & Larimer, 1999). As schools adopt a vision of twenty-first-century learning, the librarian's responsibilities extend to collaborating with students, teachers, and administrators in face-to-face situations as well as through collaborative digital tools (Johnstone, 2012). These virtual collaborative possibilities extend and expand the librarian's influence beyond the library walls.

Our librarian, Carolyn, is highly involved with technology and views herself as a technology leader and advocate. She has positioned herself as a technology advocate and has become one of the principal technology go-to people for teachers and students. As the district's chief librarian, she is highly involved with technology and always alert to new developments that may impact students, teachers, administrators, campus, and the district. She believes a librarian is positioned as a general curriculum specialist for the school, working across the curriculum to gather teaching and learning materials and to support the instruction of teachers and students. Carolyn relies on Carol Kuhlthau's (2004) information search process model which provides a framework for her professional work. Carolyn believes it is important for librarians to be comfortable with technology tools that can help students become confident of their information literacy skills. Carolyn is an active participant on the Internet through her blogs[1] and tweets[2] both as a creator and consumer of knowledge. She regularly attends and presents at professional conferences sharing her knowledge with and learning from educational professionals. Recently, Carolyn presented at the ISTE annual conference, Texas Computer Educator Association conference, Tech Forum (Austin), Computers in Libraries conferences, and SXSWEdu.

Narrative

We use a narrative approach to describe the chronology of events as the school adopted iPads. We begin in April, 2010 when the iPad was commercially launched. We conclude the narrative in May, 2012 after the first year of use at the high school. The narrative is focused to describe the librarian's leadership for the integration of iPads across academic disciplines within the high school. As such, it is not a comprehensive description of all the events in this large-scale effort, but rather provides vignettes of activities.

April, 2010

When the iPad was released, Carolyn immediately saw the potential of iPads for libraries as a mobile Internet device, e-book reader, and productivity tool through the Apple suite. Prior to the iPad launch, her library had four Kindles for student and teacher use to test e-books. The Kindles were well-received, but the purchasing model didn't support library functionality. The iPad seemed to be a viable option for library use because it could be an e-reader and more.

September, 2010

Following the enthusiasm in the general marketplace for the iPads, Carolyn worked with the district's instructional leadership team and her school administrators to develop a pilot effort. Through this initial pilot effort, six iPads were purchased and made available

1 Blog can be accessed at http://futura.edublogs.org/ipads/.
2 Follow Carolyn's tweets at http://twitter.com/#!/technolibrary.

for checkout to teachers as well as students. The iPads were loaded with apps supporting every subject area.[3] The six iPads could be checked out in three ways: (1) to teachers for four days of individual use; (2) to teachers as a class set for use in the classroom; and (3) to students for use within the library. Since Carolyn and district curriculum staff were learning about the iPad's educational potential, Carolyn asked the users to complete surveys about their iPad experience, identify apps they found useful, and describe challenges they encountered.

Carolyn worked with teachers as they used this initial set of iPads. The library was available to purchase and upload apps which teachers identified for trial. When teachers used the iPad set for a specific lesson, Carolyn met with them to plan the lesson and identify and purchase needed apps. The teachers who used the iPads were overwhelmingly positive.

Students quickly became enthusiastic users as well. Carolyn organized a small research study to compare the usability of iPad to desktop computers. A group of students accessed a library database by desktop computers and then accessed the same database via an app on the iPad. Carolyn repeated the usability test with the library online catalog. For both functions, students found it much easier and faster to use these library research tools from the iPad. The number of clicks and links to get to required information was reduced, and the process of accessing library information was streamlined. The iPad provided a better user experience.

October, 2010

Carolyn collaborated with a science teacher to plan a lesson and identify and select appropriate apps. The junior-level physics teacher utilized the iPads with her classes in a lab environment. In preparing for the lab, the teacher created a pathfinder, a step-by-step guide of activities for students, providing a sequence of apps which supported the instructional goals for a lesson on gravity. Each six-student group shared one iPad and worked collaboratively to complete the science lab. The apps in the lab included a biography app about Isaac Newton's Gravity [app], the Physics Lite [app] to practice balance and experience the force of gravity, and the YouTube [app] to watch a video. The teacher noted the advantage of groups working at their own pace rather than her presenting the material from the front of the room. With the video, students were able to control their pace by starting, stopping, and replaying it as needed. The flat-screen design of the iPad made sharing one device much easier than a laptop which would pose visibility challenges for multi-user viewing.

3 The list can be viewed at http://tinyurl.com/whsappslist.

Situated in the library, Carolyn provided support to a special education reading class which included several profoundly disabled students. The apps used included iBooks [app], Alice in Wonderland Lite—Interactive Book iBigToy [app], and the Nook for Kids [app]. The various multimedia functionalities of these apps supported students' success with reading. The screen and font could be enlarged in iBooks [app]. The Alice in Wonderland [app] provided audio-supported interactivity, so students could navigate through the story itself as well as find hidden surprises. The Nook for Kids [app] allowed students the option to have the book read to them or to read it themselves. A very interesting observation was that students with manual dexterity issues were able to turn iPad "pages" by themselves even though their disability prohibited page turning in print books. These students were able to experience a sense of reading independence through their iPads.

November, 2010

Carolyn presented her survey results and observations of the initial pilot program to a school leadership committee which includes the Director of Instructional Technology and Assistant Superintendent for Curriculum and Instruction. Based on the successful integration of iPads for a limited number of classes and the educational potential, she recommended that the school purchase more of these devices, especially for library use and the special education department. One of the unexpected benefits of adopting the iPad was the long-term financial savings. Some apps, particularly for special education instruction, were far less expensive than the equivalent software solution. For example, the Proloquo2Go [app] costs $189/single license and provides a full-featured augmentative and alternative communication (AAC) solution for people who have difficulty speaking. The app replaced ACC devices and software which can cost thousands of dollars. It was decided that the library would continue to maintain the six iPads and check them out as was done in the pilot study. Additional iPads were purchased for the special education department.

April, 2011

Shortly after the school leadership meeting, the campus principal, Director of Instructional Technology, and Assistant Superintendent for Curriculum traveled to Apple, Inc. headquarters for a workshop on iPad integration in K–12 schools. They were convinced that the iPad would be an important tool for transforming the school into a twenty-first-century learning campus. They also returned with ideas about implementing a project which would become the Westlake Initiative for Innovation (Wifi).[4] At a school board meeting, the Director of Instructional Technology presented data to convince them to fund an iPad pilot initiative.

4 http://eaneswifi.blogspot.com/.

Table 17.1 List of initial apps available to teachers and students

App Name	App Name	App Name
Audio Note	DropBox	eClicker
Evernote	Garage Band	GoodReader
Graphing Calculator HD	iBooks	iMovie
Keynote	neu.Annotate	Notarize
Numbers	Pages	Penultimate
WebDavNav+		

May, 2011

After several program revisions, the decision was made that all teachers would receive an iPad over the summer and all junior- and senior-level students would receive iPads at the start of the 2011/12 school year. Additionally, iPads would be provided to sophomore students enrolled in eleventh- or twelfth-grade courses or in specialized courses, such as robotics or computer programming.

June, 2011

During the summer, Carolyn developed a list of apps that could have educational merit. She used the information from the pilot iPad surveys, professional reviews online, Twitter feeds, and recommendations from other teachers. The site, Educational Apps Review[5], provided useful information. The app, SelfServ, was selected to facilitate the downloading of thousands of apps from school resources (see Table 17.1).

To organize teacher professional development, Carolyn assisted the Director of Instructional Technology to provide professional development for a staff of nearly 200. In-service training sessions were available before the start of the school year. During the school year, "appy hour" training was conducted during lunch-time and after school. Informally assessing training needs and coordinating with the technology department, Carolyn taught numerous training sessions. A web-page[6] was created by the campus technology coordinator to provide 24/7 information.

August, 2011

Distribution of iPads to teachers was staggered throughout the summer and all teachers had their iPads by the first week of school. On the third day of school, 1,500 students

5 http://www.iear.org/.
6 http://tinyurl.com/d359fds.

were issued iPads loaded with SelfServ [app] which allowed them to download apps the school had adopted. Students and teachers both were allowed to sync the devices to any email account they preferred and to add any apps they needed as the year progressed. Each academic department was given a pool of funds to purchase content-specific apps. Teachers and students could download free apps without approval. They could also purchase apps using their own iTunes accounts.

September, 2011

Carolyn became a member of the Campus Vision Committee which was to study the iPad initiative. One of the principal accomplishments of the committee was to create an online survey to assess the level of iPad usage in classes, how helpful or motivating the devices were to students, and the problems and distraction levels that students self-reported. The survey was designed by students and administered in the Fall, 2011 as a data baseline, and again in May, 2012.

With the iPads in the hands of all teachers and nearly half the student body, the library's role expanded. The student help desk, "genius bar," was located in the library. Carolyn worked with architects to design a space in the library for the genius bar that would also serve as an interactive space for iPad users. The area was designed so that students could congregate, charge devices, brainstorm via black plexiglass whiteboards, and sit on comfortable seating. iPads were mounted on posts at the entryway for video streaming or announcements. Students named the space *the Juice Bar*, to signify creative juices and power (juice) for the iPads. The library also became a physical space where students could use the iPad recreationally. Carolyn designated a "gaming" area where students could play with their iPads and not disrupt other library users.

The library staff became proficient at solving minor technical issues. The librarians were also the contact persons for students who had lost, misplaced, or damaged their iPads, forgotten their passwords, and any other unanticipated issues. They coordinated with the district's help desk staff (located off-campus at the district offices) to provide technical services when the Juice Bar wasn't staffed.

Finally, the librarian became the administrator and primary contributor to the campus blog[7] about the iPad project. As a librarian and avid social networker, Carolyn believed she had a professional responsibility to document the Wifi initiative for others in the library and educational technology community. She realized that starting the

7 http://eaneswifi.blogspot.com.

documentation early in the process would be important for action research purposes and also as a model for other schools. The blog has become a clearinghouse of the information for ubiquitous computing initiatives.

October, 2011

One of the significant observations Carolyn noticed about the ubiquitous computing rollout was that it created a collaborative culture. Students and teachers were learning collaboratively and in many directions: (1) students to teachers, (2) teachers to students, and (3) teachers with students. They were excited about the novelty of the device, discovering new apps, and developing instructional opportunities.

The iPads allowed students to manage their time and organizational skills with the calendar [app]. Students became proficient at self-discovered apps like Quizlet [app] that allowed them to create their own review flash cards. For teachers and the librarian, the iPad's portability allowed them to access school email, calendars, grading, and students' documents no matter where they were, thus improving their work flow. Part of Carolyn's informal role involved helping staff and students use these tools, figuring out how to email from particular apps, troubleshooting problems with WebDavNav which accesses district servers, or helping students export large files from iMovie, for example. Through her own professional use of the iPad, Carolyn was able to model iPad functionality.

The mobility of the iPad as well as the camera feature quickly led to creative uses of the devices. As the librarian helping document the pilot, Carolyn did walk-throughs of the campus and spontaneously captured video or images of students and teachers using iPads instructionally. Teachers could videotape a class and analyze their own teaching. In Languages Other Than English (LOTE), students increasingly began skits in their classes and lessons in American Sign Language. Environmental science students on field trips used the camera for photos of birds, plants, and environmental structures, etc. Returning to the classroom, they used iBirdsLite [app] or Audubon [app] to identify the wildlife observed in the field. From these pictures, students created digital portfolios of their learning.

With the embedded camera in the iPad, numerous financial and time benefits were realized. First, students and teachers could capture digital content spontaneously, without needing to plan and check out/in audio/video equipment. The school realized cost savings because the library could purchase a reduced number of audio recorders, digital film or still cameras. The library workload of maintaining and inventorying this equipment was reduced. Finally, students and teachers developed device proficiency because they were using the same equipment each time they captured video.

November, 2011

One of the most obvious functionalities of the iPad is as an e-reader. iBooks [app], Nook[app] and Kindle [app] are e-readers through which individuals purchase books. Carolyn saw the need for library delivery of e-books to students via a more efficient method that allowed for check-out of books, rather than purchase. After reviewing the many options, Carolyn selected Overdrive and its accompanying app[8] to create an e-book library collection through which students could check out e-books digitally. She created a pilot effort for one year to determine if the cost and use were reasonable in terms of the amount of use the service received. To introduce e-books, Carolyn became an "embedded librarian" and traveled to selected classrooms to demonstrate the app and e-check-out process. Students were enthusiastic and began using the service immediately, accessing both paid titles and free Project Gutenberg[9] titles.

Appropriate e-book circulation models for libraries are still emerging. Carolyn believes models are needed that recognize the different ways in which schools use books, and then develop apps to support those models. Teachers may need a large quantity of novels for only three weeks for a whole class reading assignment. Teachers may need multiple copies of multiple books for small group reading assignments. Teachers may need a large collection on a specific subject for a themed lesson. Students also need individual access to popular novels, classic works, and magazines. Currently, there are multiple vendors and the choice of books varies greatly from vendor to vendor. The segregated marketplace is a barrier to student use because of the complexity. Studies show that libraries actually increase book sales for publishers. Carolyn suggests that publishers collaborate with e-book vendors and app developers to provide young adults and children easy access to e-books through library systems. Carolyn outlined these needs in a chapter to Polanka's (2011) book about e-books in school libraries (see Carruthers, 2013).

Another need that became evident was that every student should have mobile access to the "library" from their iPads. Working directly with students in their classrooms in an embedded librarian model, Carolyn helped students set up folders on their iPads that included the library website, catalog site, database apps like Ebsco [app] and Gale's Access My Library [app] so that the library became mobile and could be accessed 24/7. Because students now have a mobile library, Carolyn becomes an embedded librarian,

8 As of May, 2012, more publisher apps and products have emerged in the market, namely Baker and Taylor's Axis360 which uses the Blio [app] and Follett Shelf which uses Follett [app], and other products from education publishers are in the pipeline. http://futura.edublogs.org/2012/05/12/adding-to-the-e-book-offerings-follett-shelf/.

9 http://m.gutenberg.org/.

going to students either physically or via Facetime. She sees this type of service delivery as a viable option as students, teachers, and librarians become more comfortable with virtual instruction and computer-supported collaborative learning (CSCL).

January, 2012

Throughout the year, Carolyn collaborated with teachers to integrate iPads into existing teaching practices. Teachers experimented with apps like Audionote [app] for note taking. For the Virtual Vietnam War Project[10], English teachers and their students used Pages [app] for storyboarding of an iMovie [app]. Side by Side [app] was used to compare/contrast two websites or literary pieces. Students in Latin class used Puppet Pals [app] to create shows with animation and audio. The students in statistics class used Numbers [app] to conduct a statistical analysis of walking abilities when they were "sober" versus "intoxicated" (wearing vision distorting goggles). During this lab experiment, students relied on the portability of the iPad device to input raw data scores while in the field performing the experiments. Returning to the classroom, the students used Numbers [app] to perform their statistical analysis and create charts.

May, 2012

As the pilot year came to an end, several important decisions were made. For the 2012/13 school year, all high school students would be provided with iPads. Those who currently had a school iPad were able to rent their device for the summer. Teachers would keep their iPads and would have access to three professional development opportunities. The brain-child of the Director of Instructional Technology, Carl Hooker, iPadpalooza would be a professional development opportunity as well as a celebration of mobile learning to be held on campus over the summer. Carolyn was a co-organizer for the conference and would present a session on iPads in libraries and different models of library use—from using iPads as learning stations, to having carts of iPads in libraries, to the challenges of one-to-one models. Teachers would also be able to participate in a series of district workshops on iPad immersion or a three-day Apple Institute led by district technology coordinators. Carolyn would present at the iPad Immersion workshop about e-book apps, research-related apps, and note-taking apps.

Conclusion

Over the past twenty-four months, Carolyn has led, witnessed, and participated in significant changes at Westlake High School and its library. She believes that these changes

10 http://www4.eanesisd.net/~vietnam/.

will continue as more educational apps appear and as more students, universities, and K–12 schools adopt iPads or tablet devices. A significant trend which Carolyn foresees is the emergence of the embedded librarian. Through embedded librarianship, librarians will conduct information literacy education in the classroom rather than the classroom visiting the library. She also sees using FaceTime and collaborative and communication apps as providing opportunities for the embedded librarian to work with students and teachers virtually. The e-book market is also altering the popularity of nonfiction print titles, moving away from reference types of titles to more recreational nonfiction titles. The creation of pathfinders, web apps, e-book collections, and management of devices will be an opportunity for librarians to support teaching and learning.

Librarians must be visionaries and technocrats who have the technology, information literacy, and pedagogy knowledge to support the development and needs of their learning community. During her two-year transformation experience, Carolyn worked with teachers at different levels of technology integration, suspending her professional philosophy. Referencing Puentedura's SAMR model of technology integration (2010), Carolyn collaborated with teachers integrating technology in different ways, all of which were pedagogically valid for the teaching and learning goals.

Table 17.2 SAMR technology integration model and library examples

Integration phase	Substitution	Augmentation	Modification	Redefinition
Phase description	Technology acts as a direct tool substitute, with no functional change	Technology acts as a direct tool substitute, with functional improvement	Technology allows for significant task redesign	Technology allows for the creation of new tasks, previously inconceivable
Library example	October, 2011 Students use Quizlet to create flashcards	September, 2010 Students and teachers use iPads to access library databases	November, 2011 Students use variety of apps for real-world statistical analysis	October, 2010 Physics lab in which students use a pathfinder to experiment and document their exploration of gravity

Throughout the two-year time period, the school's community and leadership worked to transform teaching and learning. Of the many well executed initiatives, the team was open to risk taking and experienced set-backs. Carolyn suggests the following leadership behaviors:

1. Start small but purposefully.
2. Learn about and identify key apps and their technical details.
3. Empower other experts (educators and students) as technology leaders.
4. Foster, support, and model creativity in multiple modes.
5. Allow devices to be customized to become personal and ubiquitous.
6. Understand SAMR model of technology adoption and suspend judgment.
7. Collaborate to offer training in variety of formats and times.
8. Team with instructional specialists for training and support.
9. Check project progress via surveys and adjust as needed.
10. Document, share, and celebrate stories of and for the community.

A ubiquitous technology school community will virtualize aspects of library work and expand the job description of the librarian to include technology leader. At the same time, the library will continue to be a learning hub for the school—an information literacy center, a source of reference assistance, a reading literacy center, a production center, a teacher collaboration center as well as a location for trainings, workshops, student relaxation and independent learning.

References

American Association of School Librarians (AASL). (2009). *Empowering learners: Guidelines for school library media programs*. Chicago, IL: American Library Association.

American Library Association. (1989). Presidential Committee on information literacy. Final report. Chicago: American Library Association.

Bishop, K., & Larimer, N. (1999). Literacy through collaboration. *Teacher Librarian*, 27(1), 15–20.

Carruthers, M. (2013). Book review of *No Shelf Required: E-Books in Libraries* edited by Sue Polanka. *Medical Reference Services Quarterly*, *32*(1), 126–127.

Friedman, T. (2007). *The world is flat: A brief history of the twenty-first century* (Expanded edition). New York: Picador.

Johnstone, M. P. (2012). Connecting teacher librarians for technology integration leadership. *School Libraries Worldwide*, *18*(1), 18–33.

Kuhlthau, C. C. (2004). *Seeking meaning: A process approach to library and information services*. Santa Barbara, CA: ABC-Clio.

Kuhlthau, C. C. (2010). Guided inquiry: School libraries in the 21st century. *School Libraries Worldwide*, *16*(1), 1–12.

Livingstone, S. (2008). Internet literacy: Young people's negotiation of new online opportunities. In T. McPherson (Ed.), *Digital young, innovation, and the unexpected* (pp. 101–122). Cambridge, MA: MIT.

Massey, S. A. (2009). *Digital libraries in schools: The best practices of National Board Certified library media specialists.* Unpublished doctoral dissertation. Retrieved September 12, 2012, from Dissertation Abstracts International (3359753).

New Media Consortium. (2012). NMC Horizon project preview, 2012 K–12 edition. Retrieved September 12, 2012, from http://www.nmc.org/publications/2012-horizon-report-k12.

Partnership for 21st Century Skills. (2009, December). P21 framework definitions. Tucson, AZ: Partnership for 21st Century Skills. Retrieved June 2, 2012, from http://www. p21.

Puentedura, R. (2010, December 8). SAMR and TPCK: Intro to advanced practice. Retrieved July 2, 2012, from http://hippasus.com/resources/sweden2010/SAMR_TPCK_IntroToAdvancedPractice.pdf.

U.S. Department of Education. (2010). Transforming American education: Learning powered by technology (National Educational Technology Plan). Washington, DC: Office of Educational Technology (OET). Retrieved November 20, 2011, from http://www.ed.gov/sites/default/files/NETP- 2010-final-report.pdf.

Zhao, Y., & Frank, K. A. (2003). Factors affecting technology uses in schools: An ecological perspective. *American Educational Research Journal, 40*(4), 803–840.

Chapter 18
iTeach and iLearn with iPads in Secondary English Language Arts

Tablet computers like the iPad seem to be well-suited for educational purposes, but no empirical research yet exists that examines its potential. This chapter shares the stories of Brett and Julie, two veteran high school English teachers who are integrating iPads into their classrooms for the first time as a part of a one-to-one iPad initiative at Hilly High School. We share an analysis of their practices, developed over the past year via weekly classroom observations, formal interviews, and numerous informal discussions. From these risk-taking practitioners, we identify and discuss issues related to pedagogy, assessment, new media literacies, efficiencies, student behavior, engagement, distractibility, and academic integrity. Results indicate that the iPad improves the efficiencies of learning activities but also introduces new classroom management issues. Many teaching and learning activities with the iPad can be either engaging or distracting. Our findings may prove useful to districts, schools, and practitioners who venture to establish similar ubiquitous tablet-supported educational innovations.

For Designers

Educational app designers will learn how apps are used in high school classrooms for teaching and learning, and adopted and adapted by a variety of teachers. Designers can picture everyday school practices, user preferences, and teachers' concerns, all of which factor into how a particular app is or is not used within the classroom.

For Teachers

Teachers will meet Brett and Julie, two risk-taking teachers using iPads and apps in their classrooms for the first time. You may learn successful integration strategies, set expectations for change, and predict potential pitfalls when using iPads in your class. Finally, teachers will identify strategies to help prepare for future mobile initiatives.

For Researchers

This chapter provides an ethnographic view of the ways teachers and students use ubiquitous iPads to facilitate learning in high school English language arts. We focus on content-specific learning and classroom practices. Researchers will identify the high need for more disciplined research set within PK–12 education and across content areas and may generate significant and complementary research topics to investigate in future research.

In five years, #mobilelearning will = #learning.

Gregory Russell
PhD student,
Learning Technologies,
University of Texas, Austin

Dr. Joan Hughes
Associate Professor,
Learning Technologies,
University of Texas, Austin

Gregory S. Russell is a PhD student of Learning Technologies at the University of Texas, Austin, where at present he works as an instructional designer on a blended-learning, computer science course that uses problem-based learning to address issues of diversity. Greg is also involved in research projects that examine the effects of technology integration on teaching and learning in public school contexts, interactions between humans and digital agents, and the use of geocaching in informal learning environments. Prior to joining UT, Greg was an elementary and middle school teacher at an urban charter school. Greg also played professional baseball, and he still enjoys an active lifestyle with sports, cross-training, and cycling (http://www.gsrussell.com).

Joan E. Hughes is an associate professor of Learning Technologies in the College of Education at the University of Texas at Austin. Her research examines preservice and inservice teachers' development of technological knowledge and practice of technology integration in content areas. She currently leads three ongoing projects: a longitudinal study of one-to-one laptop computing in preservice teacher education; comparative case studies of middle school technology integration, leadership, and student use in and out of school; and an ethnographic study of one-to-one iPad tablet integration in high school. Dr. Hughes has nineteen years of experience in education, as an elementary and middle school teacher and university professor. She earned her PhD in Educational Psychology at Michigan State University. Her website is TechEdges (http://techedges.org).

iTeach and iLearn with iPads in Secondary English Language Arts

In 2011 to 2012, Hilly High School (HHS) distributed an iPad to all of its junior and senior students, its faculty, and some of its staff. This chapter shares the stories of Brett and Julie, two veteran English teachers engaged in the first year of this initiative. From their examples, we can better understand how iPads are integrated into classroom practices in year one.

Context

HHS is located in an affluent suburban area of the United States and serves 2,500 students (74 percent White, 11 percent Hispanic, 10 percent Asian, 4 percent multi-race, 1 percent African-American; 3 percent economically disadvantaged; 2 percent limited English proficiency) in a small district of about 8,000 students total. Hilly High is considered high achieving, as 96 percent of its graduates attend college, and its 2011 federal accountability rating was "Exemplary." HHS and its district have invested heavily in digital technologies over the past decade. Most HHS classrooms have teacher desktop computers, digital projectors, televisions, and often have interactive whiteboards. In addition, students are also allowed to use their personally owned digital technologies, including mobile phones, if the child and his/her parent sign a BYOT[1] Acceptable Use Policy.

In Fall 2010, the HHS librarian obtained six iPads and the special education department purchased thirty iPads to use with students. The following spring, an additional twenty iPads and a few training opportunities were shared with high school department heads and instructional leaders. In May 2011, a bond levy passed, and the school board approved a plan, submitted by the district and high school, to purchase 1,500 iPads in lieu of desktop computer replacements. This iPad project plan focused on "innovation," placing "learning in students' hands," and "transforming teaching and learning."

As university researchers, we collaborated with district superintendents, the HHS principal, and the lead librarian to develop a mutually beneficial research project: an ethnographic research study that began in Fall 2011. While many PK–12 schools/districts are adopting iPad technologies (Associated Press, 2011), there is no disciplined research to date that examines iPad-based teaching and learning in these contexts (Banister, 2010). Research on laptop programs (Bielefeldt, 2006; Knezek & Christensen, 2009; Swan

1 BYOT refers to the "Bring Your Own Technology" movement within educational settings that allow students and teachers to use their own digital devices during school hours.

et al., 2005; Zucker & McGhee, 2005) suggests that iPads might affect student engagement, but there is little evidence of how teachers and students use the iPad or its apps to innovate subject-specific instruction and learning experiences. Although the larger ethnography has broader goals, our intention for this chapter is to address the following research question: How do iPads affect content-specific teaching and learning?

The data guiding our analysis and the cases presented in this chapter include weekly class observations, two formal interviews, and numerous informal chats with Brett and Julie. They also include interviews with the HHS principal, district superintendents, and both instructional and IT leaders. These data were collected between November, 2011 and August, 2012.

Brett

Brett is a fifteen-year veteran teacher at Hilly High School, beloved by his students, who often ask him to read their names at graduation. He is very personable and builds personal rapport with his students naturally, relying on this rapport heavily for classroom management purposes. For instance, he often is able to use humor with students while keeping the class focused on the learning task. Brett thoroughly enjoys his teaching position at this high-achieving school, where he is one of the few non-AP-English 4[2] teachers. In addition to teaching English 4, Brett coaches for the football and baseball teams and is married and a father of two. Brett feels that he has been successful in the classroom, on the field, and at home by working hard and focusing on one thing at a time. For instance, he does not take work home from school to grade at night, preferring to complete these tasks before school or during his single preparatory period each day. However, by his own admission, Brett's busy schedule leaves him little opportunity to discover as many "cool" ways of using the iPad as he would like, especially since iPad-specific professional development opportunities provided by HHS conflict with both his lunch and his coaching after school, neither of which he is willing to sacrifice. As a teacher, Brett aims to be innovative and engaging, while providing his students learning experiences that will help them be successful in the future. All of these factors impact how he implements the iPad into his instruction, which tends to be teacher centric.

iPad Practices in Teaching and Learning

Over the course of the first year of iPad integration, Brett experimented with a variety of apps in his English 4 classes, some of which were integrated frequently, while others

2 AP refers to Advanced Placement level course; English 4 refers to the senior-level English language arts class.

were used once and never again. In Brett's classroom, students usually chose which app to use for a given classroom activity, but at times Brett would promote the use of one app over another, such as when he required students to use Celtx for script writing. Brett often assumed that his students knew more about iPad apps than he did, and he learned more about apps from his students than from any other source. Brett rarely provided whole-class instruction on how to use any particular app, unless it was to specify formatting principles, like how to change the font size or style within an annotated text box. The most commonly used apps in Brett's classes were:

- Internet browsers (e.g., Safari)
- PDF[3] annotation tools (e.g., NeuAnnotate)
- Dropbox (a cloud-based shared storage service)
- word-processing apps (e.g., Pages, Notes)
- subject-specific apps (e.g., Aesop's Fables, Celtx).

In Brett's classes, students used their iPads as e-readers on a daily basis. E-versions of required texts were read via iBooks, a PDF annotation tool, or HTML-based versions. Most of these texts are currently in the public domain, like *The Canterbury Tales,* and available for free from multiple sources. Students rarely consumed online materials *other* than e-texts in Brett's classes. On the other hand, a great deal of classroom materials, like teacher-created handouts and assignments, were distributed as PDF files online and accessed via Dropbox by students who could then annotate the documents using apps like NeuAnnotate or iAnnotate. Students were frequently asked by Brett to take notes or complete writing tasks with their iPad during class time, for which they used a variety of apps, including native apps (e.g., Notes), handwriting apps (e.g., Penultimate), note-taking apps (e.g., Notability), and common productivity apps (e.g., Pages). A few students used styluses to interact with the iPad's touchscreen, but most used their fingers to click, drag, and use other touch-gestures to control the device.

Besides reading and writing, students in Brett's class used their iPads to produce multimedia projects that were easily shared. In these multimedia projects, students used the iPad to produce, edit, and publish multimedia artifacts in order to demonstrate their learning. For instance, after reading *Beowulf,* students worked in groups to:

- develop a script for a unique, short film that embodied one of the text's multiple themes;
- create a professional-quality movie poster for their film;
- film, edit, and publish movie trailers for their film.

3 PDF is Portable Document Format, a product of Adobe.

To complete these projects: students used the iPad's camera to film video and capture photographs; they edited the video, audio, and pictures using apps like iMovie; and they shared their final products with their peers inside and outside of the classroom and sometimes publicly online via YouTube. Additionally, one student from each group wrote the final draft of their script using Celtx, an app that scaffolds the proper formatting of scripts, which was purchased using discretionary funds from the English department. Brett also supported these group projects with explicit instruction on design principles and formatting standards and used a rubric for assessment.

During the more common instances of whole-class instruction, Brett encountered more difficulties managing students than during other small-group or individual activities. Although Brett believed that off-task behavior had not increased since the introduction of the iPads into class, he was very aware that it occurred, and sometimes frequently. At times, he called upon students who were obviously (because of their physical movement) playing video games, to re-engage them with the lesson, but he was unable to eliminate off-task behaviors entirely. He spoke of, but had not yet tried, positioning himself at the back of class, which might enable him to better view the students' iPad screens and thereby spot less noticeable off-task iPad behaviors such as movie-watching, Internet browsing, online shopping, and social networking. But Brett was not discouraged by these off-task instances, and he continued to incorporate the iPad into his instruction on a daily basis.

Pedagogy

Whole-class, direct instruction was the most common teaching strategy enacted in Brett's classroom. On a regular basis, Brett began a whole-class reading session by introducing and lecturing about an English concept with support from a Powerpoint or Prezi lecture. The students then listened to Brett lead directed reading, in which he read and analyzed the text aloud in front of the entire class. Students were asked to follow along and annotate their e-text on their iPad; however, students were only infrequently observed annotating texts at these times. Throughout these activities, Brett constantly reminded students what material would be covered on their upcoming quiz or test.

Assessment

The phrase "This will be on your quiz" was omnipresent in Brett's daily classroom. Brett's approach to assessment involved the use of weekly reading quizzes with multiple-choice, fill-in-the-blank, and short-answer questions, and summative tests, both of which were completed by students on paper. Brett felt students needed to perform well on these types of assessments in college, and therefore they were important to his instruction in high school. Like other teachers at HHS, Brett initially attempted to administer quizzes and tests via the iPad, but a "culture of cheating" developed at Hilly

High with these types of electronic assessments via the iPad. Although Brett (and other teachers) attempted to work around these cheating issues via various web-based strategies and apps, Brett ultimately returned to paper quizzes and tests to ensure student fidelity. Although the aforementioned multimedia projects were graded with descriptive rubrics, the same learning and content assessed by these projects were *also* assessed via the aforementioned quizzes and tests.

Julie

Julie is a seventeen-year veteran teacher at Hilly High School, where she is respected by her peers for both the quality of her instruction and for her innovative integration of the iPad into her teaching. Julie teaches AP English 4, leads the student council after school, and is married and a mother of one. In four of her AP English classes and in response to student and parent preferences, Julie utilizes direct-instruction pedagogies, such as lectures, independent practices, quizzes, and tests. In her two other AP English classes, Julie utilizes more student-centric learning approaches, which she prefers, to engage students with the course's content. Students in both sections maintained a positive working relationship with Julie, constantly engaging with her in witty conversations that employed humor, insight, and wordplay. Julie is an avid supporter of the iPad initiative. Although she felt that the iPad should not be the focus of any given lesson, she tried to incorporate the technology into all of her classes in order to facilitate learning opportunities that were previously less feasible, such as the annotation of images as artifacts of learning. Throughout our observations and interviews, she consistently reflected upon her practices and sought out iPad assistance with iPad integration into her teaching practices.

iPad Practices in Teaching and Learning

Students in Julie's classes used their iPads as e-readers on a daily basis, accessing texts, like *Hamlet*, via apps like iBooks or from free online resources. Besides using Internet browsers to access free e-texts and the World Wide Web, students accessed the class's online shared folder via the school website, where they downloaded classroom documents posted by Julie. Most often, these classroom documents were PDFs, which they annotated using apps like NeuAnnotate. A common assignment involved students downloading a worksheet document from the class shared folder, annotating it as instructed, and emailing the completed document to the teacher. The native email app Mail was used daily by both students and Julie as a simple means to submit short writing assignments, like poetry reflections, and for Julie to constantly assess student learning. However, these emails also posed organizational challenges for Julie, who tried, unsuccessfully in her opinion, to use email filters and folders to manage the onslaught of student materials. Julie allowed students to choose their preferred apps, but she considered requiring students to sometimes use more powerful and reliable apps (e.g., iAnnotate) to alleviate technical problems that occur with free alternatives (e.g., NeuAnnotate). Content-specific apps were occasionally used to provide opportunities for assessment via multimedia (e.g., Fotolr PS HD) or to discover materials of personal interest (e.g., Poetry).

Pedagogy

In Julie's classes, students were consistently engaged in discussions about the text they were reading. In the student-centered classes, these discussions were entirely student led. For example, during one unit, students chose from a collection of books and organized literature circles for each individual book. These groups would most often read independently at home and then discuss their thoughts and reactions to the text with each other during class time. In addition, some groups included students from other class periods in their literature circles and would hold part of their discussions asynchronously in the class's online forum. Julie monitored both the in-class and online discussions carefully, ensuring that groups were on task, and helping them address the critical themes and content of each text. Students rarely used their iPads during literature circle time, but when they did, they consulted the e-text, completed an Internet search on a related topic, or went off task (e.g., playing a video game app like Jetpack Joyride). As the facilitator, Julie listened more than she spoke, but she held students accountable for their discussions by requiring students to email her a discussion summary and a personal reflection.

In the direct-instruction classes of Julie's AP English 4 course, teacher-directed guided reading sessions and discussions were prominent, while student-led discussions were rare. During guided reading, students most often listened to audio versions of the text via a speaker system or to other students reading the text aloud, and intermittently Julie would pose comprehension or analysis questions. Although a few students were regularly observed annotating their texts and posing questions to Julie and each other, most did not. Julie felt compelled to utilize direct-instruction strategies in these classes even after the iPad initiative due to pressure from certain parents and students. She spontaneously and frequently apologized to researchers for these instructional practices, which connotes some level of discomfort with direct instruction.

Assessment

Students' emails, discussion summaries, and in-class and online discussions served as evidence of student learning, but Julie's main formal assessment strategy for both types of classes relied on quizzes and tests. Initially, Julie encountered cheating and plagiarism when administering quizzes and tests via the iPad, just like Brett and the rest of the

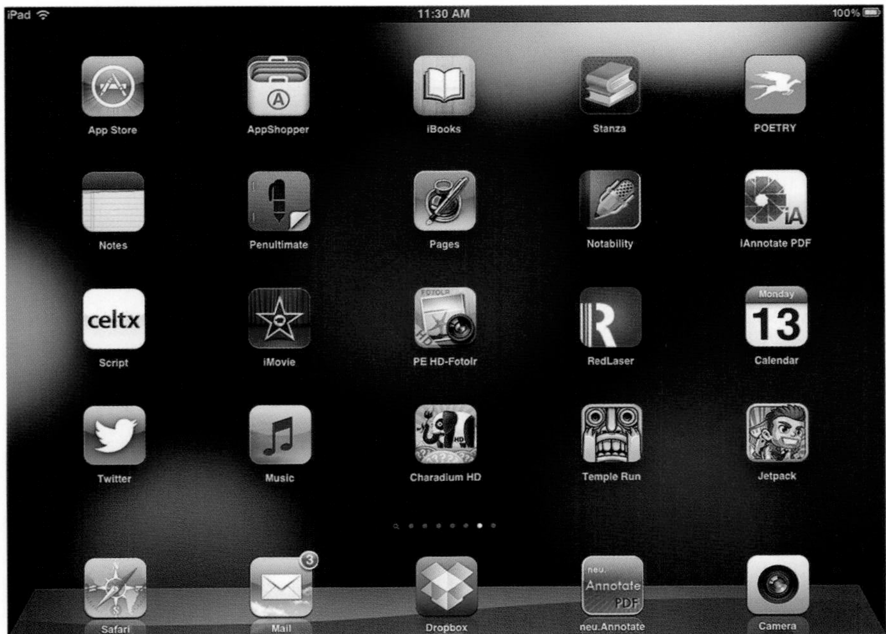

Figure 18.1
Some of the most commonly used apps by students in high school English language arts courses at Hilly High.

school. However, most of Julie's quizzes and tests used open-ended questions, which tend to make cheating more difficult than for closed questions. Toward the end of the year, Julie began experimenting with Google Apps to create alternative digital versions of quizzes and tests. With the use of Google Forms, she was able to produce multiple forms of each test or quiz, which were easily distributed to different class periods and to absent students. Julie felt confident that the open-endedness of the questions and the multiple versions of each assessment reduced the amount of cheating from earlier in the year, though she continues to hope for better solutions.

Discussion

In this section, we discuss several insights that arose from Brett's and Julie's experiences, which may prove useful to districts, schools, and practitioners who venture to establish future ubiquitous tablet-supported educational innovations.

Efficiencies

The iPad afforded vast efficiencies in Brett and Julie's classrooms, especially by expediting classroom activities and electronic communications. Email facilitated timely feedback between peers and with the teacher. The organization and distribution of learning materials via cloud-based storage spaces (e.g., Dropbox) and QR codes[4] minimized the need for teachers to print resources or make photocopies and made documents accessible to students anywhere at any time (albeit with Internet access). Students spent minimal time in class searching for learning materials like pens, pencils, paper, or past assignments. The paperless nature of these classrooms meant that absent or forgetful students could easily access important documents again via their iPads, which tended to help students organize digital materials. In addition, students were able to quickly access just-in-time information from the Internet via a variety of apps (e.g., Safari or Dictionary). All of the time gained via these efficiencies may have led to increases in learning time. However, it is unclear if any of these efficiencies were more efficient than if students were using other computing devices.

App-specific activities also facilitated new, efficient classrooms. Annotation apps like NeuAnnotate allowed students to quickly annotate e-texts, whereas annotating similar school-owned texts or textbooks would be cumbersome or prohibited. Content-specific apps also helped students focus their learning, such as how the Poetry app organizes poems by keywords and styles thereby enabling students to quickly find poetry of interest to them. Still other apps scaffolded students' task completion, such as the Celtx app that provided an organized structure for students to learn how to format and write effective screenplays.

Observation data indicated teachers and students were able to use the iPad and its apps instantly and as desired, because of the iPad's "instant on" feature and quick processing speed. There were no observed instances of IT support or technical issues arising with the iPads. No concerns about viruses or malware were observed. Furthermore, the iPad's touchscreen interface allowed students and teachers to use the device anywhere, not just on a desk. All in all, the daily, instantaneous use of numerous apps with the iPads seemed to greatly increase, and at times transform, the efficiencies of certain classroom activities.

Many of these efficiencies were developed over time. Due to time constraints and budget cuts (that eliminated most of the district's technology integrationist positions), there were limited professional development opportunities for teachers prior to and

4 Quick response (QR) codes are two-dimensional matrix barcodes that allow smart devices to scan them in order to access various types of encoded information.

throughout the school year. Teachers and district IT staff were often forced to discover solutions on the fly. For example, without a content management system, teachers decided to use email to communicate with students. However, teachers quickly learned that they needed to organize the mass influx of incoming messages so as not to become overwhelmed. File storage and sharing was also a challenge at the beginning of the year, until students and teachers became comfortable using either Dropbox or their school's shared folder system as a solution.

In response to these challenges, the district researched content management systems that the iPad could support seamlessly, which they will implement. They also purchased unlimited access to Wikispaces for classroom use. Districts must consider their available digital infrastructure and resources when deciding how to support and lead teachers and students toward iPad-friendly communication, file sharing, and collaborations that have adequate and flexible privacy controls. To make full use of these capabilities, a *robust* wireless Internet infrastructure is required.

New Media Literacies and the 4Cs

Our data reveal that iPad activities seem to engage students in becoming new media literate. For example, the iPad's hardware and apps facilitate students' creation of individual and collaborative multimedia expressions of learning, like when students used photographs to support their writing or filmed video responses to discussion questions. Students were constantly asked to apply their information literacy skills in a variety of ways. For instance, in Julie's class students were asked to find an image from the Internet that represented a theme from a particular poem. Then, students used critical thinking and creativity to alter and annotate the image, with an app of their choice, so as to make connections between the image and the poem explicit and to provide analysis on multiple levels.

Additionally, the sharing and publishing process was authentic because students easily shared their expressions with their peers, a meaningful audience. Students in Brett's class often shared their multimedia projects with each other before and after each class period, facilitated by the iPad's mobility and screen size. Other students published their work to appropriate online spaces, which expanded the audience beyond the school community, but also introduced issues of privacy, safety, and control. Nevertheless, activities that employ new media literacies are critical for young learners (Jenkins, 2006), because these opportunities provide forums for students to discuss issues related to social media, information literacy, authenticity of online materials, plagiarism and copyright, and appropriate online behavior or digital citizenship. Students would benefit from classroom practices and apps that utilize both new media literacies and digital citizenship skills.

Student Engagement

The iPad is a highly capable computing device that can facilitate numerous learning activities that may increase student engagement. Today's high school age students expect the use of digital technologies for learning (Berryhill & Durrington, 2009), and its usage can make learning more authentic. Even the mere replication of "off-line" assignments with the iPad can result in increases to both the quantity and quality of students' work, such as when Julie's students began to submit their responses to literature via email instead of paper. Furthermore, with over 200,000 apps available, in addition to vast Internet-based resources, the iPad can provide students with access to contemporary, global, media-rich, and interactive content that is highly engaging. With the iPad, students may both consume and create content by listening to, writing, or recording songs; photographing, drawing, or manipulating digital images; and filming, editing, re-mashing, and publishing videos. iPad apps like iMovie, Fotolr PS HD, Snapseed, and Comic Life allow students to complete these types of engaging, multimedia projects with only one computing device, the iPad.

Many of these engaging activities would not have been possible without the freedom provided by the HHS and district administration for teachers and students to individualize their iPads. By allowing individuals to control and personalize the apps and information on their iPads, administrators increased students' control of and engagement with their learning devices and, in turn control of and engagement with their learning. For instance, during a regular classroom activity such as note taking, students were observed to use a wide variety of apps, including: Camera, Notes, Notability, NeuAnnotate, Pages, and Penultimate. Some students used styluses as input devices, and others used stands to change the iPad's viewing angle. They directed their own Internet searches, shared files with their teacher, communicated using their own online accounts, and were self-reliant learners (at times) with their iPads. These activities would not have been as effectively integrated without control over the iPad and its apps (the relatively low cost of iPad apps was also important). On the other hand, while the rich content, the variety of apps, and the iPad's unique features might engage students with learning, these same factors may also draw students toward distraction.

Student Distraction and Academic Integrity

From cheating to video games, managing students' iPad use is challenging because the iPad provides multiple opportunities for off-task behaviors. Concerned stakeholders, like parents, teachers, principals, and politicians worry that students may only partially attend to learning tasks because iPad apps are quick to load and close, making it easy for students to access apps that can distract from the academic task-at-hand.

Our data suggest that iPads do not increase the overall quantity of off-task behavior, though iPads may make these behaviors more *visible*. Non-digital off-task behaviors like dawdling, drawing, note passing, or daydreaming are simply harder to observe than some off-task behaviors with the iPad. For instance, fast-twitch hand gestures and the use of the iPad's gyroscope during video game play are easily observable. Like many schools, Hilly High School utilizes an Internet firewall to limit student access to predetermined "distracting" sites like YouTube and Twitter, but students were (on rare occasion) observed accessing these sites or apps, most likely via proxy servers. On the other hand, according to Brett and Julie, students who were consistently off task on their iPads were the same students who were likely off task before iPads. Brett and Julie were more concerned about their students' academic integrity than about any occasional off-task behavior.

Issues of academic dishonesty became prevalent at Hilly High with the iPad initiative. Teachers and the administration discovered students were accessing the Internet, snapping photographs and screenshots of exam materials, and communicating electronically with each other during formal assessments. Teachers experimented with multiple solutions to these problems, such as using alternative assessment strategies and a variety of different apps, but they were unable to find complete solutions. Alternative or open-ended assessments were time consuming; Brett referred to one multimedia project as a "black hole" that consumed much more time than he anticipated. Eventually, both Julie and Brett came to rely mostly on pen and paper for formal assessments, whereas the majority of the rest of their assignments were digital. Still, they continued to experiment with different solutions, and they hoped to overcome these challenges in the future as solutions to these problems are developed by peer practitioners, app designers, and researchers.

Conclusion

We suggest that districts anticipate the challenges of technology integration and proactively build a knowledge base, develop personnel, and provide resources that address these challenges, including: instructional technology leadership, file management systems, acceptable use policies, tools for digital assessments, and content-specific professional development with the technology itself. Teachers will also require new media skills and access to rich curricular knowledge and resources that they can utilize within their subject-specific activities. There is a great need for the effective design of apps to support iPad implementation and multiple approaches to pedagogy and assessment.

This chapter describes the practices of two teachers, but it also illustrates the potential impact of iPad interventions on teaching and learning within formal learning environments. As similar initiatives emerge across school districts, it is critical that we learn more about the unique affordances and challenges presented by using iPads and apps for learning in schools. For that reason, we continue our ethnographic research study at Hilly High School, and we encourage other risk-taking practitioners, designers, and researchers to address related gaps.

We urge great professional care in the reading and any formation of practical or research-based implications from these two teachers' stories. This district and its high school staff are risk-takers who aim to innovate and change teaching and learning, yet we know that true educational change requires shifts in practices, beliefs, *and* materials, a change process that typically yields only slight accomplishments beginning in an initiative's *third* year of effort (Fullan, 2007). We shared two stories from the *first* year of an educational change effort. While we do not expect "true meaningful change" to have occurred during the first year, the potential to learn from practitioner risk-takers, who traverse one step ahead of other schools is immense. As researchers, we feel ethically bound to share these insights in their nascent stages with practitioners and researchers, because we believe they are valuable. We simultaneously urge readers to remember

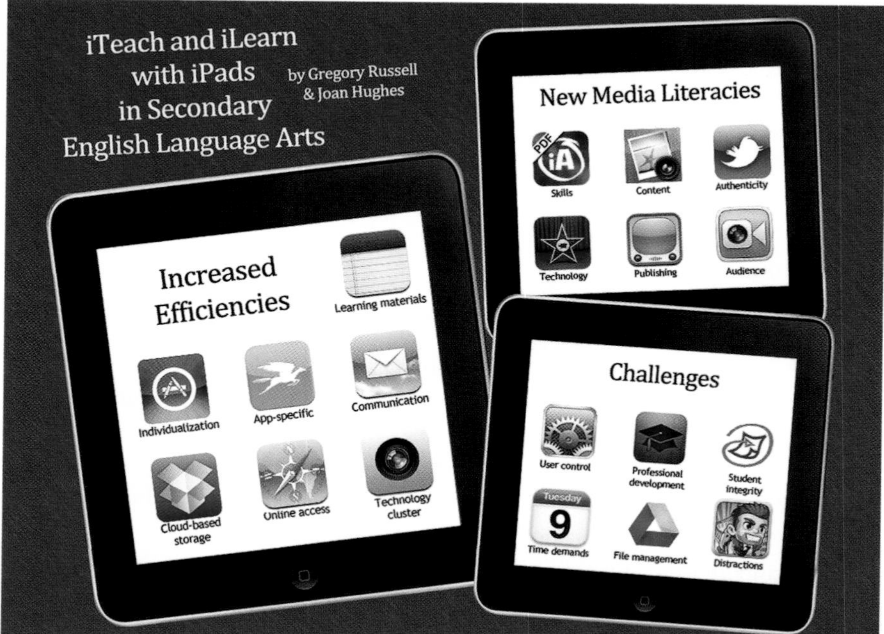

Figure 18.2
Summary of chapter's findings.

that these stories reflect two real practitioners who not only took risks in discovering how iPads might be useful for teaching and learning in their content area, but also took risks by consenting to share their perspectives with us, researchers external to their organization.

References

Associated Press. (2011, September 6). Many U.S. schools adding iPads, trimming textbooks. *eSchoolNews*. Retrieved April 1, 2010, from http://tinyurl.com/3mcesbh.

Banister, S. (2010). Integrating the iPod Touch in K–12 education: Visions and vices. *Computers in the Schools, 27*(2), 121–131.

Berryhill, A., & Durrington, V. (2009). Instructional technology investments in higher education: Are faculty using the technology? *College & University Media Review, 15*(1), 25–45.

Bielefeldt, T. (2006, July). Teaching, learning, and one-to-one computing. Paper presented at the International Society for Technology in Education, National Education Computing Conference, July 6, San Diego, CA.

Fullan, M. (2007). *The new meaning of educational change* (4th edition). New York: Teachers College.

Jenkins, H. (2006). Confronting the challenges of participatory culture: Media education for the 21st century. The MacArthur Foundation. Retrieved April 1, 2010, from http://tinyurl.com/2uztw4.

Knezek, G. A., & Christensen, R. W. (2009). Construct validity for the teachers' attitudes toward computers questionnaire. *Journal of Computing in Teacher Education, 25*(4), 143–155.

Swan, K., Van't Hooft, M., Kratcoski, A., & Unger, D. (2005). Uses and effects of mobile computing devices in K-8 classrooms. *Journal of Research on Technology in Education, 38*(1), 99–112.

Zucker, A., & McGhee, R. (2005). *A study of one-to-one computer use in mathematics and science instruction at the secondary level in Henrico county public schools.* (No. 0231147). Washington, DC: SRI International.

Chapter 19
Teacher Resiliency (Problem Solving) and Handheld Computing

Beginning teachers are under a great amount of stress as they learn how to teach. During their internship semester, while they are acting for the first time as lead teachers, they are also asked to submit a large number of artifacts such as reflections, literature reviews, and teacher candidate work samples as part of the accreditation system for their university and to the state for their teaching license. At the same time, new teachers are entering a technology-filled world of assessments, professional communications, and record tracking. Progressively school systems are utilizing technology to track student performance and to provide online teaching resources, especially for beginning teachers. New teachers can become connected nationally and globally to other teachers and teaching resources through online repositories provided by many professional organizations. Some examples of these include online courses, journals, books, and opportunities for e-mentoring and social networking. On the other hand, professional learning communities (PLCs) are increasingly hosted in the cyberspace and therefore becoming global and attracting greater expertise. In this chapter three university supervisors present their findings on bringing the promise of a management system they developed using mobile devices and have utilized with twelve preservice teachers around professional dilemmas. The goal of this research was to investigate ways in which a comprehensive teaching management system could provide protective factors and mediate risk factors known to be important to resilient individuals and successful teaching (Beltman, Mansfield, & Price, 2011). The process through which a person is developing the ability to overcome adverse situations and remain successfully adapted has been linked to the concept of "resiliency." A resilient individual in general is someone who responds to difficult situations with a resilient "nature," an individual who shapes their own learning through solving problems and ultimately as a result of persistence and practice becomes even more resilient. Resilient teachers are those who "stay in the profession [and] do not just survive, but thrive as confident and healthy professionals" (Beltman, Mansfield, & Price, 2011, p. 196). While resiliency is a mixture of personal and environmental characteristics, most agree that it can be shaped at least in part. Factors in resilient teaching that can be taught; examples include skill in teaching, ability to solve professional dilemmas (teaching problems), motivation to persist and an overall positive outlook despite other factors. Could mobile technologies assist in supporting teacher resiliency in a poor rural disadvantaged southeastern state in the US where teacher turnover rates are twice that of the state average (20 percent as compared with 10 percent)? Through interviews, observations, a pre-/post-technology use survey, a pre-/post-resiliency questionnaire, preservice teacher weekly reflections and artifacts from the apps used on the iPad during their student teaching semester, it was found that all twelve preservice teachers were able to use their iPads and the apps to manage themselves and their classrooms, to solve professional dilemmas, as a teaching tool, and as a way to relax and release stress. None of the participating preservice teachers owned an iPad or had used one before, though ten owned a smartphone. Different preservice teachers depending on the grade level and the school used the mobile device and apps in a plethora of different ways illustrating the flexibility of the technology. None of the schools in which these preservice student teachers taught provided iPads for their students; however all of the schools had a wireless network available. In fact, just the use of an iPad by the preservice teachers for teaching elevated the status of these teachers in the eyes of the students and administrators thereby contributing to their confidence. While there is no one "magic bullet" in education, due to the flexibility, mobility, connectivity, wide availability of apps, cloud computing and sharing, our research illustrated that mobile technologies have the potential to transform education through a targeted and specific teacher support system focused on teacher management.

For Designers

The need has never been greater to understand how technologies can be designed and evaluated in order to make the greatest impact. The research described in this chapter is an attempt to mediate learning using mobile technologies with the purpose of supporting teachers in developing resiliency. Through insight into the complex and dynamic task of teaching and teacher support, instructional designers can consider pedagogical frameworks for developing more comprehensive systems through the interplay of the device and the processes and interactions that become possible.

For Teachers

A portable way to organize daily activities, such as jotting down notes and reminders while in the midst of teaching, proves to be very handy. Using the device in this manner assists with not only solving the teacher's problem of individualized instruction, but the device itself serves as the solution to the teacher's problem. This chapter illustrates ways in which beginning teachers used iPads and associated apps as a personal management system and ways in which their university supervisors were able to support them. The university supervisors focused on the goal of providing technology resources that would assist them in becoming resilient teachers.

For Researchers

In this study, those teachers placed in rural and under-served schools need to develop resiliency in order to not only survive but to thrive in the profession. They need the ability to critically reflect and effectively solve professional and personal dilemmas. This chapter illustrates the purposeful teaching of professional problem solving and reflection using a mobile device such as an iPad in order to support protective factors and mediate challenges important in developing resiliency in teachers.

Mobile learning will empower people through new channels of communication and replace everyday tasks through technology.

Dr. Rita Hagevik
Director of Graduate Studies,
Science Education,
University of North Carolina at Pembroke

Heather Higgins Lynn
Postdoctoral Fellow,
Education Policy Initiative,
University of North Carolina at Chapel Hill

Dr. Irina Falls
Associate Professor,
School of Education,
University of North Carolina at Pembroke

Dr. Rita Hagevik is Director of Graduate Studies in Science Education and an assistant professor in the Department of Biology at the University of North Carolina at Pembroke where she holds a PhD in Science Education and Forestry. An environmental and science educator by training, she specializes in the use of geospatial technologies in teaching and learning. She has over twenty years of experience with conservation projects focused on wetland environments such as ephemeral pools and brackish marshes. She has authored more than thirty papers and popular articles dealing with conservation, geospatial technologies, and science teaching and learning. Her most recent titles include *Mapping Our School Site, Developing 21st Century Learning using the Power of the Globe and GPS*, and *Using Action Research in Middle Grades Teacher Education to Evaluate and Deepen Reflective Practice*.

Dr. Irina Falls, Associate Professor of the School of Education at the University of North Carolina at Pembroke, started her professional career as a child clinical psychologist in Bucharest, Romania. As a Fulbright scholar and later doctoral student at the University of North Carolina, Chapel Hill, she became interested in developmental disabilities and inclusive early childhood education. Dr. Falls was a research scientist at the Carolina Institute for Developmental Disabilities at the Frank Porter Graham Child Development Institute before joining the School of Education at UNCP. Her interest and current research focus on mobile technologies closely related to teaching online courses as well as the skills and dispositions that predict the retention and effectiveness of beginning teachers.

Heather Higgins Lynn is a postdoctoral fellow at the Education Policy Initiative at Carolina in Chapel Hill, North Carolina. She works with several initiatives in the North Carolina Race to the Top education reform grant evaluation, including the Teacher and Leader Effectiveness Evaluation (TLEE) and Educator Incentive initiatives. Prior to this appointment, Higgins served as an assistant professor of Education at the University of North Carolina at Pembroke in the Department of Professional Pedagogy and Research. Higgins holds a PhD in Teacher Education and Development from the University of North Carolina at Greensboro, an MEd from the Harvard Graduate School of Education, and a BA from Wake Forest University.

Teacher Resiliency (Problem Solving) and Handheld Computing

Introduction: The Importance of the Problem

At the beginning of the second decade of the twenty-first century we are witnessing a rapid transition to ubiquitous mobile computing in all domains of education. Teacher preparation programs are no exception to this new trend that has been often used for learning and teaching in higher education. However, presently, there are no documented attempts to apply mobile technology devices and apps to the development of teacher dispositions and personal characteristics. Teaching involves more than effective organization, instructional knowledge, and teaching skills. It also encompasses professional dispositions, also referred to as a set of values, beliefs, and perceptions that guide teachers' professional conduct. On the other hand, effective teachers possess a distinct set of personal characteristics that enable them to not just maintain their jobs (survive) "but thrive as confident and healthy professionals" (Beltman, Mansfield, & Price, 2011, p. 196). The process through which a person is developing the ability to overcome adverse situations and remain successfully adapted has been linked to the concept of "resiliency." Teacher resiliency has been linked to several processes and characteristics among which problem solving and perceived self-efficacy are crucial. Since resiliency can be learned, teacher education programs should begin shaping teacher candidates early through intentional and explicit methods and strategies. In the present technology climate, mobile technology offers a variety of modalities that can facilitate critical thinking and problem solving while in the field. This chapter explores strategies for fostering resiliency in preservice teachers with the support of mobile technology devices and innovative applications.

Teacher Resiliency

Resiliency has become an important concept that has recently made a comeback in studies about beginning teachers' effectiveness and retention. While many studies have studied the multiple challenges that teachers face in both rural (Zost, 2010) and urban areas (Castro, Kelly, & Shih, 2010; Huisman, Singer, & Catapano, 2010; Margolis, 2008; Tait, 2008), researchers recently have shifted their interest towards the concept of "teacher resiliency" by investigating the specific factors that enable certain teachers to remain and be successful in their profession (Beltman, Mansfield, & Price, 2011; Gu & Day, 2007).

Many authors argue that resiliency is a mixture of personal and environmental characteristics but most agree that it can be shaped at least in part. Bernshausen and Cunningham (Zost, 2010) identified several characteristics of resilient teachers which included:

skillful in their teaching area, a feeling of acceptance by the school and the community, the ability to adjust and prevail over challenges, a higher level of determination and a strong desire not to fail, and a positive outlook about themselves, their school, and life in general.

Fortunately, resilience should be considered not so much an innate quality of the individual to "bounce back," but rather the end result of a complex and dynamic process in which a series of factors interact (Castro et al., 2010; Day & Gu, 2007; Howard & Johnson, 2004). Thus, by responding to difficult situations with a resilient "nature," an individual learns how to shape their own learning and to improve upon problem-solving skills and ultimately as a result of persistence and practice become even more resilient.

In a comprehensive and well-structured review of the literature on teacher resilience since 2000, Beltman, Mansfield, and Price (2011) classified and found evidence of the two types of factors whose interplay leads eventually to resilience: risk/challenging factors and protective factors, which can be in turn either individual or contextual.

Individual risk factors can be low self-confidence, difficulty asking for help, conflict between personal beliefs and school practices, while contextual risk factors might be related to family, school/classroom characteristics, or any type of professional work context.

Protective factors (supports) have been also extensively studied although, like the risk factors, they were not always directly related to the concept of "resilience." Among the individual protective factors perception of self-efficacy (Tschannen-Moran & Woolfolk Hoy, 2007), capacity to problem solve (Yost, 2006), personal strengths and characteristics such as strong motivation to teach (Gu & Day, 2007), and critical reflection (Bobek, 2002; Gu & Day, 2007) are cited as being essential. Some authors stress the importance of students' ongoing reflection for analyzing and solving dilemmas and for getting a better perspective of the teaching and learning context and the role of oneself in it (Kuechle et al., 2010). Therefore, there seems to be a necessity of intentionally creating designated spaces for reflection on and making sense of the teaching context, self-performance, factors that can facilitate or hinder one's teaching, and system of support available in all internship experiences. In "Teaching Ms. Kerbin," Kuechle et al. (2010) cite Pultorak and Stone (1999) who noted that for student teachers "teacher reflectivity has the potential of moving us towards a refined description of how individuals transform from novice thinking to expert understanding" (p. 5).

In summary, although the literature points out that resiliency is playing a crucial role in the retention of novice teachers, there is no indication so far that teacher education programs are attempting to include it as one of their outcomes.

Handhelds and Problem Solving

There is an increasing emphasis on teaching methods that engage students with the context and make them more active through constructivist models. Many researchers have indicated the countless potential uses of handhelds in field investigations (Bennett & Cunningham, 2009; Franklin et al., 2007; Soloway et al., 1999). Involving preservice teachers in the learning of problem solving and resiliency-building processes using handhelds devices certainly lends to an active, constructivist learning experience.

Handhelds can play the valuable role of facilitators of the process through which teacher candidates assess the situation, search for possible solutions and decide on an action to implement. Of the two protective factors that support teacher resiliency—problem solving skills and perceived self-efficacy—we can definitely teach problem solving skills while confidence in one's professional efficiency is partially a result of performance.

Handheld devices such as iPads, in addition to their mobility, offer various applications for recording and guiding the problem-solving process as well as for solving those problems. For the purpose of developing the problem-solving process, offering solutions, and for supporting their implementation, the iPad's mobility, applications' variety and flexibility, and technological novelty constitute the most valuable features.

iPad Mobility

iPads lend themselves to jotting down notes in the classroom, on the playground, during lunch, or during a meeting. They allow the bearer to record events while still in the situation/context so that the facts are less altered by time and emotions. The notes then can be uploaded or shared through email or other social media. Using handheld devices in this manner offers the opportunity to learn how to develop resiliency through reflective problem solving by preservice teachers through reflection "in action" as well as "on action" (Schön, 1983). For this purpose there are apps such as:

- Sticky Notes—lets you write short messages and organize them on your digital bulletin board by position or color.
- iNote—Sketch and Share—the notes can be shared via email, Facebook, or Twitter.
- WhiteNote—digital notebook application for the iPad that supports free-form text positioning and basic freehand drawing as well as support for images and sound.
- Outliner for iPad—allows you to organize your thoughts, tasks, and projects. Easily create a to-do list for today, or track an entire project anywhere you are. Share your outlines, edit them online, and collaborate with other Outliner users.

- SketchPad HD is an easy-to-use app that allows you to takes notes and draw in a variety of colors, collect and browse through notes, as well as share them through email.
- Dropbox—this popular service allows you to sync your files automatically to other computers or devices.

iPad's Variety and Flexibility of Apps

The world of apps is growing at a dizzying speed and with over 225,000 apps to choose from, you can be certain to find one for your goals. For the purpose of problem solving and to clarify professional dilemmas, there was a paucity of apps but we thought that the teacher interns could find useful the following:

- I Can do for iPad—this app walks you through three easy steps to identify your blocking thoughts and feelings, and to rephrase them to be more actionable.
- iThoughts (mindmapping)—mindmapping enables you to visually organize your thoughts, ideas, and information. Typical uses: task lists, brainstorming, project planning, goal setting, concept mapping, course notes/revision, meeting notes.

iPad's Technological Novelty

The novelty of the iPad can serve multiple purposes for solving problems in the classroom. For example, the teacher can use it as a reward for children who do well as well as a way for collaborative peer groups to work together on the same task. Through its multitude of apps for children of all ages and abilities, the iPad lends itself to a diversity of uses in a variety of situations.

Research Methods

In order to explore the value of handheld computing devices for facilitating the building of resiliency through a problem-solving process during the student internship, the authors implemented an exploratory study with a group of six preservice teachers at a public university in the southeast United States. The focus was on investigating the interaction among perceived self-efficacy, problem-solving sills, and self-reflection and what it can reveal about the resiliency-building process. We decided to concentrate on the problem-solving process of the professional dilemmas encountered by the student teachers, while their measured self-efficacy and periodic reflections were considered the result of this process. A resilient teacher is one that knows how to frame a problem and how to navigate reflexively through the effectiveness of possible solutions and resources. These skills can be learned and fostered in the student teachers through this project.

Data Sources and Analysis

The preservice teacher internship is an extremely stressful time in the life of teacher candidates. In addition to their teaching for the first time as lead teachers, they are asked to submit a large amount of papers—reflections, literature reviews, artifacts, and the Teacher Candidate Work Sample (TCWS) which can be over a hundred pages. Because of their mobility, handheld devices can facilitate note taking in various contexts while ideas are still fresh. A total of six undergraduate students in their semester of student teaching were recruited. The preservice teachers were pursuing a teaching license in their internship semester (student teaching) of their plan of study, and enrolled in the following teacher education programs: three in Special Education, one in Early Childhood Education, and two in Science Education. They were enrolled to fulfill their internship in the spring semester 2012 and had never taught as lead teacher before this internship. The participants are all females, of ages between twenty-six and forty-two years of age and included the following races: White (Caucasian), three, African-American, two, and Native American, one.

The study was conceived as a mixed-methods research in which quantitative as well as qualitative data collection methods were used. Due to the fact that we only had six participants and that this is an initial exploratory study intended to clarify and guide future research strategies on larger samples, the authors relied heavily on the qualitative data collected. The survey results have been thoroughly analyzed in view of the extensive literature review conducted for this study, and we anticipate the development of new measures for capturing all the resiliency domains highlighted in the literature.

The choice of using handheld devices (iPads) to facilitate data collection, and to find and apply solutions to professional dilemmas, was made for several reasons; one primary motive was related to the availability of the hardware and software for no cost to the students. The students were issued their own iPad 2 loaded with all the required apps, a screen protector, and a protective leather case. Although most students had technology experience due to the fact that most education courses are taught online, none had used an iPad in the past. The students were allowed to experiment with the device for a couple of weeks before being required to use it for problem solving and reflect on its uses. There were several apps downloaded on their iPads including some that allowed taking notes, drawing diagrams, and visually organizing thoughts. Of particular interest is the I can do for iPad app because it established the framework of working through the problems providing the user with the following steps:

Part One: Describe the Issue

(Use these questions and choose from the options offered by the app or come up with your own to answer them.)

1. What I need to do.
2. What are my feelings (there is a drop-down menu from which you need to choose at least one)?
3. What are my blocking thoughts?

Part Two: Reconsider

(Use these questions and choose from the options offered by the app or come up with your own to answer them.)

1. My thinking was wrong because . . .
2. My thought has these distractions . . .
3. My more actionable thought is . . .

USE the app to work out the thoughts.

Seven major categories of challenging situations were offered to the preservice teachers for organizing their problem solving/dilemmas using the reflective problem-solving strategy and the handheld devices: (1) the first day of student teaching; (2) working as a team with the cooperating teacher; (3) classroom behavior management; (4) sensitivity to the needs of children with difficult home circumstances; (5) observations by the university supervisor; (6) inclusion practices; and (7) breaking through with a difficult student (Kuechle et al., 2010). However, the participants were told that they are free to add any challenging situation to these general categories.

The data collection was mainly qualitative and consisted of weekly reflections, problem solving notes on the mobile device apps, and final interviews. The interns were asked to submit weekly reflections in which they were prompted to document various professional dilemmas as well as the purposes for which they used their iPad, be it professional or personal. The exit interviews were semi-structured individual conversations aimed at gathering information about both the most important experiences and personal characteristics that may evidence resilience, as well as their use of the provided mobile devices for solving various problems.

After completing the pre-test surveys regarding their perceived self-efficacy and resiliency, the participants attended two two-hour training sessions that included the following.

Training in Problem-solving Techniques

The participants were informed about the procedures to follow in documenting and reflecting events and practices, as well as in the use of the handheld mobile devices and their applications. Procedures for getting support and coping with challenging events were also put into place by establishing communication pathways with the university supervisor, mentors, and colleagues.

Establishing the Methods, Timing, and Rules for Noting and Keeping Records of the Challenging Events and Reflections

The participants were informed on methods of recording and uploading their documents to the cloud or sending them through email. They also received a schedule for communicating with the university supervisor periodically.

Basic Training in Using the Mobile Devices (iPads) and the Applications Required for the Project

The participants were instructed to use the mobile devices (iPads) for several purposes:

1. Using their iPads efficiently for various purposes including how to prolong battery life and upload documents to the cloud;
2. Searching for possible solutions to the encountered problems/dilemmas;
3. Implementing the chosen solution such as individualizing instruction for a child, organizing activities for a group of children, behavior management;
4. Using the various productivity applications to manage scheduling, tasks, and time planning.

Findings

The pre- and post-tests (i.e. surveys) were administered through Qualtrics software and were exported to SPSS for analysis. The data analysis consisted of descriptive statistics and paired T-tests to determine if there are significant differences between pre- and post-survey results.

The reflections, problem-solving process documents submitted by the interns, and the final semi-structured interviews were qualitatively analyzed as a whole through content analysis. In analyzing these documents we looked at two categories of information: information about the types of challenges encountered in the field and the processes used by the student teachers to overcome them, and information about the use of mobile technology as a facilitator during their problem-solving and/or resiliency-development process. For the first category we used the classification of risk/challenges factors developed by Beltman, Mansfield, and Price (2011) to organize and present our data (see Table 19.1).

The Resiliency Scale administered before and after the teaching period showed significant differences. The paired T-test showed a significance of .045, which in a larger sample could be interpreted as important. However since we only had six students, we cannot draw any conclusions except that this is something to follow in a larger sample. We also intend to develop a resiliency scale that includes all the factors that the Beltman, Mansfield, and Price (2011) study identified.

The Sense of Self-Efficacy Scale did not show any significant differences between the pre- and post-tests, but again, because of the small size of the sample this is something to be followed in the future with larger samples. One has to keep in mind though that the perceived self-efficacy is not an attribute that changes in such a short time.

The Technology Use Survey did not show significant change between the two types of administration. It was surprising though that while most students seemed to have access and be knowledgeable using various types of technology tools, 67 percent of them never used online collaborative and sharing tools. Also, none of the students had access to an iPad prior to this study.

By using the classification of risk/challenges factors (Table 19.1) developed by Beltman, Mansfield, and Price (2011) to analyze and present the qualitative data, we were able to identify several themes that were frequently mentioned as challenges during the student teaching. Solving certain challenges involved the use of the iPads while others required more complex solutions.

Risk/challenge Factors

Classroom Management/Disruptive Students

This was the challenge most frequently mentioned. The student teachers clearly did not feel prepared to cope with students who had disruptive behaviors and wished they had more training. Additionally, the fact that they were not present when the classroom rules were set made them feel at a disadvantage.

The Teacher Workload in Addition to Actual Classroom Teaching

This was another challenge mentioned very frequently. The interns were surprised and felt overwhelmed by the amount of paperwork involved, and by the nonteaching activities that the special education teachers in particular were asked to perform.

Concern about Emotional Involvement with their Students

This was another frequent topic of worry for the interns. The majority were concerned about being able to separate personal from work-related involvement. One student said, "I'm concerned that my heart strings will want to take over when I am a teacher and how do I balance my emotions with all of my students?" They expressed their wish to be able to control their emotions. "Will I be able to control my emotions or will I break down and cry?" said another.

Table 19.1 Content analysis themes regarding resiliency protective and risk factors

Category	Subcategory 1	Subcategory 2
Individual Risk/Challenges		Negative beliefs/low self-confidence
		Difficulty asking for help
		Lack of control of one's emotions; stress
Contextual Risk/Challenges	Classroom/school	Classroom management/disruptive students
		Meeting needs of disadvantaged (DS)/special needs students (SpN)
		Scheduling, workload, timing, flow of workday (SCH)
		Imposed stressful times
		Relationships with students' parents

Content (**Interviews content** Reflections content)
I feel a rollercoaster of emotions. Some days I feel confident in my abilities and other days, particularly when a student has a meltdown and trashes my room, I wonder if I am making a difference.
W—no difficulty asking for help after trying herself.
My strengths were seeking information.
Desire to separate personal from work-related emotional involvements.
I'm concerned that my heart strings will want to take over when I am a teacher and how do I balance my emotions with all of my students?
Will I be able to control my emotions or will I break down and cry?
Something that I would like to improve is controlling my emotions.
I am concerned about my heart getting the best of me.
W—a boy who was hitting—try diff ways but had to step back because did not work.
S—a girl yelled at her—clinical teacher cited the rules; assistant principal also helped.
Manage students with severe behavioral issues.
I have one student in particular that I am unsure of how to get him to function in a classroom environment without acting out or shutting down.
I would like to improve my approach for when students shut down and refuse to work. Since being in the classroom I can see how easily one child's behavior can change and how that affects the entire class.
I am concerned about how to keep the class under control.
How do I respond when they become disruptive, violent, and throw things?
I had my first experience with behavior problems in the classroom.
How to handle discipline problems in the classroom.
W—students in poverty.
Meeting the needs of diverse special ed students.
Would like to know in advance how a day of work would look like, organization of events, planning.
I made the discovery that teachers have a lot of things placed on them, some at very short notice.
I feel like I have walked into a world where multi-tasking is a must.
Assessment is very stressful time for students.
Stressed and exhausted because of all the work to be done on top of teaching.
This week I feel like I am over my head, with school and with my family. I think I can be a great teacher, but what do I do about being a parent for my own child?
I am concerned about how to grade when a parent does the homework for their child.

(*Continued*)

Table 19.1 Content analysis themes regarding resiliency protective and risk factors

Category	Subcategory 1	Subcategory 2
	Professional work	Relationships with colleagues
		Scrutiny of peers, parents, principal
		Using material prepared by others
		Heavy workload, lack of time, non-teaching activities
		Difficult schools, courses or classes
		Externally imposed regulations
		Unsupportive/no mentor
		Low salary/poor funding
Individual Protective factors	Personal attributes	Altruism; moral purpose; influence of faith
		Strong intrinsic motivation – sense of vocation
		Tenacity; perseverance; persistence
		Positive attitude; enthusiasm; optimism
		Not primarily motivated by extrinsic rewards
		Emotional intelligence; emotional stability

Content (**Interviews content** Reflections content)
I am concerned about my role as a Special Education teacher and working with the General Education teachers.
I am concerned about collaborating with other teachers.
There is a lack of communication between the special education teachers and the general education teachers.
I am less confident (second guess myself) when the clinical teacher is around.
W and S would have liked to see how the rules were established at the beginning of semester.
W and S—work overwhelmed, they had to lead a classroom and submit all weekly assignments for their seminars and work on their E-portfolios, and TCWS.
Paperwork, administrative work.
There is so much more to teaching than the classroom—need to be aware of the home environment of children.
There is a lot of planning involved in teaching—overwhelming.
I watch my clinical teacher work every day on paperwork for new and existing students and it is amazing to see how she handles the stress.
I am concerned about all of the relationships that I will encounter with my colleagues. That type of relationship with your peers makes your job a lot harder than it should be. I am concerned about how to handle that type of situation if it should occur.
W and S complained about classroom rules being set before their arrival.
S—clinical teacher not technology oriented, not facilitating her use of technology.
Questioning why teachers are not paid more or more recognized for the work they do! It truly is a profession that is demanding but very rewarding.
How do teachers meet the needs of their students when funds and resources are limited?
Teachers don't receive enough money as it is and they have to spend a lot of their own money for supplies in their classroom.
Belief that all children should have the same opportunities.
W, S and M all implied a strong sense of vocation.
S—keeping telling those students they can do better—maintained high expectations for students.
Confidence in my ability to plan lessons.
All interns reaffirmed that they want to be teachers, that their place is in the classroom and they love children—became attached to the ones they taught.
I think smiling will keep me sane.

(*Continued*)

Table 19.1 Content analysis themes regarding resiliency protective and risk factors

Category	Subcategory 1	Subcategory 2
		Patience
		Flexibility
	Self-efficacy	Willingness to take risks/accept failure
		Sense of competence, pride, confidence
		Internal locus of control; belief in ability to make a difference
		Self-efficacy increases with experience
	Coping skills	Proactive problem-solving skills including help seeking
		Able to let go, accept failure, learn and move on
		Use of active coping skills
		High levels of interpersonal skills, strong networks; socially competent
	Teaching skills	Know students; help them succeed; high expectations
		Skilled in range of instructional practices

Content (Interviews content Reflections content)
W—surprised by the patience/calm attitude she had with disruptive children.
Ability to stay calm when one student was behaving poorly.
W—trying to be a more "go with the flow person."
You often have to think outside the box in order to teach your lessons effectively.
My clinical teacher's lesson plans are fluid and flexible.
My strengths this week were being flexible and going with the flow.
I have found that flexibility is very important.
W—had to learn to step back when unsuccessful repeatedly.
My strength this week was finding (and saving) resources that will be helpful for me in the future.
I feel proud of myself. I got to help make some decisions in the classroom and in the planning process.
I made huge gains with one student who has been particularly difficult to work with.
With each week that I am in this internship my confidence grows in my ability to successfully teach.
As I observed my clinical teacher this week I came to the conclusion that I am perfectly capable of doing this.
All participants considered themselves good problem solvers, but also ready to seek help when necessary.
Ability to divorce myself from the school day when I get home.
I would like to improve how I manage my time and workload.
M—uses the professional network in the school as support system.
S—high expectations.
W—committed to educate children from poverty backgrounds.
Being consistent with the children.
Strength is knowing that a child can achieve anything if we just believe they can do it and if we set small steps to build their self-confidence and self-worth.
I think my strength this week has been discipline and holding students accountable for their behavior.
I spent a lot of time helping them to deal with the frustrations they were experiencing over reading the text on their own.
I have noticed that lesson planning comes more easily and I am able to adapt instruction more easily.
My strength this week was my ability to be firm about my expectation about behavior in the classroom.

(*Continued*)

Table 19.1 Content analysis themes regarding resiliency protective and risk factors

Category	Subcategory 1	Subcategory 2
		Confidence in teaching abilities
		Time management and organization
	Self-care	Creative and explore new ideas
		Take active responsibility for own well-being
		Significant supportive relationships
Contextual Protective factors	Contextual support	School/administrative support
		Mentor support
		Support of peers and colleagues
		Working with the students
		Characteristics of preservice program
		Support of family and friends

Source: Adapted from Beltman, S., Mansfield, C., & Price, A. (2011).

Content (**Interviews content** Reflections content)
My strength this week was to help students deal with the anxiety of completing work on their assignments.
With each week that I am in this internship my confidence grows in my ability to successfully teach.
I know the routines and what needs to be done in the mornings, during class, and after school and I am able to get stuff done without anyone asking me to do it.
I have more responsibility in the classroom which is accompanied with more independence.
My strengths this week was classroom leadership. This was the first time I had the opportunity to have complete control of the classroom.
Time management and organization are not my strengths.
How to keep the big teaching picture in mind as I plan and teach in the present? Planning all the time is a little intimidating to me because I'm not sure how to plan and organize for the future and the present at the same time.
My strength would be my organization skills.
Time management would be the thing I need to work on. There is not enough time in the day to complete everything that is required.
This week my strengths were having an imagination and thinking like a child.
S—relax after hard days.
W—calendar of dancing lessons on iPad.
W—my mother was a big support.
S—both parents were teachers and I talk with them a lot.
S—university supervisor and clinical teachers have been very supportive.
W—cooperating teacher was very helpful with lesson plans.
W—university supervisor was very helpful in alleviating student's worries regarding the E-portfolio. "It will be ok; you will figure it out!"
Mentorship support implemented in the first year of teaching—all.
Use of the school network of colleagues for support—all.
The children in my class can be a joy to be around and they sure can make you feel better if you're feeling a little blue.
W and S considered that the program prepared them well to start teaching.
W—her mom was very supportive—helps her with suggestions to teach teak ideas, brainstorm strategies.
S—both parents were teachers and I talk with them a lot.

Relationships with their Colleagues

This was a concern for special education teachers who worried that regular education teachers did not communicate enough with them regarding inclusion of children with special needs.

Time Management and Organization

This was often mentioned as a significant challenge due to the multitude of tasks the teachers are expected to accomplish.

Protective Factors

Flexibility

This was the quality that the student teachers mentioned often as a necessity for coping with various situations in the classroom.

Sense of Competence, Pride, and Confidence

This was the next protective factor identified in teachers' reflections.

Helping Students Succeed and Having High Expectations of Them

This was mentioned by four of the six students as being an important ingredient of teacher success.

Through the reflections during the internship, the students discovered and commented on their personal and professional growth and the process of building self-confidence and self-efficacy as they became more experienced. As the student reflections progressed later into the semester, they were showing more confidence in their ability to teach and to handle unexpected situations such as behavioral manifestations. The common theme at the beginning was that they felt just like visitors in the classroom, whereas gradually they began to recognize they can have a role and that the students listen to and respect them as participants in the educational process. "I have more responsibility in the classroom which is accompanied with more independence," said one student, while another remarked, "I know the routines and what needs to be done in the mornings, during class, and after school and I am able to get stuff done without anyone asking me to do it." This process was not easy and during many weeks they often doubted themselves, questioning and arguing back and forth their choice to become a teacher.

Intrinsic Motivation for Teaching

In the form of declared commitment to the profession and desire to make a difference in the lives of children, intrinsic motivation was implied by all interns in one way or another during their reflections and interviews.

Use of Mobile Technology to Facilitate Problem Solving

During the exit interviews the interns revealed their use of the iPads during the student teaching period. We grouped these uses in the following categories: professional use, personal use, and use for problem solving.

Use of iPads for Professional Purposes

All students used the iPad to help them in planning their lessons, either by using it to write lesson plans on the go or by looking for applications or videos to use in their teaching. Another universally common use of the iPad was to reward the students by letting them use it for educational purposes. Still other students used the iPads to individualize instruction. For example, one intern would give the iPad to a student who needed help with reading and would let him play reading games while his classmates were involved in higher-level reading activities. Another professional use was for jotting down notes while in the classroom. "The iPad is so easy to grab and so easy to access. You jot down things that you would forget otherwise." Interns also used the iPads for networking with their colleagues and for sharing or asking for teaching tips. One science education teacher declared during her exit interview that the use of technology was a point of contention between her and the classroom teacher. She said that although the classroom was equipped with a Smart Board and the students could check out laptops, these devices were never used. In addition, when the intern suggested the use of the iPad for projecting student work on the Smart Board she encountered rejection from the teacher worded as "Let's do this at another time. For now, let's continue the way as I have always done it."This particular example shows that the new mobile technologies have more opponents than adopters and discrepancies over their use could be another professional dilemma that novice teachers will have to solve. (There are many more examples of professional uses of the iPads.)

Use of iPads for Personal Purposes

The interns admitted that it was easy to use the iPad for keeping a personal calendar, to-do lists, or for playing mindless games to relax after a long day at school. During such a stressful period as teacher internship, having an easy way to organize one's life and keep track of multiple tasks is definitely part of building resiliency. On the other hand, although it might seem that personal relaxation has nothing to do with solving professional dilemmas, one of the personal protective factors that play an important role in building resiliency is taking care of oneself (Beltman, Mansfield, & Price, 2011).

Use of iPads for Problem Solving

Although there is sufficient evidence in the data collected in this study that the student teachers used the iPad to solve many problems encountered in their internship semester, only two kept records of their challenges/professional dilemmas in a structured format as suggested by the researchers. For instance one of the interns in special education wrote this dilemma related to behavior problems in the classroom. Issue: "How do I handle a situation when a student is physical with me (tries to hit me)? I feel very frustrated, angry, a little insulted and extremely overwhelmed." The app lets the user choose the emotions experienced and grade their intensity by sliding a lever on a continuum. The user can also add feelings that are not on the list. Identifying the feelings created by a difficult situation is the first step in acquiring the emotional control that allows rational thinking. The student continued by describing her blocking thoughts (these are usually barriers to the solving process): (1) I don't want the child to feel like they have won and hitting is an acceptable behavior; (2) I want the child to take responsibility for his actions and recognize appropriate behavior—but what is appropriate?; (3) I don't want to appear like "tattling on the child" to the teacher in charge because they may see me as incompetent (i.e. I cannot handle the situation by myself). Then the student proceeds to pair each blocking thought with its "distractions" and with the description of a "more actionable thought" respectively. In the case of the first blocking thought (I don't want the child to feel like they have won and hitting is an acceptable behavior), the distractions chosen were "all-or-nothing thinking" and "I-can't-stand-it-is." The app offers a list of twelve so-called "distractions" representing the most common negative ways of thinking. The final problem-solving step is the development of "more actionable thoughts" related to the blocking thought in question. In this case the student listed "I can make the child understand that they hurt me and have the child take an appropriate action to rectify the situation such as helping me finish a task."

While the "I can do for iPad" app is a valuable tool for solving everyday life problems, there is certainly a need for developing apps that can assist with professional dilemmas. Such apps should include steps related to the process of professional growth and development, as it is described by the creators of the Connect modules (http://community.fpg.unc.edu) and include the definition of the professional dilemma, formulating it in an answerable question, looking at evidence-based practices and professional literature, making a decision, and finally evaluating the decision implementation.

All students expressed their feeling of being overwhelmed by the workload of the internship and their difficulty in following the problem-solving steps framework. The writing up of encountered problems was an additional task that was not required by the internship and therefore was perceived as optional. In future studies we will include the problem-solving steps in the required reflections in order to be able to have a periodic and documented recording of the challenges they face and the solutions they consider in solving them.

Implications

The process through which novice teachers use and possibly develop resiliency is an important component for job satisfaction and teacher retention. We focused on the problem-solving process as a main contributor to develop resilient teachers that do not only survive but thrive in adverse environments. By providing the student teachers with mobile technologies (iPads) we discovered a variety of possible apps used as strategies to cope with challenges and develop resiliency.

In an era in which mobile technology becomes the norm rather than the novelty, teacher preparation programs should explore the diverse opportunities that this offers. Although resiliency has been acknowledged as being a crucial factor in teacher retention, there are no documented approaches to date targeting it. Problem-solving skills are a crucial component of resiliency and new, more complex apps need to be developed in order to provide appropriate support to professionals in the field. The study described here is only the first stage of a series of systematic inquiries in the process of building teacher resiliency with the aid of mobile technology and at incorporating the results in teacher education programs.

References

Beltman, S., Mansfield, C., & Price, A. (2011). Thriving not just surviving: A review of research on teacher resilience. *Educational Research Review, 6*(3), 185–207. doi:10.1016/j.edurev.2011.09.001.

Bennett, K., & Cunningham, A. C. (2009). Teaching formative assessment strategies to preservice teachers: Exploring the use of handheld computing to facilitate the action research process. *Journal of Computing in Teacher Education, 25*(3), 99–105.

Bobek, B. L. (2002). Teacher resiliency: A key to career longevity. *Clearing House, 75*(4), 202. Retrieved March 2, 2011, from http://0-search.ebscohost.com.uncclc.coast.uncwil.edu:80/login.aspx?direct=true&db=ehh&AN=6519729&site=ehost-live.

Castro, A. J., Kelly, J., & Shih, M. (2010). Resilience strategies for new teachers in high-needs areas. *Teaching & Teacher Education, 26*(3), 622–629. doi:10.1016/j.tate.2009.09.010.

Day, C., & Gu, Q. (2007). Variations in the conditions for teachers' professional learning and development: Sustaining commitment and effectiveness over a career. *Oxford Review of Education, 33*(4), 423–443.

Franklin, T., Sexton, C., Young, L., & Hongyan, M. (2007). PDAs in teacher education: A case study examining mobile technology integration. *Journal of Technology and Teacher Education, 15*(1), 39–57.

Gu, Q., & Day, C. (2007). Teachers' resilience: A necessary condition for effectiveness. *Teaching & Teacher Education, 23*(8), 1302–1316. doi:10.1016/j.tate.2006.06.006.

Howard, S., & Johnson, B. (2004). Resilient teachers: Resisting stress and burnout. *Social Psychology of Education, 7*(4), 399–420.

Huisman, S., Singer, N. R., & Catapano, S. (2010). Resiliency to success: Supporting novice urban teachers. *Teacher Development, 14*(4), 483–499. doi:10.1080/13664530.2010.533490.

Kuechle, J., Holzhauer, M., Lin, R., Brulle, A., & Morrison, S. (2010). Teaching Ms. Kerbin: A unique approach to student teacher reflections and their use with preservice candidates. *Action in Teacher Education, 32*(3), 25–39.

Margolis, J. (2008). What will keep today's teachers teaching? Looking for a hook as a new career cycle emerges. *Teachers College Record, 110*(1), 160–194.

Schön, D. (1983) *The reflective practitioner: How professionals think in action*. London: Temple Smith.

Soloway, E., Grant, W., Tinker, R., Roschelle, J., Mills, M., Resnick, M., Berg R., & Eisenberg, M. (1999). Science in the palm of their hands. *Communications of the ACM, 42*, 21–26.

Tait, M. (2008). Resilience as a contributor to novice teacher success, commitment, and retention. *Teacher Education Quarterly, 35*(4), 57–75.

Tschannen-Moran, M., & Woolfolk Hoy, A. (2007). The differential antecedents of self-efficacy beliefs of novice and experienced teachers. *Teaching & Teacher Education, 23*(6), 944–956. doi:10.1016/j.tate.2006.05.003.

Yost, D. S. (2006). Reflection and self-efficacy: Enhancing the retention of qualified teachers from a teacher education perspective. *Teacher Education Quarterly, 33*(4), 59–76.

Zost, G. (2010). An examination of resiliency in rural special educators. *Rural Educator, 31*(2), 10–14.

Chapter 20
iPad-enabled Experiments in an Undergraduate Physics Laboratory

Technology has often been a catalyst for educational change and tablet computers such as the iPad are no different. For example, like a calculator, an iPad can be used as a tool to enhance education and learning. Our research involved using iPads and specific software applications ("apps") as replacement equipment for two traditional laboratory experiments in an introductory physics course. In the past, these experiments have utilized laboratory equipment to measure kinematical properties of motion (e.g., position, velocity, acceleration, etc.) and electronic properties in a circuit (e.g., voltage, resistance, etc.). The iPad and apps provided tools that allowed students to automate repetitive and multiple tasks (e.g., tracking position of a moving object and performing motion analysis), enabled simplified interfaces (e.g., virtual oscilloscope), and promoted mobility of experiments. The results of our case study show how iPads and apps provide automation and a simplified interface that can help promote student engagement, enhance measurement accuracy and consistency, and reduce student anxiety.

For Designers

Designing a functional, yet simplistic, interface can be complicated to achieve. One of the advantages of using apps over traditional laboratory equipment is the simplicity of apps' design and the automation of data collection. Additionally, apps often offer quick and instant feedback, which the laboratory environment usually lacks. In the case of our research, the design of both of the apps provided users the ability to collect and manipulate experimental data with a simple interface, and combined several operations into a single interface.

For Teachers

Integrating technology into one's curriculum can be difficult and overwhelming. However, when technology is used for very specific purposes, both the complexities of implementation and anxiety can be reduced. For example, in both of our cases, the apps were chosen for specific purposes of automating data collection and analysis while promoting student engagement with a friendly interface. Simply put, the integration and implementation of the iPads and apps enhanced instruction, because the technologies were well suited for the lab experiment.

For Researchers

When we research new implementations of technology and pedagogies it is important to consider the educational context. We noticed that students often spend too much time struggling with the operation of equipment and become frustrated with performing repetitive laboratory measurements, which interfered with their learning of physics. Being aware of the context provided us an opportunity to conduct a research project that used iPads to automate data acquisition, improve accuracy and consistency in student measurements, as well as improve students' overall educational experience.

Automative, friendly, and mobile interfaces will speed up and enhance learning.

Dr. Roberto Ramos
Associate Professor,
Physics,
Indiana Wesleyan University

Dr. Christopher Devers
Director of Research,
Center for Learning and Innovation,
Indiana Wesleyan University;
Assistant Professor,
Indiana Wesleyan University

Roberto Ramos is the Blanchard Endowed Chair of Physics and Mathematics and Associate Professor of Physics at Indiana Wesleyan University (IWU) in Marion, Indiana. He is an experimental condensed matter physicist and is published in *Science* and *Nature Communications*. His active research interests include superconductivity, quantum information, nanotechnology, and physics education. He is interested in the role of technology in improving science education. He is a native of the Philippines, received his PhD in Physics from the University of Washington, and did postdoctoral work at the University of Maryland. He is an elected member of the Philippine-American Academy of Science and Engineering.

Christopher Devers is Director of Research for the Center for Learning and Innovation and an assistant professor in the School of Education at Indiana Wesleyan University (IWU). Prior to joining IWU, Dr. Devers was a professor at the University of San Diego, where he taught graduate courses on cognition and technology. Professor Devers' research focuses on the processes and environments in which technology promotes learning. He received a PhD from the University of Illinois at Urbana-Champaign.

iPad-enabled Experiments in an Undergraduate Physics Laboratory

Educational Change and Technology

Throughout history, technology has been a catalyst for change within education; a pencil is one such example (Baron, 1999). When pencils were equipped with erasers, educators argued that quick access to erasers would cause pupils to be less studious, as they would have the option of erasing their work (Baron, 1999). However, using pencils with attached erasers did not harm education, but rather allowed students to easily revise their work. Educators and others have made similar arguments in regard to technologies such as pens, highlighters, chalk boards, dry erase boards, overhead projectors, data projectors, calculators, computers, audience response systems, etc. For example, one might argue that using a calculator may cause students to fail to memorize multiplication tables. However, we must remember that technology is simply a tool that can either aid or hinder education, and ultimately it should be used in ways that have positive effects on education. As in the calculator example, addition, subtraction, and multiplication tables still needed to be learned and memorized; using the device simply helps decrease cognitive load, which can free up mental resources that can be used for problem solving. The same argument can be said about iPads and apps. Outfitting a classroom or even an entire school with iPads does not mean that one should stop learning content or memorizing facts, simply because content and facts can easily be found on the Internet. Again, an iPad is one tool that can be used to promote learning. The challenge then becomes integrating iPads in a meaningful way that helps contribute to learning—much like the calculator example. Just as pencils promoted educational change, iPads too can provide a catalyst for rethinking how we approach education.

Advantages and Disadvantages of Technology

Technology offers the advantage of providing quick and cheap feedback. For example, students know right away if they have successfully answered a problem, and often, their answer did not cost them much capital—students do not suffer criticism from others, the device did not make noise or break, etc. More specifically, iPads offer the following quick and cheap feedback. First, they are more visually oriented than mechanical devices, which allows one to focus more on solving the problem than trying to figure out how to operate the device. Second, because they can record audio/video, one is able to capture an event in real time, and rewatch the event as many times as needed; thus eliminating the need to repeat an event multiple times. Third, iPads are simple to operate (e.g., touch interface)—students do not become confused from seeing an array of knobs, worry about turning the wrong one, or fear pushing the wrong button. Fourth, the device can easily be reset if needed. If something goes wrong using an iPad, one simply can push the home button and reopen the app. Last, iPads offer portability.

Students are able to simply move the device around as needed. For example, students might complete a lab in class and then take the device outside to repeat the lab in a different environment. These components provide a rich environment that, when utilized well, can have a positive impact on student learning.

There are disadvantages to technology as well, such as price, battery life, sustainability, etc. However, many believe that the educational advantages of technology outweigh their disadvantages. Additionally, as technology evolves, some of the disadvantages will become less of an issue. For example, iPads do not suffer some of the complexities and problems often associated with traditional computers—viruses, corrupted programs, complex navigation and general setup, and so on. Overall, given the right environment, the advantages of technology often outweigh the disadvantages.

Mobile Devices in Education

Technology is evolving as small touch-enabled devices become more and more prevalent in society; some even argue that PCs will become obsolete. With the onset of this post-PC environment, mobile touch devices can provide unique advantages and opportunities for student learning. For example, in a physics laboratory, iPads and iPods can be used instead of complicated mechanical equipment. More specifically, in the past, one might use a mouse and keyboard to concurrently control multiple 3D particles produced from holographic optical tweezers. However, research suggests that using an iPad and a specialized app (iHologram) can provide a more intuitive interaction with the particles (Bowman et al., 2011). Whereas, using a mouse and keyboard offered a somewhat limited interface with the device, an iPad allowed the app to simultaneous interpret eleven touches (inputs) at any given time (Bowman et al., 2011). Using the iPad allowed novices to interact with the equipment, whereas before, specialized training might have been required. Additionally, mobile smartphones have also been used in physics classes. A mechanical oscilloscope can be intimidating and students often have difficulty using the device—they are plagued with many knobs, dials, and buttons. However, an oscilloscope attachment developed by HMB-TEC can be plugged into either an iPhone or iPod Touch, that when combined with an app, provides a touch-enabled portable oscilloscope (Forinash & Wisman, 2012). The intuitive touch interface allows one to easily navigate the software, as well as save pictures, export data, and zoom in or out of the graph, which would be difficult to accomplish with a traditional mechanical device. Clearly, when integrated with thoughtful activities and lessons, iPads and iPods can provide educational benefits.

Overview of our Case Study

Due to the advantages and portability associated with touch-enabled devices, we used iPads as a pedagogical tool for select physics labs—the study of accelerated motion through video-motion analysis and the study of electronic circuit behavior using the iPad as a virtual oscilloscope. More specifically, we evaluated the iPad's potential for high-power visualization, manipulation, and presentation of physical phenomena in a classroom and laboratory environment. Physics is a highly technical field, where the study of abstract principles of motion and electricity can potentially benefit from the power of visualization, audio-visual data acquisition, and mobility that the iPad provides. These benefits were realized by utilizing the iPad's features, which include an onboard video-camera, microphone, accelerometers, and gyroscope. Furthermore, the intuitive and friendly touch interface provided a more familiar, less intimidating, and more educationally engaging platform for delivering and processing content in the physical sciences, particularly for non-science majors.

In this case study (Stake, 1995; Yin, 2003), we evaluated the pedagogical value of the iPad and several physics applications or "apps" based on our experience in using these in two three-credit introductory physics courses taught at Indiana Wesleyan University (IWU). The year-long course consisted of a traditional lecture class and its laboratory component. The class consisted of twenty-seven students who were not physics majors (typically pre-med, biology, exercise science, etc.). Students met weekly for three one-hour lectures, and were divided into two student lab sections that met weekly for two hours. Inside the traditional physics laboratory, students performed ten experiments that cemented their understanding of concepts learned in lectures. Up until the Fall of 2011, students had been using conventional "benchtop labs" that included blocks, strings, and inclined planes to study motion, and a standard oscilloscope to study basic principles of circuit analysis.

To many students, physics experiments involve tools which are complicated to use (as in the case of the oscilloscope, with its many knobs and switches) and somewhat disconnected from common real-world experiences (as in pulleys, wooden blocks, and masses). In this case study, we present how the iPad improved the educational experience in the traditional introductory college physics laboratory (Bush, Garriott, & Ramos, 2012). Our experiences indicate that it can be used to enhance interest and efficiency, and make connections with real-world applications. We report the impact of two types of iPad-enabled physics experiments.

1. The study of accelerated motion through video motion analysis
2. The study of electronic circuit behavior using the iPad as a virtual oscilloscope.

We also present student responses to this new pedagogy, and compare performance to conventional methods. In the lecture part of the course, the iPad was also actively used to perform visually stimulating in-class demonstrations of wave motion and audio analysis.

Video Motion Analysis in the University Physics Laboratory

Introduction to Video Motion Analysis in Physics Courses

Many students who have taken an introductory course in physics can attest that their first few laboratory experiments dealt with "classical mechanics" or the study of motion—particularly accelerated motion associated with free-falling objects or objects sliding along an inclined plane (i.e. accelerated linear motion). A second experiment typically involves projectile motion, which is a combination of two linear motions along two directions: accelerated motion along the vertical axis, and linear motion along the horizontal axis. In both experiments, the objective is to measure the position of objects at various times, from which one determines their velocity and acceleration. The "objects" involved are usually metallic weights or blocks of wood sliding on a surface. A third class of experiments usually involves some form of rotation, say of a wheel or pulley.

These tried and tested experiments have been used for decades in the instructional physics laboratory. Objects are usually tracked using a ticker tape tied to the moving object. The paper tape passes through a "spark timer" which produces a physical record of the motion by making electrical burn marks on tape at set time intervals. The velocity of the tape (and therefore, the object) is obtained by measuring the distance between burn marks, and then dividing these by the time between sparks. After plotting velocity against the total time, the slope of the resulting curve tells us the nature of the motion, whether it is uniform or accelerated. For example, for constant velocity motion, the marks on the tape will be evenly spaced while for uniformly accelerated motion, the spacing will either increase or decrease consistently. However, the use of a ticker tape is intrinsically invasive and, in many cases, not accurate. For example, if the ball being tracked rebounds after hitting the floor or if the wooden block reverses direction on its way up an inclined plane, the resulting slack in the paper tape does not result in meaningful data points. Furthermore, the act of measuring distances between many ticker-tape burn marks is tedious and susceptible to error.

With the advent of inexpensive camcorders and webcams, video analysis replaced the ticker-tape technique. Specifically, this new technique uses a video camera, with a minimum frame rate of thirty frames per second, to capture the motion of a moving object (Bryan, 2005; Escalada & Zollman, 1999; Rodrigues, Pearce, & Livett, 2001). An educational software application, such as Videopoint Physics (http://www.vpfundamentals.com/), Vernier Logger Pro (http://www.vernier.com/products/software/lp/), Measurement in Motion (http://www.learninginmotion.com/products/measurement/index.html), or Tracker (http://www.cabrillo.edu/˜dbrown/tracker/index.html), is used to capture, frame by frame, the position of a chosen point on the moving object. The software also provides the correct distance scaling by calibrating against a standardized distance (i.e. a meterstick set against the background of the recorded motion). The program can then use the coordinates to calculate, and plot position and velocity as functions of time. The software is usually located in a standalone computer or laptop, to which the camcorder or webcam has to be physically connected. Therefore, the setup consists of multiple components with multiple settings and can be cumbersome to operate.

Using an iPad provides the ability to capture, analyze, and present video, all with a single device. There are no wires, cables, and no bulky camera or camcorder on a tripod. Instead, the iPad has two (front and back) on-board video cameras with a frame rate of thirty frames per second—as good as many inexpensive webcams and camcorders. Furthermore, its mobility gives it the potential to be used outside the traditional classroom and provide access to real-world experiments. Many students also find the touchpad interface friendlier compared with the knobs and settings associated with camcorders and other equipment (e.g., oscilloscope). The ease of use tends to reduce the learning curve associated with operating science equipment and helps students focus on content versus delivery tools. Finally, the iPad has other sensors that may be used for experiments not discussed here, including a microphone to input sound for acoustic studies, an accelerometer for measuring real-time acceleration of the iPad, and a gyroscope for sensing rotation of the iPad for angular measurements.

iPad Pedagogy in Motion-based Experiments: Description and Results

Video motion analysis in this physics lab class was made possible using an iPad and the Vernier Video Physics app (http://www.vernier.com/products/software/video-physics/). The goal of the experiment was to analyze motion of a chosen object in three different cases:

1. Free-fall of a dropped tennis ball
2. Projectile motion of a tennis ball
3. Uniform circular motion of a marker on a wheel of a stationary bicycle.

Video Physics allows for the capture and storage of video clips that are recorded directly on the iPad.

For this lab experiment, we recorded short video clips representing the three cases. After the video was recorded, data points were plotted by tracking a single point on the object as it moved, frame by frame, throughout its trajectory.

Using the crosshairs that appeared on the software's interface, the user moved the crosshairs over to the point and tapped the iPad—repeating this for different points, for different time frames, yielded the data points for the objects' positions.

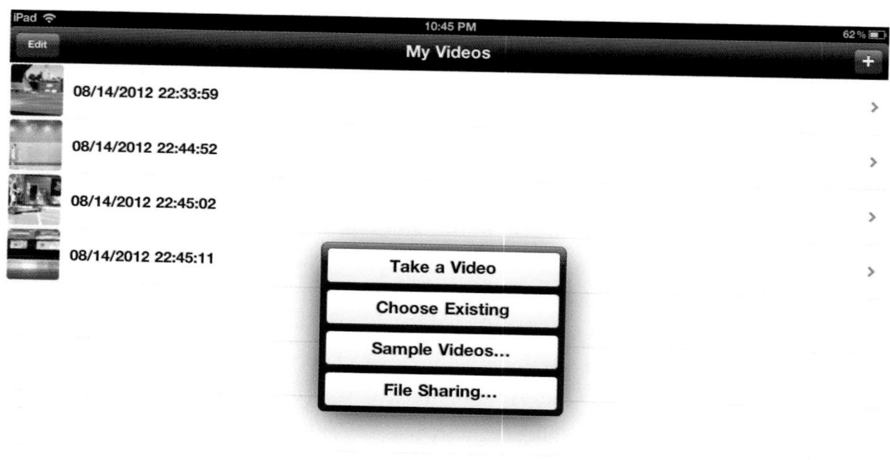

Figure 20.1
The Vernier Video Physics app start screen that allows one to capture and load video for analysis.

To determine the actual distances travelled by the object, distances on the iPad screen are calibrated against the image of a meterstick positioned near the plane of the motion. In addition, the origin of an x–y coordinate system can be positioned as desired. The software can then automatically plot the trajectory, as well as the position versus time graphs, and the velocity versus time graphs.

By taking the slope of the velocity–time curve, one can calculate the acceleration of the object.

This entire process described takes no more than a few minutes, because of the automatic data acquisition and processing by the iPad. In contrast, using a spark timer and ticker-tape system would take more than two or three times longer than the iPad, because the experimenter has to manually and tediously measure the distances between successive dots on the tape. Cases 1 (free-fall of a dropped tennis ball) and 3 (uniform circular motion of a marker on a wheel of a stationary bicycle) listed above are

Figure 20.2

A loaded video where one is able to track a moving object—in this video, a baseball (video from Vernier).

illustrated in Figures 20.5 and 20.6. In Figure 20.5, the y-components of position and velocity, as generated by Video Physics, are shown. Because the y-coordinate increases proportional to the square of time (t^2), its slope, which is the y-velocity, is increasing linearly in time. The constant slope of this y-velocity, which is shown by the drawn guide line, is in agreement with constant value of the acceleration due to gravity, $g = 9.8$ m/s^2.

In Figure 20.6, the trajectory, position- and velocity-versus time curves of a marker on a bicycle wheel are also plotted. From these data points, it is possible to obtain the angular speed of a point on the wheel. This specific example also highlights the potential of using the iPad in performing measurements in the field (in this case, the recreation center). Its portability allowed students to realize how the laws of physics can be used to describe and understand real-world applications.

In terms of accuracy and precision, the iPad performs on the same level as other inexpensive systems. There are small amounts of blur, which represent uncertainty in position, but it is only of great concern with objects moving at very high speeds.

Figure 20.3

Vernier's software can be used to capture the frame-by-frame motion of a baseball in flight. By clicking on the various positions of the ball, its position coordinates are calculated by the software and used to generate a velocity curve (video from Vernier).

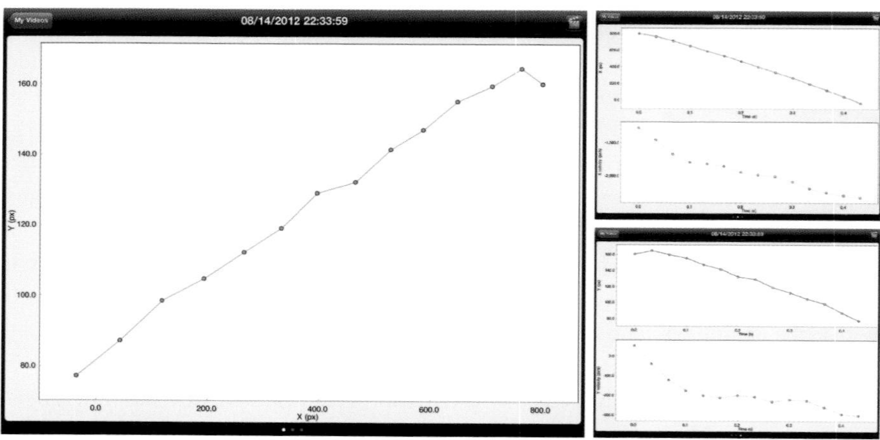

Figure 20.4

The Vernier Video Physics app calculated the velocity curve of the baseball.

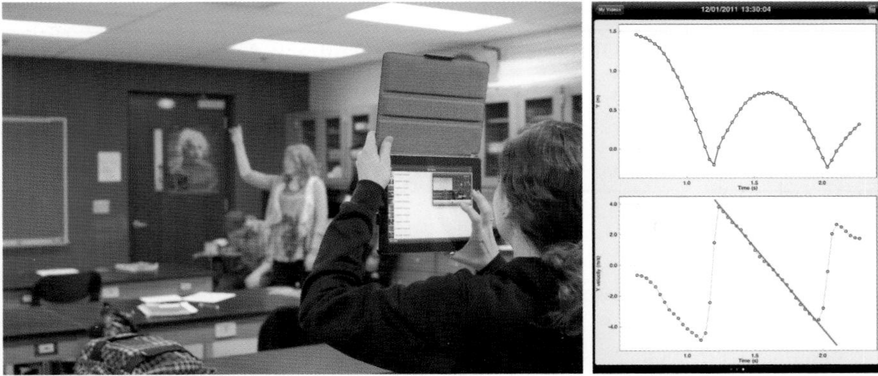

Figure 20.5
Video motion analyses of a tennis ball in flight using an iPad resulted in fast data acquisition and analysis. The Vernier Video Physics app plotted the y-position (top right) and y-velocity (bottom right) against time. The vertical acceleration of the ball due to gravity is extracted by taking the slope of the y-velocity curve.

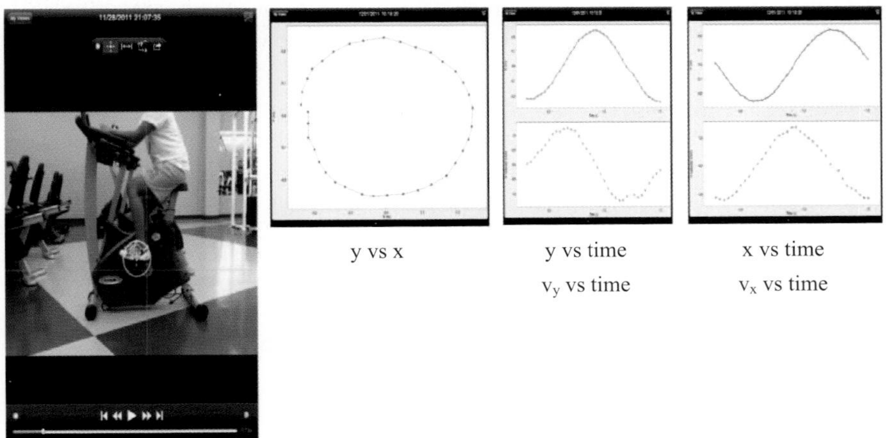

Figure 20.6
The portability of the iPad allowed students to use it to analyze the rotational motion of real-world objects like an exercise bicycle outside the traditional laboratory.

We surveyed twenty-seven students who had completed both a traditional lab that utilized the mechanical motion-based equipment and a lab with the iPad, and compared the results. Students were presented with three statements and were asked to choose their level of agreement, based on five choices: Strongly Agree, Agree, Neutral, Disagree, and Strongly Disagree. The statements are, as follows:

Table 20.1 Survey results from the mechanical motion-based equipment and iPad lab

	Strongly Disagree	Disagree	Neutral	Agree	Strongly Agree
Statement 1	0%	3.7%	3.7%	33.3%	44.4%
Statement 2	0%	3.7%	3.7%	29.6%	59.3%
Statement 3	0%	3.7%	11.1%	40.7%	44.4%

1. Statement 1. The video analysis method, as enabled by the iPad, engaged my attention more than the traditional method of using a spark timer and tape.
2. Statement 2. The video analysis method, as enabled by the iPad, enhanced the visualization of what was happening in the experiment.
3. Statement 3. The video analysis method, as enabled by the iPad, enhanced my understanding of the experiment and its goal of measuring uniformly accelerated motion and projectile motion.

From the anonymous student surveys, it is clear that the majority of the students felt that they were engaged using video motion analysis, as implemented using the iPad, versus the conventional technique of using ticker tapes. Through personal interviews of students, it was made clear that the visualization that the iPad provided, and the elimination of the tediousness of making repetitive measurements, were key factors in the labs' success. The iPad allowed students to spend more time thinking and understanding what was happening rather than mechanically performing measurements and calculations over and over. In addition, the sight of a bicycle wheel, a real-world object used in the lab experiment, allowed the students to appreciate the connection between ideas of motion and everyday objects. Finally, the ability for the students to participate in data collection and see themselves throw balls or turn wheels in the actual video, appeared to enhance the desire to understand the physics underlying their observations.

Oscilloscopes in Physics

Introduction to the Oscilloscope as a Tool to Analyze Electrical Circuits

The analysis of period electronic waveforms, or any oscillating property that can be represented by a time-varying voltage signal, is usually performed using an electronic instrument known as an "oscilloscope." It may help to think of an oscilloscope as a powerful and visual multimeter, which can plot in real time how voltage signals fluctuate over time. Used in many physics and engineering laboratory courses, it looks like a small TV with a screen that displays how a voltage signal, plotted along a vertical axis, changes as a function of time, which is plotted on the horizontal axis.

Figure 20.7
Physics students use a conventional oscilloscope in the foreground while another group uses the iPad oscilloscope in the background.

The voltage signal usually comes from the "output" of a student-assembled circuit and is compared with the "input" voltage signal fed into the circuit. This way, students figure out how the circuit functions.

For example, a typical input signal is a "square wave" voltage signal. This signal turns the voltage "on" and "off" for definite periods of time. If fed into a circuit consisting of a resistor and capacitor (a capacitor is an electronic component that can store electricity), the output voltage looks different from the input voltage. We say that the circuit modified the signal. In general, engineers and physicists are interested in how circuits affect signals. Therefore, the oscilloscope is a powerful educational tool that displays these effects.

The oscilloscope also has many knobs and switches that have many functions, including selecting the voltage scale and time scale of the display, triggering modes, the channels or inputs to probe, etc. As a result, even engineering and science majors often describe the oscilloscope to be quite intimidating and difficult to operate. The situation becomes more frustrating for non-science majors and pre-med students who do not have a particular need to learn about the other functions of an oscilloscope other than what is needed to take some simple measurements.

The iPad as a Virtual Oscilloscope in Physics: Description and Results

To answer the need for student-friendly oscilloscope experiments, we developed, tested, and evaluated experiments that use a "virtual oscilloscope" consisting of an iPad and an electronic accessory called the OSCIUM iMSO-104 (http://www.oscium.com/products/mixed-signal-oscilloscope-imso-104) to replace the conventional oscilloscope.

One of the experiments involved using an oscilloscope to determine the electronic response of a simple RC circuit—a circuit consisting of a resistor of resistance R and capacitor of capacitance C connected in series (a capacitor is an electronic component that stores electrical charge and energy) to an oscillating square wave voltage fed into the

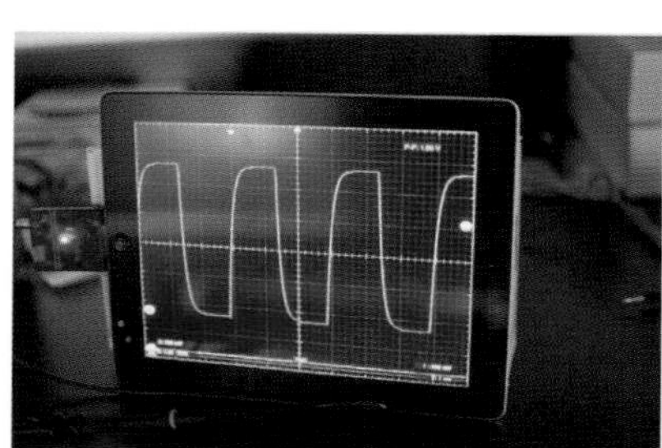

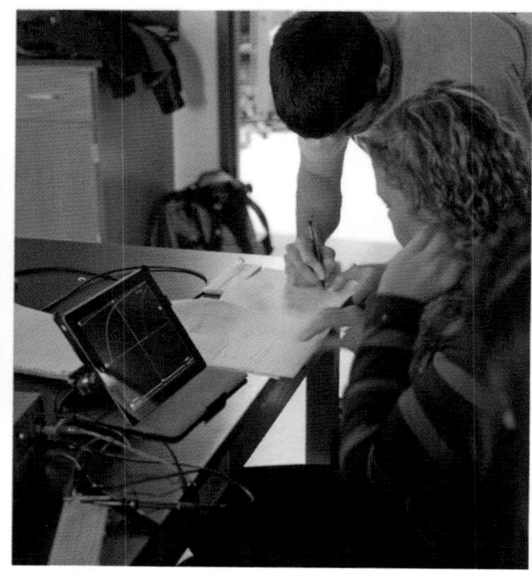

Figure 20.8
Students use the iPad/Oscium iMSO-104 as a virtual oscilloscope to experimentally measure the relaxation time constant of an RC circuit. The large display and simple interface make the iPad oscilloscope ideal for non-engineering majors studying the effect of an RC circuit on simple voltage signals.

circuit. The resulting "output voltage" of the circuit displayed how the capacitor charges and discharges energy over time. The objective was to measure the relaxation time τ = RC (the relaxation time is the product of the resistance R and capacitance C) of the charging process, which is the time it takes for the capacitor to discharge to 37 percent of its maximum energy, as observed through the oscilloscope's screen display.

Figure 20.9a shows the experimental setup consisting of a conventional oscilloscope used to read out the output voltage of the RC circuit mounted on an electronic breadboard excited by a square wave voltage from a function generator.

In contrast, Figure 20.9b displays how the standard oscilloscope has been replaced with an iPad display and the iMSO-104 accessory. There are no knobs or switches and the iPad automatically optimizes the display. Furthermore, the scale or view of the display can easily be changed by pinching the touchpad surface or dragging one's fingers across the screen. The trigger level can also be set by dragging a horizontal line with a fingertip. Thus, the read-out system is much less complicated, and the adjustments are done intuitively in a more visually friendly interface.

Unfortunately, the iPad virtual oscilloscope currently has only one analog input channel (versus the dual channels of most basic oscilloscopes) and can only probe either input or output signals of a circuit at a time. While it is desirable to be able to display both input and output signals simultaneously, this function is only crucial for experiments that involve a phase change or time delay between both signals. Also, the iMSO-104's

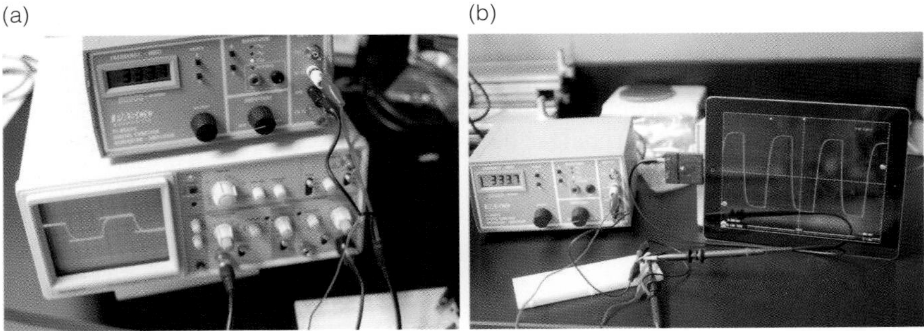

Figure 20.9
The experimental setup for measuring the relaxation time constant of an RC circuit is shown with a conventional oscilloscope (a), with its many knobs and switches; (b) shows the same experimental setup but using an iPad virtual oscilloscope (right) consisting of the iPad and the Oscium iMSO-104 attached to the iPad. The large display and the friendly interface helped students focus on the underlying physics of the experiment.

Table 20.2 Survey results from the traditional RC circuit and iPad lab

	Strongly Disagree	Disagree	Neutral	Agree	Strongly Agree
Statement 1	0%	0%	0%	13%	87%
Statement 2	20%	53%	27%	0%	0%
Statement 3	0%	0%	0%	20%	80%

maximum bandwidth is only 5 Mhz, compared with 20–30 Mhz of basic oscilloscopes, which means the iPad oscilloscope cannot capture signals oscillating faster than 5 Mhz. For standard electronic experiments in freshman physics laboratories, particularly for non-science majors and pre-meds, these limitations are not crucial.

The twenty-seven students of our two physics laboratory sections were asked to perform the RC circuit experiment, using both conventional and iPad virtual oscilloscopes. As before, students were presented with three statements and were asked to choose their level of agreement. The questions and results are as follows:

1. Statement 1. The iPad interface was friendlier than that of the conventional oscilloscope.
2. Statement 2. The absence of a second channel on the iPad negatively impacted my understanding.
3. Statement 3. I recommend using the iPad-based oscilloscope for the RC experiment.

The results suggest that all the students in both sections agreed that the interface of the iPad virtual oscilloscope was friendlier than the conventional oscilloscope. All students also recommended using the iPad oscilloscope for future RC circuit experiments. Nearly three-quarters of the students indicated that the absence of a second analog channel did not impact their understanding of the experiment. It was also observed that the students required much less time in performing the iPad-based RC relaxation time experiments, due to the reduced time needed for getting oriented with the iPad interface. Additionally, because of the iPad's large display, signal resolution was also improved.

Conclusion

We developed, implemented, and tested two classes of iPad-enabled laboratory experiments for an undergraduate physics course in a liberal arts setting. These experiments in motion and electricity have effectively replaced old setups and improved pedagogy by taking advantage of the iPad's on-board technological features and its intrinsic mobility.

In experiments that analyze the kinematical ideas of motion such as position, velocity, and acceleration of free-falling projectile and rotating objects, we have seen how the iPad, with its on-board video-camera and the Vernier Video Physics app, can provide an "all-in-one" modern tool that replaces conventional multi-component setups (ticker-tape spark timers, standalone camcorders, cables, etc.). Data were quickly acquired and efficiently processed by the iPad, therefore helping students focus more on learning. The iPad's portability enabled students to study rotational motion of real-world objects, such as an exercise bicycle, outside the traditional laboratory setting. In the area of circuit analysis, we have used the Oscium iMSO-104 electronic accessory to turn the iPad into a virtual oscilloscope to analyze the effect of an RC circuit and determine its relaxation time constant. In contrast to the conventional oscilloscope, which has numerous knobs and switches that intimidate most beginning physics students, the iPad-enabled oscilloscope has a much friendlier and intuitive touchpad interface that makes learning more enjoyable. Using surveys and personal interviews, the iPad was shown to be motivating and readily accepted by students. The majority of students stated that they recommend using the iPad for these experiments. Much like how the pencil (Baron, 1999) and calculator were "technologies" that acted as catalysts for educational change, we too have demonstrated how an iPad has changed physics labs. The iPad offered numerous

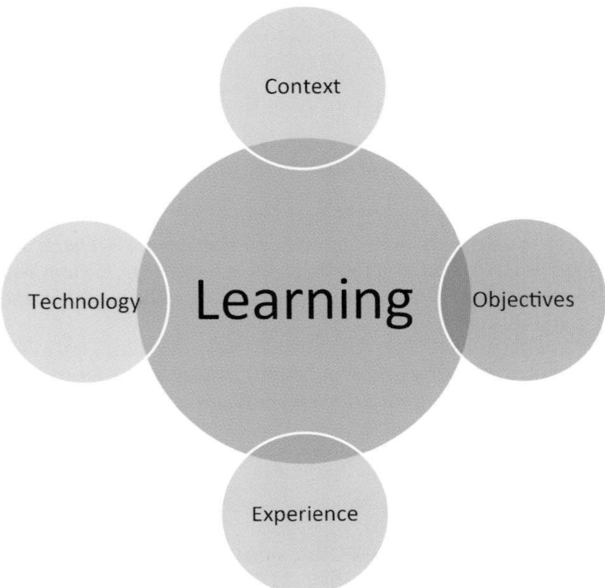

Figure 20.10
Framework developed from the research.

advantages over traditional lab equipment (e.g., touch-interface, portability, etc.), and when thoughtfully instituted for specific purposes (e.g., motion and an oscilloscope), it provided a richer user experience, which led to higher overall student satisfaction. To help represent the research findings, an illustration and framework was developed.

Figure 20.10 represents an illustration of the general framework developed from the research—context, objectives, experience, and technology. Specifically, when designing and implementing a new project, one must first consider the context. For our research, we recognized that students were losing valuable time operating complex mechanical equipment. Next, it is important to evaluate one's objectives. In our project, our objectives were for students to learn more about physics and less about operating mechanical equipment. Third, one should consider what activities students should experience. Our project was concerned with students experiencing simple and interactive interfaces, which provided the same functionality as mechanical equipment. Last, one should select a technology that can seamlessly be integrated to help enhance leaning. Due to the nature of our project, we chose to implement iPads and very specific apps. This framework—context, objectives, experience, and technology—all provide a base for implementing technology into educational environments. Specifically, the framework allowed us to successfully utilize iPads and apps in a physics class, while increasing engagement and overall learning.

References

Baron, D. (1999). From pencils to pixels: The stages of literacy technologies. In G. Hawisher & C. Selfe (Eds.), *Passions, pedagogies, and 21st century technologies* (pp. 15–33). Logan, UT: Utah State University Press.

Bowman, R. W., Gibson, G., Carberry, D., Picco, L., Miles, M., & Padgett, M. (2011). iTweezers: Optical micromanipulation controlled by an Apple iPad. *Journal of Optics, 13*(4), 044002.

Bryan, J. (2005). Physics instruction using video analysis technology. *College Board, AP Central*. Retrieved November 18, 2011, from http://apcentral.collegeboard.com/apc/members/courses/teachers_corner/48402.html.

Bush, L., Garriott, A., & Ramos, R. C. (2012). Using the iPAD as a pedagogical tool: Focus on angular motion analysis with real-world applications, *Bulletin of the American Physical Society, 57*(1). Retrieved July 18, 2013, from: http://meetings.aps.org/link/BAPS.2012.MAR.K1.6.

Escalada, L., & Zollman, D. (1999). An investigation on the effects of using interactive digital video in a physics classroom on student learning and attitudes. *Journal of Research in Science Teaching, 34*(5), 467–489.

Forinash, K., & Wisman, R. F. (2012). Smartphones as portable oscilloscopes for physics labs. *The Physics Teacher, 50*(4), 242–243.

Rodrigues, S., Pearce, J., & Livett, M. (2001). Using video analysis or data loggers during practical work in first year physics. *Educational Studies, 27*, 31–43.

Stake, R. (1995). *The art of case study research*. Thousand Oaks, CA: Sage Publications.

Yin, R. (2003). *Case study research: Design and methods* (3rd edition, Vol. 5). Thousand Oaks: Sage Publications.

Section 5
The Future of Mobile Learning

When we get asked about the future of mobile learning, we both have to laugh and smile a bit at the thought of mobile learning twenty years from now. As Kyra and Eli (Charlie's daughter and Aaron's son respectively, to whom this book is dedicated) look back on this book we believe they will also share in a laugh, as it will seem *ridiculously* out of date. Just as when we look back only a decade ago on some of the technologies that we thought would revolutionize education, the hardware and software have moved far beyond what many had envisioned for a decade later. We can now see how apps can change the future of education. However, we argue that pedagogy and practice have not followed design and development as they should. Much like Mr. Russell and Dr. Hughes noted in their chapter, "In five years, #mobilelearning will = #learning." We need to advance our design and development of apps along with our pedagogical practices, where mobile learning is synonymous with learning and education. To accomplish this feat, we have identified several practices and design features, as well as concerns that we believe are vital to the discussion.

Education Crowd-sourced App Store

By the time this book hits the press, there will be close to a million apps in Apple's App Store. As authors throughout this book have mentioned, and as we have experienced, when one does a search for apps related to education, it is much like searching for a polar bear in a snow storm; finding the exact app that meets your goals for your class is nearly impossible. Thus, if we imagine an education-specific App Store that was crowd-sourced by the teachers themselves, with reviews from users who are actually in the trenches, we will see that educators can quickly identify the apps best aligned with their instructional goals. Moreover, this will afford an evaluation system to guide the design, development, dissemination, and pedagogical practices of education-related apps.

User-generated Content

It is now time to design apps that infuse user-generated data, elevating user-generated content and ubiquitous learning to yet another level. As our work in adventure learning has grown into environments such as WeExplore, where learners are collecting and sharing their own data to develop on-the-fly explorations and investigations, it is time for apps to call upon the learner, tapping their knowledge base and research while giving them a platform to share and collaborate. Through the design of apps that inspire learners to collect data in the field via their mobile phones and tablets, we will see yet another level of sharing, storytelling, and collaboration that we, as educators, could have only dreamt about in the past.

Device-agnostic Learning

Although we are moving closer to device-agnostic mobile applications, users of many learning environments and apps continue to struggle across platforms. If we are using our iPad as we have breakfast, followed by the iPhone on the bus, and then our desktop at work, all apps, learning environments, and websites should work seamlessly across all platforms. When this simple, yet difficult-to-implement, idea becomes a reality, educators and learners will have a seamless educational experience that we have only envisioned within the context of mobile learning and education.

Teacher-developed Apps

The idea of teachers developing their own apps to use within their classrooms was only a dream, until recently. In the Learning Technologies program at the University of Minnesota, we have taught several classes over the past few where K–12 teachers, many of whom are novice designers, conceptualize, design, develop, and integrate their own educational apps their classrooms. The paradigm shift of educators from consumers to designers of mobile learning is a disruptive, yet plausible, movement. Thus, we now have educators who are content and technology specialists developing and integrating apps that afford the individualized outcomes of their curriculum. As app development becomes more accessible for all users, especially educators, we believe we will see mobile learning evolve at an exponential pace.

Mobile-specific Pedagogy

The discussions around technological, pedagogical, and content knowledge (TPACK) have flooded much of the literature within our field throughout the past years. What does this mean for mobile learning? As we approach a million apps in the App Store, how do we start learning how to integrate them within the classroom? The time is now to urge research journals to embrace mobile-specific pedagogy special issues and bring light to current practice, as well as a call for what must be achieved. We know that successful teachers are often well versed in TPACK, but what does TPACK look like for mobile learning now and in the future? We recommend the delineation of and research on pedagogical models that outline best practices for the integration of apps across all PK–20 classrooms, followed by exploratory research to guide future app development in parallel with teacher pedagogy.

The Concern

The more apps and technology bring us together, the more opportunities they have to tear us apart, in life as much as in education. Simply do a search on cell phone use with teenagers and adults and the results are astounding. It seems everyone is connected at all times—at school, driving, lunch, and even in the bathroom! What does this mean for the family circle? What does this mean for social development? What does this mean for the future of education? We don't have the answers for all of these questions at this time, but what we do know is that we need to pay attention to how often we are "connected" and what our students and children are doing when "connected." We would be doing us all a disservice if we didn't stop to remember that, like Kyra and Eli, there is more to their lives than putting an iPad in front of them to keep them busy.

What Lies Beneath the Water?

The question of "What lies beneath the water?" can be equated to the vast regions left to explore in the oceans *underneath* the tip of "the iceberg." It is said that we have explored only five to seven percent of the ocean floor and about half of a percent of the ocean in its entirety. Much like the ocean, the future of mobile learning is unexplored and the challenge and opportunity for us as educators, designers, and learners is to be that explorer, making a difference through every move we make to improve education and mobile learning. We have always said, "Life is about experiences, not conclusions."

Now is the time to take what we learned along with what we missed in the time to read this book, afford a transformational learner experience through meaningful design of a new app, apply the pedagogical practices of integrating it into the classroom, and conduct research that we will collectively build our knowledge upon. We must embrace everything yet to be explored within The New Landscape of Mobile Learning.

Dr. Charles Miller is an Associate Professor of Learning Technologies and Co-Director of the LT Media Lab in the College of Education and Human Development at the University of Minnesota. Miller's research explores opportunities to transform education through design, bridging the gap between aesthetic learning experiences and contemporary interaction design. With nearly two decades of new media design, development, and research experience, Miller has received awards from organizations such as Yahoo!, AIGA, USA Today, The Washington Post, American Scientist, IBM, Adobe, SITE, and AECT for his work on projects ranging from environmental expeditions and political campaigns to information visualization platforms and mobile education initiatives. Miller has published more than one hundred journal articles, book chapters, and conference proceedings on the role of design in education; has received more than ten million dollars in federal grant, foundation, and corporate funding; and has given hundreds of talks on design in education around the globe. When away from the office, Miller enjoys boating and fishing with his wife, Jill, and two kids, Kyra and Parker.

Dr. Aaron Doering is an Associate Professor in Learning Technologies and Co-Director of the LT Media Lab at the University of Minnesota. He holds the Bonnie Westby-Huebner Endowed Chair in Education and Technology, is a Laureate of the prestigious humanitarian Tech Awards, and a fellow for the UMN Institute on the Environment. An adventure learning pioneer, Doering has delivered online education programs on sustainability and climate change to millions of students while traveling the world—from the circumpolar Arctic, to the Amazon, to Africa, and to Australia. He gives hundreds of talks a year on online learning, transformational learning, design, and motivation. His academic writing is focused on how online learning impacts the classroom experience, designing and developing technology-enhanced learning experiences, and K-12 technology integration. When Doering isn't on a different continent, he spends his time with his wife, Amy, and their son, Eli, on acreage in the woods outside of Minneapolis, MN.